BETWEEN THE YESHIVA WORLD AND MODERN ORTHODOXY

THE LITTMAN LIBRARY OF
JEWISH CIVILIZATION

Dedicated to the memory of

LOUIS THOMAS SIDNEY LITTMAN

who founded the Littman Library for the love of God
and as an act of charity in memory of his father

JOSEPH AARON LITTMAN

and to the memory of

ROBERT JOSEPH LITTMAN

who continued what his father Louis had begun

יהא זכרם ברוך

'Get wisdom, get understanding:
Forsake her not and she shall preserve thee'

PROV. 4: 5

The Littman Library of Jewish Civilization is a registered UK charity
Registered charity no. 1000784

BETWEEN THE YESHIVA WORLD AND MODERN ORTHODOXY

◆

The Life and Works of Rabbi Jehiel Jacob Weinberg 1884–1966

◆

MARC B. SHAPIRO

Oxford · Portland, Oregon
The Littman Library of Jewish Civilization

The Littman Library of Jewish Civilization

Chief Executive Officer: Ludo Craddock
Managing Editor: Connie Webber

PO Box 645, Oxford OX2 0UJ, UK
www.littman.co.uk

Published in the United States and Canada by
The Littman Library of Jewish Civilization
c/o ISBS, 920 N.E. 58th Avenue, Suite 300
Portland, Oregon 97213-3786

First published 1999
First issued in paperback 2002
Reprinted 2004
Reprinted with corrections 2007, 2010, 2016

© Marc B. Shapiro 1999, 2007

All rights reserved.
No part of this publication may be reproduced,
stored in a retrieval system, or transmitted, in any form or by
any means, without the prior permission in writing of
The Littman Library of Jewish Civilization

This book is sold subject to the condition that it shall not,
by way of trade or otherwise, be lent, re-sold, hired out or
otherwise circulated without the publisher's prior consent in any
form of binding or cover other than that in which it is published
and without a similar condition including this condition
being imposed on the subsequent purchaser

A catalogue record for this book is available from the British Library

The Library of Congress catalogued the hardback edition as follows:
Shapiro, Marc B.
Between the yeshiva world and modern orthodoxy : the life and
works of Rabbi Jehiel Jacob Weinberg / Marc B. Shapiro
p. cm.
Includes bibliographical references and index.
1. Weinberg, Jehiel Jacob, d. 1966. 2. Rabbis—Biography.
3. Jewish scholars—Biography. 4. Orthodox Judaism—Germany—History.
5. Jews—Germany—History—1933–1945. I. Title.
BM755.W357S53 1999 296.8'32'092—dc21 [B] 99-24372 CIP
ISBN 978-1-874774-91-4

Publishing co-ordinator: Janet Moth
Design and production: Pete Russell, Faringdon, Oxon.
Copy-editing: Lindsey Taylor-Guthartz
Proof-reading: George Tulloch
Index: Sarah Ereira
Printed in Great Britain on acid-free paper by
CPI Antony Rowe, Chippenham, Wiltshire

In honour of my grandparents

THOMAS SHAPIRO

and

GWENDOLYN FREISHTAT

Preface

On Tuesday, 25 January 1966, the coffin of Rabbi Jehiel Jacob Weinberg left Jerusalem's Sha'arei Tsedek hospital, accompanied by a throng of people. It had been transported from Switzerland, where Weinberg had died the previous day. Among those accompanying the coffin to its final resting-place were many of Weinberg's students, as well as a large number of religious and political leaders, including the country's chief rabbis, government ministers, and President Zalman Shazar. As Weinberg's coffin was about to be placed in the hearse which was to take it to the cemetery in the Sanhedria district of Jerusalem, a number of yeshiva students intervened. They insisted, in accordance with Jerusalem custom, that the coffin be carried to the cemetery. After a short discussion the students had their way. A few minutes later, as the funeral procession made its way on foot to the cemetery, it was met by a number of rabbis led by Weinberg's close friend Rabbi Ezekiel Sarne, head of the Hebron-Slobodka yeshiva. Sarne ordered the students carrying the coffin to proceed to the cemetery on Har Hamenuhot. Many great Torah scholars are buried in this cemetery, and Sarne and his colleagues were adamant that Weinberg be laid to rest beside them. An argument ensued on the road, and Sarne emerged victorious. Once again the funeral plans were altered.

A funeral such as this had never before occurred in Jerusalem, and all the Israeli newspapers carried reports on this strange event. Even those who had never heard of Weinberg were led to wonder why in death he could not rest in peace, and what it was about his personality that evoked such strong feelings in different camps. One generation after Weinberg's death, we still do not have a biography of him which would enable this question to be answered. In fact, although Weinberg is often discussed in the larger contexts of Jewish law in modern times and German Orthodoxy, and there is widespread acknowledgement of his importance, there are only a couple of significant articles devoted to him.[1]

This book aims to fill this gap in modern Jewish studies by providing a complete study of Weinberg's life and achievements. In preparing this work I have often recalled the warning of Rabbi Eliezer Berkovits, one of Weinberg's leading students, that any biography of Weinberg would 'have to show the complexity of his character, the inner struggles . . . the tragedy and loneliness of his life'. I hope this book has accomplished this task, and will therefore give us a better understanding of the man, and also explain why from the beginning of his life until its very end—and even afterwards—Weinberg found himself being pulled in opposite directions.

[1] After I had finished writing this book a new article by Judith Bleich appeared, 'Between East and West: Modernity and Traditionalism in the Writings of Rabbi Yehi'el Ya'akov Weinberg', in Moshe Z. Sokol (ed.), *Engaging Modernity* (Northvale, NJ, 1997), 169–273.

I would not have been able to complete this study of Rabbi Jehiel Jacob Weinberg were it not for the gracious assistance of many people, too numerous to name. I must, however, acknowledge my two teachers, the late Professor Isadore Twersky and Professor Jay Harris, whose wise counsel enriched the book immeasurably. This book has its origin in my doctoral dissertation, which was, alas, the last directed to completion by Professor Twersky. It is a great privilege to have worked with Professor Twersky's close guidance, and I am deeply saddened that he did not live to see the appearance of this volume.

Others who have assisted me in various ways include Professor Shnayer Z. Leiman, Professor Mordechai Breuer, Professor Shaul Stampfer, Professor Daniel Schwartz, Professor Leo Trepp, Dr Louis Jacobs, Dr Abraham Weingort, Dr Yehudah Ben-Avner, Dr Jacob J. Schacter, Dr Philip Miller, Dr Gabriel Cohn, Dr Manfred Altman, Rabbi Eliezer Katzman, Rabbi Shalom Carmy, Rabbi Joseph Apfel, Rabbi Moshe Kolodny, Rabbi Jerry Schwarzbard, Mr Albert Kahan, Mr Zalman Alpert, Mr Yehudah Mirsky, Mr Arno Pomerans, Ms Susan K. Shapiro, Ms Ally Alperovich, Ms Connie Webber, Ms Janet Moth, Ms Lindsey Taylor-Guthartz, and the Corn family of Potomac, Maryland, Weinberg's only surviving relatives. Professor Lawrence Kaplan graciously read the entire manuscript and offered many helpful suggestions. Rabbi Dr Aharon Rakeffet also deserves special mention, as it was he who first introduced me to Weinberg many years ago when I was his student at the Jerusalem Torah College (BMT). Finally, I must thank the many people, too numerous to name, who gave me copies of Weinberg's letters in their possession.

I would like to thank my parents for giving me the best possible home to grow up in. Without them, this book would never have been written. My grandparents, Thomas Shapiro and Gwendolyn Freishtat, have always been a source of encouragement. The time I spend with them is truly precious. It is to them that I dedicate this book.

Contents

Note on Transliteration

THE transliteration of Hebrew in this book reflects a consideration of the type of book it is, in terms of its content, purpose, and readership. The system adopted therefore reflects a broad approach to transcription, rather than the narrower approaches found in the *Encyclopaedia Judaica* or other systems developed for text-based or linguistic studies. The aim has been to reflect the pronunciation prescribed for modern Hebrew, rather than the spelling or Hebrew word structure, and to do so using conventions that are generally familiar to the English-speaking Jewish reader,

In accordance with this approach, no attempt is made to indicate the distinctions between *alef* and *ayin*, *tet* and *taf*, *kaf* and *kuf*, *sin* and *samekh*, since these are not relevant to pronunciation; likewise, the *dagesh* is not indicated except where it affects pronunciation. Following the principle of using conventions familiar to the majority of readers, however, transcriptions that are well established (for example *tannaim*) have been retained even when they are not fully consistent with the transliteration system adopted. On similar grounds, the *tsadi* is rendered by 'tz' in such familiar words as barmitzvah, mitzvot, and so on. Likewise, the distinction between *ḥet* and *khaf* has been retained, using *ḥ* for the former and *kh* for the latter; the associated forms are generally familiar to readers, even if the distinction is not actually borne out in pronunciation, and for the same reason the final *heh* is indicated too. As in Hebrew, no capital letters are used, except that an initial capital has been retained in transliterating titles of published works (for example, *Shulḥan arukh*).

Since no distinction is made between *alef* and *ayin*, they are indicated by an apostrophe only in intervocalic positions where a failure to do so could lead an English-speaking reader to pronounce the vowel-cluster as a diphthong—as, for example, in *ha'ir*—or otherwise mispronounce the word. Here too, an allowance has been made for convention: *yisrael* has been left as it is, without an apostrophe, since interference in this familiar form would constitute an intrusive intervention of no benefit to readers.

The *sheva na* in indicated by an *e*—*perikat ol*, *reshut*—except, again, when established convention dictates otherwise.

The *yod* is represented by an *i* when it occurs as a vowel (*bereshit*), by a *y* when it occurs as a consonant (*yesodot*), and by *yi* when it occurs as both (*yisrael*).

Names have generally been left in their familiar forms, even when this is inconsistent with the overall system.

Thanks are due to Jonathan Webber of the Oxford Centre for Hebrew and Jewish Studies for his help in elucidating the principles to be adopted.

Note on Sources

IN writing this book I have incorporated information found in numerous private letters written by Weinberg, copies of which are in my possession. Since these letters are not yet available to the general public, and some may never be, I have quoted liberally from them. (In my doctoral dissertation I provided the original Hebrew text of many of these letters.) My evaluation of Weinberg's personality could not have been made without them. It is true that I have not had access to some important collections of letters written to leaders of the yeshiva world, which might have led me to re-evaluate some of my conclusions, but on the whole I believe that the picture presented here will not be substantially altered by any future revelations.

Abbreviations

LBIYB *Leo Baeck Institute Year Book*

'Lebenslauf' Weinberg, 'Lebenslauf', presented to the University of Giessen, translated here as Appendix I

Letter in *Kelei sharet* Letter from Weinberg published in Abraham Abba Reznik, *Kelei sharet* (Netanyah, 1957)

Letter to Gordon Letter from Weinberg to H. L. Gordon, published in H. L. Gordon, 'After the Death of Rabbi Jehiel Jacob Weinberg' (Heb.), *Hado'ar*, 11 Feb. 1966, 235

SE Weinberg, *Seridei esh*, 4 vols. (Jerusalem, 1977)

ONE

EARLY LIFE (1884–1905)

THE FINAL DECADES of the nineteenth century found Jews in Russia, Poland, and Lithuania coming to grips with a number of new movements and philosophies. What in the previous century had been a cohesive society had, in a hundred years, been fragmented, and abandonment of religious tradition was widespread. Although the apostles of Jewish enlightenment (Haskalah), through their propagation of new ideals, had some influence in bringing about this modernization and acculturation, there were other important factors which were independent of Haskalah, although often indirectly nourished by it.[1] Foremost among them was the need for economic improvement, which was pursued by most without any concern for, or knowledge of, the Haskalah vision. It was these economic concerns which led many young people, including women, to study at gymnasiums and universities, an extremely rare phenomenon in previous generations when those men who engaged in intellectual pursuits concentrated on rabbinic literature.[2]

By the last two decades of the nineteenth century, although most east European Jews were still traditional, the guardians of tradition were confronted with an entirely new challenge, and never before had it been so difficult to retain the allegiance of the young. Even in the smaller towns, where adherence to tradition was always stronger than in the cities, there were signs of change, and important elements of traditional society such as arranged marriages and an education system centred on the Talmud began to be questioned.

For many of the young intellectuals, who would formerly have been expected to enter the rabbinate, the Haskalah literature, in particular Hebrew belles-lettres, became the alternative to rabbinic literature. We know that even in the great yeshiva of Volozhin there were times when this literature was popular, much to the

[1] For a good summary of the major trends in 19th-cent. eastern Europe, see Lucy S. Dawidowicz, *The Golden Tradition* (New York, 1967), 27–90.

[2] For figures of Jewish attendance at gymnasiums and universities see Shaul Stampfer, *The Lithuanian Yeshiva* (Heb.) (Jerusalem, 1995), 224, who also points out that, by the mid-1880s in the tsarist realm, there were more Jewish students in the universities than in yeshivot. Regarding the beginnings of women's university study, and the reactions of the *maskilim* to this, see Shmuel Feiner, 'The Modern Jewish Woman: A Test Case in the Relationship between Haskalah and Modernity' (Heb.), *Zion*, 58 (1993), 467 ff.

displeasure of the yeshiva administration.[3] It is true that even in earlier generations yeshivot were known to be centres of the Enlightenment.[4] This phenomenon was no doubt related to the fact that many students attending the yeshivot were not dedicated to their studies but had other motives in mind, for example, finding a good wife or escaping from home.[5] However, there is no doubt that by the last decades of the nineteenth century student interest in Haskalah literature, at the expense of talmudic studies, was much more widespread than before.[6]

In the light of the challenges which faced and severely weakened traditional society in the late nineteenth century, it might appear paradoxical that the great flourishing of yeshivot occurred during this period. Yet, as Shaul Stampfer has shown, it was precisely because of the crisis in religious society that the *musar* yeshivot of Lithuania were created. As the positive response of traditional society to the inroads of non-traditional forces, these yeshivot, which followed in the *musar* tradition of Rabbi Israel Salanter (1810–83),[7] were intent on presenting a vision of life which could compete with the other ideologies for the allegiance of the young. Furthermore, as was actually pointed out by Weinberg,[8] and anticipated by Rabbi Eliezer Gordon (1840–1910),[9] the great increase in yeshivot during this period was also related to a decrease in the numbers of those studying Torah in more informal settings.[10] In other words, when local communities were full of men studying Torah, young men could stay in their home towns in order to further their Torah education. In those times the two great yeshivot of Volozhin and Mir were sufficient for those who wished to study in an institution. However, the decline of Torah study on the local level made it necessary to create centres where

[3] See Stampfer, *Lithuanian Yeshiva*, 158 ff., who discusses all aspects of student interest in Haskalah. See also Jacob J. Schacter, 'Haskalah, Secular Studies and the Close of the Yeshiva in Volozhin in 1892', *Torah u-Madda Journal*, 2 (1990), 91 ff.

[4] See Michael Silber, 'The Historical Experience of German Jewry and its Impact on the Haskalah and Reform in Hungary', in Jacob Katz (ed.), *Toward Modernity: The European Jewish Model* (New Brunswick, NJ, 1987), 114–15, 148 n. 37.

[5] See Stampfer, *Lithuanian Yeshiva*, 21. For a later period, see Jacob Katz, *With My Own Eyes*, trans. Ann Brenner and Zipora Brody (Hanover, NH, 1995), 53–4.

[6] Throughout Chs. 1–3 the words Haskalah and *maskil* are not to be taken in their technical sense, but rather as they were used in Orthodox parlance to describe a positive attitude towards secular studies and modernization, often at the expense of traditional religious practices. Although modern scholarship does not recognize the existence of a Haskalah movement in the early 20th cent., and men such as Micha Josef Berdyczewski and Ahad Ha'am were actually opponents of the Russian Haskalah, in traditional circles these not-so-subtle distinctions were totally absent. In their eyes the modern opponents of tradition were viewed in the same way as their Haskalah predecessors.

[7] See Emanuel Etkes, *Rabbi Israel Salanter and the Beginning of the Musar Movement* (Heb.) (Jerusalem, 1984), for details on Salanter's life and thought.

[8] 'Die Jeschiwoth in Russland', *Jeschurun*, 3 (1916), 120–1.

[9] See his sermon recorded in Yeruḥam Asher Warhaftig, *Shalemei yeruḥam* (Jerusalem, 1941), 3 (no pagination). See also Jacob David Wilovsky, *Beit ridbaz* (Jerusalem, 1995), introduction, 6–7, who makes the same point with regard to Volozhin's rise to greatness.

[10] See also Ehud Luz, *Parallels Meet*, trans. Lenn J. Schramm (Philadelphia, Pa., 1988), 9, and *Igerot mibeit halevi* (Benei Berak, 1993), 4, 31.

students could devote themselves to this occupation, far from the unsupportive environments of their home towns.

Having said this, two more points must be emphasized. First, even with the decline of communal learning and the flourishing of yeshivot, yeshiva study was never a necessity for aspiring scholars, and many outstanding scholars never spent time in one.[11] Second, even with the rise of anti-traditional ideologies and the decline in local Torah study, the Lithuanian Jewish population as a whole remained more supportive of their budding Torah scholars than did the populations of other lands. It is therefore no accident that there were many more of these scholars in Lithuania than elsewhere.[12]

It was into this east European Jewish society in transition that Jehiel Jacob Weinberg was born in 1884, in Ciechanowiec, a Polish town in the Grodno district.[13] He was apparently the oldest of at least six children born to Moses and Scheine (née Kuzinsky). Virtually nothing is known of his family, which testifies to its undistinguished character. Moses Weinberg seems to have worked as a miller at one time,[14] though in his later years he operated a small store.[15] It is known that Weinberg had at least two brothers, one of whom was named Isaac,[16] and three sisters named Duba, Feigel, and Anna.[17]

Ciechanowiec, which was a medium-sized town with a fairly large Jewish population,[18] has one of the largest and most complete memorial books ever published for a European Jewish community, thus providing a good picture of what life was like there.[19] Isser Smolar has described how, until the last years of the nineteenth

[11] Without my having researched this issue, the following names stand out: R. Abraham Isaiah Karelitz (1878–1953), R. Isaac Herzog (1888–1959), and R. Joseph B. Soloveitchik (1903–93).

[12] Cf. Emanuel Etkes, *Lithuania in Jerusalem* (Heb.) (Jerusalem, 1991), 64.

[13] For reasons which are not clear, but which are presumably related to the German government's attitude towards Polish Jews, Weinberg always gave Pilwishki, Lithuania, as his birthplace in official documents. This was the site of his first rabbinical position. Although he almost always gave 1884 as the year of his birth, the exact month and day are not consistent in these documents.

[14] This is the tradition of the Corn family of Potomac, Maryland, the only surviving descendants of Moses Weinberg.

[15] Told to me by Zvi Pasternack, a native of Ciechanowiec and one of the founders of the Mizrachi movement's Ciechanowiec branch; see Eliezer Leoni (ed.), *Ciechanowiec Memorial Volume* (Heb.) (Tel Aviv, 1964), 317–18. In his 'Lebenslauf', presented to the University of Giessen, Weinberg refers to his father as a 'Kaufmann'. This document is given here in translation in Appendix I.

[16] Weinberg's letter to Samuel Atlas, dated 24 Dec. 1946; his introductory essay in Shlomo Zalman Pines, *Musar hamikra vehatalmud* (Jerusalem, 1977), 10; his undated 1945 letter to the Corn family; Milton Corn's letter to Weinberg, dated 12 Aug. 1945; Zvi Mathisson's letter to Weinberg, dated 28 Nov. 1952; *SE* iii, p. 200.

[17] The first two names are found in Leoni, *Ciechanowiec*, 735. Anna came to America in the 1930s.

[18] The earliest population figures available are from the beginning of World War I, when the town had 4,000 Jews. In 1921 there were 1,649 Jews out of a total population of 3,291 people. The devastation of the war had taken its toll on Jew and non-Jew alike; see Leoni, *Ciechanowiec*, 68–9.

[19] Leoni, *Ciechanowiec*; see also the little volume by Yehoshua Rosenbloom, *My City, Ciechanowiec* (Heb.) (Tel Aviv, 1951). The fact that Ciechanowiec does not have an entry in the *Encyclopaedia Judaica* is surely an oversight, perhaps the result of reliance on the Russian *Yevreyskaya entsiklopediya*, which also omitted Ciechanowiec.

century, the social and cultural life of the community was still very much centred on the synagogue, as in many contemporary communities. Traditional life in Ciechanowiec did not yet have to confront, in any significant measure, the rising tide of new ideologies which had taken the larger cities by storm. The study of Torah, at various levels, was still the principal avocation of Ciechanowiec's Jewish residents.[20]

At the turn of the century the traditional patterns of life in Ciechanowiec began to break down, and by the early years of the twentieth century all of the new cultural and recreational interests of east European Jewry were found there. Widespread Torah study was replaced by the drama and sports clubs which were then the rage. The city also reflected wider Jewish society in housing representatives of all the different political and ideological movements to be found in Polish Jewry at this time. Needless to say, battles between traditionalists and modernists were a feature of everyday life.[21]

In his adolescent years Weinberg was thus exposed to the whole spectrum of east European Jewish life. His parents, like most other inhabitants of the town, could be characterized as traditional,[22] and although we do not know much about his upbringing or his family's economic circumstances, it is clear that they did not belong to the aristocracy, which was made up of the learned and the wealthy, and tended to send its talented sons to the yeshiva. Weinberg eventually became one of the students who broke with the traditional pattern and advanced beyond what should have been his set station in life. Students like him in fact helped create the myth that the yeshivot were institutions offering equal opportunity to all, when in fact the aristocratic element in the yeshiva was generally well established and self-perpetuating.[23]

No doubt, Weinberg attended one or more of the *ḥeder*s in the town.[24] He must have outgrown them very quickly, however, for there are stories of his brilliance as a child, although one must always be wary of possible hagiographical elements in such tales. One noteworthy story has the young Weinberg showing distinction by participating in a talmudic lecture by Rabbi Elijah Barukh Kamai (1844–1917), the rabbi of Ciechanowiec,[25] and he soon became known as the 'Ciechanowiecer *ilui*' (prodigy).

In 1900 Weinberg travelled to Grodno and studied for a year in the *beit midrash* of the Hevrah Shas. This *beit midrash*, which was established in the latter part of

20 Isser Smolar, 'The Cultural State of the Jews of Ciechanowiec at the End of the Nineteenth Century' (Heb.), in Leoni, *Ciechanowiec*, 337–9.

21 See ibid. 64 ff.

22 Told to me by Zvi Pasternack.

23 See Shaul Stampfer, 'Three Lithuanian Yeshivot in the Nineteenth Century' (Heb.) (Ph.D. diss., Hebrew University of Jerusalem, 1981), 15.

24 See Leoni, *Ciechanowiec*, 391–6, regarding these *ḥeder*s.

25 Aharon Sorasky, introduction to Weinberg, *Et aḥai anokhi mevakesh* (Benei Berak, 1966), 17; Pinhas Biberfeld, 'In Memory of the Gaon Rabbi Jehiel Jacob Weinberg' (Heb.), *Hane'eman* (Tishrei 5727 [1966]), 30.

the eighteenth century, became well known in the nineteenth century because the legendary preacher Rabbi Nahum Kaplan used to frequent it.[26] Unusually for the time, it was composed of young married men; an exception was made to admit Weinberg because of his great talmudic knowledge. While he was in Grodno his fame continued to spread and, despite his young age, he was chosen to give talmudic discourses in the 'carriage drivers'' synagogue.[27] He lectured there every day, and on the Sabbath delivered a homiletic discourse. For his services he was paid 1 rouble 20 kopeks a month.[28]

In 1901 Weinberg made an important decision, whose impact he felt until the day he died: he travelled to the Lithuanian town of Slobodka, on the outskirts of Kovno (Kaunas), to study at the famous yeshiva which had been founded by Rabbi Nathan Zvi Finkel (1849–1927) in the early 1880s.[29] Finkel, also known as the Elder of Slobodka, had been a student of one of Rabbi Israel Salanter's leading disciples, Rabbi Simhah Zissel of Kelm (1824–98). He established his yeshiva, which devoted a great deal of time to the organized study of *musar*, at a time when much of the rabbinic world was opposed to the nascent *musar* movement.

Finkel's position at the yeshiva was that of *mashgiaḥ*, an innovation of the *musar* movement, whose job was to indoctrinate the students in *musar* ideology. In this role Finkel advocated a new doctrine of *musar*.[30] Whereas earlier adherents of the movement had stressed the natural defects of the human personality and its distance from the Divine in order to encourage selfless devotion to God and to uproot negative character traits, Finkel stressed the dignity and majesty of humanity. In his view, only one who saw himself as closely bound to the Divine could be expected to devote himself to God.[31] He therefore insisted that the students' personal lives should be conducted in a manner which, in addition to gaining the respect of the masses, would, above all, instil self-respect; without proper self-respect, he thought, no one would be able to develop his spiritual potential. So, for example, students were to be impeccably groomed and dressed in the manner of contemporary bourgeois society.[32] Like much else at Slobodka, this too was an innovation.

[26] See Dov Rabin (ed.), *Encyclopaedia of the Diaspora: Grodno* (Heb.) (Jerusalem, 1973), ix. 335. Kaplan's biography was written by Israel David Miller, *Toledot menaḥem* (Petrokov, 1913), and expanded by Shemuel Yerushalmi, *Rabi naḥum hatsadik* (Jerusalem, 1970). His association with the *beit midrash* led many people, including Weinberg, mistakenly to credit him with its foundation. See Weinberg's letter in H. L. Gordon, 'After the Death of Rabbi Jehiel Jacob Weinberg' (Heb.), *Hado'ar*, 11 Feb. 1966, p. 235; hereafter referred to as Letter to Gordon (1966).

[27] Regarding this synagogue, which, as its name suggests, was frequented by the local carriage drivers, see Rabin, *Encyclopaedia*, 339.

[28] Letter to Gordon (1966).

[29] During this time students began to gather around Finkel, but since there was never a formal establishment of the yeshiva, no exact date for its founding can be pinpointed. See Stampfer, *Lithuanian Yeshiva*, 232.

[30] A comprehensive discussion of Finkel's life and work is found in Dov Katz, *The Musar Movement* (Heb.) (Jerusalem, 1982), iii. See also David Netanel Weinberger (ed.), *The Elder of Slobodka* (Heb.) (Brooklyn, NY, 1986).

[31] See Katz, *Musar Movement*, iii, ch. 8.

[32] See ibid. 288–90; Stampfer, *Lithuanian Yeshiva*, 238; Samuel Bialoblocki, *Em lamasoret* (Tel Aviv, 1971), 234.

As David E. Fishman has written: 'Slobodkaite Musar internalized the modern bourgeois values of orderliness, personal hygiene, dignity, and restraint, and magnified their importance above and beyond any position they may have held in the traditional Jewish scale of values.'[33]

Another element of Finkel's attempt to shape the personalities of his students at the most profound level was that all aspects of their lives came under the watchful eye of the yeshiva.[34] Under such conditions it was more difficult for students to become devotees of the Haskalah or Hibbat Zion than it was at the great yeshiva of Volozhin where, despite some attempts at supervision, the students' lives were not as closely monitored.[35] A further important difference between Slobodka, and indeed all *musar* yeshivot, and Volozhin was that the latter had no regard for any form of introspection designed to improve the students' characters and increase their 'fear of heaven'. The study of Talmud for its own sake was the be-all and end-all of the Volozhin yeshiva, and everything else was viewed as a distraction from this tremendous goal. Character improvement and the 'fear of heaven', while certainly important, were regarded as an automatic by-product of devotion to Talmud study, and therefore did not merit any special attention.[36]

Before Weinberg arrived in Slobodka it had already begun to attract many first-rate students. This was largely due to the closing of Volozhin, which had been shut down by the tsar's government in 1892 because of its refusal to introduce an extensive programme of secular studies.[37] Although it reopened a few years later, it had lost its two leading lights, Rabbi Naftali Zvi Judah Berlin (1817–93), who had died, and Rabbi Hayim Soloveitchik (1853–1918), who had been appointed rabbi of Brisk. Since the yeshiva did not have any of its old lustre, the gifted students who in previous years would have gone there turned instead to Slobodka. Here they could study under two of Lithuania's greatest scholars, Rabbi Isser Zalman Meltzer (1870–1954) and Rabbi Moses Mordechai Epstein (1866–1934).

Although the students at Slobodka belonged to a *musar* yeshiva, many of them still believed they could study as if they were in Volozhin, ignoring all Finkel's demands that they should concentrate on *musar*. They were encouraged by many leading rabbis, such as Rabbi Zvi Hirsch Rabinowitz (1848–1910), rabbi of Kovno, and Rabbi Moses Danishefsky (d. 1908), rabbi of the town of Slobodka, who at this

[33] 'Musar and Modernity: The Case of Novaredok', *Modern Judaism*, 8 (Feb. 1988), 42. The Slobodka form of *musar* soon became fairly standard, with only the well-known Novaredok school standing in direct opposition to Slobodka and advocating a brand of *musar* characterized by abstinence, aloofness from society, suspension of the rules of etiquette, and a strong ecstatic tendency. See Fishman, 'Musar and Modernity', and Gedalyahu Alon, 'The Lithuanian Yeshivas', in Judah Goldin (ed.), *The Jewish Expression* (New Haven, Conn., 1976), 461–2.

[34] See Stampfer, *Lithuanian Yeshiva*, 239.

[35] See ibid. 96 ff., 158 ff.; Schacter, 'Haskalah', 91 ff.

[36] See Stampfer, *Lithuanian Yeshiva*, 98–9. For R. Hayim Soloveitchik's opposition to *musar*, see *SE* iv, p. 309; Joseph B. Soloveitchik, *Ish hahalakhah: galui venistar* (Jerusalem, 1992), 67–8. (R. Hayim Soloveitchik was one of the heads of the Volozhin yeshiva.)

[37] See Schacter, 'Haskalah', 76–133.

time were leading an assault against the organized study of *musar* in the yeshivot. These rabbis argued that, in addition to creating a sect, *musar* study also threatened the hegemony of Talmud study in the yeshiva curriculum. In this latter point they were certainly correct, for the advocates of *musar* believed that it was just as important as the study of Talmud.

It soon became clear that a majority of the Slobodka students were opposed to the study of *musar*, and some even went so far as to steal the *musar* books and to disrupt Finkel's *musar* lectures. The fact that Finkel was known to have given increased financial support to some students, allegedly those who agreed with his approach, created further tension in the yeshiva. Since it was obvious to all that Finkel would never accept any compromises when it came to *musar* study, the anti-*musar* faction hoped to drive him out. They succeeded in 1897, when the controversy became so bitter that the yeshiva was forced to split.[38] Finkel retained the loyalty of about a quarter of the 250–300 students and moved to another building in the city.[39] Since Meltzer had recently left to found his own yeshiva in Slutsk, Epstein was now the sole *rosh yeshiva* of Slobodka.[40] As he was not actively involved with the *musar* movement there was some suspense while the students waited to see where his loyalties lay. The 'rebels' were very disappointed when Epstein chose to follow Finkel.[41]

The new yeshiva directed by Finkel was named Keneset Yisrael after Rabbi Israel Salanter, while the anti-*musar* yeshiva was named Keneset Beit Yitshak, after the recently deceased Rabbi Isaac Elhanan Spektor of Kovno (1816–96), widely considered to have been the leading halakhist of his time. Whereas Keneset Beit Yitshak was a continuation of the earlier yeshiva pattern seen in Volozhin, Keneset Yisrael, having apparently rid itself of anti-*musar* agitators, set out to create a synthesis of Lithuanian Talmud study and *musar* which was not found in any other yeshiva. It was Finkel who was responsible for combining the two areas of study on a large scale. In his *musar* lectures he also integrated talmudic logic and halakhic issues, thus demonstrating that the traditional focus of the yeshivot did not stand in opposition to *musar*. In fact, Finkel's students treated his *musar* lectures as they did talmudic ones, discussing and dissecting every point.[42] This was a fulfilment of the dream of Rabbi Israel Salanter, who always spoke of the need for a synthesis between Talmud study and *musar*.

However, although the yeshiva itself was dedicated to combining *musar* and

[38] See Dov Katz, *Musar Controversy* (Heb.) (Jerusalem, 1972), chs. 7, 16 section 3, and Stampfer, *Lithuanian Yeshiva*, 244 ff. Finkel used monetary incentives as part of his educational strategy; see Katz, *Musar Controversy*, 263; id., *Musar Movement*, iii. 300.

[39] See Katz, *Musar Movement*, iii. 43; id., *Musar Controversy*, 99, 264; and Stampfer, *Lithuanian Yeshiva*, 246.

[40] In addition to his talmudic lectures, he was also involved with fund-raising.

[41] See Katz, *Musar Movement*, iii. 43–4; Israel Zissel Dvortz, *The Gaon Rabbi Moshe Mordechai Epstein* (Heb.) (Tel Aviv, n.d.), 11.

[42] *SE* iv, pp. 328–9; *Musar Movement*, iii. 214.

Talmud study, and had been founded only a few years earlier as a result of disagreement over this issue, there were still many students in Keneset Yisrael who opposed *musar* study; perhaps they hoped to reform it from within. By the summer of 1901 the yeshiva was once again split into two camps, and even in the study hall the two factions sat on different sides.[43] As in the previous dispute, the students were divided between those who supported *musar* study and Finkel's leadership and their opponents who, supported by the anti-*musar* forces outside the yeshiva, wished to see Finkel removed from his position. It is likely that pressure for his removal also came from students who resented having their every movement closely watched. With Finkel out of the way they would have greater freedom to learn about Haskalah and Zionism, the two great forces which had infiltrated the yeshivot and were competing for the allegiance of the younger generation.[44]

When Weinberg entered Keneset Yisrael in 1901 it was at the height of its greatness, despite the *musar* controversy. The study hall was filled with large numbers of promising talmudists who later became some of the world's leading scholars.[45] Students continued to arrive in Slobodka despite the yeshiva's difficult economic circumstances. In fact, the institution was surviving almost entirely on the support of a Berlin philanthropist, Emil Lachmann, and there was very little food for the students.[46] Despite the objections of the yeshiva's financial administrator, Finkel would not turn anyone away.[47]

Weinberg records that when he first arrived at the yeshiva he was amazed at how crowded it was. Newly arriving students simply picked a chair and would have rights to this seat for their entire stay at the yeshiva. There was also an aristocracy in the yeshiva whose seats were located along the eastern wall. Although this aristocracy created resentment among the other students, Finkel encouraged its members and provided them with a number of additional honours, believing that this was the way to bring out excellence in a basically élitist institution. The most outstanding of the aristocracy, those who showed both brilliance and an exemplary character, were actually invited to live in Finkel's home. Actions like this prompted Kovno's last chief rabbi, Abraham Kahana Shapiro (1871–1943), to say that Finkel's love for a talented student surpassed that of a father for his only son.[48]

In the atmosphere of the yeshiva Weinberg was able to thrive and achieve great talmudic erudition. He thus became a favourite of Finkel,[49] who, according to

[43] See Dvortz, *Gaon*, 24 ff.; Katz, *Musar Controversy*, 264–7; and Stampfer, *Lithuanian Yeshiva*, 247–8. Dvortz, *Gaon*, 28, suggests that the dispute over *musar* was connected with the general intellectual ferment among young people in the years before the 1905 revolution. Since he does not elaborate on this or cite any evidence to support his view, I am unable to judge whether it is correct.

[44] See Luz, *Parallels Meet*, 248–9.

[45] The great historian of Jewish philosophy, Harry A. Wolfson (1887–1974), also frequented the yeshiva at this time, although he was officially a student at Keneset Beit Yitshak; see Hillel Goldberg, *Between Berlin and Slobodka: Jewish Transition Figures from Eastern Europe* (Hoboken, NJ, 1989), 40–1.

[46] Regarding Lachmann, see Stampfer, 'Three Lithuanian Yeshivot', 169–71.

[47] *SE* iv, p. 326.

[48] Ibid.; Weinberg's letter to Dov Katz, dated 24 June 1949.

[49] See Zvi Mathisson, 'The Tragedy of a Great Man' (Heb.), *Hado'ar*, 4 Mar. 1966, p. 284.

Weinberg, 'raised me as if I were his son'.[50] While at the yeshiva he also had the opportunity of meeting two of the other great leaders of the *musar* movement, Rabbi Naftali Amsterdam (1832–1916) and Rabbi Isaac Blazer (1837–1907), and they too left an incalculable impression on his life.[51] In fact, at Finkel's recommendation, Weinberg was chosen as Amsterdam's study partner and together they immersed themselves in the difficult halakhic work *Ketsot haḥoshen*.[52] Years later Weinberg recalled:

We, the younger students of the yeshiva of Slobodka, were proud that we had been deemed worthy of being close to him [Amsterdam]. We danced for joy because we were part of the group which comprised men of the calibre of Rabbi Naftali Amsterdam, Rabbi Isaac Blazer, and Rabbi Simhah Zissel.[53] We are fortunate in that we were privileged to behold men of such gigantic moral stature.[54]

Weinberg's detailed descriptions of the yeshiva reveal how important it was in shaping his life. He observed that it taught him that a Jew is incomplete without striving for a synthesis of Talmud study and *musar*, for only this approach can bring forth the Torah's great life-sustaining power.[55] All of Weinberg's later writings on the *musar* movement were based upon his first-hand experiences in Keneset Yisrael. Indeed, half a century after he had left Slobodka, Weinberg's memory of the yeshiva remained vivid, as can be seen from his description of the last *musar* lecture given by Rabbi Isaac Blazer in Keneset Yisrael, which took place in 1903:

I remember very clearly the talk he gave on the Yom Kippur before he went to Palestine.[56] It was in the Slobodka Yeshiva where he stood, wearing a white *kittel* and wrapped in his *tallit*. His text was: 'Cast me not away in my old age' [Psalms 71: 9]. He told a story of soldiers who deserted the army and fled the country to avoid being tried as deserters. After some years, a new king issued a pardon on condition that they return to complete their military service. One old soldier agreed to come back. But when the country's officials saw

[50] *Lifrakim*, 365 (139).

[51] Weinberg portrays these three figures in *SE* iv, pp. 296–312. He also records a number of Finkel's *musar* lectures; see ibid. 312–24 and 'From the Lectures of the Elder' (Heb.), *Keneset yisrael* (Shevat 5698 [1938]), 30–2.

[52] *SE* iv, p. 298; Weinberg's letter to Dov Katz, dated 24 June 1949. Relevant portions of this letter are printed in *Ḥidushei ba'al 'Seridei esh'*, ed. Abraham Abba Weingort (Jerusalem, 1995), 3–4 (first pagination). *Ketsot haḥoshen*, by R. Aryeh Leib Heller (1745?–1813), was widely regarded as the most challenging halakhic text, and to master it was a sign of genius. See also *SE* iv, p. 298, where Weinberg recalls a moving experience with Amsterdam that took place on Purim. Other Slobodka students who studied with Amsterdam had similar experiences: see Katz, *Musar Movement*, ii. 283.

[53] Zissel was one of Salanter's three leading students, the other two being Blazer and Amsterdam.

[54] *SE* iv, p. 304; translation adapted from Leo Jung (ed.), *Men of the Spirit* (New York, 1964), 270–1.

[55] 'Keneset Yisrael', *Hamodia*, 12 Heshvan 5672 [1911], p. 41; this article also appears in Israel Zissel Dvortz (ed.), *Keneset yisrael* (Poltava, 1912), 4–9.

[56] This lecture was also remembered by Harry A. Wolfson; see Isadore Twersky's introduction to Leo W. Schwarz, *Wolfson of Harvard: Portrait of a Scholar* (Philadelphia, Pa., 1978), p. xx; Goldberg, *Between Berlin and Slobodka*, 198 n. 76.

his age-worn body, they scoffed at him and said he was of no value any longer. In telling this, Rabbi Isaac almost collapsed and then cried out to the students, 'How fortunate you are that you are young! If you apply your time and energy you can still reach great heights. Have pity on a poor old man who wasted his time on earth.'

The effect of his talk cannot be described. We felt an electric shock pass through us. Here was a man, a giant who had not stopped studying all his life, sobbing his fear that he had not fulfilled his duty to the Almighty. Anyone who has not heard this kind of address cannot possibly understand the meaning of a true religious experience. . . . For the graduates of the yeshivot, Rabbi Isaac Blazer was such a divine guide. His sweet voice, full of grief, still echoes in my heart. Whenever Yom Kippur night arrives, I relive that sacred hour, the holy face, the awesome scene, the timeless faith. He was 'one of the patriarchs'—as close to an angel as a human being can ever be.[57]

Strangely enough, although we know that the dispute over *musar* in the yeshiva was very intense at this time, Weinberg chose to gloss over it in his published recollections of his time in Slobodka. However, in a private letter he revealed that he was persecuted by the anti-*musar* faction because of his closeness to Finkel. His opponents were jealous of the honours Finkel lavished on him, and also suspected that he was acting as Finkel's spy. 'They nearly put me in *ḥerem*, not permitting any student to study under me. This deprived me of my income, since in those days the main source of earnings for advanced students was derived from instructing [less advanced] students.'[58]

While it is true that the study of *musar* was what distinguished Keneset Yisrael from many other yeshivot, just as important was the advanced Talmud study, which bound it to the other schools. As far as this was concerned, Keneset Yisrael was no different from Volozhin in stressing the importance of Talmud study for its own sake, rather than in preparation for a career in the rabbinate.[59] As in Volozhin, social status was still very much determined by talmudic proficiency.[60] Finkel was well aware that any yeshiva that stressed character development at the expense of the traditional yeshiva curriculum would quickly develop a reputation similar to that of Novaredok, and would be seen as a yeshiva in which Talmud study was not taken seriously.[61]

The presence of Rabbi Moses Mordechai Epstein in Keneset Yisrael was enough to prevent any misunderstandings about the central role of Talmud study in this institution. Epstein employed the Lithuanian approach to Talmud study, which Norman Solomon has termed the Analytic Method, although, as he has pointed out, Epstein's approach was less conceptual than that of Rabbi Hayim Soloveitchik's circle, 'and even where he uses the Analytic vocabulary one sometimes feels that [it] is his expression rather than his content which is non-traditional'.[62] Epstein

[57] *SE* iv, pp. 307, 310 (translation adapted from Jung, *Men of the Spirit*, 249–50, 253).

[58] *Ḥidushei ba'al 'Seridei esh'*, 5.

[59] See Alon, 'The Lithuanian Yeshivas', 455–6.

[60] See Etkes, *Lithuania*, 39 ff.

[61] See Fishman, 'Musar and Modernity', 43.

[62] Norman Solomon, *The Analytic Movement* (Atlanta, Ga., 1993), 64. See also the analysis of Epstein's method in Shelomo Yosef Zevin, *Authors and Books* (Heb.) (Tel Aviv, 1959), 277–91.

also encouraged students to acquire a deep understanding of small sections of the Talmud, as opposed to wide-ranging knowledge without analytical underpinning.[63] Like other practitioners of the Analytic Method, Epstein made Maimonides' Code one of his central subjects of study. In the Analytic circle, this was regarded as the most important commentary on the Talmud, and major conceptual analyses often used Maimonides' formulations as their starting-point. Not surprisingly, all who studied under Epstein were influenced in this direction, and Weinberg's own talmudic approach had its origin in what he learnt at Keneset Yisrael.[64]

Although Weinberg was devoted to his rabbinic studies, he was also able to acquaint himself with the secular Hebrew literature of the Haskalah. His first serious exposure to this took place in the winter of 1901. Weinberg was visiting his parents in Ciechanowiec for an extended period when a friend introduced him to the writings of Abraham Mapu (1808–67) and Peretz Smolenskin (1842–85). During this winter Weinberg read through the entire works of these two writers. The discovery of Hebrew belles-lettres was an exciting eye-opener for him, as for many other yeshiva students. In contrast to the dry use of Hebrew in rabbinic literature, modern Hebrew literature showed the beauty of the language and the versatility with which it could be employed. Although, in an article written more than a decade after he had left the yeshiva, Weinberg claimed that contemporary (1916) yeshiva students had no fear of reading 'forbidden books' and were, in fact, acquainted with all the new literature being produced, this does not appear to have been the case during his time in Slobodka.[65] Weinberg certainly must have known that Finkel would not approve of his actions.

After the winter of 1901, when Weinberg returned to Keneset Yisrael, he must have shown signs of a personality change, for he was suspected of reading secular literature. Some thought was therefore given to providing him with a room-mate who would double as an administration spy. Weinberg was able to prevent this—he argued that he was obliged to room with a young boy, Zvi Mathisson, who had come with him from Ciechanowiec—and his attachment to Haskalah literature did not seem, at first, to have affected him deeply. Thus, in discussions with other students he is known to have opposed Zionism. He also read the rabbinic journal *Hapeles* and the literature put out by the so-called 'Black

63 See Epstein, *Levush mordekhai* to *Baba kamma* (New York, 1924), introduction, 6, where he explains that one who knows the entire Talmud but lacks analytical strength is regarded as an ignoramus. See also Epstein's similar comments in the introduction to his *Levush mordekhai* on *Baba metsia* (Jerusalem, 1929), 2–3.

64 Because his essays on Slobodka concern figures involved in the *musar* movement, he never mentions Epstein. There is, however, no doubt that Weinberg attended his lectures and regarded him as his teacher; see e.g. *SE* iii, p. 381, and iv, p. 218, where he refers to Epstein as *mori verabi* 'my master and teacher'. On other occasions he refers to him as *maran*, 'our master', a title he rarely used for others. See also his eulogy for Epstein in *Lifrakim*, 219–20 (269–70).

65 'Die Jeschiwoth' (1916), 122. In a letter written in 1913, Isaac Halevy made a similar point regarding east European yeshiva students; see Asher Reichel (ed.), *Letters of Rabbi Isaac Halevy* (Heb.) (Jerusalem, 1972), 205.

Cell',[66] both of which were virulently anti-Zionist and anti-Haskalah, and once rebuked Mathisson for attending a lecture of Rabbi Isaac Jacob Reines (1840–1915), the founder of the Mizrachi movement.[67] Although Weinberg still read *Hamelits* and *Hatsefirah*, he was able to convince Finkel—and maybe even himself—that his entire purpose in reading them was to learn how to respond to the enemies of *musar*, who often used these newspapers to air their complaints.[68]

During this time Weinberg also supported the new Russian Mahazikei Hadat movement,[69] a predecessor of Agudat Yisrael and the brainchild of Jacob Lifshitz (1838–1921), a leading Orthodox publicist who for years had been Rabbi Isaac Elhanan Spektor's personal secretary.[70] In 1902 Weinberg was mentioned, together with some other Slobodka students, as having given a donation to the group (1 rouble 60 kopeks).[71] Weinberg presumably backed the yeshiva administration when it confronted some forty students who had formed a Zionist society. The students refused to obey the administration's orders to disband and only gave in when it became clear that not only would they be expelled, but their chances of finding a good wife would also be put in jeopardy. Furthermore, those who had already received *semikhah* were threatened with having their ordination revoked.[72]

Yet despite his outward conformity, the contradictions in Weinberg's personality were continuing to develop. As Mathisson writes: 'Although he was firmly rooted in the traditional world of Torah and yeshivot, there were times when he played with the idea of leaving this world and crossing over to the world of the Haskalah, as it was called in those days.'[73] Mathisson recalls an interesting anecdote about Weinberg's time at Keneset Yisrael and his relationship to the Haskalah.[74] In 1903 Israel Isidor Eliashev (1873–1924), the famous Yiddish writer known as Ba'al

66 See Yair Shifman, 'The Dispute between the Orthodox and the Zionists from the First Zionist Congress until the Appearance of *Hapeles*' (Heb.) (MA diss., Hebrew University of Jerusalem, n.d.), 89–90; Isaac Levitats, *The Jewish Community in Russia 1844–1917* (Jerusalem, 1981), 180; Yosef Salmon, *Religion and Zionism* (Heb.) (Jerusalem, 1990), 272 ff.

67 Mathisson, 'Tragedy', 284. Mathisson went on to become one of the first Zionists in Ciechanowiec (see Leoni, *Ciechanowiec*, 255), and Weinberg eventually became an admirer of Reines; see *SE* iv, pp. 353–9. Despite their differences in outlook, Weinberg and Mathisson were very close during this period. In the coming years, Weinberg tried desperately, and ultimately unsuccessfully, to purge Mathisson of his religious doubts. In a letter to Mathisson from 1924 (the exact date is illegible), Weinberg wrote: 'I no longer remember exactly the circumstances which caused the break-up of our relationship, but I believe it was an incident of Sabbath violation which led to you insulting me.'

68 See his letter in *Ḥidushei ba'al 'Seridei esh'*, 5.

69 There was an earlier Galician Mahazikei Hadat movement, founded in 1879; see Aryeh Bauminger *et al.*, *Sefer krakow* (Jerusalem, 1959), 102 ff.; Salmon, *Religion*, 222 ff.

70 Lifshitz outlined the programme for his organization, which for some reason never really got off the ground, in an essay published in the Iyar and Sivan issues of *Hapeles*, 2 (5662 [1902]). Lifshitz's essay was later republished, with an additional section, in his *Maḥazikei hadat* (Petrokov, 1903).

71 *Hapeles*, 2 (Tammuz 5662 [1902]), inside front cover.

72 *Hamelitz*, 25 Feb. 1902, p. 3. A secret Zionist organization was subsequently formed. See their manifesto published in *He'avar*, 9 (1962), 106, which also expresses their dissatisfaction with the yeshiva administration.

73 'Tragedy', 284.

74 Ibid.

Makhshoves, was working as a doctor in Kovno. One day Weinberg prevailed upon Mathisson to go to Eliashev on the pretext of asking his professional advice. During the conversation Mathisson was to ask Eliashev casually whether he had received a letter from Jehiel Weinberg of the Keneset Yisrael yeshiva. When Mathisson asked Eliashev about the letter, the doctor replied that he had received it but that there was nothing he could do. It was only later that Mathisson learned from Weinberg that he had asked Eliashev to assist him in acquiring a secular education.[75]

Weinberg was not unique among Keneset Yisrael students in being attracted to the Haskalah. Indeed, even Finkel had been something of a *maskil* in his youth.[76] Having seen the error of his ways—he reportedly burnt all his Haskalah books—Finkel was determined to prevent any of his students from blundering into this path. Despite all his efforts, however, he was not completely successful. Since many of the students were from small towns and had never been exposed to secular works, it was only natural that, despite all the obstacles Finkel placed in their path, they would be attracted to this new world.[77] In fact, many students ignored the yeshiva administration's opposition and took advantage of the Jewish library in Kovno, where they were able to read all sorts of Haskalah literature.[78]

In an illuminating passage, written a decade after he left the yeshiva, Weinberg undoubtedly looked back to his own youth when he described the difficulties faced by the young rabbis of Russia:

> The most tragic figures are precisely the young rabbis who stand between two magnets. Their young hearts are pulled to where everything is exciting and alive, they hope and aspire, love and are loved. However, their feeling of Jewish responsibility tells them that it is forbidden to desert the sages and elderly righteous ones who carry the entire Jewish 'spiritual wealth' on their weak backs.[79]

Weinberg himself was just such a tragic figure, being simultaneously attracted by two opposing forces while he struggled to decide upon his direction in life. In the end, his sense of responsibility did prevent him from abandoning Orthodoxy, just as he described in this passage. Yet as we shall see, this sense of responsibility was not enough to keep him from changing the *form* of his Orthodoxy.

[75] Hayim Haikel Greenberg, a hagiographical writer interested in guarding Weinberg's reputation, was shocked that Mathisson could reveal Weinberg's youthful ties to the Haskalah. See his *Kovets rabani torani: 'Aḥiezer'—'Torat ḥayim'* (Tel Aviv, n.d.), 18, where he writes that to reveal such information is a desecration of Weinberg's memory.

[76] See Eliezer Elijah Friedman, 'The History of the Musar Sect' (Heb.), *Hator*, 29 Jan. 1926, p. 9. See also Stampfer, *Lithuanian Yeshiva*, 242 n. 68.

[77] See Stampfer, *Lithuanian Yeshiva*, 235 ff.

[78] See *Hamelits*, 25 Feb. 1902, p. 3; A. Litvin, *Yidishe neshomes* (New York, 1917), vol. iii, chapter on Slobodka towards the end of the book (which has no consecutive pagination).

[79] *Lifrakim*, 419 (333). In context this passage refers to the struggles over Zionism. See similarly his 'Schulfragen im Ostjudentum', *Jeschurun*, 3 (1916), 490–1.

When Weinberg was about 19,[80] he was ordained by two of the leading local rabbis, Zvi Hirsch Rabinowitz of Kovno and Moses Danishefsky of Slobodka.[81] It is logical to assume that it was standard procedure for the local rabbis to confer ordination in addition to any other rabbis. If this was not the case, it would be strange that Weinberg, a devoted follower of Finkel, was ordained by two of the leading opponents of *musar*, who also happened to be leaders of the anti-*musar* Slobodka yeshiva, Keneset Beit Yitshak.[82]

Weinberg remained at the yeshiva for another year, until just after Passover 1903, bringing his total stay there to about two and a half years.[83] He then journeyed to the Mir yeshiva together with Mathisson and Finkel's son, Eliezer Judah (1879–1965). The latter was engaged to the daughter of Rabbi Elijah Barukh Kamai, the former rabbi of Weinberg's home town of Ciechanowiec, who had in the meantime become head of the Mir yeshiva. The 'mission' of Weinberg and his companions, together with a number of other students sent by Finkel, was to establish Mir as a centre of *musar*. Their success made Mir one of the first of a group of yeshivot which were brought under Finkel's influence.[84] While at Mir, Weinberg also studied with the younger Finkel, having been requested to do so by both the latter and his father, with the elder Finkel putting an emphasis on the compilation of talmudic *ḥidushim*.[85] In Weinberg's eyes, it was the intensive study with Finkel which, more than anything else, was responsible for his future accomplishments as an outstanding talmudist.[86]

[80] According to his 'Lebenslauf', Appendix I, and the information he supplied for both S. Wininger, *Grosse Jüdische National Biographie* (Czernowitz, n.d.), vi. 233, and the *Jahres-Bericht des Rabbiner-Seminars zu Berlin für 1924* (Berlin, 1925), 28, Weinberg was ordained at the age of 17. As this would mean 1901, immediately after he arrived at Keneset Yisrael, I do not believe the date is accurate. The Letter to Gordon (1966) supports my estimation of the date, for it implies that his ordination did not take place until just before he left Slobodka.

[81] See Samuel Noah Gottlieb, *Ohalei shem* (Pinsk, 1912), 151, where Weinberg also mentions that he was ordained by R. Elijah Barukh Kamai, R. Eliezer Rabinowitz of Minsk, and other unnamed rabbis (the information in this encyclopedia of rabbinic personalities came directly from Weinberg).

[82] Weinberg's great respect for Rabinowitz is evident in his essay on Kovno in *Lifrakim*, 397–411 (302–16). However, Weinberg's view of the factors underlying Rabinowitz's opposition to *musar*—namely, that he was manipulated and dragged into the conflict (ibid. 405 (310))—is much too simplistic. Regarding Rabinowitz's opposition, see the more complete account in Katz, *Musar Controversy*, chs. 7 and 9.

[83] Mathisson, 'Tragedy', 284, appears to have a near-perfect memory of events, and I am relying upon him here. According to Weinberg's Letter to Gordon (1966), he spent *three* and a half years in Slobodka. This is incorrect and must be attributed to a simple lapse in memory.

[84] See Katz, *Musar Movement*, iii, ch. 4, esp. p. 64. It was common for Finkel to send his best students to assist in the direction or establishment of other yeshivot. This was part of his effort to spread the Keneset Yisrael ideology; see ibid., ch. 4.

[85] While we do not have any examples of Weinberg's *ḥidushim* from this period, there are unpublished Torah letters from Weinberg to R. Sheftel Kramer and R. Isser Zalman Meltzer which were written at a slightly later period (1904–5).

[86] Letter to Gordon (1966); Mathisson, 'Tragedy', 284; *Ḥidushei ba'al 'Seridei esh'*, 21. The time Weinberg spent with the younger Finkel gave him a lifelong love and admiration for his study partner. See his letter in *Hama'ayan*, 6 (Tishrei 5726 [1965]), 45.

During his time at the Mir yeshiva, Weinberg's interests remained broad.[87] It is clear that he was still intrigued by the world outside the yeshiva and continued to be pulled in two directions. He gives us a glimpse of this in a passage he wrote some years later recording a conversation with Kamai which reveals the gulf that had already developed between Weinberg and the older generation:

> I once remarked to him that it was not easy for members of the young generation to remain totally removed from the new life, and that one cannot require sacrifices such as this, which are more than they can handle. He gave me a clear answer: 'Why is this possible for us and why did our forefathers succeed? Everything depends on strength of will and patience. One who has no strength is lost as far as Judaism is concerned.' I was, of course, disarmed and had nothing to retort. I did not want to evoke the sad memories of what he had experienced with his own children.[88]

In other words, it was not that Weinberg agreed with Kamai that Judaism was not in need of revitalization. On the contrary, his reference to the fact that some of Kamai's own children had abandoned Orthodoxy,[89] a common phenomenon during this period even among the rabbinic élite,[90] showed that he thought the latter's approach was misguided. However, Weinberg realized that the necessary adjustments would never come from men such as Kamai, who even opposed the *musar* movement.[91] It would have to come from the younger generation, men such as Weinberg who remained faithful to tradition while recognizing the problems which existed in the traditional world. This is the unstated implication of the above-quoted passage.

In mid-1904, after a year and a quarter of study at Mir, Weinberg left the yeshiva and went to Grodno in order to study Russian. This alarmed the elder Finkel, who followed Weinberg to Grodno in order to prevent him from taking this step. Finkel also enlisted the saintly Hafets Hayim, Rabbi Israel Meir Hacohen of Radun (1839–1933) in this effort, and the latter summoned Weinberg in order

[87] From his letter to Mathisson, dated 5 Dec. 1904, we see that he had read Nahman Krochmal's classic *Moreh nevukhei hazeman* (Lemberg, 1851).

[88] 'Schulfragen' (1916), 454–5. It seems most likely that this conversation took place while Weinberg was studying at Mir.

[89] Zalman Kamai, a close friend of Weinberg, was one of the rabbi's children who forsook their father's path (interview with Shraga Abramson, a native of Ciechanowiec). He is mentioned in two letters from Weinberg to Mathisson written in 1905.

[90] The most outstanding of these young rebels from rabbinic families was probably Jacob Klatzkin (1882–1948), son of R. Elijah Klatzkin (1852–1932), who became a leading Zionist thinker. It was this phenomenon which caused the rabbinic élite to be very concerned about its children's future religiosity. See e.g. Moshe Ostroveski (ed.), *Ish yerushalayim* (Jerusalem, 1937), 68, for R. Eliezer Gordon's apprehensions that his children might give up Orthodoxy if he remained in Lithuania instead of emigrating to the Holy Land. See also Wilovsky, *Beit ridbaz*, 8 ('The sons and daughters of the rabbis are much worse than the laymen's children'), and id., *Kerem ridbaz* (Jerusalem, 1995), 46.

[91] See Katz, *Musar Controversy*, 256, 279; Mathisson, 'Tragedy', 284; Moshe Tzinovitz, *Mir* (Heb.) (Tel Aviv, 1981), 88–9; Yehoshua Ovsay, *Collected Articles* (Heb.) (New York, 1947), 130.

to persuade him to abandon his plan.[92] In an era when many of the best students were being swept away by the ideological currents of the day, it is understandable that Finkel reacted as he did, especially since he knew that Weinberg, for all his commitment to the Slobodka ideology, was still attracted by the Haskalah.

After his stay in Grodno, which appears to have been interrupted by Rabbi Israel Meir Hacohen's intervention,[93] Weinberg returned to Ciechanowiec and in due course received his exemption from military service. This was a significant moment in his life, and he expressed thanks to God that he was not forced to serve 'the wicked Russians', who had caused so much pain and hardship to the Jewish people. He also expressed relief that he would not have to fight against other Jews, 'for who knows whether I might not already have killed some of my people, who are oppressed on account of their Torah and religion, their holiness and uprightness, their righteousness and purity'.[94]

During his time in Ciechanowiec Weinberg once again tried to acquire a secular education, this time requesting assistance from Shemaryahu Levin (1867–1935), the noted Zionist author and former crown rabbi of Yekaterinoslav. From Ciechanowiec Weinberg wrote to Mathisson on 9 December 1905, and this letter reveals his state of mind:

I am able to tell you that after I received my exemption from the army I immediately informed Dr. S. Halevi[95] of this, and he answered me promptly with a long letter full of love and friendship. He wrote that he is ready to stand by me as much as possible, and advised me to wait a little while in my town until the storm passes and things calm down.[96] Afterwards I am to travel to Yekaterinoslav and he will send me the letters which I need. I

[92] Mathisson, 'Tragedy', 284; *Ḥidushei ba'al 'Seridei esh'*, 4–5; Weinberg, 'Our Education' (Yid.), *Undzer Veg*, 11 May 1951, p. 2. In a letter from Weinberg to Mathisson, dated 24 Jan. 1906, Weinberg writes a few phrases in Russian and also requests Mathisson to send him the Russian translation of Leo Pinsker's *Auto-Emancipation* as well as a book to help improve his Russian penmanship.

[93] 'Our Education' (1951), 2. In this source Weinberg claims that R. Israel Meir Hacohen 'saved' him, and that had he not intervened, Weinberg would never have achieved any success in either Torah or secular studies: 'I owe my secular education to the Hafets Hayim alone.' What Weinberg no doubt meant is that had he not waited until he was firmly grounded in his talmudic studies before tackling secular studies, he would have remained mediocre in both.

[94] Letter to R. Sheftel Kramer, dated 23 Nov. 1905.

[95] i.e. Shemaryahu Levin.

[96] He refers to the revolutionary disturbances of 1905. In his article 'Der "Masmid"', *Jeschurun*, 4 (1917), 425–30, Weinberg presents what appears to be a fictionalized account of an unnamed yeshiva affected by the revolutionary fever of 1905. (Although Weinberg refers to his story as 'recollections', he was no longer in Mir in 1905, which suggests that the story does not reflect reality.) According to his story, only a single student, out of the entire *beit midrash*, was ready to stand up against the Jewish revolutionaries who attempted to prevent the students from studying. Whether or not Weinberg's account has any historical basis, it is known that the yeshivot, especially Mir, were affected by the revolutionary fever. See Katz, *Musar Controversy*, 260, and Tzinovitz, *Mir*, 87–8. Regarding Slobodka at this time see Katz, *Musar Movement*, iii. 52–3, and for Novaredok see Fishman, 'Musar and Modernity', 45–51. See also Stampfer, *Lithuanian Yeshiva*, 249 n. 97, and for the period after 1905 see B. Schulman, 'The Revolutionary Spirit in the Yeshivot' (Heb.), *He'avar*, 12 (1965), 134–47. Regarding rabbinic opposition to the revolutionaries, see Eli Lederhendler, *Jewish Responses to Modernity* (New York, 1994), 67 ff.

followed his advice and waited, and last week wrote to him requesting that he send me the necessary letters. However, I have not received any answer. I know that this is due to the postal strike and he is not able to send me letters. Therefore, I must now linger idly in our small town. It is as if I am sitting on burning coals, for my days and years are passing like lightning and I am either staying in the same place or going backwards. What should I do now? I know that it is very wrong at a time like this to worry about private matters, when a sea of anxiety is engulfing everything. Yet a man such as I, for whom it is impossible to take part in the general tide, must certainly prepare himself for the future. In short, you now know my state of mind. My heart wanders and is empty. I lift up my eyes to the hills; from where shall my help come [cf. Psalms 121: 1].[97]

How different recent Jewish intellectual history would have been had things worked out with Weinberg and Shemaryahu Levin! Zionism and Hebrew literature would have certainly gained a great mind, but twentieth-century Orthodox Jewry would have lost one of its most creative intellects.

[97] Mathisson, 'Tragedy', 284.

TWO

PILWISHKI (1906–1913)

PRIVATE LIFE: MARRIAGE

IN 1906, shortly after writing the letter to Mathisson mentioned at the end of the first chapter, Weinberg was offered the rabbinate of the Lithuanian town of Pilwishki (Pilviškiai in Lithuanian; Pilvishok in Yiddish), about 30 miles south-west of Kovno.[1] In order to attain this rabbinic position Weinberg was required to marry Esther Levin, the 16-year-old daughter of the town's deceased rabbi, Jacob Meir Levin.[2] According to one version recorded by Weinberg, Rabbi Zvi Hirsch Rabinowitz was responsible for arranging his appointment to the rabbinate,[3] though elsewhere he portrayed Rabinowitz as merely giving his approval.[4] According to Mathisson, who was a witness to the event, it seems that Finkel realized that Weinberg was at a turning-point in his life. In order to ensure Weinberg's continued adherence to the rabbinic lifestyle, Finkel arranged the marriage or, as Weinberg himself put it, 'forced me to marry'.[5]

Mathisson recalled Weinberg's marriage as being the most tragic event of his life. He simply did not care for his bride, who was both very young and uneducated, probably knowing little more than how to read the prayer book. She was a typical Orthodox woman of the old generation, whereas Weinberg, despite his yeshiva

[1] In his 'Lebenslauf', Appendix I, and his letter to R. Isaac Herzog, dated 16 Oct. 1950, Weinberg writes that he received his first rabbinical post when he was 20 years old, i.e. in 1904. This is clearly impossible. In *Lifrakim*, 405 (310), he writes that he became rabbi of Pilwishki in 1905. This is also the date given in the *Jüdisches Lexicon* (Berlin, 1930), iv. 1360; *Jahres-Bericht des Rabbiner-Seminars zu Berlin für 1924*, 28; Wininger, *Grosse Jüdische National Biographie*, vi. 233; and Harry Scheiderman and Itzhak J. Carmin, *Who's Who in World Jewry* (New York, 1955), 803. This date must also be incorrect, since his letter to Mathisson, quoted at the end of Ch. 1, is dated December 1905, and Weinberg had not yet been appointed rabbi. In his letter published in Abraham Abba Reznik, *Kelei sharet* (Netanya, 1957), 1–2, he says that he served as rabbi for seven years, until the outbreak of World War I. This would mean that he assumed the rabbinate in 1907. However, the very reliable Mathisson, 'Tragedy', 285, claims that he served as rabbi for eight years before 1914, indicating that he assumed the position in 1906.

[2] See *Lithuanian Jewry* (Heb.) (Tel Aviv, 1967), iii. 339. According to information in the record book of the Jewish community of Helsinki (to which she later emigrated), Esther Levin was born on 19 Mar. 1890.

[3] *Lifrakim*, 405 (310).

[4] Letter to Gordon (1966).

[5] Mathisson, 'Tragedy', 284; Letter to Gordon (1966): 'The Elder of Slobodka and the heads and members of Yeshivat Keneset Yisrael forced me into this marriage. In my youth I submitted to them and through this shattered my life's course.'

training, was still somewhat of a *maskil*, who read modern newspapers and books in both Hebrew and Russian, and had a good deal of contempt for the Jewish masses.[6] As Mathisson noted, unlike the intellectually and culturally aware young women he knew from Ciechanowiec, Esther Levin had nothing to offer Weinberg, who was not prepared to seclude himself in the traditional Orthodox world of Lithuania and would obviously have preferred to choose his own wife. The relationship between Weinberg and Esther Levin appeared doomed from the start. Although he did sometimes consider calling off the wedding, Weinberg's own desire to join the rabbinate, together with the pressure both from his parents and from Finkel, prevented him from taking this step. The marriage went ahead as scheduled and Weinberg became the town's new spiritual leader.[7]

Shortly after this Weinberg passed a government examination in Lomza and was appointed crown rabbi (*kazyonny ravvin*) of the Pilwishki district.[8] In the mid-nineteenth century the tsarist government created the office of crown rabbi in order to turn the rabbinate into an instrument of government policy. Only those who had acquired sufficient secular education and knowledge of Russian were permitted to assume the office. The crown rabbi, who often had little Jewish learning and was non-observant, was almost never regarded as a spiritual leader by the traditional community.[9] Not surprisingly, he was usually relegated to a bureaucratic role, representing the community to the authorities and ensuring that births, deaths, and marriages were recorded in the communal registry. Alongside the crown rabbi, communities would also employ rabbis whom they regarded as their spiritual leaders, but who were not recognized as such by the government.[10]

However, the fact remains—and this has been overlooked in the scholarly literature on the subject—that by the first decade of the twentieth century there was a significant number of traditional rabbis who, like Weinberg, were employed as crown rabbis. This meant that the title of crown rabbi no longer carried its former stigma. It is thus no surprise that Rabbi Isaac Jacob Reines, in his defence of the Lida yeshiva's inclusion of secular studies, pointed with pride to the fact

[6] In his letter to Zvi Mathisson, dated 3 Nov. 1905, Weinberg writes: 'The masses are far removed from idealism and they only understand one language well, the language of personal gain, materialism.'

[7] Mathisson, 'Tragedy', 284; Letter to Gordon (1966). With regard to the young women Weinberg knew, in his letter to Mathisson, dated 24 Jan. 1906, Weinberg wrote as follows to one of his female friends (in Russian): 'Best wishes to esteemed Mademoiselle Dora Gachnoch. You did not manage to say good-bye to me and it made me cross with you. Still, by the time of your wedding we will make peace. After all, we were good friends at one time! Good-bye for now! I remain your respectful friend, Hile.' Although it was much more common in Weinberg's day than at present for yeshiva students to have female friends, it was certainly not typical.

[8] 'Lebenslauf', Appendix I; *Jahres-Bericht des Rabbiner-Seminars zu Berlin für 1924*, 28; Wininger, *Grosse Jüdische National Biographie*, vi. 233.

[9] There were some exceptions. For example, R. Abraham David Lavut (1815–90) served as crown rabbi of Nikolayev. See the introduction to his *Kav venaki* (Brooklyn, NY, 1985), 4. R. Isaac Ze'ev Soloveitchik (1838–1927) served for a time as crown rabbi in Kovno. See Hayim Karlinsky, *The First in the Brisk Dynasty* (Heb.) (Jerusalem, 1984), 48–50.

[10] See Azriel Shochat, *The Institution of the 'Crown Rabbinate' in Russia* (Heb.) (Haifa, 1976).

that students who studied at his institution would be able to pursue a career in the 'spiritual rabbinate, the official rabbinate, or both of them together'.[11] Similarly, Rabbi Judah Leib Zirelson (1860–1941), himself a crown rabbi, urged his colleagues to follow in his path. He argued that by receiving government recognition, 'spiritual' rabbis would raise the prestige of their office as well as ensure themselves a decent salary.[12] It is, of course, understandable that smaller communities which could not afford to employ two rabbis would have preferred a 'spiritual' rabbi who could also obtain government recognition.[13]

Pilwishki was smaller than Ciechanowiec, Weinberg's home town, and according to the 1897 census 1,242 Jews lived there (53% of the total population).[14] Although Weinberg commented that for the Jews of Pilwishki it was considered a notable event when the wire of the *eruv* came down, this is certainly something of an exaggeration from what we know of the town.[15] Despite its small size, there was a significant Zionist presence as well as a number of socialists and *maskilim*.[16] The community produced a group of distinguished personalities, among them the poet Hillel Bavli (1893–1961) and the talmudist Samuel Bialoblocki (1891–1960).[17] There were several scholars among its inhabitants, and the *beit midrash* was

[11] *Shenei hame'orot* (Petrokov, 1913), section 2, part 2, 12*b*.

[12] See his letter in Aaron Cohen, *Keneset hagedolah* (Alexandria, 1904), ii. 29*a*. See also R. Samuel Borstein's letter, ibid. 51*a*. Thirty years before Zirelson, R. Samuel Mohilever and R. Mordechai Gimpel Jaffe advanced similar suggestions which, however, had no impact. See Shochat, '*Crown Rabbinate*', 71–3. Zirelson also expressed confidence that the government could be persuaded to modify its requirement of secular education for crown rabbis, so that knowledge of the national language would be sufficient. As he noted, this was all that was required for official rabbis in Congress Poland.

[13] It would be worth compiling a list of traditional rabbis who also served as crown rabbis. In the biographical entries in Samuel Noah Gottlieb, *Ohalei shem* (Pinsk, 1912), a number of individuals are identified either as crown rabbis, or as having received government permission to assume the office, the most notable being R. Zalman Sorotzkin, R. Ezekiel Lifshitz, R. Menahem Krakowski, and R. Abraham Kahana Shapiro. From a recently published letter of R. Hayim Soloveitchik to R. Elijah Klatzkin, dated 1894, we see that the latter was crown rabbi in Mariampol. See *Festschrift in Honour and Memory of Rabbi Abraham Dov Weisfisch* (Heb.) (Jerusalem, 1992), section 2, 138 (bound with Nahum Manasseh Gutentag, *Ayelet ahavim*).

[14] *Lithuanian Jewry* (1967), iii. 339.

[15] *Lifrakim*, 224 (274).

[16] M. Z. Levinson-Lavi, 'Pilvishok', in Mendel Sudarsky *et al.* (eds.), *Lithuania* (Yid.) (New York, 1951), i, col. 1533; Berl Kagan, *Jewish Towns and Villages in Lithuania* (Yid.) (New York, 1990), 403–4.

[17] Bialoblocki resembled Weinberg in many ways. He too studied at Slobodka, and became known as the '*ilui* of Pilwishki'. (He was still known by this title as late as 1935; see the title-page of *Hama'or* (Sivan–Tammuz 5695 [1935]).) He later travelled to the University of Giessen, where he earned his doctorate only a few years after Weinberg had left. Like Weinberg, he too combined traditional and critical study of the Talmud. Yet for some unknown reason, presumably a personal conflict, Weinberg had no respect for either his character or his scholarship. See Weinberg's letter in *Hapardes* (Nov. 1966), 33, for a scathing attack on Bialoblocki after the latter was appointed as professor of Talmud at Bar-Ilan University, accusing him of every imaginable sin, not to mention lack of scholarship. He is similarly harsh in other private letters. It is thus not surprising that in his letter in Reznik, *Kelei sharet*, he does not mention Bialoblocki among the prominent personalities from Pilwishki. One should compare Weinberg's attitude with the glowing words of S. Y. Agnon and H. Z. Hirschberg regarding Bialoblocki in *Bar-Ilan Annual*, 2 (1964), 12–43.

constantly in use.[18] The local Jews' economic situation was satisfactory too; they were predominantly engaged in agriculture and poultry-raising, and most of their produce was sold in Kovno or exported over the nearby German border.[19]

These factors combined to make Pilwishki a fairly desirable position for a young rabbi, and Weinberg found the city quite pleasant, noting that he was greatly respected by Jew and gentile alike.[20] Even when the economy soured in 1913, the townspeople were prepared to accept without objection his decision to forbid any arrangements with the gentile population in order to allow work to be performed on the Sabbath, despite the fact that other local rabbis had given such permission.[21] Pilwishki's positive effect on him was such that forty years after he had assumed its rabbinate, he still fondly recalled the first halakhic discourse he had delivered there.[22] As we do not yet know enough about the Lithuanian rabbinate, it is impossible to determine how typical Weinberg's experiences were, even though he believed that his position was quite unusual.[23]

The source of Weinberg's difficulties was his failed marriage. After half a year he informed Mathisson of his situation and urged the latter to come to Pilwishki to keep him company. Mathisson acceded to this request and lived with Weinberg in Pilwishki for a year. During this time Mathisson observed that Weinberg was very lonely, wandering like a stranger through his own home. In addition to Weinberg and his wife, his mother-in-law and two of her young children also lived in the house. Yet only on the Sabbath would the entire family eat together, and, at least when Mathisson was there, Weinberg did not even sleep at home.[24]

After a few years of marriage it was clear to Weinberg that he would have to divorce his wife if he did not intend to spend the rest of his days in misery. The only question was when he would summon up the strength to do so. In a very revealing letter to Mathisson, dated 5 December 1909, we also learn that his misfortune was causing a rift in his relationship with his parents:

[18] A picture of the *beit midrash* appears in Sudarsky, *Lithuania*, i. 1534. This is almost certainly a picture of the rebuilt *beit midrash*, as the original one was destroyed in World War I; see *Lithuanian Jewry* (Tel Aviv, 1967), iii. 339. A picture of a street in Pilwishki can be seen in this book, among the pictures between pp. 350 and 351. See also *Lithuanian Jewry* (Heb.) (Jerusalem, 1959), 39.

[19] Levinson-Lavi, 'Pilvishok', col. 1533; Letter in *Kelei sharet*, 2–3,

[20] Letter in *Kelei sharet*, 2–3.

[21] Ibid. 4; *SE* ii, no. 21.

[22] *SE* ii, p. 67.

[23] The recent comments of Emanuel Etkes are too impressionistic and rely on too few sources to support any general statements. See his 'Talmudic Scholarship and the Rabbinate in Lithuanian Jewry', in Leo Landman (ed.), *Scholars and Scholarship: The Interaction between Judaism and Other Cultures* (New York, 1990), 107–32. Some might argue that Weinberg's nostalgic recollections of his time in the rabbinate, written thirty-five years after he left Pilwishki, do not reflect reality. However, at least for the beginning of his time in Pilwishki, we have contemporaneous evidence—a letter to Mathisson written on 14 June 1907—that confirms the picture found in his letter in *Kelei sharet*. In his letter to Mathisson he wrote: 'My rabbinic position is well established. Considering the state of the contemporary rabbinate, my situation is one of the very best. Another in my place would regard himself as the happiest man in the world.' The continuation of the letter is interesting in that Weinberg plainly acknowledges his ambition: 'Am I happy [with my position]? That is a difficult question to answer. There is a well-known saying: "The appetite grows by eating".' (The source of the saying is François Rabelais's *Gargantua*: 'L'appétit vient en mangeant.')

[24] 'Tragedy', 285.

There have already been many moments when I forcefully decided [to divorce my wife]. However, when the time comes to follow through on my decision, I falter. This is due to my cowardice and fear of the uncertain future. . . . I also have many debts and most importantly, my health is very weak. The realization that my weak body will not be able to withstand the storms which will descend upon me destroys my spirit and crushes my aspiration. . . . I am very confused and lonely, and unto whom shall I pour out my grief and frustration? What is your opinion? Have you met my father? How does he view matters? It is clear to me that he does not feel my anguish. He is only concerned that his imaginary honour, which I acquired for him through the sacrifice of my life, should not disappear. Do you exchange letters with anyone from Pilwishki? What have you heard of my situation? I am practically separated from humanity and have no dealings with people. Give regards to my parents. I do not have even the slightest desire to write to them.[25]

Mathisson notes that he received similar letters throughout the winter, yet Weinberg still did not attempt to end the marriage. This was certainly not an easy step to take, for divorce was very uncommon in traditional Lithuanian Jewish society, and among members of the rabbinate it was unheard of. In addition to this, Weinberg's parents and his wife's family were putting pressure on him to come to terms with the situation. They blamed Weinberg for the marital problems and stated explicitly that they would not allow him to divorce,[26] leading Mathisson to suggest that Weinberg threaten to abandon his wife without a *get* if she did not agree to end the marriage. 'He rejected this idea, arguing that [were he to do so] he would be forced to abandon his world, the world of the rabbinate. Aside from this, he was without means of support, for almost all his income fell into the hands of his mother-in-law.'[27] In a letter to Mathisson written in 1910, Weinberg also admitted that he was not able to divorce her and give up his rabbinic position—which he retained only by virtue of the marriage—for having achieved a measure of status in the Jewish community, his self-image would no longer allow him to assume the role of private citizen.[28]

A few years later, in 1912, Finkel sent a group of select students from his yeshiva to Pilwishki, hoping that if Weinberg would occupy himself teaching the boys, he would no longer be obsessed by the difficulties in his personal

[25] 'Tragedy', 285.

[26] Weinberg's letter to Mathisson, dated 4 Jan. 1910. In this letter Weinberg wrote: 'I know that I am not at fault. On the contrary, they are at fault for not informing me of many things which I needed to know before we settled the matter [i.e. the marriage], and for stubbornly exerting such pressure on me. But they see me as their murderer and will never forgive me. . . . In short, with this step [i.e. divorce] I bring tragedy upon them and myself and cause great pain and disappointment to my parents and family.' Weinberg's deep bitterness was now causing him to resent the citizens of Pilwishki. In this letter he wrote: 'I feel enmity towards the entire population of Pilwishki, who are in my eyes as vultures descending on their prey. No one feels my pain.'

[27] 'Tragedy', 285.

[28] Letter to Mathisson, dated 4 Jan. 1910: 'I am already accustomed to holding a position in the community, respected or insignificant, but a "position" nonetheless. . . . A bad quality is deeply embedded in my personality which compels me to seek a position in society and not be one of the "wretched creations" whom everyone treads on and ignores. This is not a "desire for honour" in its simple sense. No! It is a sensitive and profound conception.'

life.[29] However, by this time it was too late and there was nothing that could be done to persuade Weinberg to resign himself to his fate. He knew that he would have to end his marriage; the only question that remained was when. In the meantime Weinberg had developed a new interest which no doubt allowed him, in some measure, to escape his depressing circumstances. He had begun to assume an active literary role among the Russian and Lithuanian Orthodox intelligentsia.

PUBLIC LIFE: EARLY JOURNALISM

East European Orthodox Newspapers

His most significant work appeared in the two leading Orthodox Hebrew newspapers, *Hamodia* of Poltava (Ukraine) and *Ha'ivri* of Berlin.[30] *Hamodia* was edited by the rabbi of Poltava, Elijah Akiva Rabinowitz (1862–1917), a most interesting personality who had previously edited the monthly *Hapeles*, a magazine Weinberg had read in his youth. Rabinowitz was an enthusiastic supporter of the Zionist movement in its early years and even attended the Second Zionist Congress in 1898. When it was decided at this Congress to include 'cultural' issues among Zionist activities, however, he left the movement and became one of its bitterest opponents.[31]

Both in *Hapeles* and later in *Hamodia*, Rabinowitz used his considerable literary skill to lambaste Zionism, and these publications were two of the first examples of the 'orthodox fighting the modern world with its own weapon—journalism'.[32] When Weinberg began to write for *Hamodia* opposition to Zionism was prominent in its pages. However, articles on a variety of issues affecting the Jewish community were also published. By insisting that everything he printed be intellectually respectable, Rabinowitz ensured that the newspaper, which catered to the rabbinic élite, would not be viewed simply as a forum to attack opposing views. It was of great importance to Rabinowitz that all articles be written in impeccable Hebrew, demonstrating that even opponents of the Haskalah and Zionism were capable of expressing themselves clearly in the revived language. The opponents of tradition were thus not allowed to lay claim to the mantle of Jewish cultural creativity. As Kressel puts it: 'The paper shows the adjustment of extreme orthodoxy to modern means of expression—even though it continued fighting those who invented them.'[33]

Orthodox Hebrew newspapers were certainly not unknown before Rabinowitz, with the *Shomer tsiyon hane'eman* published by Rabbi Jacob Ettlinger (1798–1872)

[29] Letter to Gordon (1966); *Jahres-Bericht des Rabbiner-Seminars zu Berlin für 1924*, 28; Wininger, *Grosse Jüdische National Biographie*, vi. 233.

[30] Some of these articles have been reprinted in *Lifrakim*, and I will refer to this source when discussing them.

[31] See Ya'akov Barnai, 'Rabbi Rabinowitz of Poltava's Change of Mind on Zionism' (Heb.), *Sinai*, 70 (1972), 282–8.

[32] Getzel Kressel, *Guide to the Hebrew Press* (Zug, Switzerland, 1979), 51.

[33] Ibid. 48.

being the most outstanding.[34] Still, Ettlinger's journal, whose major focus was talmudic discussion, bore no resemblance to the Orthodox papers which appeared later. It is true that some of the Haskalah newspapers, such as *Hamagid*,[35] *Hakarmel*, and *Hatsefirah*, were conservative in nature and would have been acceptable to many of the enlightened German Orthodox. However, they did not correspond to the form of Orthodoxy which chacterized east European Jewry, and they occupied a position on the margins, read only by the *maskilim* and the more open-minded rabbis. On the other hand, *Maḥazikei hadat*, published by the Belz hasidim from 1879 onwards, did not have much appeal because of its religious extremism.

The creation of an Orthodox press in Russia must be credited to Jacob Lifshitz, the founder of the Mahazikei Hadat movement mentioned in Chapter 1. In an effort to combat the advocates of the Haskalah, he became involved with the newspaper *Halevanon* in the early 1870s. It was here that he launched the first intensive polemical attacks against the *maskilim*. Although he strongly opposed what they were trying to accomplish, he still appeared to support a conservative Haskalah, at least in theory. This explains his reference to the 'beloved Haskalah', which unfortunately had of late been transformed into an anti-rabbinic phenomenon. According to Lifshitz, he would have been content to see the *maskilim* devote themselves to the scholarly study of Jewish sources and the writing of apologetic literature directed towards non-Jews. The problem, as he saw it, was that they also presumed to know what was best for traditional Judaism and lectured the rabbis on how to improve matters.[36]

By publishing the journal *Hapeles* at the turn of the century, Rabinowitz followed in Lifshitz's footsteps and consolidated the place of the Orthodox press in traditional east European circles to such an extent that it is hard to believe that there was still any significant opposition to such papers by the time he began to publish *Hamodia* in 1911.[37] This was not an unimportant accomplishment, since

[34] See Yitshak Raphael, *Rishonim veaḥaronim* (Tel Aviv, 1957), 327–35; Judith Bleich, 'The Emergence of an Orthodox Press in Nineteenth Century Germany', *Jewish Social Studies*, 42 (1980), 323–44.

[35] Although *Hamagid* was published in East Prussia for a time, its primary audience was always *maskilim* in the Russian empire.

[36] See his article in *Hakarmel*, 7 (1868), 100–2, which appeared under a pseudonym (see Lifshitz, *Zikhron ya'akov* (Israel, 1968), ii. 73). See also Gideon Katzenelson, *The Literary Battle between the Orthodox and the Maskilim* (Heb.) (Tel Aviv. 1954), ch. 3; Seymour Siegel, 'The War of the *Kitniyot* (Legumes)', in A. A. Chiel (ed.), *Perspectives on Jews and Judaism* (New York, 1978), 383–408; Israel Bartal, 'Jacob Lifshitz's *Zikhron Ya'akov*—Orthodox Historiography?' (Heb.), *Millet*, 2 (1985), 412–13.

[37] See Hayim Ozer Grodzinski, *Collected Letters* (Heb.) (Benei Berak, 1970), ii. 586–7, for an appeal signed by a number of leading rabbis urging support of *Hamodia*. In 1907 Grodzinski advocated the creation of an Orthodox daily newspaper; see Reichel, *Letters of R. Isaac Halevy*, 121. R. Moses Nahum Yerushalimski argued for the establishment of a daily newspaper as early as 1903. See his letter in Cohen, *Keneset hagedolah*, ii. 20*a*. For R. Eliezer Gordon's attempt to establish an Orthodox paper, see Zalman Sorotzkin, *Hade'ah vehadibur* (Jerusalem, 1965), iii. 116–17. See also Abraham Mordechai Alter, *Collected Letters* (Heb.) (Jerusalem, 1988), 93 ff.; Ezekiel Abramsky,

many leading rabbinic figures originally opposed the creation of an Orthodox newspaper. Lifshitz himself mentioned that when he first made efforts in this direction, he was confronted by those who believed that it was impossible for this medium ever to be transformed into a proper method of advocacy for the Orthodox cause.[38]

In fact, this opposition to the newspaper format, whose basic purpose would be to polemicize against the opponents of Orthodoxy, had deep roots. Even when the Reform movement was just beginning, there were those who opposed any sort of public attack on it.[39] Once the Reform and Haskalah movements had taken off, and it was recognized that there was no hope of going back to the 'innocent' days of old, an even more significant number of Orthodox thinkers came to oppose any sort of polemics. They argued that the negative effects of polemics far outweighed any value they might have. To begin with, the distraction from Torah study could not be justified.[40] Secondly, polemics by their nature have the effect of circulating radical and dangerous ideas among people who normally would never have been exposed to them. Rabbi Joseph Saul Nathanson (1808–75),[41] Rabbi Abraham Jacob Friedman (1820–83), the *rebbe* of Sadeger,[42] and Rabbi Israel Meir Hacohen[43] are among those known to have held this position.

Needless to say, rabbinic opposition to Orthodox involvement with Haskalah newspapers was even more intense, and the *maskilim* considered it something of an event when a rabbi from the old school took to the Haskalah newspapers to defend his point of view.[44] As far as the *maskilim* were concerned, the fact that the rabbis avoided reading newspapers showed how truly isolated they were from the problems confronting the Jewish community. It is thus no surprise that many of the Orthodox, including Lifshitz, believed that the creation of an Orthodox press—a sign that the Orthodox were, in fact, interested in dealing with the challenges of modernity—would stop the attacks of the *maskilim*.[45]

The other newspaper for which Weinberg wrote, *Ha'ivri*, was very different from *Hamodia*. Published in Berlin, it was edited by Rabbi Meir Berlin (Bar-Ilan, 1880–1949), the son of Rabbi Naftali Zvi Judah Berlin of Volozhin and a leader of

Collected Articles (Heb.) (Jerusalem, 1994), 83–5; Dawidowicz, *Golden Tradition*, 210–13; Stampfer, *Lithuanian Yeshiva*, 289 n. 113; and Mordechai Breuer, 'Orthodoxy in Germany and its Eastern Counterpart at the Turn of the Century', *LBIYB* 41 (1996), 79.

38 *Zikhron ya'akov*, ii. 99, 'Habit Becomes Second Nature' (Heb.), *Hamodia*, 5 Tevet 5671 [1911], 169.

39 See Elijah Ragoler, *Yad eliyahu* (Jerusalem, 1969), i, no. 25; Zvi Hirsch Chajes, *Collected Writings* (Heb.) (Jerusalem, 1958), ii. 1016–17.

40 This was the reason behind R. Naftali Zvi Judah Berlin's refusal to allow Volozhin students to publish a newspaper or even a Torah journal. See Schacter, 'Haskalah', 104.

41 See Hayim Sofer, *Kol sofer* (Munkács, 1882), 38*a*; id., *Kan sofer* (London, 1963), no. 48.

42 See Dawidowicz, *Golden Tradition*, 198–200.

43 *Collected Writings* (Heb.) (Brooklyn, NY, 1989), 81 (first pagination), 91 (third pagination).

44 See e.g. Samuel Joseph Fuenn's comments in *Hakarmel*, 7 (1868), 105.

45 See Lifshitz, 'Lahat haḥerev hamithapekhet', *Halevanon*, 9 (1873), 273–5.

the religious Zionist Mizrachi movement. Although it resembled *Hamodia* in that it too strove to be an intellectual newspaper for the religious community, its content was very different. It published articles of modern Jewish scholarship and poetry, approved of secular studies—as might be expected from a west European newspaper—and most importantly, supported Zionism.

As contributions to a newspaper were often regarded as a signal of one's ideological commitment, the fact that Weinberg simultaneously wrote for both apparently shows that he had not committed himself one way or the other regarding Zionism. This open mind is also seen in his relationship with Rabbi Isaac Jacob Reines, the founder of the Mizrachi movement, who had started a yeshiva in Lida whose purpose was to combine Torah and secular studies.[46] Weinberg was a great admirer of Reines[47] and, at the latter's request, once delivered a lecture at the Lida yeshiva.[48] However, this did not stop him from opposing the method employed at Reines's yeshiva and, for reasons which will soon become clear, he criticized it both in conversation with Reines and in public.[49] He also believed that Reines's Zionist activities were a mistake, not because religious Zionism *per se* was unacceptable, but because Reines had adopted a path in opposition to the leading rabbinic scholars of the day.[50] At this stage of his life, Weinberg was not inclined to support independent judgements on such important issues.

Defence of the Yeshiva System

Despite his criticism of Reines, Weinberg was not tilting in the direction of *Hamodia*. He did not oppose secular studies on principle, and while in Pilwishki continued to expose himself to various fields of knowledge.[51] However, overcoming his youthful doubts, he now took his place as a faithful defender of the yeshiva system in which he was trained. In line with this, Weinberg argued strongly that yeshiva students, who need to devote their entire time to the study of Torah, should be kept far from any secular studies. Just as his teacher Finkel had been a devotee of the Haskalah, only to reject it later, so too Weinberg felt that his own youthful experiences were not something students should emulate. He had 'survived' his encounter with the secular world, but others might not be so fortunate.

In an article published in 1912, Weinberg formulated his position clearly.

[46] For discussions of the yeshiva see Alexander Manor *et al.* (eds.), *Sefer lida* (Tel Aviv, 1970), 89–134; Yosef Salmon, 'The First Reform in East European Yeshivot' (Heb.), *Molad*, 4 (1971), 161–72; id., 'The Yeshiva of Lida: A Unique Institution of Higher Learning', *YIVO Annual*, 15 (1974), 106–25; and Geulah Bat-Yehudah, *Ish hame'orot* (Jerusalem, 1985), ch. 43.

[47] See his essay on Reines in *SE* iv, pp. 353–9 (also printed in *Lifrakim*, 412–23 (326–37)). The views expressed in this article, which found great favour with the Zionists, were opposed by some of the anti-Zionist German Orthodox, and they did not want the article to appear in the Warsaw Yiddish newspaper they controlled, *Dos Yidishe Vort*; see Alexander Carlebach, 'A German Rabbi Goes East', *LBIYB* 6 (1961), 112.

[48] *SE* iv, p. 359.

[49] Ibid., p. 358.

[50] Ibid., p. 357.

[51] Even the works of the noted Bible critic Julius Wellhausen caught his interest; see *Lifrakim*, 394 (299).

Responding to those who believed that the yeshivot should teach secular studies as a way of attracting the young to traditional Judaism, he wrote:

This is a complete error which has already been disproved by experience. Those whose major purpose is a career go forth from the yeshiva and wander in other fields. Those who stray into foreign territory will not return to us because of a little European education which is given to them in a superficial manner on the stools of the yeshiva. Not from these shall Judaism be built and not in them shall Jews put their national trust. At the sound of the first shot these weaklings will abandon the battle, and would that they might not pass over into the camp of the enemy. For the nature of their education is such that they are incapable of making sacrifices for their Torah, which for them is only something to make use of. . . . The fulfilment of the Torah requires great sacrifices from us . . . our entire life must be a sacrifice. . . . Therefore, those who say that we should grab the coat corners of our young ones who are led astray and attract them with 'the beauty of Japhet so that we bring them into the tents of Shem' are making a great mistake. For when the spark of self-sacrifice has vanished from the heart, hope for Judaism is lost. . . . It is true that there are only very few who will be able to rise up against the [trends of contemporary] life,[52] but from them shall Judaism be built![53]

These words, which faithfully reflect the view of the Lithuanian yeshivot, rejected all that German Orthodoxy had come to stand for, i.e. a positive attitude towards secular studies and Western culture. According to Weinberg not only was secular education simply out of the question for yeshiva students, but in essence it was only these students, who devoted themselves exclusively to Torah study, who were the backbone of traditional Judaism.[54] The role of religious laymen, in particular those who wished to pursue a profession, had little importance for Weinberg in his deliberations on how best to ensure the survival of Orthodoxy. In contrast, it was precisely the religious laymen who were the cornerstone of the ideology of German Orthodoxy developed by Rabbi Samson Raphael Hirsch (1808–88).

The sentiments behind Weinberg's view were elaborated on some years later by Rabbi Elijah Dessler (1891–1954), a leading ideologue of the Lithuanian yeshivot whose position faithfully reflected that of the east European rabbinic élite.[55] Dessler freely admitted that the combination of Torah and secular studies advocated by German Orthodoxy had a great appeal for the masses and produced pious communities with very little attrition. However, Dessler continued, since Torah study was diluted in Germany it did not produce the outstanding scholars found in the east.[56]

[52] See Luz, *Parallels Meet*, ch. 1, who discusses the 19th-cent. conflict between 'religion' and 'life'.

[53] 'Keneset Yisrael (1)' (1911) (Heb.), *Hamodia*, 12 Heshvan 5672 [1911], 39–40. See also 'Clarifying the Essence of Jewish Ethics' (Heb.), *Ha'ivri*, 9 Sept. 1911, 409, where he warns against corrupting Jewish thought and ideals by bringing the 'teachings of Japhet into the tents of Shem'.

[54] See similarly R. Isaac Ze'ev Soloveitchik's letter in *Yeshurun*, 2 (1997), 695. One could easily find tens, if not hundreds, of such comments in the writings of the east European rabbinic élite.

[55] *Mikhtav me'eliyahu* (Benei Berak, 1977), iii. 355–8.

[56] See also the comments of Elie Munk, quoted in Immanuel Jakobovits, '*Torah im Derekh Eretz*', in Moses Rischin and Raphael Asher (eds.), *The Jewish Legacy and the German Conscience* (Berkeley, Calif., 1991), 168.

As for eastern Europe, Dessler was perfectly candid in stating that east European Orthodoxy had a much higher attrition rate among its young. Indeed, as mentioned earlier, as far back as the 1880s there were more Russian Jews in the universities than in the great yeshivot.[57] It was in hope of attracting some of these students that in 1882 Reines established a yeshiva in Sventsyany, Lithuania, which offered secular studies.[58] The project met widespread opposition, and the yeshiva was soon forced to close. Not until 1905 did Reines repeat his experiment in Lida,[59] where once again the rabbinic élite united in opposition to any changes in the yeshiva curriculum as a means of responding to the widespread abandonment of tradition.[60] As Dessler explained, this opposition was due to the unique mission of the yeshivot, which was concerned with creating outstanding Torah scholars and was never intended to have a mass appeal. Even though he realized that the majority of youngsters would not succeed in this system, and that a number would even abandon Orthodoxy completely, Dessler nevertheless recalled Maimonides' comment in the Introduction to the *Guide of the Perplexed* that the instruction of a tiny élite is more important than attempting to educate a mass audience.[61] In his own words, 'this is the price which must be paid' in order to produce saintly Torah giants. As already pointed out, this approach was diametrically opposed to the view of Hirsch, who believed that the only way to ensure the survival of traditional Judaism was by concentrating on creating pious communities, not on building yeshivot which would cater to the élite.[62]

At this time Weinberg was certainly not unaware of Hirsch's views. He even recorded a conversation he had with a leading Russian rabbi who was very impressed with Hirsch's piety. Weinberg asked this rabbi why the east European Jews should not strive to develop a German-style Orthodoxy, and the rabbi replied with surprise:

57 See Stampfer, *Lithuanian Yeshiva*, 224.

58 See Bat-Yehudah, *Ish hame'orot*, ch. 10.

59 See Reines, *Shenei hame'orot*, section 2, part 2.

60 See e.g. 'Maginei Hadat' ('Defenders of the Faith') (pseudonym), 'Temporary Dwelling' (Heb.), *Hapeles*, 5 (1905), 673–8.

61 'Let a thousand fools die and one wise man benefit.' Dessler's quotation is actually derived from Shem Tov's commentary to the *Guide* (10*a* in the standard edition). In his introduction, Maimonides himself wrote: 'I am the man who when the concern pressed him and his way was straitened and he could find no other device by which to teach a demonstrated truth other than by giving satisfaction to a single virtuous man while displeasing ten thousand ignoramuses—I am he who prefers to address that single man by himself, and I do not heed the blame of those many creatures.' See also Katz, *Musar Movement*, ii. 218, who records that R. Simhah Zissel also quoted the comment of Shem Tov, believing it to be found in Maimonides' introduction. Apparently this was a well-known quotation whose accuracy no one bothered to check.

62 See Jacob Katz, *Halakhah in Straits* (Heb.) (Jerusalem, 1992), 243. It is debatable how committed even this élite was, since R. Elijah Akiva Rabinowitz was able to state that if schools on Hirsch's model were opened in Russia, all of the yeshivot and study halls would immediately be emptied. See *Hapeles*, 5 (1905), 426.

First, we don't have any rabbis of the calibre of Hirsch. Second, do you really want to replace the *Sha'agat aryeh*[63] with the *Horeb*?[64] As long as we have young people devoted to the Torah in our yeshivot, we have no reason to renounce our Torah in favour of a small amount of 'modern education'.[65]

However, it remains doubtful whether Weinberg's knowledge of the philosophy of Hirsch, or of German Orthodoxy as a whole, was much more than perfunctory. In fact, the previously quoted passage shows Weinberg strenuously opposing the very ideas that were advocated by Hirsch. The notion of making Judaism appealing, of putting the 'beauty of Japhet into the tents of Shem', was at the centre of Hirsch's programme and was intended to apply to all people at all times.[66] Rabbi David Zvi Hoffmann (1843–1921), who was at this time rector of the Rabbinical Seminary of Berlin and Germany's leading halakhist, spoke for all of German Orthodoxy when he wrote that 'our Sages also intended through their statement ["Let the chief beauty of Japhet [i.e. the Greek language] be in the tents of Shem", *Megillah 9b*] to allow entry of the entire range of culture and learning, insofar as they ennoble humanity, into the tents of Shem, i.e. the Jewish houses of study'.[67]

Throughout Weinberg's defence of the yeshiva, we see that he was very aware of what was by then no longer a new phenomenon. Confronted with a population abandoning the tradition in ever-increasing numbers, the yeshiva students began to regard themselves as the last bastions of Judaism.[68] The assumption that the yeshivot were the only institutions preventing a total dissolution of the religion was an important theme in Weinberg's writings of this period. Side by side with this notion, Weinberg defended the yeshivot against the charge, so often heard among non-traditionalists, that yeshiva students led lives of pain and sorrow. This accusation was levelled particularly at the *musar* yeshivot, where sadness and grief were supposed to be prevalent. On the contrary, Weinberg replied, although the material circumstances of the yeshiva student were obviously not very good, happiness should not be identified with financial success: 'Anyone who has not seen the joyful life of the *beit midrash*, when it is inhabited by students of the Torah, has never seen joy.'[69] Weinberg challenged the yeshiva's critics: 'Ask the students of the Keneset Yisrael yeshiva and they will tell you: "We are not lacking anything at Keneset Yisrael. There we hear things which fill our souls and bring excitement to our hearts. Our life, in our eyes, is holy, and our purpose is clear." '[70]

63 A well-known halakhic work by R. Aryeh Leib Guenzberg (1695–1785).

64 Hirsch's classic study of the commandments.

65 'Schulfragen' (1916), 456.

66 See the complete study of Hirsch's system in Mordechai Breuer, *The Torah-Im-Derekh-Eretz of Samson Raphael Hirsch* (Jerusalem, 1970). See also Jacob Rosenheim, *Samson Raphael Hirsch's Cultural Ideal and Our Times*, trans. I. E. Lichtigfeld (London, 1951), 65; originally published as *Das Bildungsideal S. R. Hirschs und die Gegenwart* (Frankfurt, 1935). The quotations given here come from this translation.

67 'Thora und Wissenschaft', *Jeschurun*, 7 (1920), 498.

68 See Stampfer, 'Three Lithuanian Yeshivot', 8.

69 'The Yeshivot (3)' (Heb.), *Hamodia*, 9 Iyar 5672 [1912], 412.

70 'Keneset Yisrael (1)' (1911), 40.

For a long time the yeshivot had been condemned by many *maskilim* as centres of obscurantism, whose strict regimen, physical dilapidation, and intensive study of useless material was destroying the psyche of young Jews.[71] Other writers, such as Micha Josef Berdyczewski (1865–1921), though more ambivalent towards the yeshivot, still criticized them for refusing to integrate modern currents of thought in the curriculum. Although a greater appreciation of the yeshivot is apparent among certain Haskalah writers of the late nineteenth century, such as S. Y. Abramovitsch (Mendele Mokher Sefarim, 1836–1917), their main criticisms remained.[72] A well-known expression of this sentiment is found in the famous poem by Hayim Nahman Bialik (1873–1934) entitled *Hamatmid* (1895). In this poem Bialik describes the 'pent and unhappy souls' who devote themselves to the Talmud. The yeshiva student is nothing more than a 'prisoner, self-guarded, self-condemned, self-sacrificed to study the law'.[73]

It was in opposition to this widespread view held by the non-traditionalists that Weinberg elaborated on the spiritual beauty and joy found in the yeshiva. Whereas Bialik had emphasized the freedom and happiness attained outside the yeshiva walls, Weinberg turned this on its head. He argued that it was actually the yeshiva students who were the happiest and most content of the young generation, happy to study Torah and filled with a zest for life. The lack of religious idealism which was seen in the younger generation, and which was responsible for the numerous defections from tradition, was not to be found in the yeshiva, Weinberg claimed. This was so despite the fact that the yeshiva students lacked the 'freedom' of their peers. Weinberg showed that even the hated *pilpul* was an essential part of Torah study, which also had positive social effects. The nostalgic view of the yeshivot of old, still largely shared even by the non-traditional community, was not something of the distant past. Rather, Weinberg declared, this image reflected reality and could be experienced first-hand by anyone who ventured inside the yeshiva walls.[74]

Weinberg continued his analysis by emphasizing that the yeshiva was a self-sufficient world which outsiders simply could not fathom. Holding such a view, he found it understandable that non-traditionalists had a negative impression of the yeshiva. Still, he claimed to be amazed that modern writers showed no desire to understand the workings of the yeshiva, and passed judgement upon it through ignorance. Ignoring the fact that men such as Bialik and Berdyczewski *were* products of the yeshiva and that this very familiarity had bred their contempt, Weinberg argued that it was a lack of intimate knowledge of the yeshiva on the part of the

[71] See Moshe Avital, *The Yeshiva and Traditional Education in the Literature of the Hebrew Enlightenment Period* (Heb.) (Tel Aviv, 1996); Schacter, 'Haskalah', 84 ff.

[72] Avital, *Yeshiva*, ch. 6.

[73] See ibid. 211 ff. where Avital discusses this poem in the context of Bialik's overall view of the yeshivot, which was not entirely negative. See also S. Daniel Breslauer, *The Hebrew Poetry of Hayyim Nahman Bialik (1873–1934) and a Modern Jewish Theology* (Lewiston, NY, 1991), 115 ff.

[74] 'Talmudic Pilpul' (Heb.), *Ha'ivri*, 31 Mar. 1911, 153–4; 'The Yeshivot (2)' (Heb.), *Hamodia*, 20 Shevat 5672 [1912], 265; 'The Yeshivot (3)' (1912), 412.

writers and the general community which explained why attempts to alter the negative perception of yeshivot were in vain. As Weinberg put it, the outsider looks at the yeshiva and sees only disorder. However, one who understands the yeshiva knows that within the apparent disorder are the forces of an advanced moral and spiritual world-view. Since the yeshiva education was both natural and complete, Weinberg was able to assert forcefully that yeshiva students had no need for those who came '"to educate" with [modern] pedagogic literature in their hands'.[75]

In words which seem to be directed against Reines and Rabbi Chaim Tchernowitz (1871–1949), the director of a yeshiva in Odessa which had similarities to that founded by Reines,[76] Weinberg elaborated on what he believed to be one of the most significant problems facing traditional Judaism in eastern Europe, namely, the widespread desire to tamper with the structure of the yeshivot. He believed that in the face of such a challenge, one could no longer adopt a middle-of-the-road position. Rather, one had to stand either with the forces of tradition or with those of reform. Weinberg's response was simply to 'drive out the foreign spirit' which some wished to see enter the yeshiva walls: 'Either the yeshivot should be worthy of their name in the complete historical sense or they should not exist at all!'[77]

These strong words were a complete rejection of any adjustments in the yeshiva curriculum like those carried out by Reines and Tchernowitz. Weinberg realized that what he was advocating stood against the onslaught of modernity. He also realized that few would be able to follow in this path. Still, since this was the only way to secure the future of traditional Judaism, he believed that it was essential that his approach should be followed. It is very clear that, like Dessler and in contrast to Hirsch, it was more important for Weinberg to be left with a small core of support, unadulterated by any contact with modernity, than to adopt strategies which would appeal to the larger community.

Weinberg did not view his reactionary stance as doomed to failure. On the contrary, as he explained in his essays, he believed it was working because the yeshiva students appeared to be standing strong against modern currents of thought. That is, they were succeeding where he had almost failed. Once again we see that success and failure were measured by the impact of modern ideas on the yeshiva, not on

75 'The Yeshivot (1)' (Heb.), *Hamodia*, 6 Shevat 5672 [1912], 232–3; 'The Yeshivot (2)' (1912), 264–5; 'The Yeshivot (3)' (1912), 411–15; 'Concerning the Yeshivot' (Heb.), *Hamodia*, 12 Sivan 5671 [1911], 506–7; 'Keneset Yisrael (1)' (1911), 40; 'Response to Criticism' (Heb.), *Hamodia*, 22 Adar 5671 [1911], 343. This complete rejection of the value of modern pedagogy with regard to the yeshiva is important, and will be discussed later when I examine how Weinberg's attitude changed.

76 See Benjamin Hoffseyer, 'Rabbi Chaim Tchernowitz, "Rav Tzair", and the Odessa Yeshiva' (Heb.) (Ph.D. diss., Yeshiva University, 1967).

77 'Keneset Yisrael (1)' (1911), 40. See also *SE* iv, p. 358. Throughout Weinberg's lengthy essays the only words of criticism directed against the yeshivot—and he did not specify which particular yeshivot he had in mind—were that *musar* texts were not being studied sufficiently ('Clarifying' (1911), 411). This criticism loses virtually all its significance when weighed against the many pages Weinberg devoted to glorifying the yeshivot.

society at large. The yeshivot had become independent and self-sufficient entities, and their success was largely divorced from what happened in the wider Jewish community. It would seem that the plan of Rabbi Hayim of Volozhin (1749–1821) to create a yeshiva independent of the local rabbi and community had now reached its zenith.[78] The lesson Weinberg drew from the success of the yeshivot was not that Orthodoxy could confront modernity and emerge unscathed, as had been accomplished by the German Orthodox. Rather, Orthodoxy could succeed by *ignoring* modernity entirely. With the tenacity of a young ideologue, Weinberg was able to consign the widespread abandonment of tradition to a feebleness of will, a lowly ethical outlook, and a lack of patience and endurance with which to confront life's problems. Ideological sincerity was discounted as an option.[79]

At a time when Jewish nationalism had assumed a powerful position in the Jewish community, it was particularly disturbing to Weinberg that the secular Jewish nationalists did not recognize what he referred to as the national power found in the yeshivot. Logically, he felt, the Jewish nationalists should have had the greatest affinity for the yeshivot, since it was the latter which were responsible for the survival of the Jewish people and which linked Jews throughout the Diaspora. Although not noted by Weinberg, the scorn shown by Zionists for traditional life in general, and the yeshivot in particular, was a relatively recent phenomenon. When the Hibbat Zion movement first arose in the mid-1880s, many of its leaders displayed a romantic longing for the religious life of the masses. Much of what was disdained by the earlier *maskilim* was rediscovered, as it were, by these Hovevei Zion. Others, who did not share this longing, desisted from attacking the Orthodox for pragmatic reasons and expressed their willingness to broker a political accommodation with them.[80] With time, however, both the admiration and the pragmatic motivation dissipated, as the reluctance of the Orthodox to compromise on matters of religion became obvious. It was then that the nationalists picked up where the *maskilim* had left off and began to denigrate Orthodox life and culture. The life-story of the father of modern Hebrew, Eliezer Ben-Yehudah (1858–1922), which followed this pattern, is most illustrative in this regard.[81]

It was in response to this later manifestation that Weinberg stressed the important role the yeshivot could play in the revival of Jewish nationalism. As he put it, once the nationalists recognized the important position of the yeshivot, this could

[78] See Emanuel Etkes, 'The Approach and Actions of R. Hayim of Volozhin as a Response of "Mitnagdic" Society to Hasidism' (Heb.), *Proceedings of the American Academy for Jewish Research*, 38–9 (1972), 19. Stampfer, however, argues that there is no evidence to support Etkes's contention that R. Hayim consciously chose to create a fundamentally new type of yeshiva. See *Lithuanian Yeshiva*, 39 n. 57.

[79] 'The Yeshivot (1)' (1912). Cf. Søren Kierkegaard's explanation of anti-religious sentiment in Christian circles: 'People try to persuade us that the objections against Christianity spring from doubt. That is a complete misunderstanding. The objections against Christianity spring from insubordination, the dislike of obedience, rebellion against all authority' (*Journals*, trans. Alexander Dru (London, 1938), 193, no. 630).

[80] See Luz, *Parallels Meet*, 31–3.

[81] See ibid. 33–5.

be followed by joint efforts between the two camps in matters of common concern.[82] Totally lacking from his critique was any sense of the different understandings of nationalism at issue. Why the Zionists should feel affinity with a group whose 'nationalism' was only expressed through the study of Torah was not even considered by Weinberg. It is difficult to see this sort of essay, with its lack of any serious analysis, as being directed at anyone other than members of the traditional community who wished to be reassured of the justice of their position.[83] Still, Weinberg's emphasis on nationalism is significant, for it shows how a modern category was able to find its place in his otherwise conservative writing.

Criticism of the Rabbinate

It was not only the secular nationalists who were the objects of Weinberg's criticism. He also confronted the Orthodox community with their own failings, chief among them being that they did not sufficiently appreciate the yeshivot. This was seen both in the paltry sums they donated to the yeshivot and in the way they treated yeshiva students.[84] In Weinberg's mind the ultimate blame for this unfortunate situation was to be directed at the rabbis, who did little to prevent the community from developing such hostility towards the yeshivot and their students.[85] Though in earlier years the rabbis had been 'the key to the hearts of the masses', according to Weinberg it was now apparent both to the Orthodox and to their opponents that the influence of the rabbinate had degenerated, so that even the best rabbis had lost a great deal of their former authority.[86] This development was not surprising for, as Weinberg pointed out, the rabbinate was full of men who should have chosen other careers, and they were assisted in their duties by blatantly dishonest community leaders. With this comment Weinberg opened a blistering attack on the state of the rabbinate in Russia and Lithuania.[87]

The struggle to obtain rabbinic positions was necessarily associated with politics and influence, and dishonesty and back-room political dealings between community leaders and rabbis, not to mention the outright purchase of positions of religious leadership, have a long history. The latter practice is even referred to in the Talmud[88] and its prohibition is recorded in the standard legal codes.[89] Yet despite all the criticism, and a number of *ḥerem*s promulgated forbidding the sale of rabbinic offices—one rabbi went so far as to blame the massacres of 1648 on this

[82] 'The Yeshivot (1)' (1911).

[83] Cf. Elijah Akiva Rabinowitz, *Hapeles*, 5 (1905), 427: 'The objective of the Mahazikei Hadat organization is not to reach out to those who have intentionally distanced themselves from the tradition. . . . Its only goal is to prevent the faithful from abandoning Orthodoxy.'

[84] 'Keneset Yisrael (2)', *Hamodia*, 19 Heshvan 5672 [1911], 55–7 (this article also appears in Dvortz, *Keneset yisrael*, 10–13); 'The Yeshivot (2)' (1912), 264–5.

[85] 'The Yeshivot (2)' (1912). See also *Lifrakim*, 3–4.

[86] Regarding this observation see also Luz, *Parallels Meet*, 204.

[87] 'Concerning the Rabbinate' (Heb.), *Hamodia*, 10 Av 5671 [1911], 631–4.

[88] *Sanhedrin 7b*.

[89] Maimonides, *Mishneh torah, Hilkhot sanhedrin*, 3: 8–9; *Tur, Ḥoshen mishpat*, 8; *Shulḥan arukh, Ḥoshen mishpat*, 8: 1.

sin[90]—it nevertheless remained a common practice and is often referred to in rabbinic literature.[91] In the nineteenth century Rabbi Solomon Judah Rapoport (1790–1867) referred with pride to the fact that he had broken with the universal practice and refused to shower the community leaders with presents in order to ensure his appointment.[92] By this time the purchase of rabbinic positions had become so prevalent that two leading halakhists, Rabbi Isaac Schmelkes (1828–1906) and Rabbi Shalom Schwadron (1835–1911), were led to defend it. In their mind it was now regarded as acceptable because the community leadership would not even consider a rabbi's candidacy unless he paid them.[93] In fact, although

[90] See Berakhyah Berekh Shapira, *Zera berakh* (Amsterdam, 1730), introduction. See also Hayim Eleazar Shapira, *Minḥat ele'azar* (Brooklyn, NY, 1991), i, no. 6, where a similar *ḥerem* is printed, signed by such eminent rabbis as Mordechai Jaffe, Solomon Luria, Samuel Edels, Isaiah Horowitz, Ephraim Luntshitz, and Meir of Lublin. This *ḥerem* is also found in Israel Heilprin, *Pinkas va'ad arba aratsot* (Jerusalem, 1990), 62–5. For further discussion see Hayim Hillel Ben-Sasson, *Hagut vehanhagah* (Jerusalem, 1959), 221–8; and Ben-Zion Dinur, *Bemifneh hadorot* (Jerusalem, 1953), 106–8. See also Shapira, *Minḥat ele'azar*, i. 10*a* n. 1, where he refers to a rabbinical conference in 1901 which also publicized the prohibition on buying rabbinic positions. See Ze'ev Aryeh Rabiner, *The Gaon Rabbi Eliezer Gordon* (Heb.) (Tel Aviv, 1968), 149–50, for a communal ordinance prohibiting the rabbi from paying for the needs of the community either as a loan or as a gift, the latter device being simply a more indirect way of purchasing the position than paying off the community leaders. (These ordinances do, however, allow a community to require the rabbi to give some temporary support to the widow and children of his deceased predecessor.)

[91] See the numerous sources discussed in Shapira, *Minḥat ele'azar*, i, no. 6; Abraham Bornstein, *Avnei nezer* (Tel Aviv, 1964), *Yoreh de'ah*, no. 465; Berish Weinberger (ed.), *Igerot shapirin* (Brooklyn, NY, 1983), 249.

[92] See his letter in Shimon Buechler, *Shai lamoreh* (Budapest, [1895]), 34. Rapoport singled out his adversary R. Zvi Hirsch Chajes as having bought the rabbinate of Zolkiew. However, there is no reason to believe this accusation; see Mayer Herskovics, *Rabbi Zvi Hirsch Chajes* (Heb.) (Jerusalem, 1972), 94–5. See also Zvi Ezekiel Mikhaelzon, *Pinot habayit* (Petrokov, 1925), introduction, 7*a*, who writes with pride: 'I was never one of the rabbis who bought their positions.' He continues as follows (7*b*): 'One cannot describe the great desecration of God's name in our day, when this matter [of purchasing rabbinic positions] is openly practised. . . . Woe to the generation in which such a thing occurs! What will become of the Torah?'

[93] Isaac Schmelkes, *Beit yitsḥak* (Przemysl, 1892), *Yoreh de'ah* ii, no. 16; Shalom Schwadron, *Da'at torah* (Toltshava, 1911), 96 (*Hilkhot sheḥitah*, section *Darkhei shalom*, no. 8). Other defences of the practice are found in the responsa of R. Menasheh Eichenstein and R. Joshua Horowitz, in Eichenstein's *Alfei menasheh* (Przemysl, 1895), no. 8. See also Reines, *Shenei hame'orot*, section 2, part 2, 7*b*; Zvi Eleazar Lifshitz, 'Concerning the Appointment of Rabbis' (Heb.), *Yagdil Torah*, 2 (1910), 16–18; and Shmuel Yosef Agnon, *Lifnim min haḥomah* (Jerusalem, 1976), 63–4. After arguing that 19th-cent. rabbinic salaries were generally very meagre, Etkes writes: 'This phenomenon is even more striking against the background of the fact that in an earlier age the office of rabbi in Poland and Lithuania was considered a respectable source of income as follows from the numerous testimonies concerning the sale of rabbinic offices in the seventeenth and eighteenth centuries. The readiness of some individuals to invest large sums in order to obtain a rabbinic post indicates that the rabbinate was then thought of as a worthwhile financial investment.' See his 'Talmudic Scholarship', 119. Since it is clear that the practice of buying rabbinic positions was also common in the 19th cent., a fact not noted by Etkes, his description of the universally low salaries of 19th-cent. east European rabbis presumably needs to be revised. (All of the sources mentioned in the preceding few notes, as well as many others, will be analysed in much greater detail in a comprehensive article dealing with the purchase of the rabbinate throughout Jewish history.)

payments for rabbinic positions were not generally carried out in public,[94] even this was not unheard of. In the early twentieth century there is at least one example of a rabbi actually advertising in the newspaper for another rabbi, *any rabbi*, to buy his position from the community.[95]

Weinberg stressed the corruption involved in rabbinic appointments in both large cities and small towns, and his disillusionment with the state of the rabbinate was clear. Although the obvious solution would have been to reform the process whereby rabbis were chosen, something which had been attempted in previous years,[96] Weinberg realized this would not be easy to achieve. However, he noted that if the religious leaders did not bring about a change in the procedure, it would not be long before change would be forced upon them. Presumably, he was referring here to the anti-traditional elements in league with the government. Although it was true that the rabbinate no longer had significant influence, and that because of the corruption involved in appointments many qualified people refused to enter the profession, Weinberg believed that large numbers of Jews would soon experience a revulsion from secular culture and decide to seek out their heritage. It was therefore crucial that when these Jews returned to the synagogue they should be met by someone qualified to lead.[97]

The decline of the rabbinate's prestige is a constant theme in rabbinic writings and Weinberg's comments in this regard are not particularly novel. Nostalgic yearning for the days of old when the authority of the rabbi was thought to have been unquestioned and held sacred by his flock has always been the rabbinic response to communal usurpation of the rabbi's power. Although the 'golden age' of the rabbinate is a myth, it is true that it was only in the last part of the nineteenth century that the authority of the east European rabbinate was reduced in a very substantial fashion. Now, for the first time, there were large segments of the population which had no use for traditional religious life. Weinberg parted company with the normal lamentations about the decline of the rabbinate by pointing a finger at his own colleagues and accusing many of them of being part of the problem. As he put it:

We have already merited the sight of men empty of Torah and lacking wisdom ascending to the highest rungs of the ladder of the rabbinate . . . and there is no one to rebuke them

[94] See Shelomo Yosef Zevin, 'Tsiyurim Ketanim', *Hamodia*, 21 Kislev 5671 [1910], 131–2.

[95] See the Warsaw daily *Haynt*, 26 Heshvan 5671 [1910], 4. This truly amazing advertisement, printed together with more mundane offerings, reads as follows:

NOTICE TO RABBIS

I wish to leave Voshlokova, in the Grodno district, and travel, God willing, to the Holy Land, but the citizens of this town still must collect money in order to pay their debts to me, approximately 2,000 roubles. Therefore, any rabbi who has this amount can, 'with my permission' and with all certainty, come here to accept the position of rabbi in this community.

[signed] RAPHAEL GORDON, *rabbi of the above-mentioned town*

Gordon was a well-known talmudist, and is best known for his strong defence of the authenticity of Solomon Friedlaender's forged edition of the Jerusalem Talmud.

[96] See Etkes, 'Talmudic Scholarship', 123–5.

[97] 'Concerning the Rabbinate' (1911).

sternly for their insolence which breaks through all boundaries. . . . Ignorance is not satisfied with what it already has, but wishes to spread throughout, and conquer, the entire rabbinic world.[98]

In a follow-up article Weinberg continued his criticism of the rabbinate.[99] Here he added a new flaw to his list, namely, that of rabbis who spend their time acquiring secular knowledge at the expense of Torah study. In opposition to the demands of the *maskilim* and his rabbinic colleague Reines, Weinberg stressed that there was no reason why the traditional rabbi should no longer be a suitable leader for his flock. Leadership and spirituality are essential for a rabbi, and it was obvious to Weinberg that neither of these qualities was acquired through secular degrees. Weinberg was not negating the value of secular studies *per se* here, but arguing that they have no relevance to the role of the rabbi. The fact that this criticism came from the pen of a crown rabbi, who had acquired the education advocated by the *maskilim*, makes it all the more interesting.

Attacks on Secular Hebrew Writers

Weinberg had enough criticism to go around and he turned next to the contemporary Hebrew writers. These writers were regarded by the Orthodox as the ideological successors of the early *maskilim*, and Weinberg's attacks reflect the dispute between the *maskilim* and the rabbis that had been going on for two generations. Like many of his contemporaries, he accused the writers of bearing a great deal of responsibility for the rabbinate's decline. Weinberg claimed that although these writers had no real contact with the Jewish masses and although their literary skills were minor, they nevertheless succeeded in defining themselves as progressives and placing the rabbis in the category of reactionaries, a categorization whose inapplicability Weinberg did not feel the need to explain. In addition to their lack of understanding of the traditional role of the rabbi, Weinberg continued, the Hebrew writers' anti-rabbinic campaign was also a result of their own bitterness at not being able to achieve any influence in contemporary Jewish life.[100]

In attempting to bridge the gap between the two camps, Weinberg argued that a *modus vivendi* could only be established when the boundaries of each group were firmly established. Weinberg agreed with Jacob Lifshitz that there was a place for modern Hebrew literature, as long as it did not presume to act as an authority on matters of religion and society. With a clearly understood separation of this type, and with the rabbinate's pre-eminence assured, Weinberg believed that the rabbis

[98] 'Concerning the Rabbinate' (1911), 632–3. Following this article *Hamodia* printed an anonymous response which was very biting and sarcastic, and accused Weinberg of demeaning the Jewish people; see 'The Issue of the Rabbinate' (Heb.), 14 Elul 5671 [1911], 713–14. Weinberg was strongly defended in a letter which appeared in *Hamodia*, 6 Tishrei 5672 [1911], 770.

[99] 'Concerning the Rabbinate (2)', *Hamodia*, 13 Tishrei 5672 [1911], 791–4.

[100] 'The Issue of the Rabbinate and the Hebrew Newspapers', *Hamodia*, 23 Iyar 5670 [1910], 73–4; 'Concerning the Yeshivot' (1911), 507.

would be happy to listen to intelligent suggestions and criticisms offered by the writers. In other words, for Weinberg there was no opposition *per se* to modern Hebrew literature. As for the writers, Weinberg claimed that if they were truly concerned with the state of the Jewish people, they would readily adopt this suggestion. 'Let [Hebrew] literature stretch forth her hand in peace. The rabbinate has always been ready, with [its own] hand outstretched in peace, to accept those who have returned.'[101]

Despite this plea, Weinberg realized that there was little chance that the secular Hebrew writers would change their ways, and it is unlikely that his articles were actually directed towards them. Had he really desired to influence non-traditionalists he would have taken to writing for their newspapers, as did Jacob Lifshitz and Rabbi Joshua Joseph Preil (1858–96), a well-known Orthodox intellectual whose perceptive essays were taken seriously in all circles.[102] Throughout his writings of this period, Weinberg showed a deep distrust of the disseminators of the Haskalah. This was so great that even though many of the *maskilim* were saying the same things as he was, especially with regard to the rabbinate, he did not grant their views any legitimacy. For example, in explaining why many of the *maskilim* supported the *musar* movement, Weinberg claimed that their motive was simply to hurt Orthodoxy by backing a movement which was creating controversy in the Orthodox world.[103]

Despite Weinberg's strident tone in his articles in *Hamodia*, there is evidence that he was not totally set in his ways. Indeed, this stridency may have been Weinberg's way of compensating for his own inner ambivalence about many of the issues he was now publicly defending. The opposing tendencies of his personality which were noted earlier were still present, and the Haskalah that he criticized so much still held some appeal for him. Mathisson recalls that in the summer of 1911, in an attempt to attract the attention of Nahum Sokolow (1859–1936), editor of the newspaper *Hatsefirah*, Weinberg sent him an article which dealt with the way the wise and righteous are portrayed in rabbinic literature. Unfortunately for Weinberg, Sokolow informed him that although the article had good elements it was not up to the standard of those published in *Hatsefirah*.[104] If Weinberg had hoped to become a shining star on the Hebrew literary scene, his confidence must have been severely shaken. For the rest of his time in Pilwishki, any interest he might still have had in reaching an audience beyond the Orthodox literati was submerged.

Still, it was the very attitude that allowed him to break with the traditional

[101] 'The Issue of the Rabbinate and the Hebrew Newspapers' (1910), 74.

[102] Regarding him see Salmon, *Religion*, 215–21.

[103] *Lifrakim*, 404–5 (309–10). Even as conservative a writer as Katz, *Musar Controversy*, 285, recognized that Weinberg had evaluated the motivations of the *maskilim* unfairly. See also Katz, *Musar Movement*, i. 211–12.

[104] See Mathisson's letter in *Hado'ar*, 11 Mar. 1966, 302. This article later appeared in the 24 May 1912 issue of *Ha'ivri* under the title 'The Righteous and the Wise in the Sages' Conception'.

rabbinic pattern and send an article to Sokolow that also gave him a clear view of the problems plaguing the Orthodox world. The need to revamp the rabbinate and the importance of the Hebrew press were areas of concern to all *maskilim*, and Weinberg shared these concerns. The difference between them was that Weinberg wished to work within traditional boundaries to bring about the desired changes. He was too much a part of the rabbinic fold to think differently.

Support for a New Orthodox Hebrew Literature

Having recognized that the *modus vivendi* he wished to see between the secular Hebrew writers and the Orthodox would never become reality, Weinberg suggested another plan of action. Since the traditional community was unable to benefit from the highly developed Hebrew literature of the non-Orthodox, he urged the creation of an Orthodox Hebrew literaturc. Although there already were several Orthodox newspapers and journals in eastern Europe, this new literature was to be different from what was then in vogue in Orthodox circles, for the latter's primary purpose was simply to criticize the views of the non-Orthodox. As Weinberg put it, this approach only succeeded in attracting an embarrassingly low level of writing that reflected very poorly on the Orthodox. Weinberg was emphatic that this type of polemical literature would never be able to sustain Orthodoxy's younger generation.[105]

Jacob Lifshitz had often questioned why the Orthodox world showed a total disregard for all attempts at creating an Orthodox literature. According to Weinberg the reason was obvious. As he saw it, the Orthodox world would never be, and had never been, attracted to the type of negative propaganda being produced by the Orthodox publicists. Lifshitz, a veteran of precisely this type of literature, had devoted his life to reviling non-Orthodox spokesmen, both in his articles and through the anonymous publications of the so-called 'Black Cell'.[106] Indeed, when Lifshitz himself wrote about the need for the creation of an Orthodox literature, forty years before Weinberg, he specifically included the obligation to engage in polemics against non-traditionalists as one of his motives.[107] As he later pointed out, these polemics were designed to strengthen Orthodox public opinion, since he knew it was hopeless to attempt to change the attitudes of the *maskilim*.[108] It was in response to Lifshitz's approach that Weinberg decided to express his views, and he

105 'Concerning Orthodox Literature' (Heb.), *Yagdil Torah*, 3 (1911), 20–2 (arabic numerals). (The complete issues of the journal (1909–11), which was edited by R. Isser Zalman Meltzer and R. Benjamin Tomashoff, have been reprinted (New York, n.d.).) With regard to the creation of a high-quality and non-polemical Orthodox Hebrew literature, see also Elijah Klatzkin, *Devar halakhah: Miluim* (Lublin, 1923), 57.

106 Although he never admitted his membership of this organization, there is little doubt that he was one of its leaders; see Chaim Tchernowitz (Rav Tsa'ir), *Autobiography* (Heb.) (New York, 1954), 141, and Shifman, 'Dispute', 89–90.

107 'Haseder vehama'aseh', *Halevanon*, 8 (1872), 17–19.

108 *Zikhron ya'akov*, ii. 101–2.

was hopeful that the former, although many years his senior, would follow in his path.[109]

In fairness to Lifshitz, it must be pointed out that when he began to publish his polemical pieces the traditional world had just been shaken by the articles attacking the *Shulḥan arukh* published in 1869 by Moses Leib Lilienblum (1843–1910).[110] This type of article had, in earlier years, been commonplace in Germany and would no longer have caused anyone there to raise an eyebrow. Yet in Russia, attacks on the *Shulḥan arukh*, in Hebrew no less, were unheard of. It was this shock that led numerous rabbis, with the full support of Salanter, to go on the offensive and publish polemical responses in the newspaper *Halevanon*.[111] The literary response to Lilienblum's articles actually had broad historical implications, for, as Stanislawski has pointed out, 'This appropriation of a Hebrew newspaper as a central tool in the defense of the faith was a crucial milestone in the transformation of traditional Judaism in Russia into an Orthodox Judaism.'[112]

In Weinberg's mind, however, what might have once been necessary in the previous generation had lost its usefulness by 1910. Indeed, he was very proud that the negative and polemical literature received little backing from either the rabbinate or the Orthodox laity. Basically, such literature was 'not worthy of honour and support'.[113] Weinberg felt that it would have been a disgrace for the 'people of the book' to take time away from profound Torah study in order to read the superficial newspapers and journals that presumed to represent them. He described the Orthodox writers as spending their time either complaining about the lack of support for the creation of an Orthodox literature or attempting to imitate the style of the Haskalah writers. It was thus no wonder to him that they did not have any impact on the Jewish community, for they were not capable of creating a richly original literature in which polemics had no place.

Elaborating on these points, Weinberg asserted that the leading medieval Jewish philosophers did not make use of abusive language and did not write provocative polemics against their opponents. Instead, they devoted their time to serious exploration of matters of faith, and this by itself was enough to demonstrate the authenticity of their positions. Men such as these had never had reason to complain that they were being ignored, and the lesson in this for modern times was self-evident. Weinberg thus agreed with the previously mentioned position of Rabbi Joseph Saul Nathanson, Rabbi Abraham Jacob Friedman, and Rabbi Israel Meir Hacohen that one need not be concerned with refuting non-traditionalists. To do so would only distract the rabbis from their true problem, that of keeping

109 'Concerning Orthodox Literature' (1911), 20–2.

110 See S. Breiman, 'The Dispute over Religious Reforms in Hebrew Literature' (Heb.), *He'avar*, 1 (1953), 115–32; Katzenelson, *Literary Battle*, ch. 4.

111 Regarding the dispute see Michael Stanislawski, *For Whom Do I Toil? Judah Leib Gordon and the Crisis of Russian Jewry* (Oxford, 1988), 91 ff.

112 Ibid. 93.

113 'Concerning Orthodox Literature' (1911), 22.

Orthodox Jews in the fold. As they saw matters, the strengthening of the Orthodox position would, by itself, provide any necessary refutations.[114]

Following in the footsteps of Salanter,[115] Weinberg stressed that there was no reason why Jewish religious revival could not be inspired by traditional Jewish literature. The authentic Jewish thought reflected in the writings of men such as Maimonides and Judah Halevi could provide inspiration for modern intellectuals who would follow in their path. Not surprisingly, Weinberg noted that there is no need for secular studies in order for one to reach the heights of spirituality and culture, for all that is necessary in this regard is contained in the Torah. In contrast to what the Zionists were saying, Weinberg argued that the teachings of Judaism could not be understood in the context of a Hebrew nationalism which differs from other cultures in form but not in kind. On the contrary, he countered, it is precisely because Judaism is fundamentally unique that any attempt to understand it other than through itself is doomed to failure.[116]

Although Weinberg's goal of creating an Orthodox literature of intellectual worth must have seemed reasonable to many, it was much easier said than done. Whether for lack of interest, lack of ability, or opposition on ideological grounds,[117] none of the leading east European rabbinic figures were essayists. Indeed, most traditional rabbis were only able to write words of *musar*, when, as Rabbi Abraham Isaac Kook (1865–1935) pointed out, what was needed was a literature showing signs of intellectual ferment.[118] As Weinberg recalled, his colleagues even expressed their disapproval that he had chosen to enter this field.[119] Both Weinberg and Kook were well aware that it had been many years since leading rabbis had written what could be described as Jewish thought. This can be explained by the fact that traditional Jewish society was relatively static, and there was no great need for expositions of Jewish belief. All intellectual effort went into the study of Talmud and halakhah. The problem with this was that times were changing and Orthodoxy was fighting a losing battle. Its leaders were ill equipped to respond to contemporary challenges, and this explains the agitation for the creation of an Orthodox press. Although, as

114 Cf. Abraham Isaac Kook, *Arpilei tohar* (Jerusalem, 1983), 39: 'The unblemished saints do not complain about evil, but increase righteousness; do not complain about heresy, but increase faith; do not complain about ignorance, but increase wisdom.'

115 See *SE* iv, p. 372; 'Rabbi Israel Salanter and his Musar Teachings' (Heb.), in Judah Elbinger (ed.), *Halevanon* (Warsaw, 1912), 3 ff.

116 'Clarifying' (1911), 409; 'Concerning Orthodox Literature' (1911), 45, 81–3, 101–2.

117 See Elhanan Wasserman, *Kovets he'arot* (Jerusalem, 1985), 72*b*, for an example of strong ideological opposition to any form of Orthodox literature.

118 Kook, *Igerot hare'iyah* (Jerusalem, 1962), i, no. 188 (letter to R. Isser Zalman Meltzer concerning the publication of his new journal, *Yagdil Torah*).

119 *Et aḥai anokhi mevakesh* (Benei Berak, 1966), 45. Throughout his Pilwishki years, Weinberg published only one article of traditional rabbinic scholarship. It appeared in *Yagdil Torah* in 1910 and is reprinted in *SE* iii, pp. 376–9. He did, however, correspond on talmudic matters with rabbinic colleagues, although none of his letters from this period survive. For a 1908 letter from R. Elijah Klatzkin to Weinberg, see Klatzkin's *Devar halakhah: Miluim*, 39.

Weinberg admitted, few east European rabbis were able to compose a coherent analysis of the issues confronting Orthodoxy, he believed that the creation of a new form of literature would bring about a change in traditional thought patterns. This change would in turn foster a new generation of Orthodox writers able to meet the modern challenges.[120]

Of course, this new literature which Weinberg discussed would support the position of the rabbinic élite, and there would be no compromises with modernity or with popular opinion. In a striking passage Weinberg wrote:

I am not embarrassed—for fear that perhaps they will caricature me as a 'black reactionary'—to proclaim my distress publicly concerning the awesome confusion that has descended into our spiritual world from the day that we went out from the 'walls of the ghetto'. The earlier days, when the Jewish people were closed up in the 'walls of the ghetto' and totally removed from the frontiers of general culture, were better than these days with regard to wisdom and understanding. Concerning the development of the intellect—leaving aside all else—with this everyone agrees! With regard to ethical and moral development, the very day that the government decreed that the ghetto be destroyed and its gates broken down was 'as dark for Israel as the day when the golden Calf was made'.[121] The authentic Hebrew thought, which is without fault or adulteration, ceased. Broken was the historic thread which united and bound us with the earlier rabbis, upon whose authority the nation relied throughout its long years.[122]

THE WIDER WORLD: EARLY ENCOUNTERS AND INFLUENCES

German and East European Styles of Orthodoxy

With the above passage Weinberg staked out his position in the debate over the value of Jewish cultural integration in gentile society. In fact, there is no question that Weinberg's nostalgic view of pre-modern Jewish life was the prevailing sentiment of the east European rabbis and presumably of the laity too.[123] What is most interesting is that this view stands in total opposition to the position of Rabbi Samson Raphael Hirsch, which Weinberg himself was later to endorse.

Hirsch felt that the ghetto had taken from Jews the elements of a healthy political, economic, and social existence. Following from this notion, 'Hirsch was convinced that the conditions of modern life afford better prospects for the

[120] 'Concerning Orthodox Literature' (1911), 101.

[121] Cf. *Shabbat* 17*a*.

[122] 'Concerning Orthodox Literature' (1911), 81–2.

[123] See Mordechai Breuer, 'Emancipation and the Rabbis', *Niv Hamidrashia*, 13 (1978–9), 26–51. Among the few east European rabbinic leaders known to have supported emancipation are R. Zvi Hirsch Chajes, R. Zvi Hirsch Kalischer, and R. Dov Ber Meisels. See Bruriah Hutner-David, 'The Dual Role of Rabbi Zvi Hirsch Chajes: Traditionalist and *Maskil*' (Ph.D. diss., Columbia University, 1971), 91 ff.; Jacob Katz, 'Tsevi Hirsh Kalischer', in Leo Jung (ed.), *Guardians of our Heritage* (New York, 1958), 215 ff.; Efraim Kupfer, *Ber Meisels* (Yid.) (Warsaw, 1952); Moshe Kamelhar, *Rabbi Dov Ber Meisels* (Heb.) (Jerusalem, 1970).

development of Torah-living, of a life that would be more accomplished and more satisfying than under the conditions of the ghetto. . . . [T]he alienation of Israel from the achievements of general culture did not derive from the genuine character of Judaism.'[124] As I have already noted, it is questionable whether Weinberg, at this time, had a real understanding of the views of Hirsch or any of the other German Orthodox intelligentsia. Although the Hebrew translation of Hirsch's *Nineteen Letters* had long been available, Weinberg did not show any sign of having read it. He thus did not see any conflict between what he wrote and his suggestion that the works of the German Orthodox be translated into Hebrew as a means of reviving the Jewish spirit.[125]

Weinberg probably knew that some years before Rabbi Israel Salanter had also recommended translating Hirsch's works into Russian and Hebrew in order to reach the young Jews of eastern Europe.[126] However, unlike Weinberg, Salanter was well aware of the nature of German Orthodoxy. Although, as we shall see, he did not wish to see east European Orthodoxy transformed along the lines of the German model, he was more amenable to reforms in the traditional system of Jewish education than was Weinberg,[127] whose position was that of an ultra-conservative attempting to keep the floodgates firm against the torrent of social change.

Even though Weinberg seems not to have read the works of the German Orthodox, his advocacy of their writings is no surprise. Forty years earlier Lifshitz had also pointed to the German Orthodox newspapers as a model. It was the German Orthodox who were the first to confront the fact that their version of Judaism could no longer be identified with the larger Jewish community. As a means of responding to this new threat, they produced a number of intellectually stimulating works of Jewish content. The German Orthodox, in particular Hirsch, were thus the natural model for the east European Orthodox in dealing with what was for them a new phenomenon.[128] If, however, Weinberg had examined the

124 Breuer, *Torah-Im-Derekh-Eretz*, 23. See also ibid. 28 and id., 'Emancipation and the Rabbis', 45–50.

125 'Concerning Orthodox Literature' (1911), 101.

126 Katz, *Musar Movement*, i. 223; Etkes, *Rabbi Israel Salanter*, 261–2.

127 See Katz, *Musar Movement*, i. 218 ff.

128 See e.g. Moses Ahronson's translation of Hirsch's *Igerot tsafun* (Vilna, 1891), introduction, 12 (as Mordechai Breuer points out in *Tradition*, 16 (Summer 1977), 146, the common vocalization *tsafon* is a mistake); Menahem Mendel Landau, *Mekits nirdamim* (Petrokov, 1903), 28*b*–29*a*; E. L. Tzihan in *Hapeles*, 5 (1905), 426; Bat-Yehudah, *Ish hame'orot*, 163; and Elijah Klatzkin's German article quoted in Breuer, 'Orthodoxy in Germany', 79. From Weinberg's own era, see Klatzkin, *Devar halakhah: Miluim*, 57; id., *Even pinah* (Jerusalem, 1930), 61*b*; R. Isaac Eleazar Hirschowitz's translation of Hirsch's writings, *Meitav higayon* (Vilna, 1913), 24, and R. Hayim Ozer Grodzinski's approbation of this work. For other examples of interest in Hirsch, see the translations of Hirsch's writings in *Hamodia*, 2 Nisan 5672 [1912], 383–4; Erev Shavuot 5672 [1912], 481–6; 15 Sivan 5672 [1912], 500–3; 12 Adar II 5673 [1913], 377–9; 19 Adar II 5673 [1913], 392–5; 2 Iyar 5673 [1913], 479–582; 9 Iyar 5673 [1913], 495–9; 8 Sivan 5673 [1913], 557–62. See also Hermann Klein, 'Das Ostjuden-Problem', *Jüdische Monatshefte*, 3 (1916), 99: '. . . the Rabbi of Czortkow said to me: "Ask the German Orthodox, in my name, to have the works of R. Hirsch *z" l* translated into the holy tongue, so that we have something for our young people. It is modern and genuinely Jewish, even hasidic."'

writings of Hirsch, he would have seen that the aspiration to integrate Judaism in the modern world, to bring the 'beauty of Japhet into the tents of Shem', is ever-present. Yet Weinberg complained that this approach had only corrupted traditional Jewish thought.

All this raises the interesting issue of the relationship between east European Orthodoxy and German Orthodoxy, which will be discussed more fully in a later chapter. For now, it is important to call attention to the fact that among the east European Orthodox there was always a great deal of admiration for the accomplishments of Hirsch and German Orthodoxy as a whole, combined with a lack of real understanding of what German Orthodoxy was all about. The fact that most east European Jews were unable to read German Orthodox literature had a great deal to do with this ignorance. The overwhelming majority of east European rabbis were, however, convinced of one thing, namely, that German Orthodoxy should remain in Germany where it was doing a good job. They strongly opposed any attempt to transfer it to the east.[129]

If the east European rabbis had been aware of the true nature of German Orthodoxy, it is likely that many of them would not have been even this tolerant and would have agreed with the Lubavitcher *rebbe*, Rabbi Sholom Dov Ber Schneersohn (1861–1920), who saw German-style Orthodoxy as a negative influence even for German Jews. As he saw it, their combination of the holy and the secular caused the Torah and *mitsvot* to become nothing more than a body without a soul, leaving the majority of the German Orthodox 'without Torah, without prayer, and with few good deeds'.[130] A recent author has argued, probably with some exaggeration, that if the east European rabbis had been aware of the true nature of German Orthodoxy, they would never have agreed to join the German-founded and -led Agudat Yisrael movement.[131] In fact, Schneersohn made a

[129] As will be seen later, R. Hayim Ozer Grodzinski was particularly fearful of German Orthodox influence, though he did write an approbation for a Hebrew translation of Hirsch's writings; see n. 128 above. For R. Hayim Soloveitchik's view of Hirsch's method of education, see *Halikhot hagrah* (Jerusalem, [1996]), 6–7 (first pagination), and Eleazar Shakh, *Letters and Articles* (Heb.) (Benei Berak, 1996), vi. 108, 202. R. Abraham Isaac Kook's views in this regard are noteworthy, but his relationship to Torah im Derekh Eretz is more complicated and requires special treatment. See Shlomo Aviner, 'Rabbi Kook and the Distinction between Holy and Profane' (Heb.), *Hama'ayan*, 22 (Tishrei 5742 [1982]), 66–9; Raphael Auerbach, 'Rabbi Kook and his Relation to the Torah im Derekh Eretz Approach and its Advocates' (Heb.), in Hayim Hamiel (ed.), *Be'oro* (Jerusalem, 1986), 528–48; Reuven Gerber, 'The Development of National Vision in Rabbi Kook's Philosophy' (Heb.) (Ph.D. diss., Hebrew University of Jerusalem, 1991), 257–62.

[130] *Igerot kodesh* (Brooklyn, NY, 1987), v. 5, 9, 14. See also ibid. ii. 465, where he claims that the German Orthodox are lacking in 'fear of heaven'.

[131] Yerahmiel Yisrael Yitshak Domb, *Ha'atakot* (Jerusalem, 1990). Cf. Meir Bar-Ilan, *From Volozhin to Jerusalem* (Heb.) (Tel Aviv, 1971), ii. 398–9. See Jacob Rosenheim, *Memoirs* (Heb.) (Tel Aviv, 1955), 173, for Elijah Akiva Rabinowitz's complaint, at the first Agudat Yisrael convention, that the majority of the east European rabbis could not understand the German speeches, and that they should therefore be translated into Yiddish (the request was turned down). See also S. D. B. Schneersohn, *Igerot kodesh*, ii. 698. It was precisely because of R. Isaac Jacob Reines's knowledge of

similar point in explaining why Rabbi Israel Meir Hacohen and Rabbi Isaac Jacob Rabinowitz (1854–1918) supported the Agudah.[132] Of course, the reverse may also be true. Had the German rabbis and communal leaders realized that, in half a century, the Agudah would fall under the control of the east European elements and become the ideological opponent of Hirsch's vision of Torah im Derekh Eretz,[133] it is unlikely that they would have founded such an organization.

Along these lines, I have noted elsewhere that any expressions of support for Hirsch by the Hungarian rabbis who were persecuting Rabbi Esriel Hildesheimer (1820–99) must also be explained as due to this ignorance. Hildesheimer was championing an enlightened Orthodoxy, but Hirsch's philosophy was a much more radical revision of traditional thought than anything Hildesheimer had advocated.[134] In addition, Hirsch had instituted some mild reforms in the synagogue (e.g. his synagogue had a choir, he preached in German, held weddings in the synagogue, and wore a special robe for prayer). All this would have been enough for the extremist Hungarian rabbis to oppose him stridently.[135] In fact, earlier in his career, when he was in Nikolsburg, he did encounter opposition from right-wing members of his community, not to mention other Hungarian rabbis.[136]

However, after assuming his rabbinic post in Frankfurt, away from the more conservative elements he had earlier confronted, he was able to win their support in his battle with Rabbi Seligmann Baer Bamberger (1808–78), when the latter opposed his ruling that the Orthodox must not retain communal ties with the Reformers.[137] The same Hungarian Jews who now looked upon Hirsch with

the nature of German Orthodoxy that he opposed the participation of the east European Orthodox in Agudat Yisrael; see his *Shenei hame'orot*, section 2, part 1, ch. 5. See also R. Hayim Eleazar Shapira, in Weinberger, *Igerot shapirin*, 275, who comments sarcastically: 'One must not join together with them and their "righteous Doktoren" (*hadoktorim hatsadikim shelahem*).'

[132] S. D. B. Schneersohn, *Igerot kodesh*, ii. 693.

[133] See Mordechai Breuer, 'Agudat Yisrael and Western Orthodoxy' (Heb.), *Hama'ayan*, 5 (Tishrei 5725 [1964]), 15–18.

[134] So it would have seemed from the standpoint of the traditional Orthodox rabbinate. Hirsch, of course, claimed that his philosophy was a *return* to traditional thought, which had been corrupted over time.

[135] See my review in *Tradition*, 25 (1989), 98.

[136] See Leopold Greenwald, *The History of the Religious Reformation in Germany and Hungary* (Heb.) (Columbus, Oh., 1948), 54 ff.; Katz, *Halakhah in Straits*, 240.

[137] See most recently Jacob Katz, *The Unhealed Breach* (Heb.) (Jerusalem, 1995), ch. 23. It must have struck Bamberger as strange that R. Moses Schick, perhaps the most prominent Hungarian rabbi, would write to him in order to support Hirsch's stand in the *Austritt* controversy (*She'elot uteshuvot maharam schick* (New York, 1961), *Oraḥ ḥayim*, no. 306). Other than sharing similar positions with regard to remaining in a community together with the Reformers, the views of Judaism advocated by Hirsch and Schick were very different, and Bamberger was much more representative of Schick's old-style Orthodoxy. (On this point, it is of interest that Katz has argued for a fundamental bond between Hirsch's advocacy of *Austritt* and Torah im Derekh Eretz; see *Halakhah in Straits*, 228 ff.) One further point worth noting is that Hirsch's separatism was only a religious, not a national, separatism, and he never intended to exclude the Reformers from the Jewish people. Yet this extreme step was advocated by many Hungarian rabbis, among them R. Moses Sofer, *She'elot uteshuvot ḥatam sofer* (Jerusalem, 1991), vi, no. 89 (end), and Schick, *She'elot uteshuvot maharam schick, Oraḥ ḥayim*,

awe[138] would not see anything incongruous about referring to Friedrich von Schiller, the German poet, whom he revered, with the epithet 'may his name be blotted out'.[139] This same lack of understanding is seen in the assertion that Hirsch's advocacy of secular studies was in the nature of an emergency measure necessitated by the times. For example, Rabbi Barukh Ber Leibowitz (1864–1940), a prominent Lithuanian *rosh yeshiva*, elaborated on this mistaken belief, which must have been widespread in eastern Europe and finds echoes in our own day.[140]

Rabbi Israel Salanter spent a good deal of time in Germany and acquired both an appreciation and an understanding of German Orthodoxy. He too believed that German Orthodoxy was valuable, even necessary, but only on German soil where the old-style Orthodoxy was unfortunately no longer viable. In particular, he called attention to the lack of talmudic scholars in Germany. This phenomenon was directly connected with the form of Orthodoxy encouraged there, which ensured an advanced secular education for all, without, however, matching this with advanced talmudic education. In eastern Europe it was widely, and probably correctly, believed that German Orthodoxy would disrupt traditional religious life.[141] Surprising as it may seem, even Reines, the advocate of secular studies in

no. 305. It is not clear why this approach was always resisted by the German rabbinic authorities, who never gave up hope that the Reformers would return to the fold. See Yonah Emanuel, 'Chapters in the Biography of Rabbi Jacob Ettlinger' (Heb.), *Hama'ayan*, 12 (Tevet 5732 [1972]), 31–2; Judith Bleich, 'Rabbinic Responses to Nonobservance in the Modern Era', in Jacob J. Schacter (ed.), *Jewish Tradition and the Nontraditional Jew* (Northvale, NJ, 1992), 54–62; and Katz, *Halakhah in Straits*, 71–2. According to R. Solomon Eger, the German rabbis were afraid that any action on their part could backfire and threaten Orthodox control of communal religious matters. See Solomon Sofer (ed.), *Igerot soferim* (Tel Aviv, 1970), section 1, p. 84.

138 See Philip Fischer, *In seinen Spuren* (Sátoraljaújhely, 1922), introduction and ch. 1.

139 See my 'A Letter of Criticism Directed against the Yeshiva of Eisenstadt' (Heb.), *Hama'ayan*, 34 (Tishrei 5754 [1993]), 18.

140 *Birkat shemuel* (New York, 1964), *Kidushin*, 38–42. See also Joseph Isaac Schneersohn, 'A Critique of the Educational Approach of German Orthodoxy' (Heb.), *Hahed* (Av 5688 [1928]), 1–3. For more recent comments, see Moses Swift, '"External Books" in the Halakhah' (Heb.), in H. J. Zimmels *et al.* (eds.), *Essays Presented to Chief Rabbi Israel Brodie on the Occasion of his Seventieth Birthday* (London, 1967), 207; Benziyon Jakobovics, *Zekhor yemot olam* (Benei Berak, 1989), ii. 132.

141 See Lifshitz, *Maḥazikei hadat*, 11*b*; Etkes, *Rabbi Israel Salanter*, 305–9; Hirsch, *Shemesh marpeh* (New York, 1992), 282 n. 40. Isaac Halevy's comments are typical of east European rabbinic sentiment (Reichel (ed.), *Letters of R. Isaac Halevy*, 158): 'The overwhelming majority of the young [German] rabbis are ignorant. Practically all of the seminary students are uneducated, and not one of them has mastery of a few tractates. Not even in Bible [are they educated], and if they do discuss it, all they know is biblical criticism.' Ibid. 205: 'It will be harmful to send German rabbis to Russia, because despite all they [i.e. the Jewish masses] have heard they cannot imagine a rabbi lacking wide-ranging and deep knowledge of Torah, and this can certainly do damage there and cause a desecration of God's name.' See also ibid. 203, where he describes German Orthodoxy as 'bankrupt'.

It is possible that Salanter's opposition to secular studies for the east European Orthodox was based on the negative experience he had with one of his pupils; see Weinberg, 'Schulfragen' (1916), 455 n. 1. The fact that R. Simhah Zissel, one of Salanter's leading students, founded two schools

the yeshiva, took a very strong stand against transplanting German-style Orthodoxy to the east.[142]

Since this negative view of German Orthodoxy vis-à-vis traditional east European Orthodoxy was so widely held, it is no wonder that all attempts to bring the former type to the east were doomed to failure.[143] Yet it is noteworthy that Salanter did not refrain from appropriating certain aspects of German Orthodoxy if he thought they could be of value in the east. One prime example is Salanter's advocacy of the publication of Jewish books in Russian in order to reach assimilated Jews.[144] It is more than likely that he came to this decision after seeing the positive effect of Jewish texts in the vernacular in Germany. In recommending this step he parted company with virtually the entire rabbinic élite, which always opposed religious publications in the modern vernacular.[145]

Salanter's view that German-style Orthodoxy had no place in the east was opposed by Hirsch and Hildesheimer, who did not believe that the brand of Orthodoxy they were espousing was only suitable for Germany. In line with this, Hildesheimer made a great though unsuccessful effort to foster a German-style Orthodoxy in Hungary.[146] Hirsch did not involve himself greatly with any practical reforms of east European Jewry, realizing how much opposition he would meet. Nevertheless, he too strongly believed that the isolation from general culture which was the norm in the east was the unfortunate result of gentile persecution

which combined Torah and secular studies (see Katz, *Musar Movement*, ii, chs. 17–18) did not contradict Salanter's view. Salanter was never opposed in principle to the introduction of secular studies, if this could be done without a negative effect on traditional society. However, he was only willing to trust his beloved pupil to carry out this mission successfully; see Katz, *Musar Movement*, ii. 216–17. Thus, he could not support any broad-based reform of east European Jewish education. Furthermore, he remained convinced that it was necessary for aspiring Torah scholars to devote themselves exclusively to Torah studies. He encouraged talented students to broaden their horizons, but only after completing their time at the yeshiva. See Katz, *Musar Movement*, i, ch. 17. In order to prevent any possible misunderstanding of his position, he even refused to sign a letter urging Russian Jews to support the Rabbinical Seminary of Berlin; see ibid. 226–7, and Etkes, *Rabbi Israel Salanter*, 307. R. Isaac Elhanan Spektor had no such reservations; see his letter in Meir Hildesheimer, 'Writings Regarding the Founding of the Rabbinical Seminary of Berlin' (Heb.), *Hama'ayan*, 14 (Tevet 5734 [1974]), 34–6. It is clear that, although he was very supportive of the Berlin Rabbinical Seminary, Spektor would never have endorsed the creation of an Orthodox rabbinical seminary in Lithuania. In Ch. 5 we will see that Grodzinski had the same attitude.

142 *Shenei hame'orot*, ii. 23 ff. (Hebrew numerals).

143 See Luz, *Parallels Meet*, 10. One source to which Luz does not refer is Zebulun Leib, 'Dover shalom', *Halevanon*, 9 (1872), 226–7, where a writer advocating educational reform points to German Orthodoxy as a perfect model of what could be accomplished in the east. See also S. T. Neuwedal, 'The Humiliation of Judaism Due to the Negligence of the Orthodox' (Heb.), *Hamodia*, 2 Heshvan 5671 [1910], 23–5, and S. D. B. Schneersohn, *Igerot kodesh*, iv. 323–4.

144 See Goldberg, *Between Berlin and Slobodka*, 30; Hirsch, *Shemesh marpeh*, 281–2.

145 See e.g. the observation of Dov A. Friedman, 'Ḥazut kashah', *Hamagid*, 30 July 1885, 257.

146 See Mordechai Eliav, 'Rabbi Esriel Hildesheimer and his Influence on Hungarian Jewry' (Heb.), *Zion*, 27 (1962), 59–86; id., '*Torah im Derekh Eretz* in Hungary' (Heb.), *Sinai*, 51 (1959), 127–42; and my 'Letter of Criticism', 15–25.

that prevented Jews from fulfilling their God-given mission in the world completely. In his view, the time would come when east European Jewry would join their German brethren and assume their rightful place in society.[147]

Weinberg rejected the approach of German Orthodoxy to modern culture and its interaction with Judaism.[148] In his article in *Yagdil torah*, in which he advocated the ideology of the rabbinic élite of eastern Europe, he was most emphatic that modern culture has no relevance for Jews. Exclusive Torah study is their mission and only through this would the battle with the non-Orthodox be won.[149] It was precisely this view which he would later abandon.

Early Stages in Weinberg's Thought

As a result of his many essays, Weinberg's name became known even outside rabbinic circles. Because of this he was invited to contribute an article to the yearbook *He'atid*, most of whose contributors were not Orthodox.[150] In this article, and in a similar one,[151] Weinberg explored the 'essence' of Judaism. For him, it was of the utmost importance that there could be no separation of the idea of God from that of ethics, and he claimed that Judaism originated this notion. Since, he argued, the only source for the Jewish ethical system is the divine will, ethical ideals and religious practices are eternally joined. Weinberg also denied that external forces had any influence on Jewish ethical ideals, which in his eyes were derived exclusively from the Torah. Because of this he did not grant any validity to comparisons between the Jewish ethical system and general ethical insights.[152]

Although Weinberg did not mention Salanter in his articles on this topic, it is clear that little of what he said was original. He was simply expounding Salanter's ideology, which was by now well known to students of the *musar* yeshivot.[153] He did, however, show more originality in dealing with the issue of apologetics, which was then a major type of Jewish literature. The desire to show that Judaism was an 'acceptable' religion motivated a number of east European writers, much as the same rationale motivated the rise of the Wissenschaft des Judentums in

[147] See Breuer, *Torah-Im-Derekh-Eretz*, 47–50; id., 'Miba'ad limeḥitzah', *Hama'ayan*, 21 (Nisan 5741 [1981]), 42. Knowledge of this attitude might have led R. Abraham Schenker, the director of the *kolel* in Kovno, to misrepresent the institution to Hirsch when seeking a letter of support. In his letter Hirsch referred to the *kolel* as a place where both the holy and the secular were studied. Presumably, Schenker told Hirsch that secular studies had a place in the curriculum. See Etkes, *Rabbi Israel Salanter*, 294 n. 80; Breuer, *Torah-Im-Derekh-Eretz*, 47–8.

[148] See most recently David Ellenson, 'German Jewish Orthodoxy: Tradition in the Context of Culture', in Jack Wertheimer (ed.), *The Uses of Tradition* (New York, 1992), 5–22.

[149] 'Concerning Orthodox Literature' (1911), 82–3.

[150] For some reason the article, 'The Essence of Judaism', never appeared in *He'atid* but was published in *Ha'ivri*, 14 June 1912, 230–1 (see Weinberg's appended note).

[151] 'Clarifying' (1911), 409–11.

[152] Ibid. and 'Essence' (1912), 230–1. On this theme, see also *Lifrakim*, 291–2 (168–9).

[153] Perhaps he was also aware of the important works of M. Lazarus, *Ethik des Judentums*, and Leo Baeck, *Wesen des Judentums*. See Henrietta Szold's translation of the former as *The Ethics of Judaism* (Philadelphia, 1900), i. 109 ff., and Baeck, *The Essence of Judaism* (New York, 1961), 59 ff.

nineteenth-century Germany. Weinberg offered no support for these apologists. To begin with, he argued, their constant concern with what the gentile world was thinking blinded them to the actual sources of Judaism. They were so busy trying to show the similarities between Jewish and non-Jewish thought that they did not even realize they were distorting the Jewish sources in order to bring them into harmony with progressive ideas.[154] Writing in a small town in Lithuania, far from the advances of modern thought and the difficulties they presented to traditional Jewish belief, it was easy for Weinberg to look down upon all such attempts at explaining Judaism. Approaches which were *de rigueur* in the west often remained misunderstood and unappreciated in the east.

As an example of the type of distortions of Judaism that the apologists were guilty of spreading, Weinberg told the following story. He was once at a gathering where a famous writer was speaking about the mission of Judaism and the importance of Israel among the nations.[155] The speaker tried to show the value of the Torah by pointing out that it is the first source for the commandment 'Love thy neighbour as thyself'. Therefore, he argued, it was imperative for Jews not to remove themselves from their role upon the world stage. The speaker continued: 'As long as one soldier is walking outside, the mission of Israel has not been accomplished and its right to exist has not ceased.'

When Weinberg heard this he could not contain himself. He approached the speaker and objected that the Torah in no way taught such a lesson. He instead pointed to the verses 'Howbeit of the cities of these peoples, that the Lord thy God giveth thee for an inheritance, thou shalt save alive nothing that breatheth' (Deuteronomy 20: 16), and 'Unto a foreigner thou may lend upon interest but unto thy brother thou shalt not lend upon interest' (Deuteronomy 23: 21).

Although Weinberg did not explain the significance of the verses he quoted, it is obvious that he was trying to show that there are indeed parts of the Torah that do not conform to what in modern times is considered an enlightened attitude, and that the values of the Torah are not to be found in a few verses which appeal to modern thought. According to Weinberg, such an approach is degrading to the Torah, for every verse in it is of equal value, even if it is unappreciated by modern man. One must not forget, he pointed out, that before the writing of the New Testament the verses of the Torah which are now held up as models of morality were ignored and even denigrated by enlightened gentiles.[156]

He also pointed out that in future years the same phenomenon may occur with other verses in the Bible. Although in Weinberg's day the notion of letting the fields lie fallow every few years and the six-day working week were gaining support, in earlier years they had been ridiculed. Yet the Torah spoke about these topics

154 'Clarifying' (1911), 410, and *Lifrakim*, 393 (298).

155 Presumably Joseph Klausner; see Weinberg, 'At Home and Outside' (Heb.), *Hamodia*, 26 Adar II 5673 [1913], 413, for his response to Klausner's popular lectures on the messianic idea in Judaism.

156 *Lifrakim*, 390–1 (295–6).

millennia ago. All this simply reinforced Weinberg's point that the Torah, in its entirety, is both divine and eternal. To select portions of it as examples of a highly developed morality, while ignoring other less 'progressive' sections, was therefore out of place.[157]

Tied in with this approach was his view that it was futile to attempt to convince antisemites that there is value in Judaism. This was especially true, he argued, since the antisemites were well aware that the apologists only quoted selected passages from traditional Jewish sources. This led them to suspect that the rest of Jewish literature was not so enlightened. The fact that the acclaimed apologetic work of Rabbi David Zvi Hoffmann[158] did not have any effect on their outlook led Weinberg to the conclusion that one must fight them with the 'strength in one's fist', not with the weapons of logic. As far as Weinberg was concerned, any effort devoted to apologetic literature aimed at antisemites was to be regarded as nothing more than a 'Sisyphean labour'.[159]

All this was stated with regard to apologetics aimed at the outside world. However, Weinberg did not hesitate to respond to antisemitic literature when his response was directed to the Jewish community. Although he made it clear that he did not feel the need to show that Judaism conforms with modern norms, there were times when he did just that, showing that he too was uncomfortable with the notion that segments of Jewish law could, from a modern standpoint, be regarded as unethical. For example, the well-known talmudic laws that discriminate economically against gentiles were one area which Weinberg felt he must clarify.

In his essay on this topic Weinberg began by insisting that none of the discriminatory talmudic laws are aimed at modern Christians. In rendering this judgement he adopted the view of the medieval sage Rabbi Menahem Me'iri, who held that gentiles of his day who conducted themselves according to moral and religious principles were excluded from any discrimination. So much so, according to Me'iri, that even though the Talmud states that a Jew need not return the lost objects of a gentile or rectify any financial errors made by a gentile,[160] this did not apply to those gentiles who followed a standard of civilized laws.[161]

Weinberg also offered what was a common apologetic explanation for the Talmud's economic discrimination against gentiles.[162] According to him, the reason the Sages permitted one to keep the lost valuables of a gentile was not because the

[157] Ibid. 392 (297).

[158] *Der Schulchan Aruch und die Rabbinen über das Verhältnis der Juden zu Andersgläubigen* (Berlin, 1894).

[159] *Lifrakim*, 384–95 (289–300). See also ibid. 52 (23). The reason he gives for his attitude is most revealing of the way in which east European Jews, even the intellectuals, thought of antisemites: 'Their hatred is not logical, but is rather a necessary outgrowth of their biological nature' (ibid. 392 (297); cf. *SE* iv, p. 278, for his characterizations of various European peoples). See, however, *Lifrakim*, 395 (300), where he contradicts this and claims that gentile antisemitism has its root in jealousy of the Jews' unique role in history and their superior religiosity.

[160] See *Baba kamma* 113*b* and Maimonides, *Mishnah torah, Hilkhot gezelah ve'avedah*, 11: 3–4.

[161] *Lifrakim*, 384 (289), 386 (291).

[162] See e.g. Hoffmann, *Der Schulchan Aruch*, 162–3.

gentile lacked any legal rights under Jewish law. Rather, it was due to the specific socio-economic circumstances which prevailed in talmudic times. In those days the gentiles were not accustomed to return lost, or even stolen, objects to their owners. Although robbery from gentiles was forbidden, the Sages did not require Jews to adopt a higher standard than their gentile neighbours. Indeed, to do so would have been against judicial logic, which requires that all members of an economic group be treated equally.

In addition, he continued, it would have been impossible for the rabbis to have expected anything different from the Jews of their generation. It was the Jews who were being viciously persecuted, and much of this persecution took the form of simple robbery and pillage of Jewish property. Any money which a Jew kept through gentile error was simply a small compensation for the enormous amounts which gentiles had stolen from Jews. Rather than being surprised that the Sages allowed such practices, one should be surprised that they were not more 'lenient' in this area. The reason they were not, Weinberg claimed, was because they feared causing a desecration of God's name or corrupting the values of the Jewish people.[163]

In concluding this survey of Weinberg's writings from the Pilwishki period, it should again be emphasized that he was not a thinker of great originality. He had certainly developed a good reputation among the Orthodox rabbinate, but considering the low quality of writing in this camp, their endorsement is not very significant. If not for Weinberg's later career, these early essays would hardly attract anyone's interest, and their only lasting value is that they enable us to study the development of Weinberg's thought. It was only in Germany that Weinberg's full talents began to flower, and it is to this next stage of his life that we now turn.

163 *Lifrakim*, 384–5 (289–90).

THREE

THE FIRST WORLD WAR AND ITS AFTERMATH (1914–1920)

GERMAN ORTHODOXY CONFRONTS THE EAST

IN MID-1914 Weinberg travelled to Germany for medical treatment of some ailment, the nature of which is not known.[1] Not long after he arrived in Berlin on 1 August, the declaration of war against Russia and a general mobilization were proclaimed. Weinberg had journeyed alone on this first trip to Berlin, no doubt assuming that he would soon be able to return to Pilwishki. However, in the wake of the outbreak of war it was impossible to travel between Germany and Russia, and he was forced to remain in Berlin. As with the other 'transition figures' whom Hillel Goldberg has described,[2] the journey from eastern Europe to Germany was to be pivotal in Weinberg's future intellectual development.

In the first days of the war Weinberg met Rabbi Abraham Isaac Kook at a Berlin railway station. Kook, the rabbi of Jaffa and later chief rabbi of Palestine, had come to Germany in order to attend the Agudat Yisrael convention, which had to be cancelled because of the war. It was Kook who helped ease Weinberg's difficult financial situation,[3] and a short time later he paid Weinberg a memorable visit at his apartment.[4] Being a Russian national, Weinberg was not in an enviable position and was at first ordered to leave the country, although this order was soon cancelled.[5] On 8 September Weinberg wrote to Kook, thanking him for his assistance and for 'joining in my sorrow'. This letter is interesting both for the biographical details it supplies and also for the light it sheds on how Weinberg viewed the German Orthodox:

> I received your dear letter and read it with joy. I did not answer until now because I was very busy and hardly had one restful day. When I received your letter I called . . .[6] and asked when I could visit him. He replied that because he is so busy he is not able to give me any time. I can only speak to him in the synagogue during services. Needless to say, I no longer

[1] *SE* iii, p. 116.

[2] See his *Between Berlin and Slobodka*.

[3] Moshe Zvi Neriyah, *Siḥot hare'iyah* (Tel Aviv, 1979), 175, and id., *Likutei hare'iyah* (Kefar Haro'eh, 1990), 340. See also Hayim Haikel Greenberg, *One of the Great Ones of the Generation* (Heb.) (Tel Aviv, 1967), 3 (unpaginated).

[4] Hayim Lifshitz, *Shivḥei hare'iyah* (Jerusalem, 1979), 119–20.

[5] Ben-Zion Shapiro (ed.), *Igerot lare'iyah* (Jerusalem, 1990), no. 79.

[6] The publishers have deleted the names in this letter.

concerned myself with him, and because of this I also did not go to Dr. . . ., fearing that he too might push me away, which would cause me to become angry and hateful. It is better for me (so I thought) to leave some room for doubt, even though in the depths of my heart I do not believe in the sincerity of the German Orthodox, in particular concerning their relations with the Russian Jews. Now that, thank God, I no longer need him, I will visit him, God willing, as is only proper. Thank God things are well with me (actually owing to the endeavours of a Liberal rabbi from the Liberal community, as if God wishes to apportion merit to all Jews on different levels, for each has something the other lacks). They have allocated me money and, although it is limited, it comes to me in a private and honourable way. I have also found someone who will give a guarantee to the doctor on my behalf.

There are many rabbis here and they all are going through difficult times. Thank God permission has already been given to travel to Russia. Many have already done so and those that remain will soon leave. I have not yet been given permission to travel because my town is close to the border.[7]

Not long after this, the leaders of the Gemeinde[8] offered to employ Weinberg as a *kashrut* supervisor for their institutions. He refused the position, despite the fact that he was short of money. As he explained, he did not want to be put in a position where he could be pressured by the community leaders into doing something against his religious principles, for example by giving his approval to what he regarded as an inadequate level of *kashrut*.[9] His situation soon improved when he accepted the rabbinate of a small congregation on Kantstrasse in the Charlottenburg section of Berlin,[10] an area to which many east European Jews gravitated.[11] However, the meagre income he received did not completely solve his financial difficulties and he was forced to rent a small and simple room.[12]

Like all easterners, the longer Weinberg remained in Germany the more he came to understand the German Jews' apparently strange ways.[13] Unlike many of

[7] Shapiro, *Igerot lare'iyah*, no. 81 (some of this letter has been expurgated and only appears in the Jerusalem, 1986 edition of *Igerot lare'iyah*). On 1–3 Sept. German troops advanced, pushed the Russian First Army out of Germany, and occupied some Russian territory. They did not reach Pilwishki and this explains why Weinberg was unable to return to the town.

[8] i.e. the general community, which included both Reform and Orthodox institutions (often referred to as the Grossgemeinde). Some cities in Germany had both a Gemeinde and a separatist Jewish community (*Austrittsgemeinde*), which followed R. Samson Raphael Hirsch's ruling that, where allowed by governmental law, the Orthodox were not permitted to retain organizational ties with the non-Orthodox.

[9] Biberfeld, 'In Memory', 31. It is possible that this story, recorded by Biberfeld in the name of his father, is actually a garbled version of another story, that of Weinberg's refusal to assume the position of *av beit din* of the Berlin community (see Ch. 6).

[10] Letter to Gordon (1966), 235; Weinberg's letter to Samuel Atlas, dated 22 Mar. 1950; M. Pineas, 'Zum Tode von Rabbiner Dr Weinberg', in Max Sinasohn (ed.), *Adass Jisroel Berlin* (Jerusalem, 1966), 176; Max Sinasohn, *Die Berliner Privatsynagogen und ihre Rabbiner 1671–1971* (Jerusalem, 1971), 7; Wininger, *Grosse Jüdische National Biographie*, vi. 233; and Mathisson, 'Tragedy', 285.

[11] See Jack Wertheimer, *Unwelcome Strangers: East European Jews in Imperial Germany* (Oxford, 1987), appendix, table IIb.

[12] Zvi Levi, 'Gaon, Man of Character, Educator' (Heb.), *Hatsofeh*, 13 Jan. 1967.

[13] Weinberg makes particular mention of one of these, that of women singing together with men at the Sabbath table; see *SE* ii, pp. 15–16. Further illustration of how unusual this practice seemed to

his fellow *Ostjuden*, however, he was not interested in segregating himself with his peers. On the contrary, despite all German Orthodoxy's faults, which he soon singled out in his articles, he wished to be a part of the intellectual ferment of this community, which was so different from what he was accustomed to in Lithuania. One of the many new insights he gained during his early days in Germany was that, contrary to the popular perception of the German Orthodox as being talmudically ignorant, there was still serious Talmud study taking place among them. It was true, he noted, that both German rabbis and laymen, despite significant achievements in Wissenschaft des Judentums, were not on the whole learned in rabbinic lore,[14] a fact which many in the Orthodox community were now attempting to alter.[15] However, this appraisal was not universally valid, and there were circles in which even men with Weinberg's broad talmudic background could feel at home. Thus, in a letter from mid-1916 which appeared in a journal edited by Rabbi Salomon Breuer of Frankfurt, Weinberg wrote: 'It was a day of great joy for me when I saw that also in Germany scholars sit and discuss matters of Jewish law in these times of worldly tumult and trouble.'[16]

It did not take Weinberg long to begin writing again on the pressing matters of the day, but this time the language he used was German. One issue of utmost importance, which was widely discussed in German Jewish circles, concerned the situation of east European Jews in the occupied territory. That this was even on the agenda of German Jewry was significant, since before the war hardly any thought had been given to the Jews of eastern Europe. Apart from this, as Weinberg himself was discovering, those east European Jews who now lived in Germany proper were often treated with disdain.

In his book *Unwelcome Strangers*, Jack Wertheimer has shown that it is wrong to portray the German Jews as unconcerned with the fate of their east European co-religionists in Germany. Yet despite the great amounts of charity given by German Jewry, the overwhelming majority of them, the Orthodox included, never doubted that the east European Jews were culturally inferior to their western

Jews of east European extraction is seen in the fact that R. Zvi Yehudah Kook saw fit to mention it in one of the youthful letters he wrote to his father from Switzerland. See *Tsemaḥ tsevi* (Jerusalem, 1991), 106. Dr Judith Grunfeld, daughter of a learned German rabbi and among the first teachers in the Polish Beth Jacob schools, told me that she had never heard of any religious prohibition on women singing in front of men until she arrived in Poland.

14 For Weinberg's comments on this lack, see 'Schulfragen' (1916), 495–6, and *Lifrakim*, 172 (246). For an account of the way in which many German Orthodox became estranged from Talmud study, see Breuer, *Torah-Im-Derekh-Eretz*, 39 ff. See also Moshe Samet, 'R. Nahman Berlin's Views on Society and History' (Heb.), in Yehezkel Cohen (ed.), *Ḥevrah vehistoriyah* (Jerusalem, 1980), 131–2. Unlike Breuer, Samet portrays Hirsch as being somewhat of an anti-talmudist. The same approach is adopted by Howard I. Levine, 'Enduring and Transitory Elements in the Philosophy of Samson Raphael Hirsch', *Tradition*, 5 (Fall 1962), 282 ff. See also the discussion in Eliezer Stern, *The Educational Ideal of Torah im Derekh Eretz* (Heb.) (Ramat Gan, 1987), ch. 2, esp. 67–8; Joseph Elias's commentary on Hirsch's *The Nineteen Letters*, trans. Karen Paritzky (Jerusalem, 1994), 305–6.

15 See e.g. *Zur Agudas-Jisroel Jugendbewegung* (Frankfurt, 1913).

16 'Li "Terei temiḥei demidkar dekhiri" ', *Jüdische Monatshefte*, 3 (1916), 282.

brethren.[17] As an abundance of documented and anecdotal evidence illustrates, they were often blunt in informing the east European Jews how they felt about their lifestyle. Furthermore, after having been exposed to the cultural superiority of German Jewry as well as to the watchful eye of an unfriendly government, most east European Jews agreed that it would be best if they abandoned their traditional ways. How else can one explain the fact that in Germany at this time there were no traces of the varied manifestations of east European Jewish culture which existed in the United States and England? Even Yiddish literature, the staple of this culture, was not found in Germany.[18]

Before the war the culture and way of life of east European Jewry were basically unknown to the majority of German Jews, including the Orthodox. What little was known was despised by a large percentage of German Jewry, and relations between the two groups were never marked by mutual respect or understanding. Although the Agudat Yisrael organization was formed with the aim of bringing together the Orthodox of eastern Europe and Germany, it was basically a rabbinic organization which had little effect on the layman. The negative feelings for German Jewry which Weinberg expressed in his previously quoted letter to Kook were common among east European Jews, and with good reason.[19]

As Mordechai Breuer has pointed out, it was the Orthodox, together with the Zionists, who felt the most sympathy for the *Ostjuden*. Furthermore, rabbis, community leaders, and the Orthodox newspapers continuously stressed how important it was to view the east European Jews in a positive light. The fact that there was an obvious need for such admonitions is itself significant, and we even find well-known rabbis, such as Esriel Hildesheimer,[20] Solomon Carlebach of Lübeck (1845–1919), and Marcus Horovitz of Frankfurt (1844–1910), expressing distaste for aspects of the hasidic lifestyle.[21] In general, it seems that even though many of the Orthodox respected the east European Jews' piety and preservation of Jewish values, they deplored their lack of culture. It is thus no surprise that there was an almost complete lack of personal and social relations between the two groups.[22]

[17] On the condescending attitude of the Orthodox separatists in Frankfurt, see Jacob Rosenheim, *Erinnerungen: 1870–1920* (Frankfurt, 1970), 131.

[18] See Wertheimer, *Unwelcome Strangers*, 179–80.

[19] See Steven E. Aschheim, *Brothers and Strangers: The East European Jew in German and German Jewish Consciousness, 1800–1923* (Madison, Wis., 1982), chs. 1, 2, and Bar-Ilan, *From Volozhin to Jerusalem*, ii. 375–6. For further analysis of the situation of east European Jews in Germany, see S. Adler-Rudel, *Ostjuden in Deutschland 1180–1940* (Tübingen, 1959), and Trude Maurer, *Ostjuden in Deutschland 1918–1933* (Hamburg, 1986).

[20] See Moses Calvary, *Bein zera liketsir* (Tel Aviv, 1947), 12.

[21] See Aschheim, *Brothers and Strangers*, 166; Yitshak Heinemann, 'R. Mordechai Halevi Horovitz and his Perception of Judaism' (Heb.), *Sinai*, 14 (1944), 169.

[22] See Breuer, *Jüdische Orthodoxie im Deutschen Reich 1871–1918* (Frankfurt, 1986), 325–6. Breuer, ibid. 59, quotes the experience of an Orthodox woman who, although she was working for a Jewish organization before World War I, did not know that the term 'Polack' referred to a person until she came to America. See also Abuha di Samuel (Moses Auerbach), 'Jüdischer Nationalismus und gesetzestreues Judentum', *Jeschurun*, 4 (1917), 630–1.

As is well known, the turning-point in relations between German Jewry and the Jews of the east came with World War I. Although, as Wertheimer[23] and Breuer[24] have shown, the promotion of a more positive image of east European Jews can be traced to the beginning of the century, it was certainly not of major importance, at least not as far as the non-Orthodox were concerned. Only the war brought about a change of attitude on the part of many Germans, and led to what has been called the 'cult of the *Ostjuden*'. During the war many soldiers had a first-hand opportunity of seeing the way east European Jews lived, and they were attracted by the simple piety and 'living Judaism' which they found. They in turn brought these impressions back to Germany, and all the Jewish newspapers were filled with articles on life in the east.[25]

Since this issue has been explored in depth by several writers, in particular Steven E. Aschheim, there is no need to elaborate on it any further. Of more immediate interest is Weinberg's role in German Orthodoxy's attempt to come to terms with the new reality: hundreds of thousands of east European Orthodox Jews now living under German rule. As might be expected, Weinberg was thrilled by what appeared to be a rapprochement of east and west, although he feared that the German Jews were taking an interest in their eastern brethren in order to 'improve' them.[26] If this tendency were to be avoided, it was vital that German Jews should understand the spiritual world of the east, and Weinberg knew that this understanding could not come about through reading any of the popular and romantic accounts. He hoped that after the German Orthodox had begun to pierce the veil which surrounded their eastern brethren, they would part company with the non-Orthodox and would cease to regard the east European Jews as adherents of an old-fashioned Judaism which needed assistance from the modern Jews of Germany. It was with this goal in mind that Weinberg set out to write a series of articles on life in the east for the Orthodox journal *Jeschurun*,[27] which was edited by Joseph Wohlgemuth (1867–1942), a leading Orthodox intellectual and lecturer at the Rabbinical Seminary of Berlin, which was the source of the ideology reflected in the journal.[28]

Although there were some German Orthodox who were so awed by their east

[23] *Unwelcome Strangers*, 151 ff.

[24] *Jüdische Orthodoxie*, 325 ff., 'Orthodoxy in Germany', 75–86.

[25] See Aschheim, *Brothers and Strangers*, ch. 7. On the often discussed 'cult of the *Ostjuden*' see ibid., ch. 8. See also Sander Gilman, 'The Rediscovery of the Eastern Jews: German Jews in the East 1890–1918', in David Bronsen (ed.), *Jews and Germans from 1860–1933* (Heidelberg, 1979), 338–65, and Michael Brenner, *The Renaissance of Jewish Culture in Weimar Germany* (New Haven, Conn., 1996), 142 ff.

[26] See *Lifrakim*, 411 (316); 'Die Jeschiwoth' (1916), 126.

[27] See Akiva Posner, 'The Monthly *Jeschurun* Edited by Dr. Wohlgemuth' (Heb.), in Y. Tirosh (ed.), *Shai liyeshayahu* (Tel Aviv, 1955), 73–8.

[28] See 'Die Jeschiwoth' (1916), 52–3. In addition to the articles referred to in this chapter, see also 'Der "Masmid" ' (1917), 425–30; 'Ein russisch-jüdischer Gaon', *Die Jüdische Presse*, 23 Apr. 1915, 191–3; and 'Vom Geistes des Ostens', *Der Israelit*, 23 Nov. 1916, 2. For his article on Kovno which appeared in *Jeschurun* of 1916 ('Eine rabbinische Residenz und ihr letztes Fürst'), I have used the Hebrew version in *Lifrakim*, 397–411 (302–16).

European brethren that they publicly declared the superiority of the east, and forswore any attempts to modernize traditional east European Jewish society by inculcating in them a Torah im Derekh Eretz ideology,[29] this view was a striking exception. For the most part, even those who were prepared to admit that the east European Jews were 'the genuine Jews',[30] and who sensed the power of their religiosity and the need for German Jews to join them,[31] also realized that there were serious deficiencies in east European Jewish life. One of these, which spurred much discussion in German Orthodox circles, was the traditional east European school system, the *ḥeder*.[32] It was clear to the German Orthodox that the days of the *ḥeder* were numbered. A new, reformed system of education would soon be inaugurated for the Jewish masses of eastern Europe, and the only question was who would be its moving force: the Orthodox, the Zionists, or the Jewish socialists.

JEWISH EDUCATION IN A CHANGING WORLD

It is not surprising that the German Orthodox were shocked by the *ḥeder*, and like the *maskilim* of the previous generation[33] as well as a few open-minded east European rabbinic leaders,[34] they were determined to reform or, even better, abolish the *ḥeder* entirely. Apart from the lack of basic hygiene in the *ḥeder*s, there was no pedagogical method to the teaching, and untrained and unsupervised instructors initiated the students into Bible and Talmud study. The language of instruction in

[29] See Eduard Biberfeld's speech in *Agudas Jisroel: Berichte und Materialien* (Frankfurt, [1912]), 43–4. Even Biberfeld hoped that east European Jewish culture would be modernized, though with Torah study still occupying a central place. However, he was adamant that German Jews must not attempt to interfere with what could only be a natural development. See also Rosenheim, *Memoirs*, 148–50.

[30] J. Wohlgemuth, 'Beiträge zu einer jüdischen Homiletik', in *Jahres-Bericht des Rabbiner-Seminars zu Berlin für 1903/1904* (Berlin, [1905]), 3.

[31] See e.g. J. Wohlgemuth, 'Zionismus, Nationaljudentum, und gesetzestreues Judentum', *Jeschurun*, 5 (1918), 163: 'The only salvation lies in uniting with eastern Jewry, in our reassimilation to the East.'

[32] For comments and sources on *ḥeder* education, see A. M. Lifshitz, 'The *Ḥeder*' (Heb.), *Hatekufah*, 7 (1920), 294–352; Zvi Scharfstein, *The Ḥeder in the Life of our People* (Heb.) (New York, 1953); H. S. Kazdan, *From Ḥeder and 'Schools' to the Central Jewish School Organization* (Yid.) (Mexico, 1956); Zvi Halevy, *Jewish Schools under Czarism and Communism* (New York, 1976), ch. 2; Diane Roskies, *Heder: Primary Education among East European Jews* (New York, 1977); Shaul Stampfer, '*Heder* Study, Knowledge of Torah, and the Maintenance of Social Stratification in Traditional East European Jewish Society', *Studies in Jewish Education*, 3 (1988), 271–89.

[33] See Steven J. Zipperstein, 'Transforming the Heder: Maskilic Politics in Imperial Russia', in Zipperstein and Ada Rapoport-Albert (eds.), *Jewish History: Essays in Honour of Chimen Abramsky* (London, 1988), 87–109.

[34] See Aaron Cohen, *Keneset hagedolah*, ii. 14*a*, 23*a*, 30*a–b*, 32*b*, 37*a–b*, 40*a* (letters of various delegates to the 1903 rabbinic conference in Cracow); Menahem Mendel Landau, *Mekits nirdamim*, 14*a*–17*b*. (For Weinberg's great admiration of Landau, see *SE* i, p. 228.) Landau's specific suggestions were rejected by Elijah Akiva Rabinowitz in *Hapeles*, 5 (1905), 683–4. For the traditionalist response to modifications of the Jewish school system, see *Darkah shel torah* (Vilna, 1902).

the *ḥeder* was Yiddish, to which most German Jews, the Orthodox included, felt a strong antipathy. They regarded Yiddish as nothing more than the corruption of a pure language.[35] Any secular education was only provided in compliance with what the law required, and the government regulations were not always adhered to. Even the so-called 'improved *ḥeder*', which was opposed by most of the east European Orthodox, never succeeded in adequately overcoming these faults.[36] Remarkably, it is also known that many east European rabbis were reluctant to teach the children of their community, even when the *melamedim* were unqualified or there were no *melamedim* at all and the children were growing up without any Jewish education. These rabbis feared that any such involvement on their part would only further degrade the status of their office.[37]

The situation for girls was even worse, since they were given no formal Jewish education. Instead, they attended non-Jewish schools, and it is thus not surprising that the number of young women who abandoned Orthodoxy far exceeded that of the young men.[38] It can be stated without exaggeration that the reactionary opposition to providing any Jewish education for girls was responsible for thousands of Orthodox young women abandoning the tradition. Even Salanter, who so perceptively saw the problems of male yeshiva education, was not as far-sighted when it came to girls' education.[39] The spectacle of young women from hasidic

[35] See Zosa Szajkowski, 'The Struggle for Yiddish During World War I: The Attitude of German Jewry', *LBIYB* 9 (1964), 131–58; Aschheim, *Brothers and Strangers*, 166.

[36] See Zvi Scharfstein, *The History of Jewish Education in Recent Generations* (Heb.) (Jerusalem, 1960), i. 389–410. Opponents of the new, 'improved' *ḥeders* (*ḥadarim metukanim*) referred to them as 'dangerous' *ḥeders* (*ḥadarim mesukanim*); see Barukh Epstein, *Mekor barukh* (Vilna, 1928), 607.

[37] A Hungarian delegate's proposal that the town rabbi should teach the children of his community when there was no other Jewish education provided was voted down at the rabbinic conference of Cracow in 1903. Elijah Akiva Rabinowitz's reason for opposing the proposal is recorded as follows: 'Through this the dignity of the rabbis, which is debased in our day, will be further degraded. If we require this of the rabbis, the masses will regard them as simple *melamedim*.' See Landau, *Mekits nirdamim*, 12*a*, as well as *Hapeles*, 5 (1905), 617, where Rabinowitz defends his view. See also ibid., where R. Judah Leib Zirelson offers the same rationale as Rabinowitz, to which he adds: 'The rabbi has to devote himself to the study of Talmud and *posekim*, which will be impossible if he assumes the role of *melamed*.' See *Mekits nirdamim*, 12*a*–12*b*, for Landau's indignant response to what he viewed as an abdication of rabbinic responsibility. In the midst of his diatribe he writes: 'In a place where children lack teachers should the rabbi be concerned with the honour of the rabbinate while Jewish children grow up as gentiles?' (The proposal referred to at the beginning of this note reflected the circumstances in several small Hungarian towns. As pointed out in *Hapeles*, 5 (1905), 616, there were no communities in Russia and Poland which completely lacked *melamedim*. However, there were many communities in which the *melamedim* were completely incompetent, but despite this Rabinowitz, Zirelson, and many of their colleagues regarded it as beneath the rabbi's dignity to teach the children himself.)

[38] See Joseph Friedensohn, 'Beth Jacob Schools in Poland' (Heb.), *Haḥinukh vehatarbut ha'ivrit be'eiropah* (New York, 1957), 61 ff.; Landau, *Mekits nirdamim*, 26*a*–28*b*.

[39] See Reines, *Shenei hame'orot*, section 2, part 1, 23*b*, who records a conversation with Salanter in which the latter expressed opposition to formal Torah education for women. Salanter died before matters reached a critical stage, and it may be assumed that had he been alive, he would have been one of the first to challenge the traditional approach to women's education.

families mocking their pious parents is often mentioned in literature of the period,[40] and as early as 1903 Rabbi Menahem Mendel Landau (1862–1935) unsuccessfully appealed to his colleagues to abandon their practice of withholding all Torah education from girls.[41] In the words of Aaron Marcus (1843–1916), the abandonment of Orthodoxy by so many young women happened without any of the rabbis 'lifting a finger'.[42] It was only when faced with an imminent spiritual catastrophe that the Orthodox leaders of the east, in particular Poland, were roused from their stupor and began to support girls' education in the form of the Beth Jacob schools. Having no idea how to implement this concept on a large scale, they turned to the German Orthodox for assistance, and the east European Beth Jacob movement was placed under the direction of the German Orthodox educator Leo Deutschländer (1888–1935).[43]

This was done after the war, however; before then girls' education was not yet a particularly important issue, either in Germany or the east.[44] German Orthodox writers, led by Wohlgemuth, were concerned with the larger issue of how to modernize the Jews of eastern Europe.[45] It was clear to them that the east European Jews needed to adopt the cultural and educational philosophy of German Orthodoxy. In other words, traditional east European Orthodoxy was to be permanently altered. It was understood that these educational changes would also be accompanied by changes in language and dress. Yiddish was to be discarded and Western garb introduced, for without taking these steps east European Orthodoxy would never be able to rise from its primitive state.[46]

These discussions did not exist in a purely theoretical sphere, for the German government had decided to use German Jews to liaise with the communities under its occupation, and the military authorities were intent on instituting far-reaching changes in these communities. Thus everyone in Germany who wrote about the

[40] See Friedensohn, 'Beth Jacob', 61 ff.; Sara Schenirer, *Em beyisrael* (Tel Aviv, 1956), i. 45, 51–2; Aharon Sorasky, *The History of Torah Education* (Heb.) (Benei Berak, 1967), 423; Gershon C. Bacon, 'Agudath Israel in Poland: An Orthodox Jewish Response to the Challenge of Modernity', (Ph.D. diss., Columbia University, 1979), 241–2; Moses Auerbach, *From Halberstadt to Petaḥ Tikvah* (Heb.) (Jerusalem, 1987), 64–5.

[41] *Mekits nirdamim*, 26*a*–28*b*. See also Hayim David Gross, *Vayelaket yosef*, 9 (1907), nos. 46, 106, 113, 148, 166.

[42] See Rosenheim, *Memoirs*, 180–1.

[43] See the comprehensive discussion in Bacon, 'Agudath Israel in Poland', 240 ff. See also Abraham Atkin, 'The Beth Jacob Movement in Poland (1917–1939)' (Ph.D. diss., Yeshiva University, 1959); Pinhas Biberfeld, 'Leo Deutschländer z"l: Bildnis eines Erziehers', in *25 Jahre Jüdische Schule Zürich Festschrift* (Jerusalem, 1980), 223–30. Many Orthodox young women had received so little Jewish education that they were unable even to read Yiddish. In recognition of this, the *Bais Ya'akov Zhurnal* also included a Polish section.

[44] There were some exceptions. See e.g. Auerbach, *From Halberstadt to Petaḥ Tikvah*, 63 ff., and the anonymous 'Concerning Girls' Education' (Heb.), *Hamodia*, Erev Rosh Hashanah 5671 [1910], 364–5. In October 1917 Pinchas Kohn and Emanuel Carlebach opened the Chavatzelet girls' school in Warsaw, in many ways the kernel from which Beth Jacob developed.

[45] See in particular J. Wohlgemuth, 'Deutschland und die Ostjudenfrage', *Jeschurun*, 3 (1916), 1–19, 65–95, 177–210, and id., 'Erziehungsfragen in Ost und West', *Jeschurun*, 4 (1917), 1–13, 65–75, 129–53.

[46] See Aschheim, *Brothers and Strangers*, 166.

issues affecting Jews in the east was hoping that his words would have an impact on the formulation of policy. To the dismay of the German Zionists, who were trying to spread their message among the east European Jews,[47] the Orthodox anti-Zionists Rabbi Pinchas Kohn of Ansbach (1867–1942) and Rabbi Emanuel Carlebach of Cologne (1874–1927) were ultimately recognized by the German government as unofficial advisers on Jewish matters. Their 'mission', which focused on occupied Poland, included a number of social, educational, and political elements, carried out with varying degrees of success. Although Kohn and Carlebach were able to prevent any non-Orthodox group from instituting its own reforms in the traditional educational system, they themselves were almost completely unsuccessful in their 'conscious and deliberate effort to reform Polish religious Jewry in accordance with their own Torah-im-Derekh-Eretz pattern'.[48]

As Breuer has shown, it was not purely selfless consideration for the east European Jews that motivated Kohn's and Carlebach's mission. Rather, it was believed that German Orthodoxy could itself be strengthened by providing it with a base among the large Polish Orthodox population, once the latter's cultural position was improved.[49] It was also true that both Kohn and Carlebach viewed themselves as agents of German foreign policy, did their utmost to dampen any Jewish nationalistic feelings, either with regard to minority rights or Zionism,[50] and 'at times regarded the Ostjuden as pawns in a German political game'.[51] This came to the fore when a private memorandum by Kohn was published in which, among other things, he 'discussed the political "manageability" of various groups of eastern Jews in the occupied territory'.[52] He also referred to the Lithuanian Jews coming into Poland as a 'destructive element', and, as we shall see, Weinberg did not let this go unchallenged.

As mentioned above, Kohn and Carlebach wished to reform the educational system of the east European Jews and to introduce them to the method of Torah im

47 See the amusing story in Rosenheim, *Erinnerungen*, 143.

48 Carlebach, 'A German Rabbi Goes East', 122. See also Alexander Carlebach, *Adass Yeshurun of Cologne* (Belfast, 1964), ch. 3; Rosenheim, *Erinnerungen*, 140 ff.; Matthias Morgenstern, *Von Frankfurt nach Jerusalem: Isaac Breuer und die Geschichte des 'Austrittsstreits' in der deutsch-jüdischen Orthodoxie* (Tübingen, 1995), 70, and the comprehensive article by Mordechai Breuer, 'Orthodox Rabbis from Germany in Poland and Lithuania during the German Occupation (1914–18)' (Heb.), *Bar-Ilan Annual*, 24–5 (1989), 117–53. Whatever success Kohn and Carlebach did have was short-lived. See e.g. the report in *Hatsefirah*, 3 Mar. 1916, 3, about the opening of the Torah im Derekh Eretz *ḥeder*.

49 Mordechai Breuer, 'Changes in the Attitude of German Orthodoxy towards Zionism during the First World War' (Heb.), in *Proceedings of the Seventh World Congress of Jewish Studies: History of the Jews in Europe* (Jerusalem, 1981), 170; id., 'Orthodox Rabbis', 152. See also Szajkowski, 'Struggle for Yiddish', 131–2.

50 As I have already pointed out (Ch. 2 n. 47), they refused to publish Weinberg's positive portrayal of the Mizrachi founder Reines.

51 Aschheim, *Brothers and Strangers*, 167. See also Carlebach, *Adass Yeshurun*, 64 ff.; Avraham Rubenstein, *A Movement in an Era of Change* (Heb.) (Jerusalem, 1981), 38 ff.

52 *Brothers and Strangers*, 168. See also Breuer, 'Orthodox Rabbis', 139 ff.

Derekh Eretz, as well as proper, that is German, pedagogic techniques.[53] But was all this appropriate for the eastern Jews? This was the question Weinberg confronted, in particular in his article 'Schulfragen im Ostjudentum', which was published in *Jeschurun* in 1916.

Although Weinberg felt that the *ḥeder* had positive aspects, he had no difficulty admitting its faults, particularly its lack of hygiene and the fact that most of the traditional, and thus untrained, *melamedim* lacked the necessary skills. Even with regard to those *melamedim* who were qualified for their job, he argued that there was no denying that they belonged to a bygone era and that it was impossible for them to adapt themselves to what was now required from teachers.[54] Because of these faults, Weinberg saw no choice but to take his stand with the *maskilim* who wished to reform the *ḥeder*. It is interesting that Weinberg showed no opposition to identifying himself with these, admittedly conservative, *maskilim*, although he did not identify any of them by name. He further made the point that the word *maskil* need not stand in opposition to Orthodoxy, even though that is the meaning it had acquired in history. In the context in which Weinberg used it, the word *maskil* represented those who supported a curriculum of both Torah and secular studies. In this regard, there was no real difference between the conservative *maskilim* of eastern Europe and the German Orthodox, neither of whom supported a Torah-only curriculum. As Weinberg put it, there was nothing objectionable about the secular subjects that the reformers of the *ḥeder* wished to introduce, and because of this many pious rabbis were in agreement with the educational views advocated by the conservative *maskilim*.[55]

Weinberg was further prepared to acknowledge that it was only the conservative *maskilim* who had examined the educational problems facing young people from a 'rational' perspective.[56] Unfortunately, Weinberg continued, these *maskilim* did not stick to a programme of reform, which would have been successful. Instead, they attempted to uproot and abolish the entire traditional system. According to Weinberg, it was obvious to anyone who did not have an axe to grind that all reforms of the east European educational system had to take place within the framework of the old *ḥeder*. This point was also explicitly acknowledged by Wohlgemuth, the leading German advocate of reform.[57] Weinberg further pointed out that in their fervour, the *maskilim* went so far as to disrupt the study of Talmud, the basis of traditional education. Such actions, he concluded, could never have endeared the *maskilim* to the general community, and it was no wonder that their efforts had failed.[58]

[53] See *Hatsefirah*, 3 Mar. 1916, 3; Rubenstein, *Movement*, 41–2. See also Carlebach, 'A German Rabbi Goes East', 78–9, for Emanuel Carlebach's unsuccessful attempt to explain to hasidim that their method of teaching children to read was wholly inefficient.

[54] 'Schulfragen' (1916), 451, 492–3.

[55] Ibid. 446, 450–1, 504–5.

[56] Ibid. 450, 504.

[57] This is a basic point in his extensive writings on the issue. See e.g. Wohlgemuth, 'Erziehungsfragen', 74–5.

[58] 'Schulfragen' (1916), 451–3.

Although Weinberg had already shown where his sympathies lay, he carefully explained what prompted most of the leading east European rabbis to oppose any reform in the traditional school system.[59] It was not because they were unsophisticated and feared the spirit of enquiry or reason. Nor could it be said that they opposed any advance on the part of the masses. Rather, Weinberg claimed, their fear stemmed from a concern that the existence of traditional Judaism was threatened by the ideologies which permeated secular studies. Because of this they also opposed the study of foreign languages, not because there was anything wrong with the languages *per se*, but because of the secular literature expressing non-Orthodox ideas which accompanied the languages. If this opposition to acquiring a secular education meant that young Jews would find it more difficult to make a living, then the east European rabbis believed that this was a price which had to be paid. Even the study of science, whose importance had been recognized by east European rabbis since the time of Rabbi Elijah ben Solomon Zalman, the Vilna Gaon (1720–97), was now regarded as a danger to the Jewish spirit. As for studies in the humanities, even when these did not express non-Orthodox ideas they were still opposed. In the opinion of the east European rabbis the humanities simply did not have any value for Jews, for the Talmud itself gave expression to a fully developed cultural spirit, containing all that one needed to know in this regard. Why then should Jews study non-traditional texts?[60]

To be sure, the rabbis of the old school believed that they were strong enough to prevent any tinkering with the traditional system: 'As long as there is a possibility of saving the old, there is no reason to look to replace it with the new.'[61] Weinberg, on the other hand, felt that the rabbis who held this view were labouring under an illusion, and that their position was much more precarious than they imagined. It was because of this that he felt he must depart from the 'party line'. This must have been a very difficult step for him to take, and he was at great pains to justify his position. Yet however much care he took to distinguish himself from the non-Orthodox opponents of traditional education,[62] he realized that by calling for reforms he was opposing the leaders of east European Orthodoxy. Men such as Rabbi Hayim Soloveitchik, Rabbi Israel Meir Hacohen, and the hasidic *rebbe*s were not yet convinced that the old methods were unworkable. That they caused economic hardship was obvious, but this was not reason enough to embrace the new. In fact, Soloveitchik was quick to insist that in order for him to join Agudat Yisrael it would have to agree not to interfere with any aspects of traditional communal life in Lithuania and Poland. Although there were some discordant tones, the German leadership of Agudat Yisrael agreed to this demand.[63]

[59] This justification of the anti-reform party was so detailed and sympathetic that, according to Wohlgemuth, it overshadowed Weinberg's own pro-reform stand. See 'Erziehungsfragen', 66–7.

[60] 'Schulfragen' (1916), 453–4, 490–1, 497–8; 'Die Jeschiwoth' (1916), 123.

[61] 'Die Jeschiwoth' (1916), 124.

[62] See 'Schulfragen' (1916), 490 ff.

[63] See Rosenheim, *Erinnerungen*, 122–3; *Memoirs*, 126–7. Despite this agreement, R. Sholom Dov Ber Schneersohn remained suspicious of German intentions and refused to join the Agudah; see *Igerot*

By calling for reforms, Weinberg was also opposing his own earlier viewpoint, discussed in Chapter 2. Now he recognized the need for two different types of educational institution—one whose main goal would be to provide general knowledge in a Jewish atmosphere, and one which would retain its emphasis on Torah study, without overlooking the need to train students for an economically viable profession. Weinberg's new approach took all of Jewry into consideration, rather than concentrating on the élite yeshiva students.[64] It was now that he began to move into the world of German Orthodoxy. He still had some way to go before he would become a fully integrated member of this society, when he no longer felt the need to apologize so profusely for his advocacy of secular studies, but he was clearly moving in this direction.

Thus, in a total departure from the views he had expressed a few years earlier concerning the requirements of a rabbi, when he claimed that there was no reason for rabbis to acquire a secular education, Weinberg now wrote that he recognized 'the sad truth' that rabbis without any such education were severely handicapped in leading their flocks. Although, of course, he did not wish to see any degeneration in Orthodoxy, 'the fast pace of economic development, even within the Jewish community, demands different measures and a different kind of preparation for life'.[65] It was because of this, he believed, that not only was it necessary to institute reforms in the traditional education system, but that they also had to be introduced and supported by the east European Jews themselves, including the hasidim who until now had viewed any attempts at reforming the *ḥeder* as the first step to a total abandonment of Orthodoxy. If the rabbis and masses of eastern Europe did not adopt a different outlook, Weinberg continued, then all the reforms in the world would not have any effect. But he was confident that they would change their views, and that even the hasidim would not court disaster by stubbornly holding on to their old ways.[66]

It is important to note that, despite his advocacy of secular studies, Weinberg was not referring to any broad-based scheme of Torah im Derekh Eretz. There is no appreciation of Western culture here, no advocacy of a synthesis between the Jewish and the secular. Indeed, Weinberg was careful to note how unfortunate it was that reforms were necessary. It would have been preferable had economic circumstances enabled a continuation of the old system, in which case there would have been no need to dilute the high Jewish culture of the east with vocational-type

kodesh, ii, nos. 366, 368, 395, v, nos. 1044, 1044*. In 1922 R. Abraham Mordechai Alter, the *rebbe* of Gur and one of the leaders of Agudat Yisrael, wrote: 'The purpose of the Agudah must be to bring about a separation from all the beauty of Japhet, which is a danger to us.' See his *Collected Letters*, 40. The German members of Agudat Yisrael obviously did not share Alter's view of the organization. The most recent study of Agudat Yisrael is Alan L. Mittleman, *The Politics of Torah: The Jewish Political Tradition and the Founding of Agudat Israel* (Albany, NY, 1996).

[64] See in particular 'Schulfragen' (1916), 499: 'We would not fulfil our task adequately if we were only concerned with a limited group—even if it is the most important—and not the general public.'

[65] 'Schulfragen' (1916), 491.

[66] See *Lifrakim*, 410–11 (315–16), 'Schulfragen' (1916), 491.

training. Weinberg's concerns were entirely of a practical nature: how would the young be able to earn a decent livelihood later in life if they were not given the proper tools?[67] Yet, as I have noted, even these cautious reforms were a change from Weinberg's previous views, which had strongly opposed any modification of the traditional education system.[68]

WEINBERG'S EARLY ATTITUDE TO GERMAN ORTHODOXY: RESPECT AT A DISTANCE

Together with the suggested revisions of the *ḥeder* system came efforts to bring German-style Orthodoxy to eastern Europe. Weinberg strongly disagreed with this, arguing that the German form of Orthodoxy was unsuited to Lithuania, and even less so to the hasidim in Poland. As he put it, German Orthodoxy was based on a unique religious feeling which could not be appreciated except by those educated in the German manner, in which different worlds of thought were amalgamated. By ignoring this fact, all the good intentions of the German Orthodox could end up destroying what was most precious to their eastern brethren.[69]

Study of his essays clearly shows that Weinberg's heart was still in the east, and it was as a member of this community that he identified himself and opposed the introduction of German Orthodoxy to his homeland. But why in particular did he believe that the German form of Orthodoxy was unsuitable for the east? As he explained it, traditional Judaism in eastern Europe was fresh and pulsating. It was there that Torah study for its own sake, the powerful ideal of the yeshivot, still had great importance. Indeed, a man lacking in Torah scholarship was regarded as nothing less than an inferior Jew. In contrast to this, German Jews studied Torah, not for its own sake, but in order to know how to regulate their lives. Furthermore, ignorance of Torah was not viewed by the German Orthodox in such a negative light. In short, a Judaism without Torah scholarship was to the east European Jews what a Judaism without divine service would have been to the German Jews.[70]

The truth of this description is illustrated by an event which had occurred in the previous generation in Frankfurt. Although the pious Orthodox Jews of this city were proud of their devotion to the teachings and philosophy of Rabbi Samson Raphael Hirsch, when Hirsch's son-in law, Rabbi Salomon Breuer (1850–1926), attempted to establish a yeshiva in 1890, he met with fierce opposition from the local community, which refused to contribute financially to the institution. In their mind, yeshivot were for the east European Jews, had no place in the landscape of

[67] See also *SE* iv, p. 294.

[68] See Ch. 2. In Ch. 4 I will discuss Weinberg's later position, which rejected this narrow vocational approach.

[69] 'Schulfragen' (1916), 495–6; *Lifrakim*, 411 (316).

[70] 'Schulfragen' (1916), 496. 'Ein Judentum ohne Thora ist ihm dasselbe, was dem deutschen Juden ein Judentum ohne Gottesdienst ist.' See also Isaiah Wolfsberg, 'Lithuanian Jewry and German Jewry' (Heb.), *Talpiot*, 3 (1947), 7–31.

modern German Orthodoxy, and were excluded from Hirsch's educational system.[71] As Jacob Rosenheim (1870–1965) recalled, it was simply unheard of and incomprehensible for a German Jew to consider sending his son to study at one of the great yeshivot of the east.[72] The change in attitude towards east European yeshivot only began in the second decade of the twentieth century.

In his article 'Schulfragen im Ostjudentum' Weinberg elaborated on the differences between east and west, and in a strong attack on the philosophy of Torah im Derekh Eretz he wrote:

Talmud and profane knowledge are separated by a deep chasm with regard to ideological and spiritual content. It is impossible for one who is thoroughly absorbed in the ideas of Kant to immerse himself simultaneously in the talmudic commentaries of Rabbi Meir Schiff or the *Ketsot hahoshen*. One whose nature has been fashioned alongside Goethe and Schiller is not easily susceptible to the beauty of the *aggadot* of Rabba bar bar Hana. The few famous exceptions to this in Germany do not prove anything. These are just the privileged few.[73]

Once again we see that Weinberg was opposed to any attempt at a synthesis of secular and Jewish learning, even claiming that the German Orthodox had failed in this regard. He viewed the 'Talmud-only' approach of the yeshivot as the sole authentic method of acquiring Jewish knowledge, and in this context repeated his opposition to Reines's yeshiva, which combined Jewish and secular studies.[74] Put simply, nothing in Western culture was of intellectual or spiritual value for Jews in Weinberg's eyes. In fact, it stood in opposition to 'Jewish culture', and would have a negative influence upon those who wished to become Jewish spiritual leaders (*gedolim*).[75]

Yet nothing could be more in opposition to the philosophy of Hirsch. For Hirsch, the beauty of Goethe and Schiller was, as Breuer puts it, concentric with the beauty in Jewish texts. Each of these spheres fructified and complemented the other, and, contrary to Weinberg's ideas, there was no conflict between Jewish culture and the best of German culture.[76] In Hirsch's mind, the Talmud scholar

[71] See Breuer, *Jüdische Orthodoxie*, 111; Eliezer Posen, 'The Frankfurt Yeshiva', in *Ateret Zvi: Jubilee Volume Presented in Honor of the Eightieth Birthday of Rabbi Dr. Joseph Breuer* (New York, 1962), 150; Rosenheim, *Erinnerungen*, 42–3; and Yitzhak Ahren, 'Rabbiner Breuers Frankfurter Jeschiwo', *Udim*, 14–15 (1990), 28 ff. Rosenheim, *Erinnerungen*, 20 and Isaac Breuer, *Autobiography* (Heb.) (Jerusalem, 1988), 19, claim that Hirsch himself, actually intended to establish a yeshiva.

[72] *Erinnerungen*, 69–70.

[73] 'Schulfragen' (1916), 496.

[74] See also 'Die Jeschiwoth' (1916), 123; *SE* iv, p. 358.

[75] See also 'Eine Rede zur Tagung der Agudath-Yisroel in Frankfurt a. M.', *Die Jüdische Presse*, 1 Feb. 1918, 44, where Weinberg repeated his advocacy of the Torah-only approach for those who wished to become part of the Orthodox intelligentsia.

[76] See Breuer, *Jüdische Orthodoxie*, 73. In describing Hirsch's philosophy I have followed Breuer's latest presentation. In his earlier study, *Torah-Im-Derekh-Eretz*, there is at least one significant difference. On p. 24 of this work Breuer writes: '*Torah-im-Derekh-Eretz* is not a physical mixture but a chemical compound. Torah and life, Judaism and culture, do not complement each other, but achieve complete identity.' However, in his recent book *Jüdische Orthodoxie*, 73, Breuer writes that Torah im Derekh Eretz does *not* mean achieving complete identity, but rather, that both the Jewish and the secular retain a 'clearly demonstrable identity' and thus complement each other.

who had no exposure to these texts had not completely developed his character. What to Weinberg was a positive trait was regarded by Samson Raphael Hirsch and his followers as an abandonment of the Orthodox Jew's role on earth, which required an appreciation of, and involvement with, advanced culture. It is thus clear from Weinberg's writings of 1916–17 that, while he had some respect for what German Orthodoxy had achieved, he was in no way prepared to grant it the same validity as east European Orthodoxy. After all, the Orthodoxy of the east was a wholly Jewish product, whereas German Orthodoxy had been sullied through contact with gentile ideas.

Another of Weinberg's concerns during the war years was the effect of the war on the cornerstone of east European Orthodoxy—the yeshivot. Since fund-raising in western Europe was now very difficult, many of the yeshivot were experiencing a financial crisis and were threatened with closure. Weinberg regarded this as the most devastating blow of the war, and earnestly urged German Jewry to come to the rescue.[77] Although his earlier essays on the yeshivot were written to give expression to a feeling that all of his colleagues shared, his essays in Germany were written in order to expose a population to something of which they knew little. Addressing his German co-religionists, he wrote:

> In our days the yeshiva is more than a mere academy. It is a place of refuge for those few who strive for a complete preservation of their Jewish way of life, and for those who wish to escape from the foreign milieu and influences of the non-Jewish spirit. The yeshiva nowadays means a concentration of the original Jewish spirit. It is a fully developed autonomous world in which the life of the Jewish mind remains pure, free of any foreign admixture. It is a sovereign territory in which the spirit of the old Judaism can develop freely, protected from all disturbances and obstacles. . . . Thus, the yeshiva students of today are the last bearers of historic Judaism. The yeshivot are the fortresses of Judaism, and their students the only ones destined to defend them.[78]

How successful he was in convincing his readers of the tremendous importance of the yeshivot is unknown, but there was never a more impassioned adherent of a cause.

SETTLING DOWN IN BERLIN

In the early days of the war Weinberg viewed his stay in Germany as temporary, believing that he would soon return to the east where 'living Judaism' in all of its brilliance was to be found. As we have seen, his 1914 letter to Kook mentions that he had not yet been given permission to return home. By 1916, with Germany in control of the Pilwishki district, Weinberg could have returned home had he wished. Instead, he chose to remain in Germany, where he continued to participate in Berlin's Jewish cultural and intellectual life. Despite all his nostalgia for the east, he was now under the spell of the west.

[77] See his 'Rettet die Jeschiwoth!', *Der Israelit*, 11 Jan. 1917, 2–3.

[78] 'Die Jeschiwoth' (1916), 121.

Although not officially a member, Weinberg began to frequent Berlin's Beit Va'ad Ha'ivri (the Hebrew Club), which was formed in the spring of 1917. This club attracted a large number of east European intellectuals, among them Jacob Simhoni (1884–1926), Zalman Rubashov (Shazar, 1889–1974), Zalman Schneur (1887–1959), and Shmuel Yosef Agnon (1888–1970). For a time Weinberg actually lived in a pension together with Simhoni, Shazar, and Jacob Nahum Epstein (1878–1952).[79] Like Weinberg, these were men who could no longer be constrained by the limits of Jewish intellectual life in the east, and had made their way to Berlin, as if drawn by a magnet. With them Weinberg was able to find intellectual companionship and enduring friendship.[80] Gershom Scholem recalled that at the Hebrew Club's gatherings Weinberg was the only one who had no hesitations about lecturing in Hebrew, and that he did so complete with Ashkenazi pronunciation.[81] During this time Weinberg also lectured before both the student union of the Rabbinical Seminary of Berlin (on the Lithuanian yeshivot)[82] and the Union of Jewish Academicians (Bund Jüdischer Akademiker), an organization comprising mostly Orthodox university students.[83]

Weinberg and the Separatists

In 1917 Weinberg wrote a long-winded and not very profound article entitled 'The Way to Understanding with the Orthodox'.[84] In this article, which is little more than a sermon and closely resembles what he wrote in his earlier essays, Weinberg claimed that the reason why Orthodoxy was confronted with such opposition in the Jewish world was because its essence was misunderstood. This was so, he argued, even though all segments of Jewish life needed the Orthodox in order to survive. Weinberg further urged the Orthodox to speak up for their rights and to organize themselves in order to achieve their goals, which should be inner-directed, and to avoid battles with the non-Orthodox or even attempts to influence them. As he put it, the Orthodox communities of both east and west had enough faults of their own which needed to be dealt with before trying to appeal to a wider audience. His arguments suggest that he could not have been very happy with the way in which Agudat Yisrael was developing.

Although Weinberg acknowledged that it would be worthwhile for the

[79] Zalman Shazar, *Or ishim* (Jerusalem, 1973), i. 222.

[80] In 1920 Weinberg performed the wedding of Agnon and his bride, Esther Marx—against the wishes of Marx's father. See the interesting story in Reuven Avineri, 'Agnon's Wedding' (Heb.), *Ma'ariv*, 6 May 1988, 5.

[81] *From Berlin to Jerusalem* (Heb.) (Tel Aviv, 1982), 101.

[82] 'Protokollbuch des seminarischen Vereins "Dibbuk Chawerim" ', entry for 4 Dec. 1915 (Jewish Theological Seminary of America, MS 3675).

[83] *Bund Jüdischer Akademiker Korrespondenzblatt* (Summer 1917), 10. On this very influential organization, see Breuer, *Jüdische Orthodoxie*, 331 ff.

[84] The article originally appeared in the Polish Agudah paper, *Dos Yiddishe Vort*. Weinberg translated it and published it as 'Verständigung: Ein Wort für Nichtorthodoxe'. It appeared in instalments in *Der Israelit* of 1923 (21, 28 June; 5, 12, 26 July; 2, 9 Aug.). It also appeared in a Hebrew translation by Aharon Sorasky (*Et aḥai anokhi mevakesh*, 49–76). For the sake of convenience I shall refer to this edition in citing Weinberg's essay.

Orthodox to work together with other segments of Judaism on issues of common concern, this was only so when there was no possibility that Orthodoxy would be weakened in the process. As far as he was concerned, it was obvious that the guardians of tradition could not be expected to be tolerant of their brethren's abandonment of this tradition. In his rather belligerent words:

Is it easy to say to a son that he should be tolerant of them that insult his mother? Tolerance?! Will a man forgive his brother when he sees the apathy shown to him, that his brother is unconcerned with his pain or happiness? Should one perhaps have tolerance for him who forsakes his mother, his wife and his family? . . . Tolerance is a modern invention! I can love or hate my brother, but under no circumstances am I, or can I be, tolerant of him. From my brother I demand, and have the right to demand, that he should not deprive me of the opportunity to love him properly, as one loves a brother.[85]

Yet despite these comments, the fact that Weinberg was theoretically prepared to work with the non-Orthodox on issues of joint concern shows that he opposed the Frankfurt *Austritt* mentality which shunned any such co-operation.

Weinberg's differences with the German Agudah and its *Austritt* ideology appear elsewhere too. At the beginning of 1918 Weinberg, as the representative of the Slobodka yeshiva, was scheduled to give a speech at the Agudat Yisrael convention in Frankfurt. As he was unable to attend, he chose to publish the address. Because of his criticisms of the direction in which Agudat Yisrael was moving, Weinberg submitted the piece to the Mizrachi organ, *Die Jüdische Presse*,[86] rather than to *Der Israelit*, which reflected the Agudah position and would probably have refused to publish it.

Although the Agudah has by now degenerated and today engages in partisan religious politics, it must be remembered that when it was founded in 1912, there were high hopes in all sections of the Orthodox population that it would be able to rise above party and political squabbles and represent what was regarded as Torah-true Judaism. What was envisioned was a truly international group encompassing all Orthodox Jews. As time went on it became obvious that this was an unattainable goal, for, as Jacob Rosenheim describes at length in his memoirs, the religious and political differences between the various segments of Orthodoxy were too profound to be patched over. This was especially true when anti-Zionism became a hallmark of the Agudah. Yet it was those very high hopes which led Rabbi Abraham Isaac Kook to leave Palestine in order to attend the ill-fated 1914 convention, where he was to speak on issues relating to the land of Israel. These high hopes also persuaded Rabbi Meir Berlin (Bar-Ilan), the leader of the Mizrachi movement, to attend the Agudah's first conference in Kattowitz, Germany, in 1912, and to pledge his support for Agudat Yisrael as the true representative of traditional Judaism.[87]

[85] pp. 57–8.

[86] 'Eine Rede' (1918), 44–5.

[87] See his article 'Agudat Yisrael', *Ha'ivri*, 31 May 1912, 213, and the report on the conference, *Ha'ivri*, 14 June 1912, 225–30. See also Bar-Ilan, *From Volozhin to Jerusalem*, ii. 396–400, and Rosenheim, *Erinnerungen*, 125.

In his article Weinberg warned the Agudah members against drifting away from their lofty goals and turning into a political party, which by definition would have to exclude segments of the Orthodox community. At this time the organization appeared to be heading in this very direction, and the uproar over Pinchas Kohn's memorandum, in particular his negative comments about Lithuanian Jews, seemed to offer proof of this.[88] Rather than dissociating itself from what he had said, the separatist newspaper *Der Israelit* actually rallied to his support,[89] defending the man who, in Weinberg's eyes, had insulted the Jewish community out of which had arisen Judaism's leading scholars.

In fact, Weinberg was just as angered by the defence of Kohn as by Kohn's words themselves. Reflecting its *Austritt* mentality, *Der Israelit* claimed that Kohn had been misunderstood, for his negative comments about the Jews of Lithuania were actually only made with reference to the non-Orthodox. It was this type of defence which particularly infuriated Weinberg, as Kohn's memorandum was directed towards non-Jewish politicians. Weinberg, for his part, was insistent that when dealing with the non-Jewish world 'we recognize no difference between Torah-true and other Jews'. A few months later he resumed his attack against the politicization of Orthodoxy, accusing the German Orthodox of ignoring the east European Jewish masses and not showing proper concern for the feelings of the young generation. According to Weinberg, this sorry state of affairs would continue until German Orthodox life was completely democratized.[90]

This dispute between Weinberg and *Der Israelit* reflects a fundamental difference between the Orthodox communities in Germany (and Hungary) and those in Lithuania and Poland. The German (and Hungarian) Orthodox, even those who did not separate from the general community, could not have been surprised by *Der Israelit*'s defence of Kohn, in which it claimed that he was only giving the government a negative portrayal of the non-Orthodox. Ever since the rise of the Reform movement in the early nineteenth century, the German Orthodox had not shied away from involving the government in their religious disputes.[91] At the beginning, when they were still the dominant party in Judaism, they denounced the Reformers as a sect, dangerous to true religion, and urged the government to close their temples.[92]

As the century progressed and the Orthodox lost power, they once again turned to the government. This time they argued that it violated their religious principles, indeed their very freedom of conscience, to be forced to remain in a single communal framework with the Reformers. Thus, as Jacob Katz has noted, the very people who would have liked nothing better than to have the government suppress

[88] See Wohlgemuth, 'Zionismus', 1–2 (note); Breuer, 'Orthodox Rabbis', 137–47.

[89] 'Alljüdische Politik', *Der Israelit*, 17 Jan. 1918, 1–3.

[90] 'Die Demokratisierung der Orthodoxie', *Der Israelit*, 20 June 1918, 1. The editor appended a strong refutation of Weinberg's opinion.

[91] See Bleich, 'Rabbinic Responses', 62–6.

[92] See Michael A. Meyer, *Response to Modernity* (Oxford, 1988), ch. 1.

the Reformers had now become advocates of freedom of religion when it was their freedom which was threatened.[93] Clearly, the tendency of the Orthodox to look to the government for assistance in religious disputes was anything but foreign in Germany.

It was a government decision which finally allowed the Orthodox to form separate communities, and even those who remained in the general community did so with the understanding that if the Reformers crossed certain lines they too would withdraw from the community. Those who continued to belong to the generalcommunity—the overwhelming majority of the German Orthodox—justified themselves by pointing to the decision of Rabbi Seligmann Baer Bamberger permitting the Orthodox to retain communal ties with the non-Orthodox, mentioned in the last chapter. However, despite many mistaken assertions to the contrary, even Bamberger was not a philosophical supporter of the concept of one community, and on a number of other occasions agreed that the Orthodox should withdraw.[94] We thus see that the notion of Jewish unity was not a fundamental, overriding concern of nineteenth-century German Orthodoxy. Although in the years following the early battles with the Reformers the German separatists were usually careful to note that their opposition was only directed against non-Orthodox religious organizations, not individuals, there is occasional evidence that this boundary was not always carefully observed, as Kohn's negative comments attest.

The situation in Lithuania and Poland was very different. For various reasons, chief among them being the lack of any real Reform movement and the fact that Orthodox tax payments were not used to support non-Orthodox institutions, there was never a separatist Orthodoxy in these countries. Even after the non-Orthodox had become a force to be reckoned with, and the large cities had become battlegrounds between Orthodoxy and its opponents with each side struggling to control communal leadership, there was never any real attempt to form breakaway Orthodox communities from which the non-Orthodox would be excluded. Even the most vigorous Orthodox ideologues, such as Lifshitz, argued against such a

[93] See *Halakhah in Straits*, 10–14. Interestingly enough, Hirsch differed from his colleagues in that, on principle, he was completely opposed to any form of government religious coercion directed against the Reformers. See ibid. 135, 244–5; Mordechai Breuer, 'Samson Raphael Hirsch Today: Conceptions and Misconceptions', *Jewish Action* (Summer 1989), 7–10.

[94] See Simhah Bamberger, *Zekher simḥah* (Frankfurt, 1925), no. 230; Moses Auerbach, 'Seligmann Bär Bamberger', *Jeschurun*, 15 (1928), 536; Hermann Schwab, *The History of Orthodox Jewry in Germany, 1830–1945*, trans. Irene R. Birnbaum (London, [1950]), ch. 10; M. L. Bamberger, 'Seligmann Baer Bamberger', in Leo Jung (ed.), *Jewish Leaders* (New York, 1953), 192–3; David Henshke, 'A Dispute for the Sake of Heaven' (Heb.), *Hama'ayan*, 13 (Tammuz 5733 [1973]), 41–4; B. S. Hamburger's biographical essay in Seligman Baer Bamberger, *Collected Writings* (Heb.) ([Israel], 1992), 543 ff. The first significant German Orthodox figure who opposed *Austritt* on philosophical grounds was R. Marcus Horovitz. On his views see Heinemann, 'R. Mordechai Halevi Horovitz', 162–71. The most complete study of Orthodox separatism is Morgenstern, *Von Frankfurt nach Jerusalem*. For the early years of the Frankfurt community, see Robert Liberles, *Religious Conflict in Social Context: The Resurgence of Orthodox Judaism in Frankfurt am Main, 1838–1877* (Westport, Conn., 1985).

step.[95] The Orthodox were content to struggle with the non-Orthodox over all communal issues, including the appointment of the rabbi, rather than disrupt communal unity which was viewed as being of overwhelming importance, especially since they lived in lands not particularly friendly to Jews.

The sentiments behind this position were articulated by the Volozhin *rosh yeshiva*, Rabbi Naftali Zvi Judah Berlin, in a responsum in which he strongly criticized the new Mahazikei Hadat organization in Galicia, which was also pursuing a separatist agenda.[96] In words similar to those used by Weinberg, which accurately reflected Lithuanian and Polish rabbinic attitudes, Berlin emphasized the need for all Jews to be united when confronting the gentile world. As he argued, it was literally this unity which enabled the Jews to survive all attempts to destroy them.[97] In this responsum Berlin also coined his famous expression describing the separatist ideology as 'painful as a dagger in the body of the nation'. Agreeing with the previously mentioned position of Rabbi Joseph Saul Nathanson, Rabbi Abraham Jacob Friedman, and Rabbi Israel Meir Hacohen, Berlin rejected the value of polemical battles with the non-Orthodox and could only advocate an increased study of Torah as the means of returning all Jews to the proper path.

As Rosenheim recalled, the question of *Austritt* was one of the real sticking-points in the early years of Agudat Yisrael. The Hungarian delegates insisted that in cities which had separatist communities only their members should be allowed to join the new organization. This became known as the 'Hungarian Demand'. The separatist rabbi of Frankfurt, Salomon Breuer, did not go this far, but still maintained that positions of authority in the movement should be reserved for those who joined the separatist community. (The Hungarian delegates later accepted Breuer's compromise.) However, the Lithuanian and Polish delegates, led by Rabbi Hayim Soloveitchik—who had earlier been supportive of Breuer—rejected this view.[98] If these delegates did not share Rabbi Naftali Zvi Judah Berlin's negative view of the separatist ideology, they were certainly neutral on the issue and did not believe that it should be of any real importance. After all, every one of them was a member of a community which encompassed the Orthodox and non-Orthodox, and they had never attempted to duplicate the separatism of

[95] See e.g. Lifshitz's strong comments in *Maḥazikei hadat*, 7*a* (note), 29*a*. See also Reines, *Shenei hame'orot*, section 2, part 1, 24*a–b*; Moses Friedman, *Da'at moshe hashalem* (Jerusalem, 1983), 268–9; Moshe Sternbuch, *Teshuvot vehanhagot* (Jerusalem, 1992), i. 484.

[96] *Meshiv davar* (Brooklyn, NY, 1987), i, no. 44.

[97] However, when not confronting the gentile world Berlin urged the observant to keep apart from their non-religious brethren; see ibid. i, no. 9. Similarly, such leading scholars as R. Hayim Ozer Grodzinski, R. Meir Simhah of Dvinsk, R. Israel Meir Hacohen, and R. Abraham Mordechai Alter of Gur, who did not urge the creation of separate communities in eastern Europe, did support religious separatism in Palestine. See their manifesto in Moshe Blau, *Al ḥomotayikh yerushalayim* (Benei Berak, 1967), 83.

[98] See Rosenheim, *Erinnerungen*, 123–4. See also Schneersohn, *Igerot kodesh*, ii, nos. 360, 363, 366 and v, no. 1044; Hayim Eiz, 'Concerning Agudat Yisrael' (Heb.), *Hamodia*, 23 Shevat 5673 [1913], 267–8. According to Salomon Breuer's son, Isaac Breuer, *Moriyah* (Jerusalem, 1982), 207, Soloveitchik only had a tactical disagreement with the elder Breuer, but supported him in principle.

Germany and Hungary in their lands. As Gershon Bacon has pointed out in his discussion of the politics of Agudat Yisrael in inter-war Poland, the Orthodox claimed that they spoke for the vast majority of the country's Jews, and that therefore 'any hint at separatism would be self-defeating'.[99]

If the Lithuanian and Polish rabbis had agreed with Breuer's separatist agenda, even though it technically only applied to communities which already had two segments, it would have implied that their own, unified, communities were religiously problematic. Furthermore, as Rosenheim recalled, the Lithuanian and Polish Orthodox who settled in Germany hardly ever joined the separatist communities, and, coming from their east European background, they did not see any religious significance in their actions. To agree with the separatists would have meant that there was a serious religious deficiency in these east European Jews, something the majority of Lithuanian and Polish rabbis, not to mention Rosenheim himself, could never admit.[100]

German Orthodoxy and German Patriotism

Throughout 1918, with the war turning badly against Germany, Weinberg remained in Berlin. In fact, he even delivered an anti-war sermon on Rosh Hashanah of that year. In order to understand this better, some background is necessary. Germany was swept up by war fever throughout World War I. It was a time of great patriotism in which foreigners obviously had no part. Virtually the entire German Jewish community, including the Orthodox, who made up about 15 per cent of this population, had united in support of their government. With the exception of England,[101] there was no other European country in which the patriotic feelings of Orthodox Jews even approached those of the German Orthodox.[102]

[99] 'Agudath Israel', 45.

[100] See Rosenheim, *Erinnerungen*, 129–31; id., *Memoirs*, 190–4; id., *Oholai Ya'akov: Ausgewählte Aufsätze und Ansprachen* (Frankfurt, 1930), ii. 174–81.

[101] England's Chief Rabbi Joseph Hertz even went so far as to declare that *kohanim* were required to serve in the army—a position which caused an enormous amount of controversy in the Orthodox community. For the text of his statement see the *Jewish Chronicle*, 14 Apr. 1916, 18. See also Shlomo Yosef Zevin, *Le'or hahalakhah* (Heb.) (Tel Aviv, 1957), 59. Kook was in England during the war, where he strongly opposed Hertz and did his utmost to secure army exemptions for both yeshiva students and *kohanim*. As far as Kook was concerned, this war had nothing to do with Jewish interests, and it was therefore best for Jews to attempt to remove themselves from it as much as possible. See Alexander Carlebach, *Men and Ideas* (Jerusalem, 1982), 101–4, and Zvi Yehudah Kook, *Lehilkhot tsibur* (Jerusalem, 1987), 13.

[102] See the many publications listed in Louis Lamm, *Verzeichnis jüdischer Kriegsschriften* (Berlin, 1916). On the patriotism of the Zionist Rabbi Nehemiah Anton Nobel, see Rachel Heuberger, 'Nehemias Anton Nobel: Ein orthodoxer Rabbiner zwischen deutschem Patriotismus und religiösem Zionismus', *Trumah*, 3 (1992), 151–74, esp. 158 ff. See also Chaim Schatzker, 'The German-Jewish Attitude of Jewish Youth in Germany During the First World War and the Influence of the War on this Attitude' (Heb.), in B. Oded *et al.* (eds.), *Meḥkarim betoledot am yisrael ve'erets yisrael* (Haifa, 1972), ii. 187–215, who stresses the importance of Jewish interests in the younger generation's enthusiastic pro-war stand.

One of the most outstanding examples of this patriotism was Joseph Wohlgemuth, the editor of *Jeschurun*, who published a pro-German tract entitled 'The World War in the Light of Judaism'.[103] In the spirit of the times many Orthodox Jews volunteered for the army, with the enthusiastic support of the rabbinate.[104] Since volunteering for army service would inevitably require one to violate various Jewish laws, such as those related to the Sabbath and *kashrut*, this step had been opposed by Rabbi Esriel Hildesheimer during the Franco-German war of 1870–1.[105] Yet Rabbi David Zvi Hoffmann, Germany's leading halakhic authority during World War I, took a different view.[106] In any event, the patriotic atmosphere was such that even if halakhic objections were raised, they were simply pushed aside.[107]

Many Orthodox rabbis and intellectuals did not share Wohlgemuth's extreme position,[108] and did not refrain from commenting on the evils and undesirability of war.[109] Nevertheless, they did not openly criticize German war aims or speak of a Jewish interest which diverged from the interests of the Fatherland. It is thus

[103] *Der Weltkrieg im Lichte des Judentums* (Berlin, 1915). See also his *Krieg und Judentum* (Frankfurt, 1916). Juda Ari Wohlgemuth, 'Joseph Wohlgemuth', in Leo Jung (ed.), *Guardians of Our Heritage* (New York, 1958), 549, in referring to his father's pro-German attitude, writes: 'His accent, however, was not on "patriotism" but on his love for the Jewish people, whom he yearned to see redeemed from Czarist cruelty.' This judgement is a complete distortion of the elder Wohlgemuth's views. Any perusal of his essays will immediately reveal that not only is there a great deal more 'patriotism' involved than the younger Wohlgemuth is prepared to admit, but that virtually everything the elder Wohlgemuth wrote on this subject was tied up with his love for the Fatherland and his desire to increase its glory. See especially his essay 'Unser Kaiser', *Jeschurun*, 2 (1915), 1–18 (also found in *Der Weltkrieg im Lichte des Judentums*, 62–75). It must be remembered that Wohlgemuth actually declared that God was on the side of Germany, making the struggle nothing less than a holy war. Furthermore, the war was not merely directed against Russia. As a good patriot, Wohlgemuth was also prepared to see England and France be destroyed. (In later years, as something of a cruel joke, students at the Rabbinical Seminary would occasionally leave Wohlgemuth's patriotic works on his desk. See Isi Jacob Eisner, 'Reminiscences of the Berlin Rabbinical Seminary', *LBIYB* 12 (1967), 38.) The nature of German Orthodoxy's attitude towards the war effort is a most fascinating subject, which has not yet been explored in depth. For some recent and illuminating comments see Breuer, *Jüdische Orthodoxie*, 342–50, and Rivka Horwitz, 'Voices of Opposition to the First World War among Jewish Thinkers', *LBIYB* 33 (1988), 233–59. In the bibliographical note found in Breuer's English version of his book (*Modernity within Tradition* (New York, 1992), 490), he writes that there is an abundance of publications, circulars, and archival documentation on the wartime activities of Orthodox Jewry in Germany. This material can be found in the Central Archives for the History of the Jewish People, Jerusalem; Bayerisches Hauptstaatsarchiv (Kriegsarchiv), Munich; and the Bernstein Collection of Yeshiva University Archives.

[104] See Breuer, *Jüdische Orthodoxie*, 342 ff.

[105] See his letter in *Die Jüdische Presse*, 12 Aug. 1870, 54.

[106] *Melamed leho'il* (New York, 1954), i, no. 42.

[107] Although in earlier years Jews had generally tried to avoid military service, as a rule they patriotically supported their monarch. See Marc Saperstein, 'War and Patriotism in Sermons to Central European Jews: 1756–1815', *LBIYB* 38 (1993), 3–14.

[108] See Breuer, *Jüdische Orthodoxie*, 343, 486 n. 178.

[109] Particularly noteworthy in this regard is Isak Unna, 'Zeitgemässe Mahnungen', *Jeschurun*, 3 (1916), 703–9. See also Miriam Gillis-Carlebach, *Education and Faith* (Heb.) (Tel Aviv, 1979), 151–2.

significant that Weinberg actually delivered a sermon, undoubtedly before east European Jews who knew nothing of German patriotism,[110] in which he proclaimed that the war had nothing in common with Jewish interests and that Jews therefore had no reason to participate in it. As he put it, the Jew does not wish to take part in wars against others, but rather in a war against the beastliness inherent in himself, for it is this war which will in turn bring about the peaceful union of all men. In the heart of wartime Berlin Weinberg was prepared to admit that the antisemites were correct when they argued that Jews were not ready to include themselves in the sacrifices being made by the rest of the population. This was so, for although Jews were always prepared to make sacrifices for their ethical vision, they could not lend their support to 'ideals which bring destruction to humanity'.[111] Whether Weinberg had spoken out against the war earlier is not known, but there is no evidence that points in this direction. In fact, this sermon, in its entirety, was not published until the Nazi era, when Jewish patriotism during World War I no longer had any relevance.[112]

Post-War Developments

After the war came to its end Weinberg still chose not to return to Pilwishki. Yet he remained concerned with events in Lithuania, and there can be little doubt that he was the moving spirit behind a number of different projects. For example, in the spring of 1920 Weinberg, together with Wohlgemuth and Meier Hildesheimer (1864–1934), established a fund to assist Lithuanian yeshivot.[113] A few months later we find the three of them once more asking the German people to be generous in support of the yeshivot.[114] Weinberg was also involved in fund-raising for the new teachers' seminary which was established in Kovno.[115]

After the war Weinberg continued his literary endeavours. In 1918 he published his first study of the *musar* movement, Rabbi Israel Salanter's innovation which so revitalized the Lithuanian yeshivot. In fact this article, and those on the same subject which he wrote a few years later, are significant as the first detailed studies of the movement, and are still valuable both for Weinberg's insight and for the oral history which he recorded.[116] Despite Weinberg's undisguised partisanship and

110 As mentioned previously, during the war years Weinberg served as rabbi of a small congregation of east European Jews.

111 *Lifrakim*, 28 (14).

112 Most of the sermon appeared in his 'Rosch-Haschonoh-Gedanken', *Die Jüdische Presse*, 6 Sept. 1918, 343–4. In this essay Weinberg speaks generally about the evils of war. However, for obvious reasons, the passage in which he acknowledges that Jews have no desire to take part in this war has been removed. (I am taking Weinberg at his word that these passages were in the original sermon and were not simply added at a later date.)

113 See *Die Jüdische Presse*, 12 Mar. 1920, 85.

114 *Die Jüdische Presse*, 11 June 1920, 1 (Hebrew section), and 18 June 1920, 1 (Hebrew section).

115 See *Die Jüdische Presse*, 16 Apr. 1920, 128.

116 Immanuel Etkes has argued that a couple of points in Weinberg's oral history are exaggerated. See *Rabbi Israel Salanter*, 98, 158 n. 24.

the fact that he was writing as an 'insider', he was still able to provide an impartial examination of the movement.[117] In other writings of this period Weinberg discussed the relevance of the traditional prayer-book, in particular its sacrificial references, to modern Jews.[118] He also continued his eminently readable, if rather superficial, explorations into the nature of the Jewish people and its religiosity.[119]

Believing that modern Hebrew literature was too important and influential for Orthodox thinkers to ignore, Weinberg began to write a series of essays on it, though only two instalments actually appeared.[120] Weinberg's essay on Micha Josef Berdyczewski (1865–1921) includes a number of fascinating points which, unfortunately, were never fully developed. All that is left are a few glimpses of what could have been some very refreshing thoughts on the nature of faith in the modern world.

The figure of Berdyczewski was bound to be fascinating to the Orthodox, for his writings include, at one and the same time, the most strident opposition to tradition as well as an apparent pride in it. Not surprisingly, this characteristic has often been discussed in scholarly studies of the author.[121] As Weinberg put it, the key to Berdyczewski is his 'Jewish heresy'. Weinberg believed that this heresy arose from the same source as the holy, and was actually the result of deep spiritual longing.[122] Furthermore, just as a distinction must be made between the base heresy of the masses and the profound heresy of thinkers such as Berdyczewski, Weinberg argued that the same is true with regard to the opposite pole to heresy, namely belief. In his mind, belief which is characterized by calm and fulfilment is actually a sign of inner emptiness and lack of thought. A man with such feelings is a believer only because he does not have the strength to deny, and such 'belief', or rather lack of denial, can never be the source of creativity. True belief, which is both religious and creative, is also stormy and turbulent and has nothing in common with passive fulfilment.

The way Weinberg expressed himself on these latter points bears such similarity to the ideas of G. K. Chesterton that one must wonder whether Weinberg had read

[117] 'Von den litauischen "Moralisten" ihrer Ideenwelt und ihrem ersten Führer', *Jeschurun*, 5 (1918), 478–84, 585–606. A few years later he published the equally significant article 'R. Jisroel Salanter und die Mussarbewegung', *Jeschurun*, 7 (1920), 595–605; 8 (1921), 52–61, 162–8 (these articles appear in Hebrew translation in *SE* iv, pp. 276–96).

[118] 'Über Opferwesen und Opfergebete', *Die Jüdische Presse*, 21 Dec. 1917, 534–6, 28 Dec. 1917, 544–6, 4 Jan. 1918, 6–7, 11 Jan. 1918, 16–18.

[119] 'Das frohe Volk', *Die Jüdische Presse*, 20 Sept. 1918, 363–4; 'Piety and Observance of the Commandments' (Heb.), *Jeschurun*, 7 (1920), 8–11.

[120] 'Ahad Ha'am as Thinker and Guide' (Heb.), *Jeschurun*, 7 (1920), 118–22; 'The New Hebrew Literature and its Champions' (Heb.), *Jeschurun*, 8 (1921), 31–9. The first essay is merely an introduction to Ahad Ha'am from the Orthodox perspective, but the promised analysis of his work never appeared. The second essay is devoted to Berdyzcewski.

[121] See Miriam Morgan, 'The Traditional Aspect in the Views of Ahad Ha'am and Berdyczewski' (Heb.) (MA diss., Bar-Ilan University, 1979), 20 ff., and Avner Holtzman, *El hakera shebalev* (Jerusalem, 1995), esp. 59–84.

[122] Cf. Kook, *Arpelei tohar*, 2.

the latter's *Orthodoxy*, which had appeared in German translation in 1909. For example, in the following famous passage we find Chesterton making the same point as Weinberg, in his own inimitable style:

> People have fallen into a foolish habit speaking of orthodoxy as something heavy, humdrum, and safe. There never was anything so perilous or so exciting as orthodoxy. It was sanity: and to be sane is more dramatic than to be mad. It was the equilibrium of a man behind madly rushing horses, seeming to stoop this way and to sway that, yet in every attitude having the grace of statuary and the accuracy of arithmetic. . . . It is always simple to fall; there are an infinity of angles at which one falls, only one at which one stands.[123]

Weinberg wrote all the essays discussed above while he was in Germany, after the war. The fact that he remained in Berlin, rather than returning to Pilwishki, clearly shows that he was intent on remaining in Germany for good. However, for a rabbi to succeed in Germany it was necessary for him to have an advanced secular education. Indeed, only a candidate with a doctorate could aspire to one of the coveted rabbinic positions. This being the case, Weinberg set his sights on attending a university. Although he was very intelligent, fluent in a few languages, and a prolific author, none of this carried any weight as far as German universities were concerned. Having only attended *ḥeder* and yeshivot, Weinberg had never received the degree necessary for acceptance by a German university. To remedy this situation, he turned to the Jüdisches Realgymnasium in Kovno, presumably without appearing there in person, and on 30 April 1919 was granted a certificate testifying to his education.[124]

Armed with this document and a recommendation from Albert Einstein,[125] he was given permission to attend lectures at the Philosophical Faculty of the University of Berlin, although he was not officially enrolled as a student.[126] In the winter term of 1919–20 the 35-year-old Weinberg was finally exposed to university learning. During this term he attended the lectures of several professors, among them Hermann Strack (1848–1922), the famous gentile talmudic scholar.[127] He remained at the University of Berlin for only one term. It was then that he decided to leave Berlin and enrol formally at the University of Giessen, beginning in the summer term.

[123] German edn. Bonn, 1909; quotation taken from *Orthodoxy* (New York, 1990), 100–1. Cf. also Joseph B. Soloveitchik, *Halakhic Man*, trans. Lawrence Kaplan (Philadelphia, 1983), 139–43.

[124] This is the information Weinberg supplied to the University of Giessen, which is now in its archives. The information in his 'Lebenslauf' (Appendix I) has a different chronology which does not seem to be correct.

[125] A letter from Weinberg to Einstein, dated 19 Dec. 1919, in which he both thanks him for the recommendation and enquiries as to when he could pay a visit to 'the great son of our people', is found in the Albert Einstein Correspondence, copies of which are kept at both Boston University and the Hebrew University of Jerusalem.

[126] Information in the archives of Humboldt University of Berlin.

[127] 'Lebenslauf': see Appendix I.

FOUR

GIESSEN AND BEYOND (1920–1932)

GERMAN ORTHODOXY AND THE PROBLEM OF MODERN SCHOLARSHIP

THE VARIOUS religious and political disputes which were a part of German Orthodoxy in the late nineteenth century continued during the Weimar Republic. Before the next stage of Weinberg's career can be discussed, it is necessary to review a major disagreement between two important groups, the followers of Rabbi Esriel Hildesheimer and those of Rabbi Samson Raphael Hirsch, known respectively as 'Berlin' and 'Frankfurt'. The ideology of Berlin had its source in the Berlin Rabbinical Seminary, a unique experiment in Orthodox rabbinical training founded by Hildesheimer.[1] Recognizing the need for rabbis with a modern education, Hildesheimer attempted to establish a seminary while still in Hungary. After meeting unrelenting opposition from his Orthodox colleagues, he moved to Berlin where the local Orthodox community was very supportive.

The seminary Hildesheimer established in Berlin was the only institution under Orthodox auspices in which students were required to have a high level of secular education before they were admitted. It was expected that they would continue their general education at the university level.[2] Furthermore, Wissenschaft des

[1] For all aspects of the history and ideology of the institution, see S. Goldschmidt, 'Die Gründung und Bedeutung des Rabbiner-Seminars', *Jeschurun*, 7 (1920), 216–55; Moses Auerbach, 'Ziel und Wege der heutigen Rabbinerausbildung', *Der Israelit*, 15 Sept. 1932, 1–3, 19 Sept. 1932, 4, 22 Sept. 1932, 6; Bernard Perlow, 'Institutions for the Education of the Modern Rabbi in Germany' (Ph.D. diss, Dropsie College, 1954), ch. 4; Moses Shulvass, 'The Rabbinical Seminary of Berlin' (Heb.), in S. Mirsky (ed.), *Mosedot torah be'eiropah* (New York, 1956), 689–713; Eisner, 'Reminiscences', 32–52; Mordechai Eliav, 'Das orthodoxe Rabbinerseminar in Berlin', in Julius Carlebach (ed.), *Wissenschaft des Judentums* (Darmstadt, 1992), 59–73; Jörg H. Fehrs, *Von der Heidereutergasse zum Roseneck* (Berlin, 1993), 221–8; and the very important comments of Eliezer Stern, *Educational Ideal*, ch. 4.

[2] Whether Hildesheimer believed that secular studies were of inherent worth, as did Hirsch, or merely of pragmatic value is not entirely clear, as there is some ambiguity in his writings. However, most scholars agree that on the whole he leaned to the second alternative. See Breuer, *Jüdische Orthodoxie*, 125–6; Stern, *Educational Ideal*, 91 ff.; Mordechai Eliav, 'Different Approaches to Torah im Derekh Eretz' (Heb.), in Mordechai Breuer (ed.), *Torah im Derekh Eretz* (Ramat Gan, 1987), 50–1; Azriel Hildesheimer, 'Rabbi Esriel Hildesheimer's Conception of Torah im Derekh Eretz' (Heb.), ibid. 75–82; Kalman Kahana, 'The Gaon Rabbi Esriel Hildesheimer and his Seminary' (Heb.), *Hama'ayan*, 29 (Tammuz 5749 [1989]), 6; David Ellenson, *Rabbi Esriel Hildesheimer and the Creation of a Modern Jewish Orthodoxy* (Tuscaloosa, Ala., 1990), 120 ff.

Judentums was a central element of the curriculum, and was taught by some of the greatest names in German Jewish scholarship.[3] Although the training of rabbis was central to the Berlin seminary's *raison d'être*, Hildesheimer made clear in his address at its inauguration that he did not intend to create a 'rabbi factory'. Rather, in addition to rabbinic training, he hoped to make the Berlin seminary the centre of an Orthodox intelligentsia, consisting of merchants, theologians, lawyers, and doctors.[4] In this he was at least partly successful.[5]

In terms of commitment to the academic study of Judaism, there was little difference between the faculty of Hildesheimer's seminary and its counterparts at the non-Orthodox seminaries of Abraham Geiger (Hochschule für die Wissenschaft des Judentums) and Zechariah Frankel (Jüdisches-Theologisches Seminar). Indeed, Hildesheimer was always quick to defend the high academic standards at his institution.[6] The Orthodox scholars who were associated with the Berlin seminary, even those who were uncompromising separatists in matters of Jewish communal politics, had no difficulty involving themselves in scholarly pursuits with the non-Orthodox. One of their main motivations for engaging in Wissenschaft des Judentums was quite similar to that of the non-Orthodox scholars; Hildesheimer gave voice to this when he spoke of the glorification of God's name which would accompany Orthodox successes in Jewish scholarship.[7]

The only real difference between the scholars at the Berlin seminary and their non-Orthodox colleagues was in the realm of dogma, which was an important factor in biblical studies and the history of halakhah. In fact, as Mordechai Breuer has pointed out, Orthodox scholarship in these areas was looked down upon for its lack of impartiality.[8] Nevertheless, even though the Berlin seminary scholars were

[3] For student interest in Wissenschaft des Judentums see the booklet *Unser Dibbuk* (Berlin, 1899), pp. vi–xii.

[4] 'Rede zur Eröffnung des Rabbiner-Seminars', *Jahres-Bericht des Rabbiner-Seminars für das orthodoxe Judenthum pro 5634 (1873–74)* (Berlin, [1874]), 87.

[5] See e.g. *Jahres-Bericht des Rabbiner-Seminars zu Berlin für 1924* (Berlin, 1925), 10 ff.

[6] See e.g. Mordechai Eliav (ed.), *Rabbiner Esriel Hildesheimer Briefe* (Jerusalem, 1965), letter 57 (German section).

[7] *Jahres-Bericht des Rabbiner-Seminars für das orthodoxe Judenthum pro 5634 (1873–74)*, 87; Breuer, *Jüdische Orthodoxie*, 174–5.

[8] See Eliav, *Hildesheimer Briefe*, 134 (German section); Breuer, *Jüdische Orthodoxie*, 186. Breuer seems to be mistaken in pointing to the dispute over the authenticity of B. H. Auerbach's edition of the *Eshkol* as an example of this phenomenon. To begin with, the main assault on Auerbach was led by Shalom Albeck (1858–1920), himself an Orthodox Jew. Secondly, this dispute had nothing to do with dogma interfering with scholarship, but was simply a question of whether Auerbach had forged the text. Finally, it is not so clear that Albeck's attempt failed, as Breuer would have it. On the contrary, the authenticity of Auerbach's edition is still highly questionable. See Zevin, *Authors and Books*, i. 106–7. For other possible examples of forgery by Auerbach, see Albeck's *Kofer ha'eshkol* (Warsaw, 1911); M. S. Samet, 'Moses Mendelssohn, N. H. Wessely, and the Rabbis of their Generation' (Heb.), in A. Gilboa *et al.* (eds.), *Meḥkarim betoledot am yisrael ve'erets yisrael lezekher tsevi avneri* (Haifa, 1970), 235–6. See also Meir Benayahu, *Shaving on Ḥol Hamo'ed* (Heb.) (Jerusalem, 1995), 102 n. 243. Auerbach was defended vigorously by Issachar Dov Bergman, 'Biography of the Author of *Naḥal eshkol*' (Heb.), in Sidney B. Hoenig and Leon D. Stitskin (eds.), *Joshua Finkel Festschrift* (New York, 1974), 59–79.

candid about their dogmatic assumptions, they believed that their scholarship, which upheld traditional views, was not based on dogma but was the result of an impartial examination of the evidence.[9] Whereas many of the Orthodox, in particular the followers of Hirsch ('Frankfurt'), ignored the works of non-traditional scholars and even rejected the fundamentals of modern scholarship, the instruction at the seminary, which accepted the assumptions and methodology of university scholarship, could not ignore the biblical criticism of scholars such as Wellhausen but needed to disprove these heretical views. Hildesheimer and his successors believed that it was essential in modern times to confront directly views opposed to tradition. Any attempt to avoid this task would be self-defeating, since the students would inevitably be exposed to modern scholarly trends.[10]

The seminary leadership was convinced that it was no longer possible to ensure theological conformity through the traditional arguments which had been advanced by men such as Judah Halevi. It was also impossible to advocate a theology based on faith alone, when this theology was at odds with modern scholarship. Rather, the students had to be convinced that the traditional view was also in accord with the highest standards of scholarship. With great confidence—indeed over-confidence—the seminary faculty believed that the conclusions of Wissenschaft des Judentums and modern biblical studies need not oppose traditional Jewish dogma, and could even be used to provide scholarly support for the traditional approach. The seminary's academic study of the Bible was therefore designed to show the scholarly weaknesses of biblical criticism. Before graduation all seminary students were to be taught how to present the traditional approach in a convincing, i.e. scholarly, manner.[11]

Rabbi David Zvi Hoffmann, a native of Hungary who succeeded Hildesheimer (d. 1899) as rector of the seminary, was also Germany's leading halakhic authority in the early twentieth century. In addition to this, he had been a practitioner of critical Talmud study for years and was an outspoken supporter of Wissenschaft des Judentums.[12] Although Hoffmann was a staunch opponent of the theories of

[19] See e.g. Hoffmann's introductory remarks in his commentary on Leviticus (Berlin, 1905), and his *Die wichtigsten Instanzen gegen die Graf-Wellhausensche Hypothese* (Berlin, 1904). On Hoffmann's approach in this area, see Tchernowitz, *Memoirs*, 260–2; Carla Sulzbach, 'David Zvi Hoffmann's *Die wichtigsten Instanzen gegen die Graf-Wellhausensche Hypothese*' (MA diss., McGill University, 1996).

[10] This is a common theme in the literature of the Berlin seminary. See e.g. S. Grünberg's comments in *Zum hundertjährigen Geburtstage des Rabbiners und Seminardirektors Dr. Israel Hildesheimer* (Berlin, 1920), 14–15. See also Abraham A. Fraenkel, *Lebenskreise* (Stuttgart, 1967), 117; Joseph Abraham Wolf, *The Era and Its Problems* (Heb.) (Benei Berak, 1965), 111; and Weinberg, *Lifrakim*, 269 (322). For the opposing view, held by Hirsch's disciples, see Rosenheim, *Bildungsideal S. R. Hirschs*, 25–7.

[11] See *Studien und Prüfungsordnung des Rabbiner-Seminars zu Berlin* (Berlin, 1928), 5.

[12] See his 'Thora und Wissenschaft', 497–504, and my 'Rabbi David Zvi Hoffmann on *Torah u-Madda*', *Torah u-Madda Journal*, 6 (1995–6), 129–37. See also David Ellenson and Richard Jacobs, 'Scholarship and Faith: David Hoffmann and his Relationship to *Wissenschaft des Judentums*', *Modern Judaism*, 8 (Feb. 1988), 27–40; Hans-Joachim Bechtoldt, *Die jüdische Bibelkritik im 19. Jahrhundert* (Stuttgart, 1995), ch. 8.

Wellhausen, that is, of Higher Criticism, and in the introduction to his commentary on Leviticus advocated unambiguous acceptance of the masoretic text, he was well aware of the difficulties it presented. It is not surprising, therefore, that he was willing to grant the possibility of textual corruption and minor post-Mosaic additions to the masoretic text.[13] However, he argued that since it was impossible to determine beyond all doubt what the original text must have been in these examples, all conjectural emendations should be avoided.[14]

This was Hoffmann's view concerning the Pentateuch, and there can be no question that his approach was more liberal when it came to the non-Mosaic books. Still, it was not Hoffmann's views of the Bible which created controversy. This was left to Hildesheimer's son-in-law, Jacob Barth (1851–1914), another leading figure at the seminary who was also one of the world's leading semitists.[15] His research into biblical Hebrew was based upon a comparative philological study of the other semitic languages, especially Arabic. This research was carried on by his pupils, the most noteworthy of whom was Samuel Grünberg (1879–1959), who also taught at the seminary. Barth's scientific approach to the Hebrew language in general and to the Bible in particular, while in accordance with the most advanced standards of scholarship, was 'cold' scholarship which did not provide his students with a sense of the sacred. Indeed, followers of Hirsch argued that it was lecturers like Barth who prevented the students from acquiring a true love of, and dedication to, Torah. For them, Barth's courses hardly differed from those taught at the University of Berlin, where no distinction was made between the study of holy and profane texts.[16]

Hirsch himself had written similarly, some years before, in the midst of a lengthy assault on Wissenschaft des Judentums:

Has this new 'Science of Judaism' ever attempted to delve into the *language* of the Word of God, the language of our ancestors, drawing from it the basic, timeless ideals of the Jewish spirit so that our sons and daughters should become eager to know that language and to allow it to shape their own thoughts and emotions? Could this new 'Science of Judaism' inspire our sons and daughters to develop their own spiritual lives from the roots of that spirit? . . . Has this new 'Science of Judaism' delved into the historical and prophetic *substance* of our Book of Books, into the *substance* of the literature of our Sages? And has it ever attempted to derive from these sources the Divinely-revealed origins and objectives, the Divinely-revealed past, present and future of mankind in general and Israel in particular? . . . Has the 'Science of Judaism' interested our contemporary generation in drinking deeply, and on their own, from the wellsprings of Judaism in order to enlighten their minds, warm their hearts, and gain sufficient energy and courage for vital, active, personal involvement in the pulsating life of our present day?[17]

13 See Calvary, *Bein zera liketsir*, 37–8.

14 See the introduction to his commentary on Leviticus.

15 See Joshua Blau, 'Jacob Barth', in S. Federbush (ed.), *Ḥokhmat yisrael bema'arav eiropah* (Jerusalem, 1958), 47–52.

16 See Rosenheim's comments in *Erinnerungen*, 54–5; id., *Oholai Ya'akov*, i. 217–24; and Isaac Breuer, 'Rückblick auf das Jahr 5662', *Der Israelit*, 3 Dec. 1903, 2131.

17 *Collected Writings of Rabbi Samson Raphael Hirsch* (New York, 1992), vii. 39–40.

Hirsch had built up an elaborate speculative etymological system, based on the uniqueness of the Hebrew language. In his view, since Hebrew was a holy tongue, it could only be studied through itself or through Aramaic, which was also viewed as a Jewish language.[18] The academic approach in comparative linguistics and philological research, as well as in broader cultural and historical fields, was anathema to the 'Frankfurt' school when applied to things Jewish.[19] As might be expected, they regarded Barth's attempt to understand biblical Hebrew through Arabic and other semitic languages as a complete waste of time which did nothing to inspire religiosity.[20]

Furthermore, and most controversially, Barth both accepted and taught the Deutero-Isaiah theory, which was regarded as bordering on the heretical by many Orthodox, particularly the followers of Hirsch.[21] Even though Barth argued that his questioning of the unity and traditional dating and authorship of Isaiah, as well as of other post-Mosaic prophetic works, violated no religious principles,[22] this did not convince the members of the 'Frankfurt' school, for whom dogma in these areas was much more rigid. The fact that Barth could advocate a theory which had almost no basis in traditional Jewish exegesis, and which incidentally had been adopted by scholars of Frankel's Breslau seminary,[23] gave the impression that his true loyalty was to scholarship rather than to Orthodoxy. As Breuer puts it, 'his lectures confirmed some of his students in their doubts rather than in their Orthodoxy'.[24]

It is no wonder, then, that the seminary's Orthodoxy was challenged in certain circles. Even Hoffmann did not escape this scrutiny. Although he was careful to

18 See his *Gesammelte Schriften* (Frankfurt, 1912), v. 143–99.

19 See Hirsch, *Gesammelte Schriften*, vi. 519, and also Isaac Heinemann, 'The Relationship between S. R. Hirsch and his Teacher Isaac Bernays' (Heb.), *Zion*, 16 (1941), 63, for a more complex interpretation.

20 See the anonymous 'Über jüdische Bibelexegese', *Jeschurun* (Frankfurt), 7 May 1885, 289–92; Isaac Heinemann, *The Reasons for the Commandments in Jewish Literature* (Heb.) (Jerusalem, 1993), ii. 110. On the medieval debate regarding the value of Arabic in understanding Hebrew, see A. S. Halkin, 'The Medieval Jewish Attitude toward Hebrew', in Alexander Altmann (ed.), *Biblical and Other Studies* (Cambridge, Mass., 1963), 242–3. It is worth noting that on a number of occasions Rashi himself explains biblical words by pointing to an Arabic origin. See the examples cited by Yaakov Hayim Sofer, *Tal ḥayim* (Jerusalem, 1994), 82–3.

21 See Zvi Weinberg, 'The Lectures of Jacob Barth on the Book of Isaiah at the Rabbinical Seminary of Berlin' (Heb.), in Uriel Simon and Moshe Goshen-Gottstein (eds.), *Iyunei mikra ufarshanut* (Ramat Gan, 1980), 229–41; Calvary, *Bein zera liketsir*, 36, 38; Fraenkel, *Lebenskreise*, 117–18; Breuer, *Jüdische Orthodoxie*, 173. (When Breuer writes that Barth never explicitly mentioned Deutero-Isaiah, he must refer to Barth's written work, for there was no such reticence in his lectures.)

22 See Barth, 'Die Entstehungzeit des Buches Hiob', in *Jahres-Bericht des Rabbiner-Seminars für das Orthodoxe Judentum pro 5636 (1875–76)* [Berlin, 1876]; Zvi Weinberg, 'Jacob Barth's Notes to Isaiah, Song of Songs and Ecclesiastes', *Beit Mikra*, 31 (1986), 78–87. Barth also argued that the Song of Songs was not originally intended as an allegory: see ibid.

23 See Heinrich Graetz, *Geschichte der Juden* (Leipzig, 1876), ii, part 2, 59 ff.; Marsha L. Rozenblit, 'Jewish Identity and the Modern Rabbi: The Cases of Isak Noah Mannheimer, Adolf Jellinek, and Moritz Güdemann in Nineteenth-Century Vienna', *LBIYB* 35 (1990), 121.

24 *Jüdische Orthodoxie*, 173.

point out that nothing he wrote in the area of Wissenschaft des Judentums should affect the practical halakhah, his research into rabbinic literature revealed halakhic development in ancient times. In Hoffmann's opinion, the halakhah had been influenced by historical and sociological factors, as well as by the personalities of the men involved. He adopted this approach in his very first work, his doctoral dissertation entitled *Mar Samuel*.[25]

Hoffmann was also open to criticism from the right for the detached and scholarly way in which he quoted and discussed the views of authors regardless of their religious affiliations. As one critic put it, he 'mentioned Rashi and Ramban in the same breath as Kittel and Wellhausen'.[26] Although this is an essential element of modern scholarship and was expected to be adopted by all seminary graduates in their own research, it was this very method which was deplored by Hirsch and his followers, as well as by the leading Orthodox historian of the talmudic period, Rabbi Isaac Halevy (1847–1914).[27] These men refused to grant legitimacy to non-Orthodox scholars. Therefore, unlike Hoffmann, they never quoted the research of Abraham Geiger, Heinrich Graetz, or Isaac Hirsch Weiss in support of their own historical conclusions. When Geiger and the others were quoted it was only to polemicize against their positions. It is thus not surprising that the Frankfurt school regarded the seminary's approach as a dangerous concession to the spirit of the university.[28] Indeed, after examining *Mar Samuel*, Hirsch himself declared it heretical. He also expressed doubts as to whether the seminary as a whole could be considered Orthodox.[29]

Rabbi Seligmann Baer Bamberger of Würzberg shared these doubts. According

[25] (Leipzig, 1873).

[26] See 'Von der Frankfurter Jeschiwah', *Jüdische Monatshefte*, 4 (1917), 170; Breuer, *Jüdische Orthodoxie*, 191. Cf., however, Joseph Wohlgemuth, 'Nachwort des Herausgebers', *Jeschurun*, 7 (1920), 511, where Hirsch is portrayed as more sympathetic to Hoffmann's biblical scholarship.

[27] See Reichel, *Letters of R. Isaac Halevy*, 132. Halevy's comment is very typical: 'Our group is not like the Berliners, for whom it does not matter if one writes for or against the Torah.'

[28] Note also the Festschrift published jointly by the Berlin Gemeinde and the Berlin Rabbinical Seminary in honour of Jakob Freimann, *Emet leya'akov* (Berlin, 1937). The non-Orthodox contributors included Leo Baeck, Ismar Elbogen, Max Wiener, Abraham Joshua Heschel, Immanuel Löw, and Gershom Scholem. Hirsch's disciples, on the other hand, would never include a contribution by a non-Orthodox author. See e.g. their *Festschrift für Jacob Rosenheim* (Frankfurt, 1931). Meier Hildesheimer, the director of the seminary and a leader of the Berlin separatist community, contributed to a volume in honour of Leo Baeck. See Breuer, 'Orthodoxy in Germany', 83 n. 22. In 1935 Weinberg published an article in the *Hebrew Union College Annual*; see below, n. 51. After the war, he agreed to contribute to a Festschrift in honour of Chaim Tchernowitz (Rav Tsa'ir), who was teaching at the Reform Jewish Institute of Religion at the time; letter to Samuel Atlas, dated 4 Aug. 1948.

[29] See Eliav, *Hildesheimer Briefe*, letter 74 (German section); Alexander Marx, *Essays in Jewish Biography* (Philadelphia, Pa., 1947), 204–6; Breuer, *Jüdische Orthodoxie*, 170 ff.; id., 'Three Orthodox Approaches to Wissenschaft' (Heb.), in Shaul Yisraeli *et al.* (eds.), *Sefer yovel likhevod morenu hagaon rabi yosef dov halevi soloveitchik* (Jerusalem, 1984), ii. 860; Yehoshua Markowitz, 'Rabbi David Zvi Hoffmann' (Heb.) (MA diss., Bar-Ilan University, 1968), 40–3; Hile Wechsler, *A Warning to Israel* (Heb.), ed. Rivka Horwitz (Jerusalem, 1991), 38–9 (first pagination). It is surprising that the correspondence of Hoffmann, Hirsch, and the others involved in this dispute has not yet been published.

to Hildesheimer, Bamberger believed that the Berlin seminary was even more dangerous to Orthodoxy than Geiger's institution.[30] Emil Lachman, the well-known Berlin philanthropist and supporter of the Keneset Yisrael yeshiva, also agreed with this position. He went so far as to revile the seminary students and to cast doubt upon their religious sincerity.[31] Although it is true that, in time, Hirsch's followers, together with the rest of German Orthodoxy, made their peace with the seminary and its faculty, they nevertheless retained a deep suspicion of any Orthodox efforts in Wissenschaft des Judentums.[32] Some even went so far as to claim that the only true Wissenschaft des Judentums was the Written and Oral Law. In their minds, all other areas of research were best described as *Wissenschaft vom Judentum*, that is, not the real thing.[33]

Unlike the faculty of the seminary, Hirsch's followers could never have imagined sending a letter of encouragement to mark the opening of the Hebrew University of Jerusalem, even if, as in the case of the seminary's letter, it expressed the hope that the studies carried out in Jerusalem would uphold the glory of the Torah.[34] In fact, almost immediately after the Hebrew University opened they criticized it harshly.[35] It is thus only to be expected that, although followers of Hirsch did often earn doctorates, they kept away from areas of Jewish scholarship for the most part. These areas were viewed as dangerous to the faith, and it is known that the Frankfurt school's outlook was even capable of influencing some seminary students.[36]

In the light of this approach it is understandable that the Frankfurt Orthodox separatists and their sympathizers were intolerant of views which differed from

[30] Eliav, *Hildesheimer Briefe*, 50 (Hebrew section); Stern, *Educational Ideal*, 107.

[31] Eliav, *Hildesheimer Briefe*, 74 (Hebrew section).

[32] On the attitude of Hirsch and his students to Wissenschaft des Judentums, see Breuer, *Jüdische Orthodoxie*, 160–79, and id., 'Three Orthodox Approaches', 856–65. Hirsch himself coined the famous phrase: 'Better a Jew without Wissenschaft than Wissenschaft without Judaism'; see his *Gesammelte Schriften*, vi. 393. See also Stern, *Educational Ideal*, 106–8.

[33] See Hermann Klein, 'Das Judenthum in seinen Grundzügen', *Der Israelit*, 5 Dec. 1904, 2069; Michael A. Meyer, 'Jewish Religious Reform and Wissenschaft des Judentums', *LBIYB* 16 (1971), 35.

[34] *Der Israelit*, 8 Apr. 1925, 6. See also the Agudat Yisrael supplement in *Der Israelit*, 25 June 1925. In 1937 the Berlin Rabbinical Seminary sent the Jewish Theological Seminary of America greetings on the occasion of the latter's fiftieth anniversary. See *Jahres-Bericht des Rabbiner-Seminars zu Berlin für die Jahre 1936 und 1937* (Berlin, 1938), 10. As with the Hebrew University, the disciples of Hirsch regarded the Jewish Theological Seminary as a centre of heresy which certainly did not deserve any acknowledgement on its anniversary. Interestingly enough, although Hoffmann believed that it was essential for the Orthodox to involve themselves with the Hebrew University, he insisted that there be a financially independent Orthodox faculty in the areas of biblical and talmudic studies. See his letters in the Central Archives for the History of the Jewish People, P40/169. It is also worth noting that Bernard Revel, president of Yeshiva College, sent the Hebrew University a flowery letter of congratulation upon its inauguration. See Sinai Leichter and Hayim Milkov (eds.), *Olei hasertifikatim* (Jerusalem, 1993), 337.

[35] See the Agudat Yisrael supplements in *Der Israelit*, 23 Apr. 1925; 11 June 1925. For criticism before the university's official opening, see *Der Israelit*, 12 Feb. 1925, 3.

[36] See Rosenheim, *Erinnerungen*, 54–5; *The Blessing of Eliyahu* (London, 1982), 11.

their own, particularly on issues such as Reform, Zionism, communal unity, and varying conceptions of Orthodoxy.[37] When one of their own strayed from the path, as Raphael Breuer (1881–1932) did when he published a commentary which interpreted the Song of Songs literally,[38] they were quick to criticize him.[39] This led Breuer to publish a second commentary which was more acceptable to his Orthodox circle.[40]

The intolerance of Hirsch's followers is seen even more clearly in the way they treated the Gemeinde Orthodox rabbi of Frankfurt, Marcus Horovitz (1844–1910). Horovitz's scholarship and piety could not possibly be questioned. Yet many of the Frankfurt separatists treated him as no different from a Reform rabbi, regarding his synagogue as forbidden territory. These separatists, who regarded themselves as the true representatives of Orthodoxy, saw refusal to join their community as a terrible error. Though this error was forgivable as far as laymen were concerned, a rabbi who followed this path was guilty of nothing less than an unpardonable rebellion against Torah values.[41]

This extremism was absent in the Berlin separatist community, which was described by Ze'ev Jawitz (1847–1924) as combining the holiness of the Land of Israel, the Torah scholarship of Vilna, and the culture of Paris.[42] The members of this community had a very good relationship with the Gemeinde Orthodox, and both segments of Orthodoxy were represented among the Berlin Rabbinical Seminary's faculty, student body, and financial supporters.[43] In contrast to the situation in Frankfurt, leading members of the separatist community in Berlin

[37] See the comment of Bar-Ilan, *From Volozhin to Jerusalem*, ii. 376. See also the important study by Yaakov Tsur, 'German-Jewish Orthodoxy and its Relationship to Organized Jewry and to Zionism' (Heb.) (Ph.D. diss., Hebrew University of Jerusalem, 1982).

[38] *Die fünf Megilloth: Hoheslied* (Frankfurt, 1912).

[39] See e.g. *Der Israelit*, 18 July 1912, 9. Breuer defended his approach in *Zur Abwehr* (Frankfurt, 1912). Some of the Frankfurt separatists cited his commentary as a reason why Breuer should not inherit his father's position as rabbi of their community. See Katz, *With My Own Eyes*, 74; Yehudah Ben-Avner, 'The Dispute over the Rabbinate of Frankfurt's Adass Jeschurun in the 1920s' (Heb.), *Sinai*, 106 (1990), 74. For other attacks on Breuer's commentary, see 'Die Tragödie des Hohenliedes', *Die Jüdische Presse*, 10 May 1912, 177–9; 'Die Komödie der "Abwehr" ', *Die Jüdische Presse*, 30 Aug. 1912, 334–6; and Reines, *Shenei hame'orot*, section 2, part 1, 25b.

[40] *Lied der Lieder* (Frankfurt, 1923).

[41] See Breuer, *Autobiography*, 10–15.

[42] See Ze'ev Zvi (Hermann) Klein, *Oraita begaluta* (Buenos Aires, n.d.), introduction.

[43] See Kahana, 'Gaon', 8; Binyamin Ze'ev Jacobson, *Memoirs* (Heb.) (Jerusalem, 1953), 58–9; Jacob Levy, 'Youthful Memories from the Adass Jisroel Community in Berlin' (Heb.), *Hama'ayan*, 4 (Tammuz 5724 [1964]), 7–8; Michael L. Munk, 'Austrittsbewegung und Berliner *Adass Jisroel*-Gemeinde 1869–1939', in Herbert A. Strauss and Kurt R. Grossmann (eds.), *Gegenwart im Rückblick* (Heidelberg, 1970), 144–5. As Moses Auerbach recalled, the difference between the Berlin separatist community (of which he was a member) and its Frankfurt counterpart was that 'In Frankfurt they said, "How fortunate that we are able to separate [from the Gemeinde]." In Berlin they said, "How sad that we have reached the point where we must separate." ' See Yaakov Tsur, 'Torah im Derekh Eretz and Torah ve'avodah' (Heb.), in Breuer, *Torah-Im-Derekh-Eretz*, 98. See also Isaiah Wolfsberg, introduction to Abraham Berliner, *Selected Writings* (Heb.) (Jerusalem, 1969), p. xi: 'In contrast to the Frankfurt community, the leaders in Berlin never rejoiced at this separation.'

were involved with Zionism[44] and Wissenschaft des Judentums. Furthermore, they were prepared to join forces with the Reform community if general Jewish interests were at stake.

It is very significant that despite the separatism, opposition to Wissenschaft des Judentums, and general extremism of Hirsch and his followers, Hirsch's religious philosophy of Torah im Derekh Eretz became a guiding light for the overwhelming majority of Germany's bourgeois Orthodox, finding popularity in all circles, including the Berlin Rabbinical Seminary. Rejection of Hirsch's religio-political programme, which Hirsch himself regarded as being of fundamental importance, was thus coupled with adoration of his 'pure' religious philosophy. It is with this latter point in mind that one can speak of a German Orthodox ideology shared by all segments of what is often called neo-Orthodoxy.[45]

A TALMUDIST AT THE UNIVERSITY

After this brief elaboration of the different strands of German Orthodoxy, our attention can now return to Weinberg's life during the Weimar years. Although at this time he had little academic training in Wissenschaft des Judentums and semitic languages, this was soon to change. In the summer of 1920 he travelled to the University of Giessen to pursue his academic studies full-time.[46] It was there that he received his first intensive exposure to the world of modern scholarship. At first it might appear strange for Weinberg to have left Berlin, the intellectual and cultural capital of Orthodoxy—not to mention Germany as a whole—in order to settle in Giessen, which had only about a thousand Jews.[47] Indeed, many who lived through that period would agree with Reform Rabbi Joachim Prinz (1902–88): 'If I could choose a time to live in, any place, I'd choose the 1920s in Berlin.'[48] During the Weimar years Berlin was also teeming with east European Jewish intellectuals, including many of the greatest names in Hebrew literature.[49] Weinberg would not have lacked intellectual companionship had he remained in Berlin. Yet Giessen boasted a teacher unique in Germany, the great semitic and masoretic scholar Paul Kahle (1875–1965), who was also a pious Christian and a vigilant defender of Jewish literature against antisemitic attacks.

Although by now much of the work of Kahle and his students has been rejected, when Weinberg journeyed to Giessen there was no serious challenge to Kahle's views, and he was regarded by many as the world's leading authority on the

[44] For a couple of exceptions to this generalization, see Breuer, *Jüdische Orthodoxie*, 329.

[45] Although 'neo-Orthodoxy' is a common term, its validity has been challenged by Julius Carlebach, 'The Foundations of German-Jewish Orthodoxy: An Interpretation', *LBIYB* 33 (1988), 88–91.

[46] Unless otherwise noted, all biographical information relating to Weinberg's stay in Giessen is taken from the University of Giessen Archives.

[47] See *Encyclopaedia Judaica* (Jerusalem, 1971), vii. 560.

[48] Otto Friedrich, *Before the Deluge: A Portrait of Berlin in the 1920s* (London, 1974), 11.

[49] See Brenner, *Renaissance of Jewish Culture*, ch. 7.

Masorah and Targumim. Twenty-five years later Weinberg nostalgically recalled the university's pleasant atmosphere, where colleagues of different religions and nationalities were united in their commitment to scholarship under Kahle's guidance.[50] Weinberg concentrated on biblical studies, which, as far as the 'Frankfurt' school was concerned, was the most dangerous of all fields of university scholarship; his choice proves the depth of his commitment to the seminary's outlook.

Kahle himself was in for something of a surprise, for never before had he encountered a student quite like Weinberg, who was only a decade his junior. He found him to be a man with massive knowledge of biblical, targumic, and rabbinic literature. At the same time, however, there was a great deal that Weinberg needed to learn in terms of method. Not only did he lack the skills to engage in critical examination of the texts he knew so well, but the entire fields of Wissenschaft des Judentums and modern biblical studies were foreign to him. It was in these areas that Kahle was to have an enormous impact on Weinberg's scholarly development. Yet it was not only Weinberg who profited from these years in Giessen, for Kahle himself paid tribute to the great assistance Weinberg offered him in his research.[51] In addition to his work under Kahle, Weinberg also studied two subsidiary subjects: Old Testament under Professor Hans Schmidt and philosophy under Professor Ernst von Aster.

Kahle was very pleased with Weinberg's progress and soon asked him to accept an appointment as lecturer in Jewish studies, beginning with the summer term of 1921. Although this new job would have eased his difficult financial circumstances, there was one problem which had to be confronted before he could accept the position, namely, an undisputed *halakhah* which states that Jews may not teach gentiles Torah.[52] Weinberg was able to solve this problem with a responsum in which he showed that teaching gentiles Torah solely for academic purposes is not proscribed.[53] It is obvious that the basis of this responsum was the fact that Weinberg was now acquainted with men such as Kahle, who were interested in Torah study

[50] Letter to Paul Kahle, dated 23 Mar. 1947.

[51] Kahle, *Masoreten des Westens*, i (Stuttgart, 1927), 78, ii (Stuttgart, 1930), 3 n. 1. Kahle and Weinberg later jointly published 'The Mishna Text in Babylonia: Fragments from the Geniza', *Hebrew Union College Annual*, 10 (1935), 185–222.

[52] See Isaac H. Mann, 'The Prohibition of Teaching Non-Jews Torah: Its Historical Development', *Gesher*, 8 (1981), 122–73; J. David Bleich, *Contemporary Halakhic Problems* (New York, 1983), ii, ch. 16.

[53] See *SE* ii, no. 92 (this responsum was addressed to R. Mordechai Gifter, but for some reason his name was omitted when it was published). For responsa on the same theme, see also *SE* ii, no. 90, and *Moriah*, 13 (Kislev 5745 [1984]), 64–6. Surprisingly, Weinberg did not mention that Salanter was in favour of Talmud being included in the curriculum of German universities. See Etkes, *Rabbi Israel Salanter*, 259–60. Weinberg's responsum also justified what was already a common practice in Germany among Orthodox Jews who were involved with academic scholarship, and thus in contact with gentile scholars. To give one example, it is well known that Hoffmann gave Hermann Strack a great deal of assistance in his rabbinic studies. (However, Hoffmann was opposed to teaching Torah to gentile youth: see *Melamed leho'il*, ii, no. 77.)

Faculty of Oriental Studies, University of Giessen, July 1923. Left to right: Weinberg, Mehmed Ali Bey, Paul Kahle, Anton Richter, Julius Lewy.

Reproduced by courtesy of the University of Giessen archives

purely for intellectual stimulation. It is certainly doubtful whether it would have been possible for Weinberg to reach the same halakhic conclusion while still in Pilwishki, for in eastern Europe gentile study of the Torah was usually understood to be related to gentile attacks on Judaism.[54]

An even greater problem which confronted Weinberg was that of biblical criticism. Although the conclusions of Higher Criticism were regarded as dogma in German universities, it was impossible for an Orthodox Jew like Weinberg to share this approach. Yet this did not mean that all forms of biblical criticism were off-limits to him. In fact, the dogmas of Orthodoxy with regard to critical study of the Bible were fairly broad, relatively speaking, when viewed from the perspective of the intellectuals associated with the Berlin Rabbinical Seminary.

As a follower of the seminary's approach, Weinberg could uphold the traditional view of the complete Mosaic authorship of the Pentateuch and still regard himself as a critical scholar. Confident that the traditional view was defensible on scholarly grounds, Weinberg was not reticent about presenting this view in his lectures. Isidor Grunfeld, the well-known translator of Hirsch's writings, attended Weinberg's classes as a young student and recalled:

> His lectures were always crowded. Not only students of theology and oriental languages, but also students of other faculties and even university professors sat at his feet, impressed by the depth of his thought and enchanted by the slow and deliberate manner of his lecturing and his deep sonorous speaking voice. I can never forget his brilliant strictures against Bible criticism and his convincing arguments in favor of the authenticity of Jewish tradition. Few were able to combine talmudic and biblical scholarship as Rabbi Weinberg did. With his sharp dialectical mind and his wide range of knowledge, this proud Lithuanian Jew did not find it difficult to impart, even to non-Jewish listeners, a deep respect for Jewish traditional values.[55]

In late 1921 or early 1922 Weinberg returned to Pilwishki for the first time. This was an important period, as the Jewish communities had been granted national autonomy in the newly formed independent Lithuanian commonwealth. These communities had undergone many changes, the most significant being that the younger generation had attempted, often successfully, to seize the reins of leadership. The elders, formerly the backbone of the Jewish community but now seen as reactionaries, were forced to resign their positions of authority and were relegated to obscurity. Confronting the tension brought about by this generation gap, and acting in his rabbinic mode—although he had been gone for over seven years he

[54] For expressions of such sentiments, see Solomon Luria, *Yam shel shelomo* (New York, 1953) to *Baba Kamma* 38*a*, and Aaron Walkin, *Zekan aharon* (New York, 1977), ii, no. 71. Such a fear continues to guide many *posekim* who confront this issue. See e.g. Israel Veltz, *Divrei yisra'el* (Benei Berak, 1980), ii, *Yoreh de'ah*, no. 37: 'Those who have some knowledge of our history are aware that most of the hardships of the Jewish people in their exile were brought about by gentiles who had a smattering of Torah knowledge.'

[55] 'The "Ba'al Seride Esh"', in Nisson Wolpin (ed.), *The Torah Personality* (Brooklyn, NY, 1980), 103–4.

was still considered the rabbi of the town[56]—Weinberg delivered a sermon which was an attempt 'to make peace between the old and young and to bring them together through mutual understanding'.[57] However, this sermon was the extent of Weinberg's efforts in this regard, for only a short time later he left Pilwishki again. This time, however, he was no longer a married man. His wife had finally accepted a divorce, after sixteen years of marriage, and Weinberg was now ready to start a new life in Germany.[58] Although in later years he spoke and wrote with great feeling about the importance of marriage, even repeating Hirsch's comment that one who is unmarried is not truly a man, Weinberg himself never remarried.[59]

Returning to Giessen, Weinberg immersed himself in the writing of his doctoral dissertation and began his studies of Greek. The dissertation was to be an analysis of the Syriac translation of the Bible, the Peshitta, focusing on its exegetical method and its relationship to both Jewish and other ancient versions. At the same time, Weinberg taught courses in Bible, Mishnah, and Talmud for beginners and advanced students. In the summer of 1923 Weinberg took his oral examinations, in which he was tested by Kahle, Schmidt, and von Aster. He passed these examinations with the mark 'ausgezeichnet (1)'—the top grade. During this summer he also handed in his dissertation, which received favourable judgements from the referees, Kahle and Schmidt. Both of them recommended that it should be accepted by the university on condition that it be revised. For some unknown reason, however, Weinberg never submitted a revised version. Thus, contrary to his own testimony on many occasions, he was never officially granted a doctorate.[60]

His dissertation has not survived,[61] and all that he ever published on targumic matters was one article which appeared in instalments in the newspaper *Jüdisches Wochenblatt* in 1924.[62] Although this article does not contain any ground-breaking

[56] See Weinberg's 16 July 1921 letter from Giessen to the communal leaders of the town, YIVO Archives, Lithuanian Towns, File 846, no. 36646, and M. Z. Levinson-Lavi's letter in *Bitsaron*, 8 (1943), 278.

[57] *Lifrakim*, 223 (273).

[58] Weinberg's letter to Zvi Mathisson from 1924 (the exact date is illegible). According to information in the record book of the Jewish community of Finland, Weinberg's former wife married the rabbi of Helsinki, Samuel Nathan Bukanz, a man more than thirty years her senior, on 29 June 1923. They emigrated to Palestine in 1926. An interesting bit of hagiography has R. Nathan Zvi Finkel fasting for forty days when Weinberg decided to settle in Germany. I heard this from R. Bezalel Rakov, who heard it from his father-in-law, R. Naftali Shackovitsky. Rakov is currently the rabbi of Gateshead and was very close to Weinberg after World War II.

[59] *Lifrakim*, 128 (86). Hirsch's remark appears in his commentary on Genesis 2: 18.

[60] In late 1927 the university attempted to contact Weinberg with regard to the revisions, but with no success. In early 1928 it discontinued his programme of study. Kahle no doubt regarded Weinberg as worthy of the degree, even if it was never officially awarded, for he always referred to Weinberg as 'Dr'. Similarly, Weinberg often signed his name 'Dr. J. Weinberg', even in letters he wrote to Kahle.

[61] The dissertation, or a revised version of it, would seem to be identical with his oft-cited unpublished book on the Targumim. See *SE* iv, pp. 49 n. 1, 103.

[62] 7 Aug., p. 208; 14 Aug., p. 218; 28 Aug., p. 236; 11 Sept., p. 254. It was later republished as 'Zur Geschichte der Targumim: Eine Darstellung der Entstehung und Entwicklung der aramäischen Targumim', *Festschrift für Jacob Rosenheim* (Frankfurt, 1931), 237–58, and appears in Hebrew trans-

research, it does include interesting suggestions about the nature of targumic literature and its influence,[63] as well as offering illustrative examples of the development of rabbinic aggadah. This latter point is itself significant, for Weinberg showed that he was quite comfortable describing aggadah as a creative genre rather than as real history, which is how it was viewed by many traditional scholars who were—and still are—unaware of how aggadah actually developed.

DEVELOPMENTS IN BERLIN

While Weinberg was in Giessen, significant events were occurring in Berlin, chief among them being the death of Rabbi David Zvi Hoffmann in 1921. In addition to serving as rector of the seminary, Hoffmann was also senior lecturer in Talmud and Codes. He thus bore the main responsibility for training young men studying for the rabbinate. A couple of years before his death Rabbi Abraham Elijah Kaplan (1890–1924) had been appointed to assist him, and he now assumed Hoffmann's role.

Kaplan was a native of Lithuania who had studied in the yeshivot of Telz and Slobodka (Keneset Yisrael).[64] Despite the fact that he had had no formal secular education, he was sympathetic to German Orthodoxy, and even assumed the task of translating some of Hirsch's writings into Hebrew. Kaplan, who was also a poet and an unabashed Zionist, was a talmudist of the first rank who created something of a sensation in rabbinic circles when in 1924 he published the first instalments of his planned comprehensive commentary on the Talmud in the seminary's journal, *Jeschurun*.[65] Had Kaplan remained at the seminary, there is no doubt that this many-talented man would have left a profound impression on German Orthodoxy and on Jewish history as a whole. Alas, this was not to be. In May 1924, at the young age of 34 and in the midst of editing Hoffmann's responsa, he suddenly passed away.[66]

lation in *SE* iv, pp. 267–75. Alexander Sperber, who was later to become a great biblical and targumic scholar, was Kahle's assistant at one time. In his article 'Peschitta und Onkelos', in Salo W. Baron and Alexander Marx (eds.), *Jewish Studies in Memory of George A. Kohut* (New York, 1935), 554–64, he advanced a number of suggestions which resembled those that Weinberg had proposed in his dissertation. Because of this, Weinberg suspected that Sperber might have seen his thesis and stolen some of his ideas. This information is contained in Weinberg's letter to Samuel Atlas, dated 24 Dec. 1946, and in his letter to Kahle, dated 10 Feb. 1949.

[63] See esp. *SE* iv, p. 268, where Weinberg uses the Targum to offer an intriguing solution to the old problem of why Hillel formulated a 'negative Golden Rule' when the biblical text (Lev. 19: 18) is stated positively.

[64] In his letter to Samuel Atlas, dated 9 June 1965, Weinberg refers to Kaplan as his former student. Perhaps Kaplan was one of those sent by Finkel to study with Weinberg in Pilwishki.

[65] See I. Grunfeld, *Three Generations: The Influence of Samson Raphael Hirsch on Jewish Life and Thought* (London, 1958), 76; Fraenkel, *Lebenskreise*, 183.

[66] For biographical information on Kaplan, see the introduction to his *Divrei talmud* (Jerusalem, 1958), i. 11–14, and M. Altmann, 'Rabbi Abraham Elijah Kaplan' (Heb.), in Samuel K. Mirsky (ed.), *Ishim udemuyot beḥokhmat yisra'el* ([New York], 1959), 324–37.

Although Kaplan's years at the seminary were short, they had a great impact. At this time German Jews, positively affected by their encounter with the east, were striving for higher levels of religious enthusiasm and were once again beginning to take the study of Talmud seriously, and he gave great encouragement to this trend.[67] In this he was assisted by a few other important Lithuanian immigrant rabbis, such as Zalman Barukh Rabinkow of Heidelberg (1882–1942),[68] Samuel Josef Rabinow of Hamburg (1889–1963), and Moses Schneider (1884–1954), who founded a yeshiva in Frankfurt.[69]

As early as the war years, an organization called the Thorabund had been formed, which aimed at spreading Torah study.[70] By 1920 Wohlgemuth was able to declare that the east European influence which had dominated German Judaism in the days before Moses Mendelssohn had once again been renewed. It was this influence which was responsible for German Orthodoxy's changed outlook with regard to the traditional study of Jewish texts.[71] The situation in Frankfurt had also changed dramatically, and in the post-war years a significant percentage of students in Salomon Breuer's yeshiva were native-born. Furthermore, in contrast to the situation at the time of the yeshiva's establishment, the community now assumed financial support of the school.[72]

In recognition of this new phenomenon, the saintly moralist and halakhic authority Rabbi Israel Meir Hacohen sent, via Kaplan, an open letter to German Jewish students, encouraging their talmudic studies and recommending that they

[67] See *Lifrakim*, 172 (246); *Jahres-Bericht des Rabbiner-Seminars zu Berlin für 1924*, 8; Joseph Wohlgemuth, 'Westjüdisches und ostjüdisches Empfinden', *Jeschurun*, 10 (1923), 1–8; Wolf, *Era*, 111–13; Alexander Carlebach, 'Were Rabbi Esriel Hildesheimer's Educational Initiatives Failures?' (Heb.), *Niv Hamidrashia* (1972), 205–6; and R. Joseph B. Soloveitchik's letter in Abraham Elijah Kaplan, *Be'ikvot hayirah* (Jerusalem, 1988), 285–6.

[68] See Isak Unna, *Lema'an ha'ahdut vehayihud* (Jerusalem, 1975), 40–4; Isaiah Wolfsberg-Aviad, 'Autobiography' (Heb.), in Yitshak Rafael (ed.), *Sefer aviad* (Jerusalem, 1986), 14–15, 56–60; Abraham Bick, 'Rabbi Zalman Barukh Rabinkow' (Heb.), ibid. 89–91; Jacob J. Schacter, 'Reminiscences of Shlomo Barukh Rabinkow', in Leo Jung (ed.), *Sages and Saints* (Hoboken, NJ, 1987), 93–132; Peter Honigmann, 'Jüdische Studenten zwischen Orthodoxie und moderner Wissenschaft: Der Heidelberger Talmudistenkreis um Salman Baruch Rabinkow', in Julius H. Schoeps (ed.), *Menora* (Munich, 1992), 85–96. Before Weinberg was chosen, Rabinkow was offered the position of lecturer in Talmud at the Berlin Rabbinical Seminary, but he declined; see Schacter, 'Reminiscences', 99.

[69] During his years in Giessen, Weinberg was sometimes seen at Schneider's yeshiva (interview with R. Gedaliah Schneider).

[70] See Breuer, *Jüdische Orthodoxie*, 325.

[71] 'Nachwort', 509. See also his address in *Das Rabbiner-Seminar zu Berlin: Ansprache aus Anlass des fünfzigjährigen Bestehens* (Berlin, 1923), 16; Miriam Gillis-Carlebach, 'The Concept of the Yeshiva and the Distinctiveness of the Lithuanian Yeshiva in the Eyes of Rabbi Dr. Joseph Zvi Carlebach' (Heb.), in Breuer (ed.), *Torah im Derekh Eretz* (Ramat Gan, 1987), 147–60; *Agudas Jisroel: Berichte und Materialien* (Frankfurt, [1912]) 11; *Zur Agudas-Jisroel Jugendbewegung*, 12–13; *Was will, Was ist Agudas Jisroel* (Hamburg, [1919?]), 6; Moses Auerbach, 'Die Bildungsfrage in der Thora-Treuen Judenheit Deutschland', in A. E. Kaplan and Max Landau (eds.), *Vom Sinn des Judentums: Ein Sammelbuch zu Ehren Nathan Birnbaums* (Frankfurt, 1925), 231; Sinasohn, *Adass Jisroel Berlin*, 177.

[72] See Katz, *With My Own Eyes*, 63–4; Posen, 'Frankfurt Yeshiva', 151.

devote themselves exclusively to Torah study for a few years.[73] Together with this increased devotion to Torah study, which was clearly visible among the students at the Berlin seminary, there was a noticeable decrease in these students' interest in Wissenschaft des Judentums.[74] This was made easier by the loss of the seminary's leading practitioners of this form of scholarship—Barth (d. 1914), Abraham Berliner (d. 1915), and Hoffmann (d. 1921).

Kaplan introduced the seminary's German students both to *musar* and to the Analytic Method of Talmud study popular in Lithuania, which was very different from the straightforward approach offered by Hoffmann.[75] Thanks to this, Wohlgemuth asserted, Kaplan was responsible for a revival of Talmud study at the seminary.[76] The results were impressive and in 1922, after only two years at the institution, Kaplan was able to comment that although in 1920 he could not deliver a talmudic lecture from Telz in Berlin, he was now able to deliver a Berlin talmudic lecture in Telz. He also noted how the German students had adopted the method of free-flowing argumentation between student and teacher, which was a hallmark of the Lithuanian yeshivot.[77] No longer could anyone truthfully remark, as Isaac Breuer had done in an article originally published in 1917, that the students at the Berlin seminary were 'wissenschaftlich', but did not 'learn' Talmud.[78]

After Kaplan's death the seminary was in need of another esteemed talmudist to continue his work. This is where Weinberg came into the picture. There is no doubt that the seminary would have preferred a native German to take Kaplan's place, but it was no secret that it had been a long time since Germany had produced its own talmudic scholars.[79] Biblical scholars, practitioners of Wissenschaft des Judentums, and philosophers could be found, but not talmudists. It was precisely for this reason that Kaplan had been chosen as Hoffmann's successor. Weinberg, now living in Berlin and working as a rabbi at one of the Gemeinde synagogues,[80] was well known at the seminary. As early as December 1915 he had delivered a Hebrew lecture on the Lithuanian yeshivot before the seminary's student union.

[73] *Jeschurun*, 10 (1923), 1–3 (Hebrew section). The complete letter was first published in Kaplan, *Be'ikvot hayirah*, 269–71.

[74] See Shulvass, 'Rabbinical Seminary', 695.

[75] See Joseph Wohlgemuth, 'R. Awrohom Elijo Kaplan', *Jeschurun*, 11 (1924), 233–45. I emphasize 'German students', since during this period sometimes as much as half the seminary's student body was from the east, and they were presumably somewhat familiar with the Lithuanian method of Talmud study; see Eisner, 'Reminiscences', 41. Kaplan himself attempted to bring Lithuanian yeshiva students to study at the seminary, seeing this both as the way to quench the thirst for Torah among young German students and to bring about 'the union of east and west about which people have spoken a great deal in the last years, although little has been done about it'; letter from Kaplan to Samuel Grünberg, dated 17 July 1920.

[76] 'R. Awrohom Elijo Kaplan', 238.

[77] *Be'ikvot hayirah*, 204. See also ibid. 119.

[78] Isaac Breuer, *Programm oder Testament* (Frankfurt, 1929), 22.

[79] See Hoffmann's introduction to *Melamed leho'il*, 2.

[80] Weinberg's letter to Zvi Mathisson from 1924 (the exact date is illegible); Weinberg's letter in Reznik, *Kelei sharet*, 2.

Berlin Rabbinical Seminary, 1928. *Front row*: fourth from right, Weinberg, fifth from right, Joseph Wohlgemuth, sixth from right, Samuel Grünberg, seventh from right, Moses Auerbach; first on left, Meir Hildesheimer. *Second row from back*: seventh from left, Alexander Altmann.

From the Altmann Family Archive; reproduced by courtesy of Manfred Altman, London

According to the report of his talk, it was received with 'lively applause'.[81] During the war years Weinberg was even asked to become Hoffmann's successor, before the seminary backed away from this offer in favour of Kaplan.[82]

More important in establishing his reputation among members of the seminary circle were the many articles he had published in *Jeschurun*, the seminary journal. Whereas his earlier articles had placed him somewhat in opposition to the ideals of German Orthodoxy, it was clear to all that his views had evolved in the intervening years. Weinberg's combination of Lithuanian-style Talmud study and conservative Wissenschaft des Judentums also corresponded exactly to the seminary's curricular focus. A prime example of Weinberg's writing which reflects this approach is his article on women's hair-covering in the 1922 *Jeschurun*.[83] This essay is a wonderful synthesis of traditional halakhic learning and modern scholarship. It is complete with textual emendations of rabbinic literature, philological analysis of the crucial word פרע, discussion of linguistic aspects of Hebrew, comments on the nature of *gezerah shavah* exegesis,[84] and citations from the Peshitta, the Septuagint, and modern Christian exegetes. It was this method which was advocated by Hoffmann and which so annoyed the Frankfurt Orthodox.

It was because of Weinberg's sympathy with German Orthodoxy and his approach to rabbinic literature that the seminary felt confident in offering him the position of lecturer in Talmud and Codes, effectively making him the resident halakhist of the seminary. The new position also established him as the supreme halakhic authority for the numerous communal rabbis who were seminary graduates, as well as for many others who had no formal connection to the institution. He was thus ensured a central role in German Orthodox life, despite his modest claim that he 'was not worthy to publicize opinions and decide halakhah for the masses'.[85] Weinberg accepted the appointment and joined the seminary staff in October 1924.[86] Another sign of his increasingly important role in German Orthodoxy came in 1925, when he was asked to become head of the Berlin Gemeinde *beit din*. He refused this position because the community would not agree to his suggested procedural improvements in the areas of *kashrut* supervision and the granting of divorces.[87]

[81] 'Protokollbuch des seminarischen Vereins "Dibbuk Chawerim" ', entry for 4 Dec. 1915 (Jewish Theological Seminary of America, MS 3675).

[82] Letter to Samuel Atlas, dated 9 June 1965.

[83] Reprinted in *SE* iii, no. 30. This article was also reprinted, with slight changes and one significant addition, in *Hama'ayan*, 5 (Tishrei 5725 [1964]), 3–8. On p. 8 Weinberg added a lengthy paragraph explaining the importance of married women covering their hair, but he also noted that this should not be made the be-all and end-all of women's Judaism.

[84] See Eliezer Berkovits, *Was ist der Talmud?* (Frankfurt am Main, 1962), 26, for Weinberg's understanding of *kal vaḥomer*.

[85] *SE* i, p. 3.

[86] *Jahres-Bericht des Rabbiner-Seminars zu Berlin für 1925, 1926, 1927* (Berlin, 1928), 4. For an overview of the seminary and its faculty during this period, see Auerbach, *From Halberstadt to Petaḥ Tikvah*, 74–91.

[87] Weinberg's letter to Moshe Klein, dated 8 June 1948.

Weinberg proved a fitting successor to Kaplan. Like him, he exposed the students to the Lithuanian method of Talmud study, a method he described as 'reaching the deepest content of a *halakhah* by collecting its details and then unifying them into an overall conceptual picture'. He continued, 'only then can one grasp the fundamental idea that underlies the details of a *halakhah*, and finally reach a logical definition of the halakhic principle and thought-category'.[88] Yet Weinberg surpassed Kaplan in that he combined the traditional method of Talmud study—in its Lithuanian form—with the critical approach, making him Hoffmann's true successor.[89] Although he had never studied under Hoffmann, the training Weinberg had received in Giessen opened his eyes to modern methods of source and text criticism, in particular the skill of responsible textual emendation, which he used successfully in his own teaching and research.

Despite his exposure to modern scholarship, Weinberg argued that one could never acquire a true understanding of Talmud without having also been trained in the traditional yeshiva method. He therefore advised capable German students to undertake study at one of the great Lithuanian yeshivot.[90] On the other hand, he warned students from eastern Europe, who had only been exposed to the yeshivot, against studying at the seminary. As he explained to a hasidic woman who wished to send her son there:

> The sons of Germany are not like the sons of Poland. The Germans have already adapted themselves to a cold environment and they therefore successfully digest secular studies. However, the transition to German Orthodoxy is dangerous for those raised in the hasidic climate of Poland which is totally infused with enthusiasm and ardour. German Jewry is not capable of inspiring those who possess a different temperament.[91]

WRITINGS OF THE WEIMAR YEARS

Halakhic Works

Although Weinberg wrote many responsa during his first few years at the seminary, only a few of them have survived, thus preventing any comprehensive evaluation

[88] 'Die Jeschiwoth in Russland' (1916), 117. In *Hama'or* (Heshvan 5693 [1932]), 39, Weinberg's method of study was described as similar to that of R. Joseph Engel. No specific reasons were offered for this comparison. For an analysis of Weinberg's method, see Abraham Abba Weingort, 'From Rabbi Jehiel Jacob Weinberg's Method of Study' (Heb.), *De'ot*, 31 (1967), 19–22, expanded upon by Pesah Paul Glavsky, *De'ot*, 32 (1967), 123–4; Weingort, 'Concerning the Essence of Acquiring a Wife' (Heb.), *Hama'ayan*, 24 (Tammuz 5744 [1984]), 41–57, and *Ḥidushei ba'al 'Seridei esh'* with Weingort's introduction and commentary.

[89] See Akiva Posner, 'The Study of Talmud in the Rabbinical Seminary of Berlin' (Heb.), *Hadarom*, 12 (1960), 192–3.

[90] Shulvass, 'Rabbinical Seminary', 703; Pineas, 'Zum Tode', 176; Jehiel Jacob Weinberg and Pinhas Biberfeld (eds.), *Yad sha'ul* (Tel Aviv, 1953), 7; Aharon Sorasky, *Or elḥanan* (Los Angeles, 1978), i. 124 n. 12.

[91] *Yad sha'ul*, 5. This translation is taken from Aaron Rakeffet-Rothkoff, 'The Spiritual Legacy of Rabbi Jehiel Jacob Weinberg', *Niv Hamidrashia*, 11 (1974), 95.

of his halakhic writings from this period. During this time, one of the important questions he was asked dealt with transferring human remains from a Jewish cemetery in Silesia, no longer German territory, to Breslau. He considered all aspects of this problem in a small book entitled *Pinui atsamot metim*.[92] Although he had some reservations, Weinberg advanced very strong reasons to permit the transfer. Another question he was asked concerned the permissibility of a *mikveh* to which the water was transferred from a well by means of an electric pump. Here too Weinberg found room to be lenient, and his view was approved by Rabbi Moses Mordechai Epstein, Rabbi Hayim Ozer Grodzinski (1863–1940), and Rabbi Barukh Ber Leibowitz (1866–1939).[93] When asked if it was permissible to convert a man who for medical reasons could not be circumcised, Weinberg wrote two lengthy responsa in which he ruled in the negative. His opinion was supported by such leading figures as Grodzinski, Kook, and Rabbi Abraham Shapiro of Kovno.[94]

Sometimes Weinberg's halakhic decisions brought him into conflict with east European scholars. An example of this is his dispute with the idiosyncratic Rabbi Joseph Rozin of Dvinsk (1858–1936), a most formidable opponent.[95] Without question Rozin had one of the greatest talmudic minds in history, and Bialik is said to have remarked that out of him one could fashion two Einsteins.[96] Aware of his brilliance, Rozin acted as if he were a medieval authority, showing a total disregard, or often even contempt, for post-medieval sages. As for the *Shulḥan arukh*, the basis of Jewish law in modern times, he simply ignored this work when arriving at halakhic decisions.[97]

At the beginning of 1929 a question came to Weinberg regarding Rozin's daughter, whose husband, Rabbi Israel Zitron of Petah Tikvah, had died childless

92 (Frankfurt, 1925). Weinberg's lengthy responsum originally appeared in the 1925 *Jeschurun*, and was reprinted in *SE* ii, no. 125. It was greatly praised by R. Hayim Judah Ehrenreich, *Otsar haḥayim*, 3 (1927), 72–4.

93 *SE* ii, no. 88. Leibowitz's responsum appears in Esriel Hildesheimer and Kalman Kahana (eds.), *Memorial Volume for Rabbi Jehiel Jacob Weinberg* (Heb.) (Jerusalem, 1969), 33–9.

94 *SE* ii, nos. 102–3. Grodzinski's responsum is included in *Seridei esh*. Kook's responsum is found in his *Da'at kohen* (Jerusalem, 1969), no. 150. That Shapiro agreed with Weinberg is clear from Weinberg's letter to Kook in B. Z. Shapiro, *Igerot lare'iyah*, no. 210. Hoffmann, *Melamed leho'il*, ii, no. 86, ruled similarly, but his opinion had not yet appeared in print when Weinberg wrote his two responsa. On this issue see Shmuel T. Rubenstein, 'Men Who Cannot be Circumcised Due to Health Reasons: Can They Convert?' (Heb.), *Torah shebe'al peh*, 29 (1988), 28–32; Menahem Finkelstein, *Proselytism: Halakhah and Practice* (Heb.) (Ramat Gan, 1994), 168 n. 14.

95 See *SE* iii, nos. 44–5.

96 See Zevin, *Outstanding Men and their Intellectual Approaches* (Heb.) (Tel Aviv, 1966), 82 n. 7.

97 On Rozin's methodology see Zevin, *Outstanding Men*, 91–152; Menahem Kasher, *Mefaneaḥ tsefunot* (New York, 1959); Moshe Shlomo Kasher (ed.), *The Rogochover Gaon and his Teachings* (Heb.) (Jerusalem, 1958); id., *Introduction to the Teachings of the Rogochover* (Heb.) (Jerusalem, 1966); id., *The Teachings of Rabbi Joseph Rozin* (Heb.) (Jerusalem, 1976); Moshe Grossberg, *Tsefunot harogochovi* (Jerusalem, 1976); Menahem Mendel Tenenbaum, *The Method of Study of the Rogochover* (Heb.) (n.p., 1987). See also the recollections of Chaim Tchernowitz (Rav Tsa'ir), *Autobiography* (Heb.) (New York, 1954), 162–5.

in 1927.[98] As he was survived by brothers she was obligated to participate in the *ḥalitsah* ceremony. However, it was not clear which of her two brothers-in-law should perform the ceremony. One brother-in-law, who was completely non-observant, lived in Leningrad, where he could not be reached. The other brother-in-law lived in Königsberg and had converted to Christianity. Rozin ruled that the Berlin rabbinical court should perform the ceremony with the man from Königsberg. His reason was that one who rejects the entire Torah, like the man in Leningrad, is halakhically no better than one who actually converts to another faith. Thus, it made no difference which of the brothers performed the ceremony.[99]

Weinberg, showing confidence in his own halakhic knowledge, wrote a responsum in which he did not hesitate to disagree with Rozin's opinion. To bolster his case he cited two authoritative sources, Rabbi Moses Isserles and Rabbi Moses Sofer. In addition to the halakhic evidence upon which his ruling was based, there was another consideration which was a motivating factor in the position he took. Weinberg felt that a sharp distinction must be made between one who converts to another faith, thereby rejecting the Jewish people, and one who despite his complete non-observance has not formally excluded himself from his spiritual heritage. According to Weinberg, there was no question that the latter must be regarded as a full and complete Jew. Weinberg feared that if Rozin's view were accepted, it would allow religious extremists to brand as apostates those Jews who were not entirely observant. This would bring the very definition of the term 'Jew' into dispute.[100]

For his part, Rozin was contemptuous of Weinberg and even humiliated him in the presence of others. He rebuked him: 'You follow the gleaners[101] and I follow the Babylonian and Jerusalem Talmuds.'[102] In similar fashion he requested that Rabbi Meier Hildesheimer instruct the Berlin rabbinical court 'not to gather from the gleaners in order to cause a woman to become an *agunah* needlessly, God forbid'.[103] Weinberg informed Hildesheimer that next to Rozin's his opinion was insignificant, but that Hildesheimer should consult the leading sages of Lithuania, Poland, and Hungary. If they should disagree with Rozin, Weinberg continued, the rabbinical court should act accordingly, even if Rozin thought that the opinions of these sages were worthless. Weinberg also sent copies of his responsum to a number of leading authorities, many of whom, incidentally, disagreed with him.[104]

198 See Meier Hildesheimer's letter to Rozin, dated 5 May 1929, in the Rozin Archives, Yeshiva University; Atlas, 'A Portrayal of the Gaon Rabbi Jehiel Jacob Weinberg' (Heb.), *Sinai*, 58 (1966), 285; Sternbuch, *Teshuvot*, ii. 370.

199 *Tsafenat paneaḥ* (Jerusalem, 1968), i, no. 80.

100 See *SE* iii, nos. 44–5; Atlas, 'Portrayal', 285. Weinberg's 'sociological' reason was transmitted to Atlas but does not appear in the responsa, which are purely legalistic.

101 That is, figures lacking originality and significance, referring here to Isserles and Sofer.

102 *SE* ii, p. 67. For an example of Rozin insulting the renowned R. Isaac Elhanan Spektor, see Tchernowitz, *Autobiography*, 164.

103 *SE* iii, p. 158.

104 In addition to the responsa printed in *SE* iii, nos. 44–5, see *Yad sha'ul*, 313–15; Moses Mordechai Epstein, *She'elot uteshuvot levush mordekhai* (Jerusalem, 1946), no. 64; Elijah Klatzkin,

Evidently unfamiliar with Rozin's irritable personality, Weinberg commented: 'As for his words of contempt, I do not wish to respond. However, I am very shocked that a man as great as he would be offended by one who disputed with him for the sake of Heaven. Is this the way of Torah? How strange!'[105] Weinberg also took offence at Rozin's characterization of Isserles and Sofer as the 'gleaners', and during the dispute declared: 'I will not listen to him because the law is not in accordance with his opinion. Rather, I am obliged to obey Rabbi Moses Isserles and Rabbi Moses Sofer, who have been accepted among our people as final authorities.'[106]

Philosophical Writings

In addition to his halakhic writings in the Weimar years, Weinberg also tried to don the philosopher's mantle, penning a lengthy article entitled 'Thoughts about Judaism'.[107] This article, picking up themes he had discussed earlier, deals with a variety of different aspects of Judaism and religion as a whole. Weinberg was particularly interested in the nature of religious faith and the complicated psychological factors underlying belief and unbelief. In fact, he claimed that any attempt to understand religious faith must come from the discipline of psychology, rather than from philosophy as was attempted in medieval times.

As far as Weinberg was concerned, the logic-based approach of Maimonides and other medieval philosophers has nothing to do with true religious faith. It therefore cannot contribute to an understanding of the nature of this faith.[108] Religious faith for Weinberg is identified with feelings and states of being. It cannot be proved in the fashion of a mathematical formula as the medieval thinkers attempted to do. Indeed, once faith is based on observable facts, it has passed into a different realm, that of thought and understanding. As Weinberg had emphasized in his essay on Berdyczewski and now repeated, faith is a psychological state reached after travelling through tempestuous waters.

Because Weinberg argued that religious faith is a purely psychological state and is not based upon observable reality, it was easier for him to claim that the Jewish people have an innate gift for interacting with the divine. He argued that whereas

Devarim aḥadim (Jerusalem, 1931), no. 54. When Weinberg wrote that 'all the sages' agreed with him (*SE* ii, p. 67), he was obviously exaggerating, although presumably he did receive the consent of a number of scholars whose responsa have not survived. For a large collection of responsa which discuss the question of *ḥalitsah* with an apostate, and of which Weinberg was unaware, see *Takanot agunot* (Odessa, 1887). This volume, and a subsequent one on the same theme, were reprinted in *Ets ḥayim* (Haderah, 1985).

105 *SE* iii, p. 158.

106 *SE* ii, p. 67. See also *SE* i, p. 245.

107 It was published in Kaplan and Landau, *Vom Sinn des Judentums*, 109–35, and was reprinted in Weinberg's *Das Volk der Religion* (Geneva, 1949), 19–63. It also appeared in Hebrew in *Lifrakim*, 366–80 (139–54), with a couple of insignificant changes.

108 See also *Lifrakim*, 97–8 (66–7).

all nations can obtain knowledge about God, true faith, the basis of religiosity, is inherited. This genius for religious faith inherited by the Jewish people also has its parallels in other nations, who have excelled in areas close to their spirit. For example, the Greeks found their genius in art.[109]

In this essay's lengthy discussion of the Jewish people's religious nature, Weinberg was careful to stress that he was not referring to religion in its narrow sense—primitive religion, which is directed outwards and answers questions about how and why the world functions. Rather, he was dealing with religion in its most advanced state, when it enables man to discover his inner being. This type of religion is exemplified by Judaism, and finds its creativity in the commandments and the variety of interpretations offered in explanation of them.

As in his earlier attempts at philosophy, there is no great originality of thought or striking ideas here. In fact, it would be incorrect to describe Weinberg as a philosopher. As I have said, although he tried to write like a philosopher, his essays ended up reading like sermons. Despite having studied philosophy at Giessen, he does not seem to have been ready to confront, or even to have been aware of, the serious philosophical issues of his day. His discussion of the nature of the Jewish people and the differences between the Greeks and Jews simply followed what had once been a widespread belief in national uniqueness (*Volkgeist*), popularized by a number of writers, notably Johann Gottfried Herder.[110]

One point which is of interest, however, is Weinberg's description of the Jews as 'das Volk der Religion'. In coining this phrase he probably had in mind the distinction Hirsch made between the Hebrew words גוי and עם, both of which characterize the Jewish people, and 'Volk', which is not a valid designation for the Jews 'unless we are able to separate from the term the concept of common territory and political power'.[111] In referring to the Jews as 'das Volk der Religion', Weinberg was adopting Hirsch's view that the Jews are not a 'Volk' in the classic sense, since their national character is of a purely spiritual nature. Therefore, a common homeland is not essential. Because of this, Weinberg concluded, the Jews are a nation unlike any other in the world.[112]

[109] See Hildesheimer's similar formulation in *Jahres-Bericht des Rabbiner-Seminars für das orthodoxe Judenthum pro 5634 (1873–74)*, 85.

[110] Although he does not mention it, Weinberg's view may have been based on that of Krochmal, who was himself influenced by Herder. See Jay M. Harris, *Nachman Krochmal: Guiding the Perplexed of the Modern Age* (New York, 1991), 75 ff. See also the present volume, Ch. 1 n. 87, where it was noted that even in his youth Weinberg read Krochmal.

[111] Hirsch, *Neunzehn Briefe über Judentum* (Altona, 1836), 87 (sixteenth letter). See also Eliyahu Meir Klugman, *Rabbi Samson Raphael Hirsch* (New York, 1996), 132, and the sources cited ibid. 376 n. 1.

[112] See also *Lifrakim*, 294–5 (171–2). Weinberg had been convinced of this basic idea for a long time. In a 1905 sermon he delivered in Grodno, he 'proved from history that Jewish nationality is different from that of all the nations because its nationality is only spiritual, and this spirituality consists of only Torah and *musar*' (letter to R. Sheftel Kramer, dated 29 May 1905). In *SE* iii, p. 258, Weinberg expressed himself in a similar way to Hirsch: 'The land is only the platform

In Defence of German Orthodoxy

At this stage of the discussion an important point must be made about the development of Weinberg's thought. We have previously observed his lukewarm and even negative attitude towards secular studies; any approval he expressed was in the context of vocational training. He specifically rejected the notion of a Hirschian synthesis of the Jewish and the secular,[113] arguing that the *aggadot* of the Talmud and Schiller could not exist simultaneously in one mind. However, shortly after his stay in Giessen he had clearly developed a much more positive view of secular studies.

In an article written in 1924 Weinberg briefly confronted the view that secular education had driven Jewish youth away from Orthodoxy.[114] He rejected this position outright. First, he argued, it was contradicted by the experience of German Orthodoxy, in which secular education was combined with commitment to tradition. Secondly, to blame secular education for defections from Orthodoxy was to advance a shameful proposition, namely, that Orthodoxy could only exist through ignorance and obscurantism, but had no chance of survival in the modern world. In a later essay Weinberg continued his defence of the German Orthodox, arguing that if they increased their Torah knowledge they could be a model for all, including the east European Orthodox.[115]

Another glimpse of Weinberg's thoughts during this period comes from a eulogy he delivered in 1927 in memory of Rabbi Hanokh Ehrentreu of Munich, who in addition to being an outstanding talmudist was also a first-rate critical scholar. Speaking before the Bund Jüdischer Akademiker, of which he was a member,[116] Weinberg for the first time completely identified himself with the ideals of German Orthodoxy, in particular the Berlin variety which approved of academic Jewish studies.[117] Using Ehrentreu's life as his model, Weinberg was led to discuss the special problems confronting the Orthodox intellectual living in the modern world.

Weinberg noted that the Orthodox intellectual struggled to create a synthesis

[upon which stands] the spiritual inheritance of the Torah, but the inheritance itself, that which is the basis for our life and existence, is only the Torah. . . . We must explicitly declare that the national territory is the Torah, and that the land is ours only on condition that it is tied to the spiritual inheritance. In this we differ from every other nation, and whoever does not acknowledge this denies the basic principle of Judaism.' For a post-war comment, affirming that all Jews possess some religiosity, see 'Simhat Torah with Rabbi Israel Salanter', *She'arim*, 30 Sept. 1953, 5.

113 I have used the word synthesis since this is the term Weinberg used. See 'Schulfragen' (1916), 497; *Lifrakim*, 163 (233). However, in his most recent work Mordechai Breuer has objected to describing Torah im Derekh Eretz as a synthesis. See above Ch. 3 n. 76.

114 'Eine ר"ה Predigt für meine ostjüdischen Brüder', *Der Israelit*, 25 Sept. 1924, 3 (Hebrew translation in *Lifrakim*, 31).

115 'Das Jeschiwoh-Problem', *Jüdisches Wochenblatt*, 14 Aug. 1925, 349.

116 See *Lifrakim*, 160 (230). For a later period see *Verzeichnis der Mitglieder des Bundes Jüdischer Akademiker nach dem Stande vom 1. Februar 1929* (Berlin, 1929), 11.

117 *Lifrakim*, 159–64 (229–34).

between the elements of modern culture, in particular critical research, and tradition. Yet he was heavily outnumbered, with opposition coming from both sides. On the one hand, there were the non-Orthodox Jews who had no binding ties to tradition and rejected whatever they chose. Weinberg saw no need to explain why this position was unacceptable. On the other hand, he continued, a large segment of the Orthodox community had isolated itself from modern intellectual trends, and was therefore not confronted with any intellectual challenge to tradition. Although the apostles of isolationist Orthodoxy claimed that it was precisely this lack of any challenge which was the best argument in favour of their approach, Weinberg pointed to the heavy price paid by this form of Orthodoxy: obscurantism and lack of intellectual sophistication.

In comments which developed a view originally formulated in his essay on Berdyczewski, Weinberg stressed that true Orthodoxy meant more, rather than less, struggle. It did not offer simplicity by avoiding modern intellectual problems, but brought with it more difficulties as well as more responsibility. This was not to be regarded as an unfortunate but unavoidable outcome of modernity. On the contrary, in Weinberg's mind the uneasy interaction of tradition and modernity was the essence of what Orthodoxy was all about. Weinberg acknowledged that this confrontation had a tragic element, yet, as he pointed out, all the great ideas in philosophy, science, and the social sciences had their origin in the struggle between received wisdom and new insight.[118]

The reason German Orthodoxy was so esteemed throughout the Jewish world, Weinberg continued, was because it had been able to create a synthesis between Judaism and modern learning and culture. It was this frame of mind that had produced men of the calibre of Hirsch, Hildesheimer, Hoffmann, and Barth. Furthermore, he argued, it was precisely because of this that the opponents of tradition viewed German Orthodoxy as a threat, for it was German Orthodoxy which showed how traditional Judaism could survive in modern times. Although the opponents of tradition expected east European Orthodoxy to wither away, it was clear to them that this was not going to happen to German Orthodoxy. This expectation, it should be added, was bolstered by the massive defections from Orthodoxy in eastern Europe during this period, compared to the relatively minor attrition in German Orthodoxy.[119]

Weinberg continued this theme, admitting that there were precious few who had been able to achieve a profound understanding of both Torah and modern civilization. 'Yet these few, and Rabbi Ehrentreu at their head, will be an example for us.' That is, even though ultimate success was not assured, the quest should not be abandoned. Weinberg believed that it was from men such as Ehrentreu that re-

[118] Cf. Kook, *Orot hakodesh* (Jerusalem, 1964), ii. 314: 'One whose soul does not roam the expanses, who does not seek the light of truth and good with all his heart, will not suffer spiritual destruction, but he is likewise without authentic construction.'

[119] See Breuer, *Jüdische Orthodoxie*, 352–3.

ligious academics and university students should take their lead. From them they would discover that there was a great deal to learn both from the sages of the east, with whose exalted character not many in Germany were familiar,[120] and from the sages of Germany. Weinberg declared that only if the best of both of these worlds were combined would there be success, leading to the sanctification of God's name.

Turning to his audience of religious academics and students, Weinberg declared that it was their task to continue in the path of their predecessors and to work for the synthesis of Jewish ideals and secular civilization. This synthesis was not to be relegated to the more technical aspects of daily life. That is, it did not mean the creation of 'Shabbat belts' which allow people to carry on the Sabbath, or similar inventions which enable the Orthodox to have an easier life in the modern world. Rather, the synthesis of which Weinberg spoke included all facets of life and human experience. Weinberg added that those who achieved this synthesis, in the way Hirsch envisioned it, would not experience any dulling of their religious sensibilities, as had been alleged by the opponents of Torah im Derekh Eretz.[121]

This last comment is quite significant, for Weinberg himself once shared this opinion. In the previous decade he had described the state of German Orthodoxy thus:

> The German Orthodox do give the example of pious Jews who at the same time take an active interest in the products of worldly culture, but they have never succeeded in blending the old spirit of Jewry and the young European spirit of knowledge to some sort of higher synthesis, in such a way that a creative and renewing impulse for the Jewish personality could emerge from it.[122]

Having spent a decade in Germany, Weinberg had discovered that there were men such as Ehrentreu who did achieve the higher synthesis of which he had written. The combination of German culture and respect for critical scholarship with the 'pure' Judaism of eastern Europe was not entirely lacking in Germany, and it was this path that Weinberg chose to follow. For the first time he was not merely identifying with the ideals of German Orthodoxy, but was even defending them against detractors.[123] In so doing he was arguing that German Orthodoxy's approach to modernity, in particular as represented by the Berlin Rabbinical Seminary, was superior to that of east European Orthodoxy, which chose to ignore the new challenges, hoping that they would disappear on their own without causing religious havoc.

Socially, Weinberg still considered himself a stranger in Germany, and his heart lay with his people in Lithuania.[124] Intellectually, however, he now belonged to

[120] See also *Lifrakim*, 166 (240) and 171 (245).

[121] See also Weinberg, 'Our Education', *Undzer Veg*, 23 Apr. 1951, 2.

[122] 'Schulfragen' (1916), 496–7.

[123] Only two years earlier, Weinberg had still claimed that the best career path for one seeking to become a *talmid ḥakham* was blue-collar work. Academic studies, he asserted, often destroy the harmony of the Jewish outlook. See 'Das Jeschiwoh-Problem' (1925).

[124] See *Lifrakim*, 162 (232), 181–2.

Germany. Since east European Orthodoxy was the safer course in his eyes, Weinberg was understandably still reluctant to expose its 'pure' Jewish culture to the modes of thought found in Germany.[125] He was also as adamant as ever that the basic curriculum of the advanced yeshiva must remain unaltered.[126] Yet the fact remains that as far as Weinberg was concerned, east European Orthodoxy was unable to respond creatively to the challenges of modernity.[127] Therefore, thinking Jews had to look towards German Orthodoxy as the way of the future—a most frightening prospect for the old-time rabbis of the east.

EASTERN TRENDS IN GERMAN ORTHODOXY

It is most interesting that at the same time as Weinberg was finding his way to the Hirschian approach, others, who had been brought up in the ideology of Torah im Derekh Eretz, were turning their backs on it. The previous generation had looked upon Hirsch as the saviour of German Orthodoxy, and this had prevented any significant criticism of his approach. Indeed, his popularity increased so greatly after his death that much of German Orthodoxy was sustained by his Torah im Derekh Eretz ideology.[128] However, by the beginning of the twentieth century, members of the new generation did not feel the same awe as their parents, and they were prepared to criticize Hirsch's approach. Although they admitted that it was necessary in its time, they did not believe that it continued to have a positive effect on Jewish life, and were thus ready to modify, or even reject, Hirsch's philosophy.

In his essay on Ehrentreu, Weinberg defended Hirsch against those in the German Orthodox community who had recently begun to criticize him. These critics argued that Hirsch's *Weltanschauung* was generally unattainable and instead led to a cold and unfeeling form of Judaism.[129] Although a decade earlier Weinberg had agreed with this position, now, carried away by his enthusiasm for the Hirschian approach, he sharply limited the validity of such criticism. Nevertheless, it is difficult to deny that his earlier approach, which claimed that the Hirschian synthesis could never have more than individual successes, was correct. This was admitted by the rabbi and physician Eduard Biberfeld (1864–1939), one of the rare few who were able to achieve the higher synthesis advocated by Hirsch. In fact, even before the war Biberfeld observed that Torah im Derekh Eretz was basically a fiction. What took its place was a form of Orthopraxy that was inferior to the Orthodoxy of eastern Europe, which, despite its cultural backwardness, gave a proper emphasis to Torah study.[130]

[125] See *Yad sha'ul*, 5; 'The Yeshivot in Russia' (Heb.), *Hatsefirah*, 5 Sept. 1920, 2.

[126] See 'Das Jeschiwoh-Problem' (1925).

[127] In Ch. 7 I quote his criticism of the east European Orthodox for their apathy towards women's education, in contrast to the German Orthodox who achieved great success in this area.

[128] It has been pointed out earlier in this chapter that Hirsch's ideology of Torah im Derekh Eretz achieved widespread influence, even among those who rejected his religious separatism and opposition to Wissenschaft des Judentums.

[129] *Lifrakim*, 163 (233).

[130] *Agudas Jisroel: Berichte und Materialien*, 43–4. See also Stern, *Educational Ideal*, 128.

Since it is only the rare spiritual personality, such as Hirsch, who can find religious meaning in Schiller's poems or in the mountains of Switzerland, it is no surprise that instead of a synthesis of Jewish and secular, the Hirschian approach was producing a dualism among the German Orthodox. Although halakhah was adhered to, in many cases with extreme punctiliousness, these Jews' lives were not generally filled with much Jewish content. In this regard, it was almost as if all that separated the Orthodox from other Jews, indeed even from gentiles, was their adherence to halakhah. In other words, the vision of Moses Mendelssohn, the leader of the Enlightenment, which saw Judaism as nothing more than revealed legislation, had triumphed. It was precisely with this in mind that Joseph Carlebach (1882–1942), a leading German rabbi and a follower of Hirsch's teachings, could give a talk in 1929 on the *conflict* between Torah and Derekh Eretz, an unheard-of topic among disciples of Hirsch in the previous generation.[131]

Although Eugen Mayer exaggerated when he claimed that religion had become a sport,[132] there is no denying that true religious feeling was not central to the mind-set of the German Orthodox bourgeois. It certainly left much to be desired when compared with the 'warmth' found among Orthodox east European laity. This led Isaac Breuer (1883–1946) to ask 'was not Gerhart Hauptmann[133] more meaningful to us' than all the pious and learned rabbis?[134]

With the secular severed from the holy, as was the case for so many Orthodox Jews in Weimar, it was only natural that religious people would begin to downplay the importance of the former element. It would certainly continue to have vocational value, but would not have any place in moulding the Jewish personality, in contradiction to Hirsch's vision. After being exposed to the exclusively Jewish education of the east, opposition to Hirsch grew among those for whom religion, and especially Torah study, had become a central facet of their life. They no longer saw any need for what they viewed as German Orthodoxy's compromises with secular culture. Instead, they chose to incorporate the 'pure' Judaism of eastern Europe into their lives. As Eliezer Stern noted, this turn to the east by the German Orthodox, culminating in the founding of Agudat Yisrael, was nothing less than an admission that they had failed in their attempt to create a Torah im Derekh Eretz utopia.[135]

[131] See Gillis-Carlebach, *Education*, 22; Julius Carlebach, 'Orthodox Jewry in Germany: The Final Stages', in Arnold Paucker (ed.), *The Jews in Nazi Germany 1933–1943* (Tübingen, 1986), 91.

[132] 'Räumet, räumt, macht Bahn!' in *Gabe: Herrn Rabbiner Dr Nobel zum 50. Geburtstag* (Frankfurt, 1922), 85.

[133] 1862–1946; German playwright, poet, novelist, and winner of the Nobel Prize for literature in 1912.

[134] Breuer, *Programm oder Testament*, 21. This reference, as well as that mentioned in n. 132, are both quoted by Breuer, *Jüdische Orthodoxie*, 321.

[135] See the discussion in Breuer, *Jüdische Orthodoxie*, 317 ff., which was my main source for this section, and Stern, *Educational Ideal*, 126 ff. See also Mordechai Breuer, 'Orthodoxy and Change' (Heb.), in id. (ed.), *Torah-Im-Derekh-Eretz*, 85–95; Moshe Ahrend, 'German Orthodox

In fact, there are signs that this transformation in German Orthodoxy had begun even earlier in the century. In 1909 Rabbi Sholom Dov Ber Schneersohn (1866–1920), always a perceptive observer, sensed that the German Orthodox had begun to realize that something was missing in their Judaism. They identified it as a lack of sufficient Torah study, but Schneersohn believed they suffered from a lack of true 'fear of heaven'.[136] Even Jacob Rosenheim, a leading advocate of Hirsch's views, came under the spell of the east.[137] While not entirely abandoning his earlier views, he began to urge that rabbis devote themselves exclusively to Torah. Rosenheim argued that intensive Torah study simply did not leave time to study the writings of Immanuel Kant and Friedrich Schelling.[138] This was a new approach, for while advocates of Torah im Derekh Eretz generally did not dispute the fact that the 'Torah-only' approach was valid in certain countries, they agreed that the rabbinate of German Orthodoxy should not adopt this path. Since, in Rosenheim's conception, the laity was presumably to continue along the Hirschian path, it was inevitable that this approach would soon produce a cultural gap between the masses and their rabbis, something German rabbis were always careful to avoid and which would prevent them from ever endorsing Rosenheim's view.

Rosenheim was no doubt led to this view because Hirschian philosophy had become stale. Indeed, no real advances had been made in the conception of Torah im Derekh Eretz, and almost everything said and written on the topic was a rehash of the master's words.[139] As Rosenheim pointed out, Hirsch had created a model religious community and Hildesheimer had trained rabbis and academic scholars. Yet neither was able to produce significant figures in the field of religious philosophy who would be able to carry on as ideological leaders of the Torah im Derekh Eretz movement. Wohlgemuth and Isaac Breuer were the two exceptions that proved the rule.[140]

New anti-religious philosophical trends, developments in science, biblical criticism, resurgent antisemitism, and Zionism also contributed significantly to the transformation of German Orthodoxy. This transformation was so far-reaching that, at its peak during the post-war years, many of the German Orthodox no longer viewed themselves as part of cultured German society. Even the basic principle of Hirsch's thought, that emancipation was a positive step in Jewish history, was being questioned, and as early as 1900 emancipation was being identified with assimilation.[141]

The traumatic period following Germany's defeat, which together with economic disaster brought about a questioning of comfortable old values, only strengthened

Spokesmen Before the Holocaust' (Heb.), ibid. 133–46; and Baruch Kurzweil, *Bema'avak al erkhei hayahadut* (Jerusalem, 1970), 286–7.

136 *Igerot kodesh*, ii. 465.

137 See Breuer, *Autobiography*, 111–12.

138 *Oholai Ya'akov*, i. 190–1.

139 See Breuer, *Jüdische Orthodoxie*, 151 ff., 317 ff.

140 *Oholai Ya'akov*, i. 184–8.

141 'Rückblick', *Der Israelit*, 11 Jan. 1900, 59, 81.

disillusionment with a German culture now viewed as irrelevant and in need of replacement by 'true' Jewish values such as Torah study, hasidism, and *musar*. Although in earlier years it had been the Orthodox of eastern Europe who had felt somewhat inferior when confronted with the pious and cultured Orthodox of Germany, the tables had turned and it was now the German Orthodox, especially the young, who were embarrassed by their form of Orthodoxy. Their cultural superiority no longer counted for much, and they felt inferior when comparing their level of Torah knowledge with that of their east European brethren. Many of the young Orthodox were no longer interested in grappling intellectually with religious and philosophical problems. Rather, they were looking for an easy solution, which they found in east European Orthodoxy. The Orthodoxy of the east, with its mystical or Talmud-centred approach, was much simpler than German Orthodoxy, lacking as it did all the intellectual and cultural baggage of the latter.[142] As Weinberg would have put it, to 'believe' meant so much less for the east European Orthodox than it did for the followers of Torah im Derekh Eretz.

At the same time that many of the German Orthodox were beginning to reach out for other interpretations of Judaism, Weinberg was doing the same—except that he was turning to neo-Orthodoxy. In this regard, Weinberg was no different from the first generation of Hirsch's students. Like them and the few twentieth-century followers of Hirsch in eastern Europe,[143] he found this new philosophy so full of life and potential that he was able to overlook its shortcomings. Weinberg's intellectual development is thus strikingly similar to that of Maslow, the protagonist of Selig Schachnowitz's 1912 novel *Luftmentschen*, who forsakes Lithuania and the world of the yeshiva only to find religious renewal through Hirsch's philosophy later.[144]

Nevertheless, the fact remains that despite his embrace of neo-Orthodoxy, Weinberg himself had something to do with the changed atmosphere in Germany which contributed to the abandonment of the Torah im Derekh Eretz ideology. Mention has already been made of the increase in Torah study which began in Germany, most significantly after the war, and of the significant role Weinberg played in this. This new emphasis on 'learning', or as Weinberg put it, 'love of Torah',[145] was bound to weaken the hold of Torah im Derekh Eretz on the intellectuals of the younger generation. In addition, during Weinberg's tenure at the seminary, it was a common occurrence for him to invite great Lithuanian Torah

[142] See Moses Auerbach, 'Zur geistigen Struktur der deutschen Orthodoxie der Gegenwart', *Festschrift für Jacob Rosenheim*, 206 ff.

[143] See *Unser Weg* (June 1929), 58–9; (Apr. 1930), 54–5. Sarah Schenirer, the founder of the Beth Jacob movement, was also greatly influenced by Hirsch. See Klugman, *Rabbi Samson Raphael Hirsch*, 67.

[144] See Michael Brenner, 'East and West in Orthodox German-Jewish Novels (1912–1934)', *LBIYB* 37 (1992), 311–13.

[145] *Lifrakim*, 172 (246). See also 'Das Jeschiwoh-Problem' (1925).

scholars who happened to be passing through Berlin to give talmudic lectures at the institution. This further exposed the students to the yeshiva mode of study.[146] It has already been noted that Weinberg encouraged his advanced students to study in the Lithuanian yeshivot. This was an entirely new concept; only a few years earlier any German boy who expressed a desire to study in the east would have been regarded as demented.[147] Even after this practice had become fairly common, many parents, not to mention German rabbis, viewed it with less than sympathetic eyes. They understandably feared that it would lead to a rejection of Torah im Derekh Eretz Judaism.[148]

Although it is obviously impossible to know what went through Weinberg's mind, one can assume that he expected those students whom he encouraged to study in Lithuanian yeshivot to return to Germany without having abandoned the Hirschian approach. To do so would mean to adopt the path of the east European rabbinate, which was not equipped to serve a secularly educated Orthodox community integrated into German society.[149] Weinberg was not blind to the fact that serious Talmud study was almost always accompanied by a rejection of Torah im Derekh Eretz, and that advocacy of the latter usually went hand in hand with a lack of talmudic achievement. Yet this did not absolve him from trying to create a new type of student, one who took both Talmud study and Torah im Derekh Eretz seriously—just as he did.

AN INDEPENDENT STAND

Throughout his time in Berlin during the Weimar Republic, Weinberg kept away from internal Jewish political disputes. In fact, in his eulogy for Ehrentreu he called attention to the latter's ability to rise above all party allegiances, noting that not everyone would regard this as worthy of praise.[150] Although other teachers at the seminary were leading activists in either the Mizrachi movement or Agudat Yisrael, Weinberg kept his distance from both. Though he maintained close personal relations with leaders of both groups, he would not embrace the political agenda of either. As Eisner put it: 'He was too critical and too subtle to see only one side of any problem, and this made it very difficult for him to fit into any rigid framework. Many organisations competed for his adherence, but hardly any, with the exception of the seminary itself, really succeeded.'[151]

146 See e.g. *Jahres-Bericht des Rabbiner-Seminars zu Berlin für 1925, 1926, 1927*, 4.

147 Rosenheim, *Erinnerungen*, 24; interview with R. Simon Schwab.

148 See Breuer, *Jüdische Orthodoxie*, 353, 491 nn. 11, 12.

149 See *SE* ii, no. 8.

150 *Lifrakim*, 159 (229). See also his comments regarding Moses Auerbach, ibid. 270–1 (323–4), and 'Eine Rede' (1918), 45. In 'Our Programme' (Yid.), *Di Yidishe Tsaytung*, 24 Mar. 1933, 8–9, Weinberg identified himself as a 'non-partisan Jew'. In 'Our Education' (1951), 2, Weinberg argued that rabbis should avoid politics and remain aloof from any party affiliation.

151 Eisner, 'Reminiscences', 45.

When some members of the Mizrachi movement tried to win him over to their side, Weinberg responded with an answer that became legendary among his students: 'You know the difference between Mizrachi and Agudah? The Mizrachi tastes better, but the Agudah is more kosher.'[152] When Rabbi Meir Bar-Ilan later asked Weinberg to become one of the leaders of the Mizrachi movement, Weinberg responded in a more serious vein. He declined the invitation, claiming that the pre-eminent rabbis of Lithuania were opposed to the organization.[153] In this reply Weinberg was not commenting on the inherent value of the organization, or even denying that he personally supported it. Rather, he was merely explaining that he could not take a leadership role in an organization which was faced with such rabbinic opposition. As will be seen later, Weinberg's primary concern was with the ideal of Zionism, not the politics surrounding it.

Although attempts have been made to associate him with Agudat Yisrael,[154] there is no truth in this: Weinberg was never a member of the organization. Indeed, we have already seen that his view of the larger Jewish community stood in stark contrast to the separatism which characterized the German Agudah. Furthermore, he could never accept the Agudah's denial of Mizrachi's religious authenticity. Although he did appear as a signatory to some of the Agudah declarations, all of these dealt with matters that had nothing to do with the ideology of Agudat Yisrael *per se* (e.g. the need to strengthen religious education in Palestine).[155]

Weinberg also maintained good relationships with, and was supportive of, both the Gemeinde Orthodox and the separatists. Weinberg himself was a member of the Gemeinde,[156] and had for a time served as a Gemeinde rabbi. In addition, most of his students went on to hold Gemeinde pulpits. Yet all the evidence suggests that this attachment to the Gemeinde was not an ideological stance for him. He could just as easily have served in a separatist synagogue, even though he was never an active partisan of this cause.[157]

By refraining from endorsing the separatist agenda, that is, by regarding it as only an option, not a religious obligation, Weinberg rejected a central facet of Hirsch's and Salomon Breuer's religious ideology. However, this stance was to be expected, for as with virtually all Russian and Polish immigrants the issue of religious separatism had no real significance for him. He did not believe in judging religiosity by whether one attended a separatist Orthodox synagogue or a Gemeinde Orthodox synagogue.

[152] Ibid.

[153] Heard from R. Bezalel Rakov, who heard it from Weinberg.

[154] See *Hamodia*, 26 Jan. 1966, 1.

[155] See e.g. the Agudat Yisrael supplements to *Der Israelit*, 21 Feb. 1929, 27 Feb. 1930, and 26 Feb. 1931. For a later period, see *Der Israelit*, 19 Nov. 1936, 14. Even the leading opponent of Orthodox separatism, R. Isak Unna, had no objection to appearing as a signatory to declarations of this type.

[156] Weinberg's letter to R. Isak Unna, dated 1 Feb. 1925.

[157] See his letter requesting financial support for the Berlin separatist community in *Hahed* (Elul 5693 [1933]), 7–8, and his letters in Klein, *Oraita begaluta*, introduction, and id., *Kahana mesayea kahana* ([Berlin], 1938), 5–6.

Just as Weinberg did not cast his lot with the separatists, so too he did not join the Achduth organization, whose leading thinker was Isak Unna (1872–1948), rabbi of Mannheim and grandson of Rabbi Seligmann Baer Bamberger. Founded in order to oppose the separatism of Agudat Yisrael, Achduth was intent both on organizing the Gemeinde Orthodox on an inter-communal basis and on unifying all Orthodox Jews regardless of their stand on religio-political questions such as Zionism and *Austritt*. This ideology, which stood in opposition to that expressed in *Der Israelit*, was supported by the newspaper *Jüdisches Wochenblatt*.[158]

Following in the footsteps of his teacher Rabbi Marcus Horovitz and the latter's successor Rabbi Nehemiah Anton Nobel (1871–1922),[159] Unna argued in favour of remaining within the general community and working with the non-observant in matters of communal concern. Confronting Hirsch, Unna argued that there was some ambiguity in his writings on the issue of *Austritt*, that his halakhic arguments were flawed, and that the religious situation in Germany had changed drastically since his time. To begin with, the existence of Orthodoxy was no longer threatened by Reform, something even the separatists admitted.[160] Furthermore, the modern Reform Jews were very different from their grandparents. This meant that rather than separating from them one had an obligation to bring them back to the fold, which could only be done through a unified community.[161] Unna's argument was a particularly important one for the Gemeinde Orthodox to hear, since many of them felt a sense of religious inferiority when confronting the separatists, who portrayed themselves as the only authentic Jews.[162]

Unna was hoping that the Rabbinical Seminary of Berlin would add its voice to the dispute that was rocking German Orthodoxy. Weinberg, however, informed him that he and his colleagues at the seminary were in complete agreement that both the institution as well as its faculty must avoid all such disputes. As Weinberg put it: 'Because of our many sins matters have become complicated in Germany, and the entire dispute about "separation or unity" has ceased to be a religio-halakhic question but has become the basis on which the parties attack one another.'[163]

158 See the complete discussion in Moshe Unna's introduction to Isak Unna, *Lema'an ha'aḥdut*, ch. 8. See also Morgenstern, *Von Frankfurt nach Jerusalem*, 86–7.

159 See Rachel Heuberger, 'Orthodoxy versus Reform: The Case of Rabbi Nehemiah Anton Nobel of Frankfurt a. Main', *LBIYB* 37 (1992), 45–58.

160 See e.g. Eduard Biberfeld's comment in *Agudas Jisroel: Berichte und Materialien*, 44.

161 See 'Das Trennungsprinzip und die Zusammenarbeit der Gesetztreuen', *Jeschurun*, 13 (1926), 403–18; 'Die Frage des Trennungsprinzips: Eine Replik', *Jeschurun*, 14 (1927), 87–90; and other relevant publications listed in the bibliography of Unna's writings in *Lema'an ha'aḥdut*, 375–91. In support of his position, Unna often cited R. Isaac Elhanan Spektor's view that religious Jews are obligated to use all means at their disposal in order to prevent the non-religious from sinning (*Ein yitsḥak* (Vilna, 1889), i, *Even ha'ezer*, no. 1). Spektor's view was to become a major weapon in the hands of Achduth supporters. See e.g. *Jüdisches Wochenblatt*, 19 June 1924, 133.

162 See Moshe Unna's introduction to *Lema'an ha'aḥdut*, 69–70.

163 Letter to R. Isak Unna, dated 1 Feb. 1925.

While he would not commit himself ideologically to either side, in 1929 he did join the halakhah commission of the Vereinigung Traditionell-Gesetzestreuer Rabbiner, which was fairly moderate and comprised mainly those rabbis who were connected to the Gemeinde.[164] Many of the rabbis in the Vereinigung were also members of the Allgemeiner Rabbinerverband, which was made up of both Reform and Orthodox rabbis, and Weinberg himself had no objections to his students joining this organization.[165] Those rabbis who refused to be part of an organization which permitted its members to join the Allgemeiner Rabbinerverband formed the Verband orthodoxer Rabbiner, which was committed to Hirsch's separatist ideology.[166]

In his only published essay dealing with the communal unity versus separatism dispute, which was notably short, Weinberg again showed his independence by rebuking both sides for engaging in journalistic excesses and challenging the religious authenticity and sincerity of their ideological opponents.[167] However, he was ambivalent with regard to the issue itself. Although he admitted that the actions of Hirsch had saved German Orthodoxy, he also recognized that the changed circumstances complicated matters, making the value of *Austritt* no longer self-evident. As Weinberg put it, to decide whether communal unity or separatism is the correct approach is something which can only be left to prophets and the passage of time, and future historians will pass judgement on which position was more sensible. Not surprisingly, they are still in dispute on this point.[168]

[164] Weinberg's letter to R. Moses Schlesinger, dated 20 June 1929. See also Yehudah Ben-Avner, 'Activities of Orthodox Rabbis in Germany' (Heb.), *Sinai*, 91 (1982), 142.

[165] See my 'Between East and West: The Life and Works of Rabbi Jehiel Jacob Weinberg' (Ph.D. diss., Harvard University, 1995), 304–5 (letter from Jacob Horovitz to Isak Unna).

[166] See Alexander Altmann, 'The German Rabbi: 1910–1939', *LBIYB* 19 (1974), 36–40. It is worth noting that in some German states separatist communities were not officially sanctioned. However, this did not stop people from establishing autonomous communities within the wider community, whose only connection with the latter was the payment of taxes. Furthermore, there were a number of small, officially non-separatist communities, which for all intents and purposes were Orthodox. Thus, even though there were only a few official separatist communities, this does not reflect the number of rabbis and laymen who actually shared the separatist ideology.

[167] See 'Das Jeschiwoh-Problem' (1925).

[168] In his later essays on Hirsch Weinberg avoided any discussion of the former's religio-political views, a point which he stressed in his letter to Samuel K. Mirsky, dated 2 Dec. 1959.

FIVE

RESPONSE TO THE NEW NAZI GOVERNMENT (1933–1934)

THE MOST SIGNIFICANT YEAR in recent German history, 1933, began under a cloud. The government was in turmoil and the new chancellor, Kurt von Schleicher, was having no success in achieving parliamentary support. The National Socialists had won a third of the seats in the Reichstag elections of November 1932, and refused to take part in any government unless Hitler was given the chancellorship. At the end of January, Schleicher was forced to resign, like the previous chancellor, Franz von Papen. It was then that President Paul von Hindenburg invited Adolf Hitler to form a government. On 30 January Hitler took the oath of office and soon afterwards persuaded Hindenberg to order new elections for the Reichstag. These took place on 5 March, with the National Socialists receiving nearly 44 per cent of the vote. Chancellor Hitler was now firmly in power.

CONTROVERSY: WEINBERG AND THE NAZIS

Ever since Hitler's assumption of power in January, the world Jewish community had been expressing grave concern over the future of German Jewry. This was not shared by Weinberg, who had a very hopeful and, even for March 1933, naive view of the new government. In mid-March he travelled to Mukachevo (Munkács), Czechoslovakia, where he had been invited by his good friend and ideological opponent, Rabbi Hayim Eleazar Shapira (1872–1937), to attend his daughter's wedding. While there, Weinberg gave an interview to the local Jewish paper, *Di Yidishe Tsaytung*, about the situation in Germany.[1] In this interview he played down the antisemitic nature of the new regime, denied that Jewish political rights or livelihoods were at risk, and expressed optimism for the Jewish future in Germany, a country based on the rule of law.

A few days later, on his way back to Berlin, Weinberg stopped in Vienna where he gave another interview,[2] this time to the Vienna Orthodox weekly *Die Jüdische Presse*.[3] Here he reaffirmed and expanded upon his optimistic view that the Jews had nothing to fear from the Nazis. He also claimed that individuals and govern-

[1] 24 Mar. 1933, 7 (this issue of the newspaper is reprinted in *Rosh simḥati* (n.p., 1992), a book commemorating the wedding).

[2] This trip is mentioned in *SE* ii, p. 362.

[3] 31 Mar. 1933, 1.

ments outside Germany were sharply exaggerating the extent of antisemitic incidents in order to further their own political interests. He claimed that any actions by foreign governments on behalf of Germany's Jews were being taken against the wishes of the German Jews themselves.

Weinberg went on to say that it was the Jews, in particular the Orthodox, who understood and sympathized with the new national movement that had swept Germany. It was the religious Jews who understood how thankful they had to be to Hitler for his fight against communism and atheism, which had brought such spiritual destruction on the Jews of Russia. Weinberg admitted that there had been some anti-Jewish excesses, yet he claimed that neither the government nor the Nazi party could be held responsible for these. He saw Germany developing in a manner similar to that of Italy under Mussolini, who had succeeded in cleansing the country of antisemitism. Although a prohibition on *sheḥitah* was a central tenet of the Nazi programme, Weinberg did not believe the government would institute such a measure; since it would only affect religious Jews it would do nothing to solve the 'Jewish question'. Furthermore, it would greatly damage the country's image abroad.

As can be imagined, these comments touched off something of a storm. Before discussing this, however, it is necessary to put into context statements which today appear shocking. To begin with, the tendency to downplay the anti-Jewish nature of the new regime was common in the weeks following Hitler's assumption of power. It was widely believed, and virtually all German Jewish newspapers expressed this view, that the antisemitic Nazi diatribes were merely propaganda designed to garner votes among the masses. There was also general agreement that life would soon return to normal, with Hitler assuming a more moderate stance.[4]

This illusion was not restricted to German Jewry, as can be seen in the fact that the London *Jewish Chronicle*, which was relentless in exposing Nazi persecution, was also able to hold out hope for the future. In the *Jewish Chronicle*'s words, 'the Nazi chiefs may acquire, in office, that sense of responsibility which they could not feel when wooing the passions of the rabble'.[5] It was actually the separatist Orthodox *Der Israelit* which expressed the most caution of all the German Jewish papers. Although it too doubted that Hitler would act in accordance with his party's rhetoric, it forthrightly declared that 'not to be aware of the seriousness of the situation would be criminally optimistic'.[6] It was such 'criminal optimism' of which Weinberg and so many others were guilty.

In focusing on the Nazis' opposition to communism, Weinberg was reflecting the views of many. As Kurt Blumenfeld wrote: 'The complacency and blindness of

[4] See Margaret T. Edelheim-Muehsam, 'Reactions of the Jewish Press to the Nazi Challenge', *LBIYB* 5 (1960), 316–17; Wolfgang Hamburger, 'The Reaction of Reform Jews to the Nazi Rule', in Herbert A. Strauss and Kurt R. Grossmann (eds.), *Gegenwart im Rückblick* (Heidelberg, 1970), 150–64; Sidney M. Bolkosky, *The Distorted Image: German Jewish Perceptions of Germans and Germany, 1918–1935* (New York, 1975), 170.

[5] 8 Feb. 1933, 7.

[6] 'Die neue Lage', *Der Israelit*, 2 Feb. 1933, 2.

the Jews was disturbed only by the fear of communism. It was always: one should not forget that Hitler is communism's fiercest opponent. Jews listened to the ghastly screamings of Hitler's election speeches and invariably only heard the anti-communist notes.'[7] This feeling of anti-communism also helps explain Weinberg's positive comments about Mussolini, which were not unusual; many Jewish newspapers and commentators spoke favourably of the achievements of Italian fascism. Indeed, there is reason to believe that a good percentage of the German Jewish bourgeois would have been happy with a non-antisemitic dictatorship, and many believed that Hitler's Germany would come to mirror Mussolini's Italy in this regard.[8] Weinberg himself later described how Judaism could be given a boost through the development of a 'Hebrew spiritual fascism', modelled on the political fascism advocated by the Italian dictator.[9] It is most significant that Weinberg was prepared to link the name of Mussolini with Jewish spiritual matters, illustrating once again that the ideology of the Duce was not unacceptable in his eyes.

Although Weinberg was not the only apologist for Hitler during this period, his views were widely reported in eastern Europe because of his standing as a leading Orthodox rabbi. It is true that there were other well-known Orthodox figures who had publicly denied the atrocity reports, but these men were inside Germany and it was believed, rightly or not, that their comments were made under duress. This belief was reinforced when it became known that, on 25 March, Hermann Goering had met with a number of leading Jews in Berlin and had demanded that they contact newspapers outside Germany to deny that there were any Nazi-organized assaults on Jews.[10] Undoubtedly, this is the context within which one must view the telegram sent on 25 March by Ezra Munk (1867–1940), an important Orthodox rabbi in Berlin, to Rabbi Leo Jung in New York. In this telegram Munk urged Jung to publicize in all the American papers that the reports of atrocities were not true.[11] In response to the Goering meeting, similar telegrams were also sent by leaders of

[7] *Erlebte Judenfrage. Ein Vierteljahrhundert deutscher Zionismus* (Stuttgart, 1962), 202 (and see also p. 182). My translation is taken from Jacob Boas, 'The Jews of Germany: Self-Perceptions in the Nazi Era as Reflected in the German Jewish Press 1933–1938' (Ph.D. diss., University of California-Riverside, 1977), 67.

[8] See Boas, 'Jews of Germany', 65; Rudolf Kaulla, *Der Liberalismus und die deutschen Juden: Das Judentum als konservatives Element* (Munich, 1928); Elie Munk, *Judentum und Umwelt* (Frankfurt, 1933), 21 ff.; Klauss J. Herrmann, *Das Dritte Reich und die deutsch-jüdischen Organisationen 1933–1934* (Cologne, 1969), 1 ff.; Donald L. Niewyk, *The Jews in Weimar Germany* (Baton Rouge, La., 1980), 198; Yehudah Ben-Avner, *Vom orthodoxen Judentum in Deutschland zwischen zwei Weltkriegen* (Hildesheim, 1987), 18.

[9] *Lifrakim*, 82.

[10] See Martin Rosenbluth, *Go Forth and Serve* (New York, 1961), 250–4; Leonard Baker, *Days of Sorrow and Pain: Leo Baeck and the Berlin Jews* (New York, 1978), 153–4.

[11] See Munk's telegram (lacking the date) and other documents from influential Jewish citizens, organizations, and newspapers, published in Jacow Trachtenberg, *Atrocity Propaganda is Based on Lies Say the Jews of Germany Themselves* [Berlin, 1933]. The complete telegram appears in Michael L. Munk, 'Austrittsbewegung und Berliner *Adass Jisroel*-Gemeinde 1869–1939', in Herbert A. Strauss and Kurt R. Grossmann (eds.), *Gegenwart im Rückblick* (Heidelberg, 1970), 146, and in Appendix II below. See also 'Gegen die "Greuel"-Propaganda', *Der Israelit*, 30 Mar. 1933, 3.

other segments of German Jewry.[12] However, Weinberg's comments differed from those of other Jewish figures in Germany in that he was never subjected to governmental pressure to portray the regime in a positive light. On the contrary, his opinion was expressed voluntarily. East European Jews, therefore, did not doubt that his optimism about the future of German Jewry and the Nazi regime was genuine.

Many east European Jews expected such statements from the Reform Jews of Germany, whom they viewed as lacking Jewish pride, and there was little surprise when certain Reform and anti-Zionist figures began apologizing for Hitler. There was also no surprise when right-wing groups such as Max Naumann's Verband Nationaldeutscher Juden defended the Nazis, arguing that the atrocity reports were irresponsible exaggerations, and that publicizing them could put the Jews in a precarious situation.[13] Weinberg joined in this chorus and, because of his standing in the rabbinic world, and the fact that he was an east European and not a patriotic German, there was great shock in the east when his comments in *Di Yidishe Tsaytung* became known.[14] Weinberg also surpassed most of his colleagues, not only in absolving the Nazis of all blame for the anti-Jewish excesses, but in showing that he sympathized with the Nazi movement and would be ready to lend his support if it would abandon its antisemitism.[15]

[12] See Trachtenberg, *Atrocity Propaganda*; Lucy S. Dawidowicz, *The War Against the Jews* (New York, 1975), 53. Even many German Zionists were opposed to world Jewish criticism of the regime. See e.g. Stephen Wise, *Challenging Years* (New York, 1949), 248; Carl Hermann Voss, 'Letters from Stephen S. Wise to a Friend and Colleague: Morton Mayer Berman', in Charles Berlin (ed.), *Studies in Jewish Bibliography, History, and Literature in Honor of I. Edward Kiev* (New York, 1971), 483. See also the letters of the Zionist Federation of Germany in Herrmann, *Das Dritte Reich*, 63–4.

[13] On these groups see Carl Jeffrey Rheins, 'German Jewish Patriotism 1918–1935: A Study of the Attitudes and Actions of the *Reichsband Jüdischer Frontsoldaten*, the *Verband Nationaldeutscher Juden*, the *Schwarzes Fahnlein*' (Ph.D. diss., SUNY Stony Brook, 1978). Naumann actually formed a special group, the Aktionsausschuss der jüdischen Deutschen gegen die anti-deutsche Hetze, designed to combat anti-German propaganda.

[14] See 'Idiocy and Wickedness' (Yid.), *Yidishe Shtimme* (Warsaw), 31 Mar. 1933, 2. Interestingly enough, Weinberg's later comments in *Die Jüdische Presse*, which were even more favourable to the Nazis, do not appear to have been known in the East.

[15] Another Orthodox rabbi, Elie Munk of Ansbach (1900–80), expressed himself in words similar to those of Weinberg: 'Without the antisemitism National Socialism would find in Orthodox Jews its most loyal followers. . . . [The Nazis] have taken up the war against the loosening of morals and respect for law, as well as against the emancipation of the female sex. They have replaced the democratic principle of majority rule with the principle of *Führertum*. They have put a stop to the progress of the collectivist economic system. All these steps are fully in accord with the direction of our religious will' (*Judentum und Umwelt*, 34–5). It is significant that both Weinberg and Munk, whose livelihoods depended on communal support, felt comfortable in expressing themselves in this way. Their position, while certainly in the minority, would thus seem to have been regarded as one which reasonable people could adopt and which would not bring about communal outrage. All this changed after the Nazi boycott of 1 Apr. 1933. To add some further context to Weinberg's statements, it should be noted that some Revisionist Zionists defended Nazism in a fashion similar to that of Weinberg: one said, for example, 'Were it not for Hitler's antisemitism, we would not oppose his ideology. Hitler saved Germany.' See Tom Segev, *The Seventh Million*, trans. Haim Watzman (New York, 1993), 23. Max Naumann endorsed the Nazi party and stated that he would have joined it had it been possible. Presumably, most members of his organization, which numbered at least 10,000, agreed with him. In fact, in February

One prominent attack on Weinberg's remarks and the pro-German messages of two Reform rabbis was penned by S. Dorfson, the Prague correspondent for the Warsaw daily *Der Moment*.[16] From his article, entitled 'Hitler Sends Messengers Throughout the World in Order to Calm the Jews', we get a glimpse of the impact of Weinberg's interview. According to Dorfson, Weinberg's comments were widely reprinted by Nazi and Nazi-supporting newspapers as proof that German Jews were not being persecuted.[17] Dorfson also accused Weinberg of stating that the real tragedy for the Jewish people was not the Nazi regime but Zionism. He continued by describing how Weinberg had been warmly received by the German ambassador in Prague, who had thanked him for his sympathetic stand and publicly proclaimed Weinberg as a distinguished preacher of Nazi ideology.

Dorfson's accusations against Weinberg were echoed by Yehiel Meir Blumenfeld (1893–1942), a leading Mizrachi rabbi from Warsaw who published an 'Open Letter' in the Warsaw paper *Baderekh*. Although Blumenfeld was certain that Weinberg had not become 'a paid spokesman for Hitler', as had the Reform rabbis of Germany(!), he was shocked by the newspaper reports that Weinberg had favourable things to say about the German leader. Particularly objectionable was Weinberg's assertion that Hitler only opposed the Zionists, a view that even the anti-Zionist Orthodox rejected.[18] Blumenfeld demanded that Weinberg publicly deny all that had been attributed to him. If such a denial was not forthcoming, Blumenfeld feared—rather prophetically—that any persecutor would be able to claim that he was not antisemitic but only anti-Zionist.[19]

1935 the government had to issue a decree in order to prevent nationalist-oriented Jews, eager to display their allegiance to the regime, from hanging swastikas on the front of their homes and shops. In August 1932 Robert Weltsch wrote that his newspaper, *Die Jüdische Rundschau*, understood the psychological and intellectual basis of Nazism, respected its goal of national renewal, and believed that a nationally conscious Jewry could coexist with the new German nationalism, once it was freed from its crude antisemitism. See John V. H. Dippel, *Bound Upon a Wheel of Fire* (New York, 1996), 39, 56–7, 70, 143. See also Saul Friedländer, *Nazi Germany and the Jews* (New York, 1997), i. 15–16. Erwin Reisner writes: 'In the first years of the National Socialist regime, one could hear the opinion—expressed by Germans, but also by many Jews—that antisemitism was only an accidental concomitant of National Socialism, principally due to Hitler's personal hatred of Jews, which he had imported from his Austrian homeland where antisemitism had always been endemic, as throughout eastern Europe' (*Die Juden und das Deutsche Reich* (Erlenbach, 1966), 204–5).

[16] 30 Apr. 1933, 5.

[17] I have not been able to find any references to Weinberg in any of the contemporary German papers, including the Nazi *Völkische Beobachter, Der Stürmer*, and *Der Angriff*. However, the late R. Joseph Apfel of Leeds, one of Weinberg's students in Berlin during this time, told me that he remembered a headline in the sensationalist Berlin daily *BZ* which played up Weinberg's comments. Unfortunately, no copies of *BZ* have survived from the period under discussion.

[18] In fact, the Nazis were more favourably inclined to the Zionists than to other segments of the Jewish population. See Boas, 'Jews of Germany', 111.

[19] *Baderekh*, 4 May 1933, 6. See also G. Kressel, 'Hitler Only Persecutes Zionists' (Heb.), *Ma'ariv*, 15 Oct. 1985, 11, who relies on Blumenfeld's letter to attack Weinberg for his 'anti-Zionist' defence of Hitler. Kressel writes that he searched the Jewish newspapers for a denial on Weinberg's part and did not find any. Had he looked a little harder, he would not have accused Weinberg of an offence of which he was innocent.

Following these two public attacks, and presumably many private communications, Weinberg responded forcefully in an open letter entitled 'An Advocate, But for Whom?' This letter appeared in another Warsaw paper, the Orthodox *Yidishe Togblat*.[20] Directing his response to Dorfson, who was responsible for publicizing and distorting his interview, Weinberg exclaimed, 'I never dreamt that someone would accuse me of being a mouthpiece for Hitler in Czechoslovakia.' Weinberg explained matters as follows. When he had left Berlin for Mukachevo on 13 March, the situation in Germany was not so bad. It was true that the newspapers had been carrying antisemitic articles and that some Jewish businesses had been closed, but he had believed that these were only passing incidents which could be attributed to the revolutionary frenzy that had engulfed the masses. He was confident that in time things would settle down. As for Dorfson's assertion, subsequently picked up by Blumenfeld, that Weinberg singled out Zionism as the real problem for the Jews, he declared that this was a complete lie, for nowhere in his interview was Zionism even mentioned. Weinberg then pointed out—and this is of the utmost importance—that he gave his interview a few weeks before the organized Nazi boycott of Jewish shops on 1 April. At this time no one had any idea that the very livelihood of Jews was going to be taken away.

Weinberg also denied Dorfson's report of his visit to Prague. According to Weinberg, the truth was as follows. While returning to Germany he had read in the newspapers that the Jews were being threatened with a boycott because they had been spreading horror stories in the foreign media and calling for a world-wide boycott of German merchandise. It was because of this that he had decided to stop in Prague. There he gave another interview, which was designed to calm German fears. He also went to the German embassy but the ambassador, Walter Franz Koch, was not in. He therefore spoke to his assistant, Rudolf Holzhausen, and assured him that German Jews were strongly denying the atrocity reports. He urged Holzhausen to inform his superiors of this, in order to help put a stop to any boycott of Jewish shops.

Although Dorfson pointed out that Weinberg was honoured for his service to the Reich, Weinberg insisted that he made it clear to the embassy that he did not want any recognition. His actions were not intended to be of service to the government in calming the fears of Jews outside Germany, but were for the benefit of those Jews who lived in Germany. Upon returning to Berlin, Weinberg informs us, he immediately wrote to two 'influential, rich German ministers'[21] and 'warned them that it is in their own interest not to enter into a war with both the Jewish and the entire civilized world, which will not remain silent when they see the torture of the German Jews who have contributed so much both to Jewish society and to the

[20] 19 June 1933, 4.

[21] At this time only three of the eleven cabinet posts were held by Nazis. With the exception of the Chancellorship, both were second-rate—Wilhelm Frick as Minister of the Interior and Hermann Goering as Minister without Portfolio.

intellectual world as a whole. They have spread German science and culture throughout the entire learned world and are therefore in no way deserving of such hatred.' Weinberg ended his letter to the ministers by appealing to them not to create another black day in Jewish history, which would be remembered in Jewish prayers together with the destruction of the Temple and the expulsion from Spain.

We thus see that Weinberg did indeed admit that his confidence had been misplaced. After the Nazi boycott of 1 April he no longer had such a sanguine view of the Jewish situation in Germany.[22] However, although his illusion was shattered he did not go to the lengths of Rabbi Leo Baeck (1873–1956), who in 1933 declared, in a now famous speech, that 'the thousand-year history of German Jewry has come to an end'.[23] Like most others at the time, Weinberg believed Baeck was exaggerating. Despite the new difficulties, Weinberg was still hopeful that the government would moderate its course.[24]

Although Weinberg was no longer arguing that the anti-Jewish excesses had been exaggerated, his opposition to the boycott of German goods was not affected in the least.[25] This view was shared by all the important Jewish organizations in Germany. Even if it was true that their denials of the atrocity reports were only made under extreme pressure, their opposition to the boycott was genuine. Indeed, there can be no doubt that the overwhelming majority of German Jews of all political and religious persuasions opposed a foreign boycott. Apart from their patriotic feelings, these Jews correctly understood that a boycott would do nothing to safeguard Jewish rights, and, on the contrary, would bring about governmental and popular reprisals.[26] This explains why Jacob Rosenheim of Frankfurt, president of World Agudat Yisrael, expressed his willingness to co-operate with the German government in order to put a stop to the boycott in Poland. However, he noted that, because of Jewish public opinion there, any such co-operation would have to be kept quiet.[27] A number of Jewish groups in the United States, Europe, and Palestine also opposed the boycott,[28] as did the renowned Rabbi Hayim Ozer

[22] In April 1933, Weinberg sent a letter to the leaders of the Berlin Jewish community with suggestions on how to provide economic aid to those whose livelihoods had been destroyed or were being threatened. A draft of this letter survives.

[23] Robert Weltsch, *An der Wende des modernen Judentums* (Tübingen, 1972), 67. See also Joachim Prinz, *Wir Juden* (Berlin, 1934).

[24] See his interview in *Lubliner Togblat*, 20 Sept. 1933. In this interview Weinberg again mentioned his belief that German National Socialism would eventually follow in the path of Italian fascism by ridding itself of antisemitism.

[25] Ibid. In this interview Weinberg mentioned that he had written two articles denouncing the boycott.

[26] See Bolkosky, *Distorted Image*, 170 ff. For Orthodox reaction, see e.g. *Der Israelit*, 14 Sept. 1933, 5; 6 Nov. 1933, 5. For Isaac Breuer's opposition to the boycott, see Morgenstern, *Von Frankfurt nach Jerusalem*, 275. For Baeck's opposition, see Baker, *Days of Sorrow*, 174.

[27] Appendix III.

[28] See Moshe Gottlieb, *American Anti-Nazi Resistance, 1933–1941* (New York, 1982); Segev, *The Seventh Million*, 26 ff.

Grodzinski of Vilna, whose opinion carried more weight among the east European Orthodox than that of any other rabbi.[29]

SHEḤITAH UNDER ATTACK

Shortly following the anti-Jewish boycott day, and under the guise of preventing cruelty to animals, Hitler shocked the Jewish community by signing a decree on 21 April 1933 forbidding *sheḥitah* throughout Germany unless the animal had previously been stunned. At the same time it was decreed that poultry must be killed by the head being instantly severed from the body. Although Hitler had always pledged to introduce such laws, and even before his rise to power the Nazi party had succeeded in passing similar laws in Bavaria, Brunswick, and Oldenburg, most German Jews shared Weinberg's view that once in power the Nazis would never dare provoke negative world opinion through the institution of such a blatant anti-Jewish measure. Furthermore, 'animal rights' organizations had been trying to ban *sheḥitah* throughout Germany for some seventy years, but the various state governments had always refused to surrender to their pressure. Having emerged victorious from the long and hard battle for *sheḥitah*, most Jews found it simply incomprehensible that all their efforts could be overturned with the stroke of a pen. Yet this is exactly what happened, with the Nazi government taking the high moral ground and condemning the Jewish ritual as lacking basic human decency.[30] Strangely enough, the central government did not ban the import of ritually slaughtered meat. Yet since this was very expensive, and could not provide nearly enough meat to satisfy the demand, the German Orthodox were immediately thrown into a quandary.[31]

[29] See Grodzinski, *Collected Letters* (Heb.) (Benei Berak, 1967), i. 296; *Der Israelit*, 20 Sept. 1933, 9. Nevertheless, Grodzinski did not publicly oppose the boycott once it was proclaimed; see Joseph Elijah Henkin, *Writings* (Heb.) (Jerusalem, 1989), ii. 217. Henkin also records R. Elhanan Wasserman's opposition to the boycott, which was not inspired by fear of possible repercussions against German Jewry, but by a talmudic statement that Jews are forbidden to rebel against the nations (*Ketubot* 111*a*). For other examples of Orthodox opposition to the boycott, see Joel Teitelbaum, *Al hage'ulah ve'al hatemurah* (Brooklyn, NY, 1982), 11; Moshe Blau, *Writings* (Heb.) (Jerusalem, 1983), 250–1; Mordekhai Savitsky, *Nezir eḥav* (n.p., 1988), introduction (on R. Joseph Rozin); Menachem Friedman, 'The Haredim and the Holocaust', *Jerusalem Quarterly*, 53 (Winter 1990), 86–114; and Abraham Fuchs, *The Holocaust in Rabbinic Sources* (Heb.) (Jerusalem, 1995), 24–5. For Orthodox support of the boycott, see Judah Leib Zirelson, *Lev yehudah* (Jerusalem, 1961), 70 ff.; Isaac Gruenbaum, *The Wars of Polish Jewry* (Heb.) (Tel Aviv, 1941), 330–1; Immanuel Meltzer, 'The Anti-German Economic Boycott by Polish Jewry in 1933–1934' (Heb.), *Gal-ed*, 6 (1982), 154.

[30] Many commentators outside Germany described the Nazi action by quoting Hosea 13: 2: 'They that sacrifice men kiss calves'.

[31] Detailed information on all aspects of the 1933 anti-*sheḥitah* decree appears in the two volumes of primary sources edited by Eliyahu Munk and Michael L. Munk, *Edut ne'emanah* (Jerusalem, 1974) and *Shechita: Religious and Historical Research on the Jewish Method of Slaughter* (Brooklyn, NY, 1976). Much of the information in both of these books is taken from the archives of the Berlin Central Office of Sheḥitah Affairs. On the pre-1933 prohibitions against *sheḥitah*, see Isaac Lewin *et al.*, *Religious Freedom: The Right to Practice Shehita* (New York, 1946), 54–71; Zorah Warhaftig, 'The

The poultry issue was relatively simple to solve. As Weinberg showed, even though Rabbi Moses Isserles wrote that the custom was to forbid severing the head immediately following *sheḥitah*,[32] other leading authorities disagreed. Furthermore, it was not even regarded by Isserles as halakhically forbidden. Thus, in a time of great need there was adequate halakhic support to permit the consumption of poultry when the head had been severed.[33]

After receiving the verbal consent of many important east European scholars, Weinberg prepared a long responsum explaining his views. As was his practice, he sent this responsum to the world's leading halakhists, many of whose replies have been preserved.[34] Grodzinski agreed with Weinberg, though only for those parts of Germany where the community was unable to obtain imported meat. Grodzinski concluded his letter by stressing that it was incumbent on the halakhic authorities to exert all their efforts to find room for leniency, so that Jews should not be led to consume non-kosher food. He also noted that his opinion was only theoretical. Whether this *heter* should be acted upon in practice was to be determined by the rabbis in Germany, for it was they who would have to ensure the competence of slaughterers carrying out the new method of *sheḥitah*, as well as making sure that his lenient ruling was applied only where properly warranted.[35] Other rabbis who supported Weinberg's view included Leib Rubin of Vilkomir,[36] Menahem Mendel Hayim Landau of Zawiercie,[37] Judah Leib Zirelson of Kishinev,[38] Aaron Baksht of Shavli (1867–1941),[39] Isak Unna of Mannheim,[40] Joseph Susmanovitz of Slobodka (1894–1941),[41] and Solomon Zalman Ehrenreich of Sziláysomlyó (1863–1944).[42] Some rabbis, however, opposed Weinberg, among them Joseph Rozin of Dvinsk,[43]

Historical and Legal Struggle over *Sheḥitah*' (Heb.), *Torah shebe'al peh*, 5 (1963), 151–9; Yehudah Ben-Avner, 'Antisemitism in the Weimar Republic as Reflected in the Jewish Newspapers' (Heb.), *Sinai*, 107 (1991), 274–5. On the difficulties in importing meat, see Munk and Munk, *Shechita*, 23–7, and Jeremiah J. Berman, *Shehitah: A Study in the Cultural and Social Life of the Jewish People* (New York, 1941), 264–9.

32 *Shulḥan arukh, Yoreh de'ah*, 24: 5, 28: 20.

33 *SE* i, pp. 173 ff.

34 See *SE* i, pp. 173–246.

35 Ibid. 218–21; Munk and Munk, *Edut ne'emanah*, 89; Hayim Ozer Grodzinski, *She'elot uteshuvot aḥiezer* (Jerusalem, 1986), iv, no. 17. According to Weinberg, only a few communities actually made use of this *heter*. See *SE* i, p. 376.

36 *SE* i, pp. 226–7. See also the text of the Vereinigung's statement in Unna, *Lema'an ha'aḥdut*, 56–7.

37 *SE* i, pp. 228–31. Landau was not only adamant that Weinberg was correct and that his opponents' view would lead thousands to consume non-kosher poultry, but he also argued that it was improper for *anyone* to adopt a private stringency. This latter point was opposed by both Weinberg (ibid. 194, 245) and Grodzinski (ibid. 220; *Letters*, i. 89), who assumed that the especially pious would choose not to rely on any leniencies.

38 *SE* i, p. 235.

39 Ibid. 235–7.

40 Ibid. 237–8; Unna, *Sho'alin vedorshin* (Tel Aviv, 1964), no. 19.

41 *SE* i, pp. 238–45. R. Hayim Eleazar Shapira was careful to point out that he would take no stand on the issue, since he saw valid points on both sides; ibid. 223–6. It is therefore strange that Weinberg, ibid. 245, cites him in support of his *heter*.

42 Menahem Mendel Kirschbaum, *Menaḥem meshiv*, ii. 405–12 (found in Kirschbaum's *Tsiyun limenaḥem* (New York, 1965)).

43 *SE* i, p. 222.

Hermann Klein of Berlin,[44] Jonah Zvi Horovitz of Frankfurt,[45] Moses Samson Wasserman of Breslau (d. 1962),[46] Menahem Mendel Kirschbaum of Frankfurt (1895–1943),[47] and Nahum Wiedenfeld of Dombrowa (1874–1940).[48]

The motives of those opposing Weinberg were not purely halakhic in nature, but also took into account wider, subjective considerations, which are generally brought to bear in halakhic decision-making. Because such non-formal considerations are not grounded in explicit texts and cannot be refuted in the fashion of traditional halakhic argumentation, they may be referred to as 'meta-halakhic' considerations. As an example of such meta-halakhah, Klein argued that if the rabbis were to agree with Weinberg, then both the Jewish masses and the Nazis would conclude that in difficult times all is permissible. This could in turn lead the Nazis to even harsher decrees. Horovitz offered similar reasons for his opposition. For example, he was concerned that if the rabbis gave permission to eat poultry in accordance with the Nazi decree, the masses would eventually be led to eat meat which had been stunned before *sheḥitah*. He also feared departing from traditional Jewish practice and, like Rozin, believed that the decree would eventually be rescinded. Finally, in a 'pure' halakhic argument, Horovitz claimed that the situation in Germany was one of religious persecution (*shemad*), with the gentiles intending to force the Jews to violate their religion. According to the halakhah, in such periods no compromises are allowed.[49]

With the exception of the last point made by Horovitz, all these arguments are meta-halakhic. They are not subject to proof or disproof on the basis of textual sources, but depend on an overall view of which halakhic ruling will best serve the community—a view which other authorities need not share. Opposition to altering the method of slaughter because of fears about how it will affect future decisions of the government or the Jewish citizenry is clearly different from opposition to this step because the food is thereby rendered non-kosher.

In this case, those rabbis who regarded a strict ruling as essential in order to prevent the breakdown of fundamental religious boundaries, and who felt that halakhic texts by themselves could not adequately support this ruling, were forced to resort to the meta-halakhic considerations mentioned above. It was these very considerations which were decisively refuted by Unna, who also added a meta-halakhic consideration of his own, directed against those 'whose stringency is in reality a leniency'. He feared that thousands of Jews would begin to eat non-kosher food if they were not permitted to eat poultry slaughtered in accordance with Weinberg's *heter*. The rabbis who were strict would have to answer on Judgement Day and explain why, because of their hesitations, they had allowed an entire country to forsake the Torah's commandments. As for the suggestion that the Nazi

[44] Ibid. 221–2. He does, however, agree that the sick can rely on Weinberg's *heter*.

[45] Ibid. 237–8, 377.

[46] *She'elat moshe* (Tel Aviv, 1957), no. 85.

[47] *Menaḥem meshiv*, ii, nos. 1–3.

[48] *SE* i, pp. 399–405.

[49] See *Sanhedrin* 74*a–b*; Maimonides, *Mishneh torah, Hilkhot yesodei hatorah*, 5: 3.

decrees fell within the category of religious persecution, this was incorrect because Jews were never *required* to eat non-kosher meat. This meant that the anti-*sheḥitah* decree was no different from the removal of teachers from their positions or the boycott of Jewish shops. It was simply another way to oppress the Jews, but was not to be regarded as *religious* persecution.[50]

Weinberg responded strongly to those who disputed with him, agreeing with a number of points made by Unna.[51] In a letter to one rabbi who had pointed out that certain leading rabbinic figures did not accept Weinberg's position, the latter freely admitted that one could find halakhists who opposed him, but added:

> Are you too stubborn to rely on an explicit ruling with which Rabbi Hayim Ozer Grodzinski, the Gaon of Munkács, and other sages have agreed? If you wish to adopt a personal stringency you may, and there is no need to seek out leading authorities upon which to base this stringency. However, where others are concerned, and where it is a matter of life and death for many and there is the possibility, God forbid, of them stumbling into sin, in this situation you have no right to be stringent.[52]

The issue of quadrupeds was much more complicated. It was generally believed by Orthodox halakhists and laity that stunning an animal before slaughter rendered it non-kosher. Indeed, any interference with the slaughtering process was regarded as unacceptable, and in former years the leading German rabbis had refused to permit any procedure which caused the animal to become senseless before slaughter.[53] Another factor complicating matters was that the Berlin Gemeinde was considering purchasing non-kosher meat for community institutions such as the hospital and old-age homes. Although the Gemeinde leadership was dominated by Reform members, the *kashrut* of its institutions had always been under the supervision of the Orthodox. However, since meat was believed to be essential for the diets of the sick and elderly, the Gemeinde leadership felt that it no longer had any choice but to serve non-kosher meat. Furthermore, it was clear that many of the non-Orthodox Jews who up until this time had observed the dietary laws were not prepared to give up meat. They would instead purchase the non-kosher variety unless some halakhically valid method was found to permit stunning before slaughter.[54]

This was the situation facing Weinberg and his colleagues on the Halakhah

[50] *SE* i, pp. 238, 387. See also the comments of R. Efraim Lassmann, ibid. 134, 139, and R. Leib Rubin, ibid. 226. All these writers agreed that the German government had no interest in forcing Jews to violate religious laws. Lassmann even argued that the 1935 Nuremberg legislation forbidding marriages between Jews and Germans strengthened Judaism more than anything done by the rabbinate. For more positive comments regarding this aspect of the Nuremberg laws, see Fuchs, *Holocaust*, 14–15, and Moses Avigdor Amiel, *Linevukhei hatekufah* (Brooklyn, NY, 1980), 310.

[51] *SE* i, pp. 245–6.

[52] Ibid. 245.

[53] See Munk and Munk, *Edut ne'emanah*, 29, 34–6, eid., *Shechita*, 55–67, and the responsum by Hoffmann published in *Hama'ayan*, 34 (Tevet 5754 [1994]), 10–12.

[54] *SE* i, p. 6; Weinberg's letter to Grodzinski published in my 'Between East and West', 323.

Commission of the Vereinigung Traditionell-Gesetztreuer Rabbiner Deutschlands. They decided to turn to the leading halakhic authorities of eastern Europe to see if there was some way, under these trying circumstances, that stunning could be permitted. They were not joined in this appeal by the members of the separatist-oriented Verband Orthodoxer Rabbiner, who adamantly rejected all attempts at finding a way to alter the system of ritual slaughter.

As the Vereinigung's leading halakhist, Weinberg was chosen to travel to the east and discuss the situation with prominent scholars. He left Berlin in September 1933, journeying first to Marienbad, Czechoslovakia, where many of the east European rabbis took their holidays. Following this he travelled to Kovno, where he spoke to Rabbi Abraham Shapiro, the rabbi of Kovno, and Rabbi Joseph Susmanovitz of Slobodka, the son-in-law of Rabbi Moshe Mordechai Epstein and a leading scholar in his own right. From Kovno he went to Cracow, and from there to Lublin and Warsaw, where once again he found himself in the midst of controversy.

Rabbi Dr Meier Hildesheimer, Weinberg's close friend and one of the directors of the Berlin seminary, had recently travelled to Warsaw to confer with Orthodox Jewish leaders in an unsuccessful attempt to persuade them not to join the anti-German boycott. His visit was supposed to have been secret, but the local Jewish newspapers soon found out about it. These newspapers reviled him as an agent of the Nazis, helping to doom the mission. Although Hildesheimer was forthright in explaining that a boycott would have a negative impact on the German Jewish community, and this was certainly his firm belief, it was not known that his journey to the east had been undertaken after a warning from the government that if nothing were done to halt the boycott movement in Poland, there would be repercussions against German Jewry.[55]

Although Weinberg tried to keep his visit a secret, it too was exposed. The newspapers reported that he had come to Poland for the same purpose as Hildesheimer, and he was branded an agent of Hitler.[56] This forced Weinberg to state publicly that his trip had no connection with Hildesheimer.[57] Despite this disavowal, he still thought it wise to curtail his visit, though not before he had a chance to travel to Vilna in order to confer with Grodzinski. Grodzinski made it clear to Weinberg that he would not consider the halakhic permissibility of stunning until all possible halakhic objections had been satisfied. This was Weinberg's job in the responsum

55 See *Der Israelit*, 20 Sept. 1934, 9; *Haynt* (Warsaw), 17 Sept. 1933, 7 (interview with Hildesheimer); Binyamin Ze'ev Jacobson, *Esa de'i lemeraḥok* (Benei Berak, 1967), 123–4; interview with Esriel Hildesheimer (son of Meier); Appendix II.

56 See *Naye Folkstsaytung* (Warsaw), 22 Sept. 1933, 5; 23 Sept. 1933, 5 (Weinberg is referred to as 'der Hitler-Rabbiner'); *Unzer Lebn* (Białystok), 24 Sept. 1933, 2; *Nasz Przegląd* (Warsaw), 24 Sept. 1933, 7; *Lubliner Togblat*, 24 Sept. 1933; 25 Sept. 1933; *Yidishe Togblat* (Warsaw), 27 Sept. 1933, 6.

57 See *Lubliner Togblat*, 20 Sept. 1933 (interview with Weinberg); 27 Sept. 1933 (declaration by R. Meir Shapiro); *Unzer Lebn*, 28 Sept. 1933, 4; *Naye Folkstsaytung*, 9 Oct. 1933, 2 (Weinberg's letter).

he was to compose. However, even assuming that Weinberg could satisfy the halakhic objections, Grodzinski indicated that his decision would still have to take into account the fact that the *sheḥitah* problem did not affect German Jews alone. He feared that any lenient ruling on stunning could endanger the *sheḥitah status quo* in other countries and lead to widespread legislation mandating stunning.[58]

The other leading halakhists agreed with Grodzinski that they should withhold their opinions until Weinberg had prepared a complete halakhic analysis of the issue. This analysis would have to confront the fact that stunning damaged an animal in a number of ways, apparently rendering it non-kosher. The Orthodox doctor Salomon Lieben of Prague had enumerated the following halakhic problems resulting from stunning: (1) internal injury caused by the animal's collapse; (2) damage to the brain; (3) damage to the lung tissue and the adhesions of the lung; (4) blood being absorbed in the organs; (5) signs of injury on the animal's bowels; (6) blood being found in the heart tissue, indicating that the heart is weakened by the electric current.[59]

Before Weinberg studied this complex issue, he was faced with some fundamental questions as to whether it was even desirable to try to find a halakhic way of permitting stunning. Should the method of slaughter which had been practised for thousands of years by the religion which taught the world about kindness to animals be abandoned because of antisemitic pressure? If Jews began to stun animals before slaughtering, would this not be an admission that *sheḥitah* was inhumane?

These were weighty considerations, and at first Weinberg was prepared to issue a ruling with other German rabbis entirely forbidding stunning. Yet he soon changed his mind, emphasizing that the meta-halakhic considerations just mentioned did not compare to the threat that thousands of Jews might begin to consume non-kosher meat. Furthermore, he added, 'it is up to the leaders of Israel to show that they are not unyielding, God forbid, but that they too share in their people's pain and will do all they can to reach the gates of deliverance'.[60] Having come to the conclusion that stunning should be permitted if there were halakhic grounds to do so, Weinberg set to work on his lengthy responsum, which was to be sent out to leading rabbinic figures throughout the world.[61]

In this responsum, which is actually a lengthy treatise, Weinberg advanced a number of reasons in support of a *heter*. Weinberg himself did not declare that stunning was permitted, for his purpose was only to present a case to the leading halakhists, not to issue a practical ruling. Nevertheless, he was fully confident that with modern methods of stunning the animal would not be rendered non-kosher,

[58] *SE* i, pp. 6, 370–1, 376.

[59] Ibid. 4–5.

[60] Ibid. 7; translation in Robert Kirschner, *Rabbinic Responsa of the Holocaust Era* (New York, 1985), 49.

[61] *SE* i, pp. 6–8, 370, 375; Weinberg's letter to R. Isak Unna, dated 20 Nov. 1933.

and all of his arguments led in this direction.[62] Yet even with these arguments in favour of leniency, Weinberg was convinced that the leading halakhists, the hasidim, and a large percentage of the Orthodox masses would never agree to alter the time-honoured practice of *sheḥitah*. This was something that their ritual instinct would not permit.[63]

Almost every rabbi who responded to Weinberg opposed any change in the traditional method of *sheḥitah*, under all circumstances. Rabbi Elhanan Wasserman (1875–1941), Rabbi Aaron Kotler (1892–1962), and the rabbinate of the Frankfurt separatist community even argued that stunning should not be used when slaughtering animals for those who were medically required to consume meat. The rationale behind this extreme view was that any such *heter* might also lead healthy people to eat meat from animals which had been stunned. Furthermore, foreign governments would conclude that stunning is not really forbidden, endangering *sheḥitah* in other countries.[64]

The pressure against change was so great that those who initially agreed with Weinberg later retracted their opinions when confronted with the weight of opposing rabbinic authority. Many of those who opposed Weinberg's lenient position did so not because they disagreed with his halakhic conclusions, but because they were afraid to assume responsibility for such an important decision. Others were not even interested in his halakhic argumentation, since nothing could persuade them to acquiesce in altering the method of *sheḥitah*. This was especially true with regard to Grodzinski, who had initially suggested that Weinberg should write a responsum on the topic.

At first, Grodzinski had been prepared to examine Weinberg's responsum impartially. He also made it clear that he would not oppose any leniencies granted by the German rabbinate, unless his opinion was solicited in an official manner.[65] Even if the German rabbinate asked for his decision and he issued a stringent ruling, he saw no need to take a public stand on this issue or to put a stop to slaughterers who were stunning animals. There were many non-Orthodox Jews who would not give up eating meat, and Grodzinski believed that it would be preferable for them to eat meat of questionable *kashrut* than to eat meat which was definitely non-kosher. As already noted, in his responsum concerning the slaughter of poultry,

[62] See his interview in *Lubliner Togblat*, 20 Sept. 1933. In *SE* i, p. 7, and Munk and Munk, *Edut ne'emanah*, 248 (letter from 1960), he wrote that he was unable to dispel all doubts, since the scientific tests were inconclusive. However, Weinberg did not show any such hesitation regarding the scientific tests during the crisis of 1933 and, on the contrary, was confident in the correctness of his view. Certainly, as we shall see, he was not being candid when he remarked, 'I attempted to find a leniency, but was unsuccessful' (*Edut ne'emanah*, 248).

[63] *SE* i, pp. 6–7, iii, p. 285; Weinberg's letter to R. Moses Schlesinger, dated 9 June 1932.

[64] See Munk and Munk, *Edut ne'emanah*, 203–9, 217–23.

[65] See also ibid. 43, 45, for letters from Grodzinski written in 1927 in which he regards the stunning issue, which was a pressing concern even in the pre-Hitler era, as an internal German affair. In fact, he writes that if the rabbis of one German state are forced to issue a lenient ruling, they should not request the approval of rabbis in other states, for any such approval could endanger *sheḥitah* there.

Grodzinski wrote that it was incumbent upon the halakhist to find any and all grounds to be lenient in order to prevent Jews from giving up kosher food. Furthermore, in a letter written in 1927 he argued that stunning should be permitted in extreme circumstances if the halakhic issues could be resolved.[66]

However, he soon adopted an entirely different approach. At the same time that Weinberg was publicly expressing his 'regret' that a halakhically permissible method of stunning had not yet been developed, Grodzinski was declaring his opposition to stunning no matter what new medical tests might reveal. In order not to give rise to any false hopes, he opposed the continuation of these tests and would not even consider what Weinberg had to say. As far as he was concerned, there was simply nothing to discuss. He also attempted, ultimately with success, to prevent Weinberg from publishing his treatise. (Had the treatise already been published, he would have wanted Weinberg to insert a note stating that, since the leading Torah scholars had rejected stunning, all of his arguments must remain theoretical.)[67]

According to Weinberg, Grodzinski abandoned his earlier view after being confronted with the burgeoning anti-*sheḥitah* movement in eastern Europe.[68] Grodzinski now realized that any decision to permit stunning in Germany—even a decision by the Reform movement—was not simply an internal German matter. The implications were much greater, for any such decision would be regarded by east European governments as a green light to ban *sheḥitah* without prior stunning in their own countries, no matter what the local Orthodox rabbis said. This consideration had not been present earlier.

Weinberg also pointed to the great pressure brought to bear upon Grodzinski by rabbis in both Germany and eastern Europe, who were adamant that Weinberg's arguments should be rejected outright. These men flooded Grodzinski with letters and telegrams. For his part, Grodzinski denied that his opinion was influenced by any such factors. In order to ensure that Weinberg's arguments for a *heter* would make no progress, he asked the leading east European rabbis not to respond to Weinberg. Rather, they were to send any comments regarding his responsum to Grodzinski himself. The logic behind this would seem to have been that in the event that a halakhist did express support for Weinberg, Grodzinski would then have been able to pressure him to change his position without Weinberg knowing anything about it. The result would be a unanimous negative reply to Weinberg's responsum.

That the views in opposition to Weinberg were based more on emotional and

[66] Munk and Munk, *Edut ne'emanah*, 43.

[67] With regard to stunning *after sheḥitah*, with which there are no real halakhic problems, Grodzinski was prepared to be lenient; see his *Letters*, i. 98. He obviously did not believe that this *heter* would have the negative repercussions he so feared when discussing stunning before *sheḥitah*. Whether an animal could be struck on the head after *sheḥitah* had been disputed by Hirsch and Hildeshimer. See Esriel Hildesheimer, 'A Selection of Letters between Rabbi Esriel Hildesheimer and Rabbi Samson Raphael Hirsch and his Supporters' (Heb.), *Yad sha'ul*, 248–51; Eliav, *Hildesheimer Briefe*, 226–8.

[68] On Poland, see Szymon Rudnicki, 'Ritual Slaughter as a Political Issue', *Polin*, 7 (1992), 147–60.

political considerations—meta-halakhah—than on pure halakhic analysis was privately acknowledged by Weinberg, as well as by some of his colleagues, both during the crisis and years later. Although in his letters Grodzinski continuously claimed that there were halakhic difficulties with stunning before *sheḥitah*, he never elaborated on them, despite repeated requests to do so. Weinberg quoted a private conversation in which Grodzinski told him that the leading halakhic scholars were unable to refute his view on halakhic grounds, but were still afraid to grant permission to stun. In a post-war communication Weinberg claimed that these scholars were motivated by three factors: (1) a general religious conservatism; (2) the view that any acquiescence in altering the method of *sheḥitah* would be used by antisemites to bolster their claim that the standard *sheḥitah* procedure was inhumane; (3) a refusal to cave in to the demands of antisemites who were intent on destroying Jewish religious life. However, during the crisis this information about the meta-halakhic basis of the opposition to stunning was kept quiet so as to prevent a weakening of rabbinic authority. When Reform leaders, in an attack on the Orthodox, also asserted that the opponents of stunning were motivated by other than pure halakhic reasons, Weinberg strongly denied this. Similarly, in a letter to the Central Office of Sheḥitah Affairs, Weinberg again denied that the opposition to stunning was based on anything other than formal halakhic sources.

Because Weinberg knew that many rabbis *were* basing their positions on meta-halakhic considerations, and because he did not wish this to become public knowledge, he was alarmed after reading an article by Rabbi Ezra Munk (1867–1940) which he believed could foster this impression. He even feared that some halakhists, who were supposed to examine the evidence impartially, might be swayed from ruling leniently because of the reasons advanced in Munk's article. As for his own public statement that stunning was absolutely forbidden, in a private letter he admitted that this did not represent his true view but was only intended for public consumption.[69]

Weinberg and his colleagues on the Halakhah Commission of the Vereinigung were hopeful that Grodzinski and other leading east European scholars could be persuaded to grant permission to stun. Even after Grodzinski publicly declared his

[69] For documentation of the preceding paragraphs see *SE* i, pp. 7, 122–3, 219, 371, 378–80, 382, 386; Weinberg's letters to Unna, R. Isaac Herzog, and Saul Weingort, published in my 'Between East and West', 306–10, 339; Julius Jakobovits's letters, published ibid. 297–8, 301–3; Weinberg's letter to Pinhas Biberfeld, dated 8 Apr. 1959; Weinberg's letter to Hillel Medalié, dated 7 Jan. 1954; Weinberg's letter to Unna, dated 4 May 1934; Weinberg's declaration in *Der Israelit*, 17 May 1934, 2; Munk and Munk, *Edut ne'emanah*, 123, 175, 176, 181, 184, 187, 190, 193, 218, 302; Munk and Munk, *Shechita*, 64–6; Grodzinski, *Letters*, ii. 358; id., *She'elot uteshuvot aḥiezer*, iv, no. 16; Grodzinski's telegram of 21 Oct. 1931 to Ezra Munk, Agudath Israel of America Archives, box B33 (II/10); Grodzinski's letter of 17 Apr. 1932 to Unna, Institute for Holocaust Research, Bar-Ilan University, File 102/3:18; Greenberg, *One of the Great Ones*, 2 (unpaginated). According to the last-mentioned source, Weinberg believed that because of his responsum the halakhists who opposed stunning could declare it forbidden, but were not able to say that stunned meat was *nevelah* (from an animal not ritually slaughtered).

opposition, they still hoped that he might change his mind. During the two years following the anti-*sheḥitah* decree, Weinberg and his colleagues corresponded with scholars in the east and travelled there to plead their case in person. Although they were unable to persuade anyone to issue a halakhic ruling permitting stunning, Weinberg was still hopeful, as he wrote in May 1934 to Isak Unna, that the east European scholars would accept a scenario whereby 'the German rabbis will themselves issue a *heter* and they [the east European halakhists] will not protest'. However, once Grodzinski made it clear that nothing could persuade him to alter his decision to oppose stunning publicly, no other east European scholar would dare contradict him on this matter. Weinberg did not now see any purpose in further delegations of German rabbis journeying to the east.[70]

Although Grodzinski probably believed that this put an end to the issue, this was not the case. There was still the possibility that Weinberg would unilaterally issue a ruling permitting stunning. Indeed, in previous years he had argued that the Halakhah Commission of the Vereinigung should issue rulings even if they would not be accepted by all segments of the Orthodox population. However, the *sheḥitah* issue was much more delicate, since any unilateral *heter* would have brought about a split within German Orthodoxy. It would also have caused east European Jews to question the *kashrut* of German meat.

Furthermore, there is no doubt that a lenient ruling on Weinberg's part would have brought him into open conflict with Grodzinski, who, despite his friendship with Weinberg, would have been forced to take steps to delegitimize the latter's authority. When questioned as to whether he would rule against Grodzinski, Weinberg responded that he would need to think long and hard about this, but as Rabbi Julius Jakobovits perceptively added, 'I understood from his words that at present he is not ready to do so.' Indeed, it was precisely because Weinberg realized the global nature of the problem that he was reluctant to issue a ruling independently, insisting instead that the world's leading halakhists should be consulted.[71]

For those who knew Weinberg, it was a foregone conclusion that he would not unilaterally issue a halakhic ruling while facing such opposition in the east. To do so would have meant standing alone, since even those scholars who might have agreed with him would not dare challenge Grodzinski's authority. However, there was one more avenue to explore—Palestine. The only other rabbinic figure with the stature to oppose Grodzinski was Chief Rabbi Kook, and a lenient opinion from him would have been supported by the many scholars of Palestine who were under his influence.

[70] Weinberg's letter to Unna, dated 4 May 1934; Munk and Munk, *Edut ne'emanah*, 177, 181. On the refusal of scholars to take issue with Grodzinski on this matter, see also Unna, *Sho'alin vedorshin*, no. 21.

[71] Weinberg's letter to Moses Schlesinger, published in my 'Between East and West', 277–8; Julius Jakobovits's letter, published ibid. 297–8; Biberfeld, 'In Memory', 31.

With this in mind, Weinberg wrote to Kook twice at the end of 1934.[72] He hoped that Kook would have 'mercy' on the German Jews who were spending great amounts of money to import meat, on the many families who had already given up kosher meat, and on the many more who would do so if a solution was not found. As Weinberg put it, Kook had to decide if it was proper to allow thousands of Jews to consume non-kosher meat because of fear of what *might* occur in other lands.[73] There is no question that Weinberg regarded this approach as improper, but as he explained, 'we who are inside [Germany] cannot take upon ourselves the responsibility [for issuing a lenient ruling]'. For some unknown reason—perhaps Grodzinski was responsible—Kook never responded to either of Weinberg's letters.

Without any support from Kook, Grodzinski's view could not be opposed. Unlike some of his colleagues,[74] Weinberg resigned himself to the fact that there would be no permission given to stun, regardless of what new technologies were developed. Therefore, even though his responsum *did* advance grounds to permit stunning, in response to enquiries he was forced to deny this. He also let it be known that the Berlin Rabbinical Seminary unequivocally supported Grodzinski. Weinberg himself, in a speech to his surprised colleagues, even presented the meta-halakhic reasons behind Grodzinski's opposition to any leniency.[75] When Weinberg eventually did publish his responsum after the war, he was careful to point out that his arguments in favour of leniency were not intended for practical application.[76] Still, there is no doubt that he was sure of the correctness of his view. In line with this he noted that, if the problem should arise again, the halakhists confronting it would concentrate on his arguments in favour of leniency, not on his

[72] Shapiro, *Igerot lare'iyah*, no. 347.

[73] The same point is made in R. Jacob Hoffmann's letter to Grodzinski, *SE* i, p. 123. See also the lengthy letters of R. Efraim Lassmann, ibid. 123–40.

[74] See Unna, *Sho'alin vedorshin*, no. 21, who as late as 1938 was still pleading with the foremost halakhists to permit stunning. He specifically asked Grodzinski to permit stunning with nitrogen, based upon the positive results of tests that had been carried out in Stockholm. Arguing in the same fashion as did Weinberg in his letter to Kook, Unna attempted to convince Grodzinski that fear of what *might* occur in other countries if permission were given to stun in this fashion could not outweigh the facts of the present, namely, that thousands had been led to abandon *kashrut*. Although in his response to Unna (Institute for Holocaust Research, Bar-Ilan University, File 102/7:18) and in a letter to R. Isaac Herzog (*Edut ne'emanah*, 302) Grodzinski promised to examine the results of the Stockholm tests, since any permission, even for nitrogen stunning, threatened far-reaching repercussions, it is hardly likely that he could ever have agreed to permit such stunning. See also Simeon Federbush, *Binetivot hatalmud* (Jerusalem, 1957), 215–16, for R. Solomon David Kahana's responsum on the topic. Kahana admitted that there was no formal halakhic objection to stunning with nitrogen, but, adopting Grodzinski's approach, argued that there were meta-halakhic reasons, in this case political in nature, which ruled out a lenient decision. See also Kirschbaum, *Menaḥem meshiv*, ii, no. 33, for a responsum of 1937 in which he argued for the permissibility of nitrogen stunning.

[75] See Munk and Munk, *Edut ne'emanah*, 178–80, 183; eid., *Shechita*, 65–6.

[76] See *SE* i, p. 7.

words of caution regarding the practical implementation of his view. If that should happen, Weinberg asserted, 'I am sure they will agree with my opinion.'[77]

Weinberg and his colleagues in the Vereinigung did not slacken in their efforts, which lasted for over two years, until it became obvious that neither Grodzinski nor any of the other leading halakhists would support them. Yet in Germany as well there was significant opposition to Weinberg's lenient approach. The separatist-oriented Verband Orthodoxer Rabbiner made it very clear that it would never agree to permit stunning. In its eyes, all the complicated scientific tests being carried out were a waste of time. The members of the Verband agreed with Grodzinski that no matter what could be established halakhically, there were important meta-halakhic reasons why stunning could not be permitted.[78]

The leader of the Verband was Rabbi Jonah Zvi Horovitz, originally from Hungary and now rabbi of the Frankfurt separatist community. At the same time that Weinberg was sending copies of his responsum on stunning to leading east European halakhists, Horovitz was sending letters on behalf of the Verband urging these halakhists, 'for the sake of the eternity of the Torah', not to issue any rulings with regard either to stunning or to severing of the heads of poultry before *sheḥitah*, unless enquiries had been made of them by Germany's two Orthodox rabbinic organizations.[79] By insisting that both organizations should be represented in any appeal, he was effectively precluding the possibility that there would ever be such an appeal. Needless to say, it was very difficult for any halakhist to rule leniently on the stunning question after being confronted with the fact that even German rabbis were expressing their opposition to such a step. Weinberg himself was aware of a number of rabbis who, because of Horovitz's intervention, refused to involve themselves in the matter—which was precisely Horovitz's intention.[80]

Weinberg's response to Horovitz came in a strongly worded letter to Isak Unna. From this letter we see how incensed he was that Horovitz felt free to interfere in the affairs of rabbis who were not members of his organization.[81] Even more offensive to Weinberg was Horovitz's implication that those who were looking for a way to permit stunning were in some way at odds with the eternity of the Torah. Furthermore, for Horovitz to speak of rabbis who were 'trying to find leniencies in order to alter the traditional method of ritual slaughter' was equally slanderous, because it was the Nazis, not the rabbis, who were responsible for altering the

[77] See Leo Jung's eulogy in *No'am*, 10 (1967), 11 (quoting Weinberg's oral remark); Greenberg, *One of the Great Ones*, 3.

[78] As with Grodzinski, their position hardened over time. At the very beginning of the crisis they issued a joint statement with the Vereinigung, promising that efforts to develop a halakhically acceptable method of stunning would continue. See *Der Israelit*, 30 May 1933, 5.

[79] *SE* i, p. 374.

[80] *SE* i, pp. 111, 375, 382; Weinberg's letter to Herzog, published in my 'Between East and West', 310–11; David Menahem Mainish Babad, *Ḥavatselet hasharon* (Bilgoraj, 1938), no. 25.

[81] *SE* i, pp. 374–7. See also R. Jacob Horovitz's letter published in my 'Between East and West', 304–5, and Weinberg's letter to Unna, dated 17 May 1934. In Ch. 4 attention was drawn to the separatists' belief that they were the true representatives of Orthodoxy.

traditional method. Weinberg and his colleagues were simply forced to deal with this situation in order to try and prevent Germany's Jews from turning to non-kosher meat.

As Weinberg correctly observed, according to Horovitz there was no reason for him to have taken the trouble of composing his lengthy halakhic treatise or of discussing the matter with the leading east European scholars, since by definition no modification of the traditional method of *sheḥitah* could ever be sanctioned. Horovitz's other reasons (fear that a lenient ruling would be improperly extended by the masses and fear of a split in the Jewish community) were also dismissed out of hand by Weinberg, for once again, if these reasons were to be accepted then by definition there was no way that a lenient ruling could ever be issued, and thus no need for any halakhic analysis. This, of course, was exactly Horovitz's point; he was even more extreme than Grodzinski, for the latter agreed with Weinberg on the question of severing the heads of poultry. The Weinberg–Horovitz dispute provides a clear demonstration of the differences between those who were concerned with the wider community and wished to prevent its members from eating non-kosher meat, and the separatist Orthodox, who rejected any compromises in religious standards designed to make life easier for those whose commitment to halakhah was not absolute.

THE SEMINARY IN SEARCH OF A REFUGE

At the same time that discussions about the *sheḥitah* issue were going on, Weinberg was once again confronted by Grodzinski, this time over plans to transfer the Berlin Rabbinical Seminary to Palestine.[82] Although Weinberg did not play a central role in this episode, it must be discussed for the further insight it gives into the relationship between east European talmudists and the modern rabbinical seminary.

In the winter of 1933 Meier Hildesheimer, the son of Esriel and one of the directors of the seminary, visited Palestine in order to lay the groundwork for the

[82] For an earlier treatment of this episode, see Daniel R. Schwartz, 'Early but Opposed—Supported but Late: Two Berlin Seminaries Which Attempted to Move Abroad', *LBIYB* 36 (1991), 267–83. Fortunately, I have obtained important unpublished material which was unavailable to Schwartz, allowing my presentation to complement his. (Only the last four pages of Schwartz's article are actually devoted to the transfer of the Seminary. The rest of the article discusses the relationship between the German Orthodox and their east European counterparts. Although I agree with the main thrust of what he writes, one point must be made in opposition to Schwartz's presentation. While it is true, as Schwartz points out, that many east European talmudists were contemptuous of the halakhic learning of German rabbis, Weinberg was never challenged in this regard and these talmudists never considered him a 'German' rabbi. The sole example Schwartz quotes in support of his mistaken contention to the contrary is the dispute between Rozin and Weinberg discussed in Ch. 4. Schwartz writes: 'This episode showed Weinberg—the Seminary's Lithuanian credentials, so to speak—being treated highhandedly by a Lithuanian rabbi as if he were a virtually negligible German rabbi.' As I have already noted, Rozin was anything but typical and he showed the same disdain for his eminent Lithuanian colleagues as he did for Weinberg.)

seminary's move. With the Nazis in power, Hildesheimer believed that Jewish life could not productively continue in Germany and that there was no reason for the seminary to remain there. Furthermore, he was convinced that moving the seminary to Palestine would have a strong impact on the development of religious life in the Holy Land. Although Hildesheimer and his colleagues realized that this plan would meet with opposition from the extreme Orthodox elements in Palestine who opposed any sort of modern education, they mistakenly believed that the opposition would not include men of more moderate leanings such as Grodzinski.

Yet when news of the prospective transfer first became known, Grodzinski began taking steps to prevent it. In his letter to Hildesheimer urging him to abandon the plan, he agreed that when the elder Hildesheimer had established the seminary it was an excellent idea and had done a great deal to strengthen Orthodoxy in Germany. However, Grodzinski continued, the elder Hildesheimer's idea of training rabbis who would also be secularly educated was only an emergency measure, designed to protect German Orthodoxy from the inroads of Reform. In Palestine, which already had great yeshivot and faced no Reform menace, there was no need for a 'factory' to produce rabbis for whom secular studies would be primary and Torah study secondary.[83]

Although he was very friendly with Hildesheimer, Grodzinski informed him that 'the truth is to be loved above all else'. He left no doubt that he would not back down but would do all in his power to thwart Hildesheimer's plan. In this approach, which came as a complete surprise to Hildesheimer, Grodzinski showed his total opposition to the Torah im Derekh Eretz philosophy as being anything more than a measure of last resort, designed to salvage what was left of crumbling Orthodox communities. As he made clear, this situation did not exist in Palestine.[84] In a letter to Kook, Grodzinski further revealed his hostility when he referred to the proposed establishment of the seminary in Palestine as 'a foreign plant in the vineyard of the House of Israel in the Holy Land, planting there the German culture which has already struck many dead, and we saw what it brought them'.[85]

Grodzinski proceeded to engage in a vigorous campaign of opposition to Hildesheimer's plan, writing to the leading rabbis in Germany and Palestine and urging them to tell Hildesheimer of their objections to the seminary's

[83] Supporters of the seminary always denied that it was a 'rabbi factory', and in his address at the seminary's inauguration Esriel Hildesheimer stressed that his institution would not degenerate into this role. See *Jahres-Bericht des Rabbiner-Seminars für das orthodoxe Judenthum pro 5634 (1873–74)*, 87. It is worth noting, however, that in their appeal for German Jews to aid the yeshivot of the east, Meier Hildesheimer, Joseph Wohlgemuth, and Weinberg felt constrained to point out that these yeshivot were *not* rabbi factories. See *Die Jüdische Presse*, 11 June 1920, Hebrew supplement. The obvious implication is that the yeshiva with which the German Orthodox were familiar—the seminary—*was* popularly regarded in this way. Grodzinski also referred to the Warsaw Tahkemoni Seminary as a rabbi factory; see his letter in *Orayta*, 14 (1984), 215. (See also Shapiro, *Igerot lare'iyah*, 335, where, in a different context, Grodzinski used the term *bet ḥaroshet* (factory) in a sarcastic manner.)

[84] Grodzinski, *Letters*, ii, no. 290.

[85] Shapiro, *Igerot lare'iyah*, 458 (translation in Schwartz, 'Early but Opposed', 281).

transfer.[86] This led Rabbi Reuven Katz (1880–1963), the chief rabbi of Petah Tikvah, and one not given to any sort of extremism, to write an article listing numerous reasons why the seminary should not be transferred. From this article, which quotes excerpts from one of Grodzinski's letters to Katz, we see once again how fearful Grodzinski was of the basic characteristics of German Orthodoxy.[87]

Both Weinberg and Hildesheimer responded to Grodzinski. On 20 December 1933, Weinberg wrote to him, acknowledging his own opposition to the transfer of the seminary and expressing his belief that Hildesheimer's efforts were doomed to failure. However, he added that his opposition was based on different considerations from those that motivated Grodzinski. Weinberg did not reveal what these considerations were, although they were probably related to his often-expressed belief that the situation in Germany would soon improve.

Weinberg took great exception to Grodzinski's negative comments about the seminary; he simply did not understand why the latter had such an unfavourable opinion. In particular, he was upset by Grodzinski's use of the phrase 'rabbi factory' to describe the seminary. On the contrary, Weinberg replied, it was the seminary which instilled the love of Torah into German Jewry and influenced many young Jews to study at the east European yeshivot. Demonstrating his complete identification with the institution, Weinberg asserted that the seminary glorified God's name and battled against ignorance and heresy with more success than the heads of yeshivot in Lithuania and Poland. There was no reason why such a positive influence should not continue in Palestine.

Rather than being denigrated as a 'rabbi factory', Weinberg continued, the seminary should be regarded as a yeshiva in the complete sense of the word. Not only were its standards just as high as those of many east European yeshivot, but it was actually much more difficult to receive rabbinic ordination at the seminary than in the east. As for secular subjects, Weinberg replied that it was true that students at the seminary studied Bible and Jewish history, yet he wondered whether these could in any way be considered 'secular'.[88] Weinberg asked Grodzinski to remember that he was not merely the leader of the yeshivot, but the leader of Orthodoxy as a whole. Because of this, the seminary looked to him to defend it against detractors, not to join in their derision.[89]

Hildesheimer's response was rather different from that of Weinberg.

[86] Grodzinski, *Letters*, ii, nos. 289, 291; Shapiro, *Igerot lare'iyah*, nos. 316, 318, 320, 325; Weinberg's letter to Grodzinski, published in my 'Between East and West', 323–4.

[87] 'Concerning the Rabbinate in Palestine' (Heb.), *Hahed* (Shevat 5694 [1934]), 9–10. Rabbi Binyamin (Yehoshua Radler-Feldman) replied to Katz in this issue of *Hahed*. See also succeeding issues of this journal, where Hildesheimer's plan was the subject of lively debate. Weinberg was greatly irritated by what he regarded as the foolish and insulting manner in which Katz treated the seminary in his article; see Weinberg's letter to Abraham Arazy, dated 28 Feb. 1934.

[88] By saying this Weinberg missed Grodzinski's point, which was that seminary students were also expected to undertake study at the university.

[89] Weinberg's letter to Grodzinski, published in my 'Between East and West', 323–4.

Grodzinski had expressed his amazement that Hildesheimer would embark on such a plan without consulting the leading Torah scholars in Palestine and the Diaspora. He mentioned in particular the Council of Torah Sages of Agudat Yisrael. To this, Hildesheimer responded that he had obtained the permission of Kook, Chief Rabbi Solomon Aronson of Tel Aviv (1863–1935), and many other rabbis who enthusiastically supported the project.[90] As Hildesheimer explained, the prime motivation behind the planned move was that because of the political situation the seminary would soon have no foreign students and very few German students, meaning that it would have to close. However, since the seminary had never regarded itself as an exclusively German institution but viewed its influence as world-wide, it was only natural for it to be relocated.

As for moving to Palestine as opposed to other countries, Hildesheimer stressed the traditional love for the Holy Land. He also showed great foresight in noting that other European lands could also go the way of Germany. Finally, Hildesheimer was convinced that the seminary would be able both to bridge the gap between tradition and modernity then afflicting Palestinian Jewry, and to prevent the establishment of a rabbinical seminary under the auspices of the Hebrew University. Since Grodzinski had argued that the philosophy of the seminary was only valid for a society under siege, this was exactly the point that Hildesheimer picked up, pointing out that the situation in Palestine was ripe for religious disaster if steps were not taken to counter it.[91]

Despite the great initiative shown by Hildesheimer, his plan never came to fruition. The opposition of Grodzinski and the rabbis in Palestine whom he had won over to his side forced even Aronson to abandon his earlier approval.[92]

[90] According to Katz, 'Concerning the Rabbinate', 10, Kook informed him that he only gave his permission for the establishment of a teachers' seminary. Grodzinski asked Kook to clarify his opinion (Shapiro, *Igerot lare'iyah*, 465, 468), but as far as we know this was never done. Dr Esriel Hildesheimer, who accompanied his father to Palestine, informed me that he remembers Kook giving his permission to transfer the seminary, but suggesting that it be established in Tel Aviv, not Jerusalem.

[91] See Hildesheimer's three letters to Grodzinski, published in my 'Between East and West', 312–22. Although Weinberg never actually supported Hildesheimer's plan, it seems that by early 1934 he had been swayed somewhat by Hildesheimer's arguments. He wrote again to Grodzinski, this time mentioning that perhaps it would be better to relocate the seminary in order to prevent the Hebrew University from opening its own rabbinical seminary. He also pointed out that secularly educated rabbis were the wave of the future. The content of Weinberg's letter can be gathered from Grodzinski's response, dated 16 Feb. 1934 and published in *Ḥidushei ba'al 'Seridei esh'*, 578. In Grodzinski's response he toned down the harsh opposition to the characteristics of German Orthodoxy expressed in his letter to Katz. Writing to Weinberg, he agreed that a religious intelligentsia would be a positive factor in Palestine. However, such an intelligentsia must not include the rabbis, who, for the present at least, must remain members of the old school. In a lecture given to celebrate the *aliyah* of a member of the seminary's faculty at the end of 1934, Weinberg expressed the hope that the seminary too would soon be in Palestine, where it would be a blessing for both the land and the people of Israel (*Lifrakim*, 271–2 (324–5)). However, one must understand these words in the utopian sense of 'next year in Jerusalem', i.e. that in messianic days the seminary would be transferred to the Land of Israel.

[92] See his letter to Hildesheimer in Yitshak Alfasi, *The Great Sage* (Tel Aviv, 1985), 116–17.

The opposition of the seminary's board of directors and faculty was also impossible to overcome. Even while Hildesheimer was trying to change Grodzinski's mind, Weinberg, Auerbach, and Grünberg, the seminary's three senior lecturers, wrote to the chief rabbis of Tel Aviv to inform them that it would be unconscionable for the seminary to abandon the Jews of Germany at this time of great spiritual need.[93] Although Hildesheimer continued to advocate his cause, forcing Grodzinski to complain again to Weinberg in June 1934,[94] his efforts were short-lived. In July 1935 he died, and today one can only speculate about how religious life in Palestine–Israel would have developed had he succeeded in his efforts.

Although the seminary was to remain in Berlin, there were soon questions about whether Weinberg would remain there with it. Shortly after the controversy over the seminary's transfer had ended, there was a new turn of events in Weinberg's life. Rabbi Samuel Isaac Hillman (1868–1953) had recently resigned his post as head of the London Beth Din and emigrated to Palestine. In the wake of his departure, the leadership of the United Synagogue of England, together with representatives of the English Federation of Synagogues, began the process of locating a successor. Most people expected that their choice would fall on Rabbi Ezekiel Abramsky (1886–1976), a well-respected scholar who was then rabbi of the London Machazike Hadath congregation. Very few knew that in meetings at the end of October 1934 the United Synagogue leadership had removed Abramsky from active consideration because of their political and personal difficulties with him.[95] This meant that a new man had to be found, who had to be both a reputable halakhist and sensitive to the concerns of those in the wider community, the majority of whom were only nominally Orthodox.

It was Britain's Chief Rabbi Joseph Hertz (1872–1946) who suggested Weinberg. Although he did not know Weinberg personally, and was sure that he did not speak English, he was familiar with Weinberg's reputation. He assumed Weinberg would be a good choice, as he was 'a European celebrity of great culture, respected throughout the orthodox Community of the world'.[96] When asked if he would be interested in the appointment, Weinberg responded in the affirmative. In order to avoid the gossip that would ensue should Weinberg come to London, it was arranged for him to be interviewed at The Hague on 8–9 November by Sir Robert Waley Cohen, at the time first vice-president of the United Synagogue, and Dayan Asher Feldman, a member of the Beth Din.[97]

Upon returning to London after the interview, Cohen gave a very positive

[93] See their letter published in my 'Between East and West', 325–6 (English trans. in Schwartz, 'Early but Opposed', 300–1); Grodzinski, *Letters*, ii. 443.

[94] *SE* i, p. 379.

[95] Honorary Officers of the United Synagogue minutes, 24 and 25 Oct. 1934.

[96] Ibid., 24 Oct. 1934 (Sir Robert Waley Cohen quoting the chief rabbi).

[97] Ibid., 26 Oct. 1934; letters from Hertz to Weinberg, dated 26 Oct. 1934 and 1 Nov. 1934, included with the minutes.

preliminary report of his meeting with Weinberg.[98] In the following week he made a full report of his visit, in which he stated:

Dayan Feldman spent a day with him, and then we had a long talk about it the next morning, and I spent the afternoon in a long discussion with the gentleman.[99] He made a most favourable impression upon me. He is undoubtedly a first-rate scholar with very high ideals and a strong sense of communal responsibility. He belongs to the ultra-orthodox section of the German Community, but showed himself fully conscious of the responsibilities attaching to the position of a Dayan serving the whole orthodox Community. He said he was unacquainted with conditions in this country, and that before definitely entertaining the idea of offering himself as a candidate for the appointment, he would wish to come over here and spend a fortnight in London. . . . If everything proves as favourable as I expect, then I think he will make a very suitable candidate for the vacancy.[100]

Back in Berlin Weinberg was seriously considering the position offered in London, and it is obvious that he did not view himself as inextricably tied to the seminary. Although we do not know what gave Weinberg the impetus to leave Berlin, no doubt the knowledge that religious life would be much more fulfilling outside the clutches of the Nazis was an important factor. Furthermore, Weinberg's financial position in Berlin was not very secure.[101] However, Weinberg feared that, if he left, the seminary would be unable to find a suitable replacement, since it was highly unlikely that any east European scholar would be willing to settle in Germany. Lacking such a replacement, the seminary would no longer be an institution of serious talmudic scholarship. Grodzinski reinforced this fear,[102] as did the directors of the seminary, who even wrote to Hertz telling him that Weinberg's departure would create problems for them. They also tried to convince Weinberg that his position in Berlin was more significant than that offered in London. All of these considerations had an effect, and four months after his interview at The Hague Weinberg informed the United Synagogue that he would not be a candidate for the position.[103] He had chosen to place his fate with that of German Jewry.

98 Honorary Officers of the United Synagogue minutes, 12 Nov. 1934.

99 Weinberg did not speak English and Erwin Altmann of The Hague, a former seminary student and the brother of Alexander Altmann, served as interpreter (interview with Manfred Altman). Weinberg thanked Erwin Altmann in a letter dated 19 Nov. 1934.

100 Honorary Officers of the United Synagogue minutes, 20 Nov. 1934. In his letters to Anna Corn (his sister), undated but written in 1945, and Moshe Klein, dated 8 June 1948, Weinberg claimed that he was offered a lifetime contract, but there is no evidence to support this in the United Synagogue minutes.

101 See Grodzinski's letter in *SE* i, p. 380.

102 Ibid.

103 Honorary Officers of the United Synagogue minutes, 26 Feb. 1935, 13 Mar. 1935; Weinberg's letter to Moshe Klein, dated 8 June 1948; interview with Alexander Altmann.

SIX

THE NAZI ERA (1933–1945)

AFTER THE SHOCK of the Nazi ascent to power had worn off, German Jews were forced to come to terms with their new status as second-class citizens. The majority response was to remain calm and wait for the inevitable fall of Hitler, a view shared by Weinberg.[1] However, this was not enough for many Jews, who chose instead to leave Germany. This fuelled an exodus that continued until the outbreak of war.[2] For those who remained, there was a whole range of new challenges, both political and religious, which had to be confronted.[3]

It was noted in Chapter 5 that the newspaper of the Orthodox separatists, *Der Israelit*, stood out from other Jewish papers in its awareness that Hitler's accession to power was not something to be shrugged off lightly. However, this awareness did not lessen the separatists' desire for a communal life independent of the Gemeinde. An antisemitic regime was certainly not going to cause them to give up their supreme value. Although they would co-operate with the Reichsvertretung der Deutschen Juden[4] when the legal and economic status as well as the honour of the German Jewish community were at stake, they would not give up their autonomy. Unlike the non-separatist Orthodox, they did not recognize the Reichsvertretung as the supreme communal authority.[5]

[1] Levi, 'Gaon', 4; Elhanan Scheftelowitz, *500 Years: The History of a Jewish Family* (Heb.) (Jerusalem, n.d.), 37; Weinberg's letters to Joseph Apfel, dated 19 May 1948 (excerpt in Apfel, 'Letters from Rabbi Jehiel Jacob Weinberg' (Heb.), *Hane'eman* (Nisan–Elul 5743 [1983], 52)) and 9 Jan. 1951, and interview with Apfel, a student of Weinberg during the Nazi years.

[2] For details see Herbert A. Strauss, 'Jewish Emigration from Germany: Nazi Policies and Jewish Responses', *LBIYB* 25 (1980), 313–61, and 26 (1981), 343–409, and Doron Niederland, *German Jews: Emigrants or Refugees* (Heb.) (Jerusalem, 1996). One of the possible destinations was Spain, which brought up the question of the alleged ban on settlement in this land, an issue which Weinberg discounted. His opinion is found in a note to the responsum he composed on severing poultry heads following *sheḥitah* (a copy exists at the Jewish National and University Library, Jerusalem). Weinberg also published this responsum in the rabbinic journal *Kol Torah*, and the note appears in the Tevet 5694 [1934] issue, p. 10. For some reason this note was omitted when the responsum was published in *Seridei esh*. On settlement in Spain, see my 'The Herem on Spain: History and Halakah', *Sefarad*, 49 (1989), 381–94.

[3] On religious challenges, see Malkah Tor, 'German Jewry's Spiritual and Intellectual Resistance to the Nazi Regime, with Special Emphasis on the Response of the Orthodox' (Heb.) (MA diss., Hebrew University of Jerusalem, n.d.).

[4] An organization established in September 1933, intended to represent all German Jews.

[5] See the declaration of Ezra Munk and Isaac Breuer, *Der Israelit*, 3 Oct. 1935, 1; Yehudah Ben-Avner, 'Unity and Separatism in German Orthodoxy in 1934–1935' (Heb.), *Keshev*, 1 (Dec. 1985),

It was precisely the separatists' acute awareness of the seriousness of the situation, which became ever more apparent with the passage of time, that led their leaders to send an amazing letter to Hitler in October 1933.[6] This letter, never previously published in full, has been described by Alexander Carlebach as 'by and large a courageous and dignified document in spite of a certain amount of double-talk and apparent sycophancy which can be understood and judged only by those who have lived in the suffocating, nauseating atmosphere that pervaded Germany in the Nazi era'.[7] In the letter the separatist leaders begin by stressing the Jewish commitment to anti-communism, the contributions that Jews have made to Germany, both through the Old and New Testaments and in World War I, and the fact that they are strong opponents of the world-wide boycott effort against Germany.

The letter then turns to the impossible economic situation in which governmental restrictions and popular prejudice have placed German Jews.[8] Without a change in the situation, German Jewry will be condemned 'to a slow but certain death from starvation'. The authors tell Hitler that they do not believe it is the intention of the government to destroy German Jewry, which loves the German soil and people and is bound to its culture. Even though some individuals might have this intention, 'we do not believe that it meets with the approval of the Führer'. However, if they are mistaken in this assumption, and if the government does desire to eliminate Jewry from Germany, 'then we would rather cease nurturing illusions and learn the bitter truth. . . . We would then consider your intentions a matter of fact and accommodate ourselves to them.'

In concluding the letter the authors stress that they are not requesting the immediate abolition of anti-Jewish restrictions, for they do not wish to create difficulties for the government. They are ready to accept certain restrictions for the present. Distancing themselves from the Reform, in a manner which Weinberg strongly opposed,[9] the authors stress the uniqueness of Orthodoxy. They point out that Orthodox Jews never intended to acquire excessive economic influence, since the Sabbath laws prevent this. Furthermore, Orthodox Judaism has always been strongly opposed to intermarriage and Jewish apostasy. What the Orthodox desire, they continue, is the ability to practise their religion freely and earn a living without threats or abuse. They conclude: 'In accordance with our religious obliga-

5–14; Unna, *Lema'an ha'aḥdut*, 83–6; Jacobson, *Memoirs*, 59; Abraham Margaliot, 'The Dispute over the Leadership of German Jewry (1933–1938)', *Yad Vashem Studies*, 10 (1974), 133–4; and Azriel Hildesheimer, 'The Central Organization of German Jewry During the Years 1933–1945' (Heb.) (Ph.D. diss., Hebrew University of Jerusalem, 1982), 62 ff.

[6] See Appendix II.

[7] Carlebach, *Adass Yeshurun of Cologne*, 132.

[8] Somewhat disconcertingly for modern readers, the authors protest against being 'equated with the coloured races'.

[9] Ch. 3 included a discussion of Weinberg's opposition to religious separatism when dealing with the gentile authorities. In early 1933, when Weinberg claimed that Orthodox Jews in particular sympathized with the new regime, he was being interviewed by a Jewish newspaper and speaking to a Jewish audience.

tions we shall always remain loyal to the government of the country. As part of the German people, the German Jew will gladly help in the reconstruction of the German nation, and do what he can to gain it friends outside the German borders.'

This letter combined the expressions of loyalty which were standard for all German Jews and the common belief that the government did not really intend to destroy German Jewry. However, the separatists distinguished themselves from other segments of German Jewry by at least recognizing that there was a possibility that the government was intent on a total removal of Jews from all aspects of German life.[10] Jews outside Germany, Orthodox included, had immediately declared Hitler to be the leading enemy of Jewry. German Jews, however, were forced to assume the role so often carried out by their east European brethren—that of proclaiming, publicly at least, their loyalty to an antisemitic ruler.

The separatists continued to follow their own path, and in March 1934 sent another letter to Hitler. This time they described the religious differences between themselves and the non-Orthodox which forced them to establish their own representative organization, guided by Orthodox principles.[11] After this incident, however, Rabbi Leo Baeck, the head of the Reichsvertretung, requested that in future they should abstain from all such steps. He argued that adopting a non-unified front in dealing with the government would have negative repercussions for German Jewry as a whole. At the very minimum, he asked the separatists to inform his organization when they intended to have political dealings with the government. Because of the new political realities, the separatist leaders soon realized that Baeck's requests were justified. It was becoming clear to them that in the present era a policy of strict *Austritt* was no longer feasible. They therefore began to co-operate with the larger community in a closer manner than ever before.[12]

HALAKHIC CHALLENGES

Aside from the political challenges in the new Germany, there were many pressing religious issues brought on by the policies of the regime. As already seen with regard to the *sheḥitah* issue, it was in this area that Weinberg assumed a prominent role.[13] It is therefore worth mentioning a few of the halakhic issues with which he

[10] Such an awareness is not apparent in the letters sent to Hitler by either the Zionistische Vereinigung für Deutschland or the Reichsvertretung. These letters are reprinted in *In Zwei Welten: Siegfried Moses zum Fünfundsiebzigsten Geburtstag* (Tel Aviv, 1962), 119–27. English translations of the letters are found in Lucy S. Dawidowicz, *A Holocaust Reader*, (West Orange, NJ, 1976), 150–9.

[11] This letter has been published in B. H. Auerbach, *Die Geschichte des 'Bund gesetzestreuer jüdischer Gemeinden Deutschlands' 1919–1938* (Tel Aviv, 1972), 70–1.

[12] See Hildesheimer, 'Central Organization', 65 ff.

[13] In a letter to Moses Shulvass, dated 23 Feb. 1935, Weinberg commented on how busy he was: 'I am swamped by the many questions addressed to me from all over Germany, and even from outside the country. It is not to be believed!'

had to deal, not for his halakhic method, which is not at all unusual, but in order to illustrate the difficult circumstances in which Orthodox Jews found themselves. It hardly needs to be said that in times like these halakhic authorities usually bend over backwards, and make use of generally ignored sources, in order to ease the halakhic burden facing their communities.

Many halakhic problems related to the difficulties of earning a livelihood. Although in his Pilwishki years Weinberg had not agreed to any sort of subterfuge whereby Jews could keep their businesses open on the Sabbath,[14] this attitude changed during the Nazi era, when the economic situation of many Jews reached a crisis stage. Thus, in 1935 he allowed a man to keep his shop open on the Sabbath if he 'sold' it to a gentile every week. Weinberg explicitly stated that the reason he permitted this procedure was because of the emergency situation in which German Jewry found itself. At such a time, he continued, it was crucial to make life as easy as possible for the Jewish community, in order that they should not be driven to abandon the Torah entirely.[15]

A few years later Weinberg again gave a similar decision, noting that he was motivated by the fact that 'the gentiles attempt to deprive the Jews of their livelihood and cause them to forfeit their possessions'.[16] This discrimination was also seen in the refusal of non-Jews to help Jewish neighbours milk their cows on the Sabbath. The rabbi of Würzburg asked Weinberg whether the Jews were permitted to perform the milking themselves. Weinberg had reservations about granting such permission, even when the milking was performed in a manner approved by certain halakhists. However, because of the Jews' difficult economic situation he advised the rabbi to avoid giving a decision either way. He explained that it would be better for Jews not to milk the cows, but if they chose to do so the rabbi need not protest, since halakhic support could be found for their action.[17]

What to do with threatened Jewish cemeteries in Germany was another problem Weinberg had to confront. In early 1936 he was asked by Joseph Carlebach, the rabbi of Altona and Hamburg, whether it was permissible to exhume bodies from a cemetery which was not guarded and bury them in a cemetery which could be protected. As far as 'pure' halakhah was concerned, Weinberg replied in the affirmative, and in another responsum spoke of the 'very great fear' that gentiles would exhume Jewish bodies.[18] However, just as the *sheḥitah* issue was influenced by numerous meta-halakhic policy considerations, so too in Weinberg's response to Carlebach it was these which carried the day. Thus, Weinberg advised the rabbi not to permit the transfer, for he believed, as did his colleague Rabbi Hermann Klein, that such a step would show the government that exhumation was permissi-

[14] See Ch. 2.

[15] *SE* ii, no. 155. He concluded the responsum as follows: 'May God have pity on the remnant of His people Israel, so that they should have no need for these types of "leniencies" which make the Torah fraudulent.' See also the concluding words of *SE* ii, no. 74.

[16] Ibid., no. 21.

[17] Ibid., no. 24.

[18] Ibid., no. 129.

ble. This, in turn, could lead to widespread forced exhumations, which the Nazis had not yet ordered.[19]

When the government refused to allow Jews to gather publicly anywhere but the synagogue, Weinberg was asked if it was permitted to hold lectures on secular topics and have concerts there. The questioner called attention to the fact that not only were these an important element in encouraging Jews in their dire straits, but that lacking such cultural events in their own synagogues, Orthodox Jews would begin to frequent Reform temples where they might be affected by the latter's ideology. After examining the halakhic permissibility of using the synagogue for purposes other than that of prayer, and taking into account the difficult times, Weinberg concluded that secular lectures, by Orthodox speakers, were permitted. He added that it would be best if some words of Torah were used to open the lecture. Concerts, in particular those without a religious theme, were forbidden. However, if the community was insistent, and a refusal would embroil the rabbi in a dispute, Weinberg believed that religious concerts could be permitted.[20]

THE SEMINARY UNDER THE NAZIS

Despite the many difficulties encountered by German Jewry during the Nazi era, Weinberg and the Berlin Rabbinical Seminary were actually going through a very productive period. Thanks to the exclusion of Jews from general society, Jewish institutions were now playing a central role in providing social, cultural, and educational services, with little government interference.[21] As the leading Orthodox institution in Berlin, the seminary became a focus of attention. Lectures and events held there assumed a more important role than in former years. As already observed, it was precisely because of the moral and religious support that the seminary gave to German Jewry that Weinberg and his colleagues refused to

[19] Ibid., no. 127. In the following year the Nazis did order the exhumation of the ancient Jewish cemetery; see Naphtali Carlebach, *Joseph Carlebach and his Generation* (New York, 1959), 191–5. There is a similar case in *SE* ii, no. 128, where Weinberg discusses possible government confiscation of the Jewish cemetery. See also Grodzinski's letter in *SE* i, pp. 378–9, which shows that Weinberg also refused to allow the sale of synagogues to Christian groups, even if there were no longer enough Jews to maintain them.

[20] *SE* ii, no. 12.

[21] See Hans Lamm, 'Über die innere und äussere Entwicklung der deutschen Judentums im dritten Reich' (Ph.D. diss., University of Erlangen, 1951), ch. 5; Ernst Simon, 'Jewish Adult Education in Nazi Germany as Spiritual Resistance', *LBIYB* 1 (1956), 68–104; Munk, 'Austrittsbewegung', 143; Joachim Prinz, 'A Rabbi under the Hitler Regime', in Herbert A. Strauss and Kurt R. Grossmann (eds.), *Gegenwart im Rückblick* (Heidelberg, 1970), 231–8; Boas, 'Jews of Germany', 88–9, 121 n. 23; Kurt Düwell, 'Jewish Cultural Centers in Nazi Germany: Expectations and Accomplishments', in Jehuda Reinharz and Walter Schatzburg (eds.), *The Jewish Response to German Culture* (Hanover, NH, 1985), 294–316; Yehoyakim Cochavi, 'German Jewish Cultural and Religious Activities (1933–1941) as a Response to the Challenge of the Nazi Regime' (Heb.) (Ph.D. diss., Hebrew University of Jerusalem, 1986); and Wolfgang Benz, *Die Juden in Deutschland 1933–1945* (Munich, 1988), 75–267.

support Meier Hildesheimer's planned transfer of the institution.[22] Furthermore, although Hildesheimer, in his letter to Grodzinski, worried that the seminary would have only a few students if it remained in Germany, this was not the case. The list of students who attended during this period, many of whom later assumed important roles in Jewish political and intellectual life, shows this clearly.[23]

Confronted with a student body no longer permitted to study at the university, the directors of the seminary allowed their students to attend lectures on secular subjects together with the students of the Reform Hochschule. This was something the Frankfurt separatists would never have sanctioned, and illustrates once again the ideological differences between 'Berlin' and 'Frankfurt'. The only restriction on which the seminary insisted was that the lectures be held at a neutral site. Some faculty members even admitted that they had no objection to their students attending lectures at the Hochschule, but because of Orthodox public opinion, they were not able to give their approval to this possibility.[24]

During the Nazi years the most important figures at the seminary, aside from Weinberg, were Jakob Freimann (1866–1937), lecturer in Jewish history, Alexander Altmann (1906–87), lecturer in Jewish philosophy, Samuel Grünberg, lecturer in the Bible and Hebrew language, and Esriel Hildesheimer (1901–98), lecturer in geonic literature and librarian. It was they who set the tone of the institution and ensured that the synthesis of traditional learning and modern scholarship would continue. The opening of each term at the seminary was always something of an event, with students and members of the community gathering to hear one of the faculty members deliver a learned lecture. The lectures were usually in various areas of modern Jewish scholarship rather than traditional talmudic dialectics. The latter, while suitable for the study hall, was not deemed especially fitting for a public forum. Two lectures offered by Weinberg were 'The Necessity of Investigation into the Sources of Halakhah'[25] and 'The Relationship of Onkelos to the Masorah and the Halakhah'.[26]

The first lecture, which took place in the spring of 1934, was later published in

[22] In the years after Hildesheimer's death there were renewed efforts to transfer the seminary. In a letter to Moses Shulvass, dated 19 Sept. 1937, Weinberg reaffirmed his opposition.

[23] See Eisner, 'Reminiscences', 50–1, and Ernst G. Lowenthal, 'In seinen Hörern noch lebendig . . . Das Rabbiner Seminar zu Berlin', *Emuna*, 9 (1974), 103–10.

[24] See Richard Fuchs, 'The "Hochschule für die Wissenschaft des Judentums" in the Period of Nazi Rule', *LBIYB* 12 (1967), 20–2. Fuchs also mentions the high regard in which Weinberg was held by the Hochschule faculty. This esteem was apparently also shared by the great semitic scholar Gustaf Dalman, for in 1938 he chose to address a question to Weinberg dealing with Maimonides' attitude towards gentiles. Weinberg's response is published in my 'Between East and West', 329–33. It is known that Dalman often came to the seminary when he needed help on talmudic matters. See Chanan Lehrmann's introduction to Weinberg's *Das Volk der Religion*, 12. Dalman himself wrote a great deal on the issue of Jewish attitudes towards gentiles; see Julia Männchen, *Gustaf Dalmans Leben und Wirken in der Brüdergemeinde, für die Judenmission und an der Universität Leipzig 1855–1902* (Wiesbaden, 1987), 93–114.

[25] See *Der Israelit*, 26 Apr. 1934, 6, and 3 May 1934, 14.

[26] See ibid. 29 Oct. 1936, 14.

Berlin Rabbinical Seminary, *c.*1933. Front row, fourth from left, Eliezer Berkovits; on his left, Meier Hildesheimer, Samuel Grünberg, Moses Auerbach, Weinberg, Alexander Altmann.

Reproduced by courtesy of the Leo Baeck Institute, New York

Berlin Rabbinical Seminary, *c.*1936. Front row, second from left, Jakob Freimann; on his left, Samuel Grünberg, Weinberg.
Reproduced by courtesy of the Leo Baeck Institute, New York

Weinberg's *Lifrakim*.[27] Its importance is readily apparent, for here Weinberg elaborated on how he viewed the ideology of the seminary, and in particular the relationship between traditional and modern methods of Talmud study. Weinberg began by explaining why in the past he had departed from precedent and opened the semester with a 'pure' talmudic lecture rather than focusing on an area of Wissenschaft des Judentums. He agreed that the opening lecture should be *wissenschaftlich*, but disputed the popular notion that only modern talmudic study could be termed 'scientific': 'If the meaning of "scientific investigation" is the clarification of concepts, the extrapolation from cognate ideas of the fundamental concepts and their logical and methodical construction', then the traditional study of Talmud may appropriately be described as scientific.[28]

In advocating this position Weinberg was adopting a very unpopular stand as far as academic Jewish scholars were concerned. At this time, most 'modern' talmudic scholars concentrated on issues of text history and philology. They did not appreciate the conceptual understanding of Talmud and saw no scientific value in the detailed elucidation of talmudic concepts offered by rabbinic scholars. Weinberg, on the other hand, argued that the only unscientific thing about traditional Talmud study was the aberration of extreme *pilpul*, yet this bore no resemblance to the method of study carried out by the great minds of the yeshiva. As for moderate *pilpul*, it was the essence of Talmud study, and 'whoever eschews *pilpul* will not escape from the logical conclusion that he must reject the Talmud too'.

Having said this, Weinberg turned to the traditional talmudists who had no interest in Wissenschaft des Judentums.[29] He argued that it was they who often erred in that they accepted the text they had in front of them without realizing that it was faulty. Often this corrupt text would contradict other authoritative texts, forcing the traditional talmudists into intellectual acrobatics in order to resolve the supposed conflict.[30] One valuable aspect of modern scholarship was that it provided a method of establishing proper texts. It was this facet of Wissenschaft des

[27] *Lifrakim*, 258–63 (115–20). All excerpts are taken from Shalom Carmy, 'R. Yehiel Weinberg's Lecture on Academic Jewish Scholarship', *Tradition*, 24 (Summer 1989), 15–23.

[28] Cf. Harry A. Wolfson's similar comment: 'Now, this method of text interpretation is sometimes derogatorily referred to as talmudic quibbling or pilpul. In truth it is nothing but the application of the scientific method to the study of texts' (*Crescas' Critique of Aristotle* (Cambridge, Mass., 1929), 27). See also *Lifrakim*, 219–20 (269–70), regarding the talmudic works of R. Moses Mordechai Epstein: 'When we shall be worthy of having a true Hebrew science, they will recognize and understand the value of the great ideas spread throughout his books.'

[29] For a good example of the traditionalists' criticism of Wissenschaft des Judentums-oriented talmudists, see Moses Avigdor Amiel, *Hamidot leḥeker hahalakhah* (Jerusalem, 1939), ch. 1 of the introduction. See also Zevin's comment on Amiel's position in his *Writers and Books*, ii. 42–3.

[30] See also *SE* iii, pp. 346–7, for the following post-war comment: 'It is not worth engaging in mental gymnastics in order to make sense of the mistakes of authors and their copyists. . . . God forbid that we should produce laws (*leḥadesh dinim*) on the basis of corrupt manuscripts or on the basis of mistakes which crept in because of incompetent copyists or printers.' In his letter to Samuel K. Mirsky, dated 28 Feb. 1960, Weinberg also stressed the importance of enlightening traditional talmudists with the modern scientific method.

Judentums which Weinberg stressed and illustrated, noting that it would require another lecture to deal with other aspects of modern talmudic studies.[31]

Responding to the students' well-founded fear that if they adopted Weinberg's approach they would be deprecated by traditional talmudists, Weinberg called their attention to the former rectors of the seminary, Esriel Hildesheimer and David Zvi Hoffmann. In addition to their great talmudic learning, and the respect offered them by all, these men were also among the founders of Wissenschaft des Judentums.[32] Turning to the students, Weinberg urged them not only to be satisfied that his approach had a basis in tradition, but also to encourage others to follow in this path. Weinberg concluded:

> A double vocation rests upon you: to introduce the love for the old *beit midrash* to those circles which viewed it as the remnant of a dated, vanishing past, and then to bring a new awareness and love for science and inquiry to those for whom the Torah and the literature and lifestyle connected to it are the highest attainment.

The method which Weinberg espoused in this lecture, and in which he instructed his students, is also apparent in his first book on rabbinics, *Meḥkarim batalmud*.[33] The inspiration for this book appears to have been the discovery by Kahle of a Targum which differs from the traditional rabbinic interpretation of Exodus 22: 4.[34] In his own analysis, Weinberg dealt with many aspects of the verse and its talmudic interpretation, taking into account the Jerusalem Talmud and halakhic *midrashim*, sources which were often ignored by traditional talmudists. There is also a magnificent interweaving of modern scholarship and traditional learning in this book. For example, Weinberg's citation of the Samaritan version of the Pentateuch to illuminate a tannaitic opinion,[35] while a natural step for him, is entirely unheard of in traditional talmudic exegesis.

Similarly, his dating of various strands of a *sugya*—source criticism—and his

[31] It is noteworthy that Weinberg did not discuss another important aspect of modern talmudic studies, that of source criticism. Perhaps he did not think that a public lecture was the proper forum to raise such a complicated and, from the standpoint of tradition, problematic issue. For a more complete analysis of the differences between traditional and critical Talmud study, see Menahem Kahana, 'Talmudic Research at the University and Traditional Yeshiva Study' (Heb.), in id. (ed.), *Beḥevlei masoret utemurah* (Rehovot, 1990), 113–42. See also David Weiss Halivni, 'Contemporary Methods of the Study of Talmud', *Journal of Jewish Studies*, 30 (1979), 192–201.

[32] In his introduction to *Melamed leho'il* (New York, 1956), Hoffmann himself had called attention to the vast gulf which separated traditional Talmud study from its more modern variety.

[33] (Berlin, 1937–8), vol. i (see p. 199 for the explanation of this strange publication date). The war prevented the publication of any further volumes. This work is reprinted, minus the introduction, in the fourth volume of *Seridei esh*. Professor Yaakov Sussman has called my attention to the fact that the otherwise fine publishing house, Mosad Harav Kook, engaged in a bit of censorship when it reprinted the volume. In *Meḥkarim batalmud*, 114, Weinberg refers to the noted talmudist Efraim Urbach as *heḥakham* and *harav heḥakham*. In the reprint, *SE* iv, p. 82, these titles have been omitted! For detailed discussion of *Meḥkarim batalmud*, see Samuel Atlas, 'Lishe'elat hilkhat idit', *Ḥorev*, 9 (1946) 59–78, and Michael Wilensky, 'Be'inyan hilkhat idit', *Ḥorev*, 10 (1948), 35–56.

[34] See the excursus to this chapter.

[35] *SE* iv, p. 20.

willingness to posit textual corruptions in order to answer talmudic difficulties—text criticism—are characteristic of a scholar trained in Wissenschaft des Judentums. Weinberg also pointed out the fact that the Talmud, *saboraim*, and *geonim* offered explanations to amoraic statements which were then integrated into the statement itself, confusing later scholars who did not distinguish between the original statement and the addition.[36] Although this view is now a commonplace among critical scholars, when Weinberg advanced this argument it was—and still is—completely foreign to traditional talmudists.

Weinberg was absolutely correct that similar explanations could be found in traditional sources, and throughout his work he was at pains to demonstrate the religious legitimacy of his approach.[37] As far as he was concerned, the only difference between him and his predecessors was one of degree, not of kind. Yet the difference between them would appear to be more significant than Weinberg claimed, for the pre-modern scholars entirely lacked a critical methodology. Any critical explanations were of an *ad hoc* nature and were only offered as a last resort, when traditional methods of solving a problem did not work. Furthermore, and most importantly, these critical explanations did not arise from a new conception of how talmudic literature should be analysed. Weinberg, however, did have such a new conception, and in his book one finds a deliberate attempt to incorporate both traditional and modern methods of scholarship, leading consistently to insights which can be termed 'critical'. As he explained in the introduction to *Meḥkarim batalmud*, Weinberg hoped that his work would mark a new approach to the study of Talmud and enable scholars to tackle the most difficult task in this field, that of illuminating the simple, and true, meaning of the text.[38]

Yet on the whole Weinberg's approach was quite conservative, and this marks an important difference between his method and that of other academic scholars. Because of this conservatism one must question whether, in spite of his numerous 'critical' insights, Weinberg can properly be categorized as a critical scholar, in accordance with how this term is currently understood. For example, although in the introduction to *Meḥkarim batalmud* Weinberg agreed that there are many saboraic and even geonic additions to the Talmud, and in his discussions of the formation of *sugyot* pointed to numerous such occurrences, nevertheless, relying upon the famous letter of Sherira Gaon he rejected the notion that the *saboraim* actually composed the Talmud. By declaring that all contrary theories, however brilliant, cannot stand before the testimony of Sherira, Weinberg confronts us with traditionalism rather than impartial scholarship, which would have no difficulty in rejecting Sherira's view if it was found to be lacking. Similarly, when

[36] See ibid., pp. 20–2, 121–5.

[37] See esp. ibid., pp. 119–20.

[38] 'In truth, there is nothing as difficult as arriving at the *peshat* of a *sugya*. The unembroidered *peshat* is more profound and abstruse than anything else' (*Meḥkarim batalmud*, p. iii). In his letter to Joseph Apfel, dated 23 Jan. 1953, Weinberg wrote: 'The *peshat* is not as simple as people think. It requires more effort than the creation of a wonderful *pilpul*.'

Weinberg rejected—with good reason—a hypothesis of Rabbi Joseph Duenner (1833–1911) which was based on an extreme form of source criticism, one senses that in addition to the scholarly considerations which led to this conclusion, there lurked a dogmatic attitude in the background. If this was not the case, how else are we to understand his exclaiming 'God forbid' that the Babylonian and Jerusalem Talmuds could misunderstand a tannaitic passage?[39] As Weinberg saw it, this was a conclusion which, in all but exceptional cases,[40] was out of bounds for dogmatic reasons, quite apart from any scholarly refutations which could be offered.

In addition to the topics mentioned above, *Meḥkarim batalmud* also includes a number of interesting digressions that deal with areas as diverse as Rabbi Abraham ben David of Posquières's view regarding the law of half-damage payment,[41] the formation of the Tosafot,[42] the nature of the Peshitta,[43] interpolations of Rashi's commentary into the printed text of the Talmud,[44] and the method of study of the medieval sages.[45] In this book Weinberg also discussed questions of biblical criticism. Following in the path of Hoffmann, he did not simply denigrate it and support himself with the authority of tradition. Rather, he seriously discussed the views of the critics and pointed out, in a scholarly fashion, what he considered to be their errors.[46]

It was during the period of Nazi rule that Weinberg reached the pinnacle of his career, as he was chosen to become rector of the seminary. Unfortunately, no record seems to have survived attesting to the exact date he assumed this office. In *Der Israelit* of 28 December 1934, Weinberg's name is not distinguished in any way from those of the seminary's other faculty members, but in a letter dated 26 February 1935, he is referred to as the rector of the institution.[47] In issues of *Der Israelit* after this date he is also referred to as rector. The choice of Weinberg as rector was only natural, as he was by far the most distinguished member of the faculty. The reason it took so long for him to be chosen was probably because Wohlgemuth, who had served on the faculty since 1895, might have taken offence. However, in the early 1930s an illness forced Wohlgemuth to retire, thus clearing the way for Weinberg's appointment. He was now responsible for deciding who would be accepted for study at the seminary, who would lecture, who would be ordained, which students would become candidates for vacant rabbinic positions, and similar administrative matters.[48]

[39] *Meḥkarim batalmud*, 38, 91.

[40] Ibid. 91: 'All the more so that we are not permitted, based on such a hypothesis *whose weakness is apparent*, to assert that both Talmuds erred, God forbid, in explaining the Tosefta' (emphasis added). A similar comment is also found on p. 38. The emphasized words imply that with more compelling proof, such a conclusion would not be rejected out of hand.

[41] *SE* iv, pp. 62–5.

[42] Ibid., pp. 82–8.

[43] Ibid., pp. 103–4.

[44] Ibid., pp. 116–18.

[45] Ibid., pp. 132–7.

[46] Ibid., pp. 44–7.

[47] See Jakob Horovitz's letter published in my 'Between East and West', 304.

[48] See Zvi Kurzweil, *Siyum vereshit* (Tel Aviv, 1992), 81–2.

WRITINGS OF THE NAZI ERA

Weinberg's other noteworthy writings from this period include an article, co-authored with Kahle, on the Mishnah,[49] important notes to Rabbi Abraham ben David's commentary on the talmudic tractate *Baba kamma*,[50] and a lengthy philosophical study of repentance, with special emphasis on Maimonides' views.[51] Lawrence Kaplan has made a close study of this essay,[52] and calls attention to the fact that Weinberg leaned heavily on Max Scheler's 'On the Eternal in Man', in particular in his identification of repentance with contrition and his downplaying of the significance of resolve for the future. As Weinberg pointed out, this was also the approach of his teacher Rabbi Isaac Blazer, and Kaplan has concluded that 'it was Weinberg's Musar inclinations that made him so open to accepting Scheler's general approach to repentance without any serious modifications'. However, it must also be noted that Weinberg, who was later to accuse so many other scholars of plagiarism, himself paraphrased large sections of Scheler's essay without acknowledgement.[53]

Also during this period Weinberg wrote a laudatory article on Theodor Herzl, whom he identified as a penitent with great religious power, not entirely brought to fruition.[54] In fact, as Weinberg saw it, Herzl's nationalism had its origin in his religious nature, and is to be seen as a *return* to tradition rather than a rebellion against it. Relying on this interpretation, Weinberg explained Herzl's negative attitude towards the inclusion of 'culture' in the Zionist programme, a stand which distinguished him from other segments of his movement. Although his adversaries, led by Ahad Ha'am, saw Herzl's opposition as a sign of his complete assimilation, and of his disillusionment with all things Jewish, Weinberg regarded it as an expression of his fundamental religiosity, which would not allow the ideals of the

[49] 'The Mishna Text in Babylonia: Fragments from the Geniza', *Hebrew Union College Annual*, 10 (1935), 185–222.

[50] *Ḥidushei harabad al masekhet bava kama*, ed. Samuel Atlas (London, 1940). Against Atlas, Weinberg argued that this work was mistakenly attributed to Rabbi Abraham ben David of Posquières (Rabad), the well-known critic of Maimonides (he also argued against Rabad's authorship of the *Sifra* commentary attributed to him); see ibid. 378–9, 383; *SE* iii, p. 357, iv, pp. 213–14; *Yad sha'ul*, 83–4. For a rejection of Weinberg's views, see Isadore Twersky, *Rabad of Posquières* (Cambridge, Mass., 1962), 80 n. 16, 99–100.

[51] *Lifrakim*, 334–51 (121–38). See Hayim Barukh Friedman, 'Repentence in the Thought of Rabbi Dr. J. J. Weinberg' (Heb.), in *Teshuvah veshavim* (n.p., 1980), 109–15, who summarizes Weinberg's major points.

[52] In his as yet unpublished paper, 'Rabbi Joseph B. Soloveitchik's Conception of Repentance'.

[53] In Kaplan's words, 'Weinberg's essay is, in effect, a free reworking of Scheler's essay, garnished and decked out with appropriate rabbinic references, particularly at the beginning and the end, and thereby suitably "Judaized".'

[54] 'Herzl, the Man of Religion' (Heb.), *Ha'olam*, 18 July 1935, 460–1. An earlier version of this essay appeared during World War I in the Warsaw *Yidishe Vort*; see the editor's note to Weinberg, 'The Magical Name—Herzl' (Yid.), *Undzer Veg*, 23 July 1948. Since no copies of the issue with Weinberg's essay survive, I was not able to discuss it in Ch. 3.

Torah to be replaced by an artificial modern Hebrew culture. Furthermore, it was precisely this religiosity which explains why Reines and the Mizrachi movement supported Herzl's plan to establish a Jewish homeland in Uganda, according to Weinberg. They sensed that Herzl understood the central religious significance of the Land of Israel, and knew that Uganda could never be more than a temporary abode. As Weinberg explained, it was because of Herzl's lofty character that the opponents of Zionism—he refers to those in Lithuania and Poland—were careful not to attack him personally, although they certainly could not agree with the Mizrachi movement that the title 'rabbi' should be affixed to his name.[55]

With this last article in mind, it is worth discussing Weinberg's attitude towards Zionism during this period. Although he never devoted a substantial article to the subject, it is possible to glean some relevant thoughts from his writings. For example, his sermons reveal his excitement at the activity of Jews in Palestine in the period following the Balfour Declaration and World War I.[56] In one sermon, Weinberg discussed in glowing terms the sacrifices made by the *ḥalutsim* to build up the Land of Israel.[57] Although, to be sure, these people were not Orthodox, Weinberg regarded the devotion they showed to the Jewish people and its homeland as incredible. He was adamant that these Jews must be embraced, for it was precisely the *ḥalutsim* who provided the Jews of the Diaspora, including the Orthodox, with a place of refuge should they need it. Since the Orthodox did not take part in the difficult task of building up the land, did not suffer for the land, and did not have the idealism of the *ḥalutsim*, Weinberg argued that they had no right to criticize the latter. This approach is a fine example of religious Zionist ideology, which was willing to overlook the religious failings of the pioneers and focus instead on the positive aspects of their work.[58]

It was Kook, in his classic *Orot*, who elaborated on the role of the non-religious in performing holy work. Weinberg shared this view, if not in Kook's mystical sense, certainly in the practical sense.[59] This ideology, however, was strongly

[55] Lawrence Kaplan's comments have helped me sharpen some of the formulations in this paragraph. R. Abraham Elijah Kaplan, Weinberg's predecessor at the seminary, was also attracted to Herzl's personality. See his essay in *Be'ikvot hayirah*, 85–91. Among Orthodox intellectuals, even Isaac Breuer, a staunch opponent of Zionism, could not overlook Herzl's greatness; see Mordechai Breuer, 'Four Eulogies for Theodor Herzl by an Opponent' (Heb.), *Hama'ayan*, 36 (Tammuz 5756 [1996]), 7–16. Weinberg's point about Herzl having started on the path of religious repentance was also made by Isaac Breuer; see ibid. 14.

[56] See *Lifrakim*, 139 and 225 (275).

[57] Ibid. 114–20 (73–9). Portions of this sermon were translated by Nathaniel Helfgott in *Jewish Action* (Spring 1991), 22–5.

[58] See also *SE* iv, p. 375, where Weinberg writes that the Land of Israel has been sanctified through the selfless efforts of the *ḥalutsim*. With regard to the religious *ḥalutsim*, Weinberg wrote as follows in a letter to Moses Shulvass, dated 26 Mar. 1937: 'I love most the simple workers who perform the labour of the nation and the land in holiness and purity. But what am I in their eyes? Can I come to them and express "my love"? They will not believe me and will laugh at me.'

[59] He did not, however, share Kook's view of the essential importance of the Land of Israel. See the citations of Weinberg quoted above, Ch. 4 n. 112. Compare this with Kook's opposing words in *Orot* (Jerusalem, 1992), 9 (trans. Bezalel Naor (Northvale, NJ, 1993), 89–90): 'The Land of Israel is not

opposed by Agudat Yisrael. The position of the latter was that the non-religious settlements were a completely negative force, whose members should receive absolutely no financial assistance from the religious community. This approach was rejected out of hand by Kook[60] and Weinberg.[61]

As Weinberg put it, before speaking to the *ḥalutsim* about religion, one must thank them for all that they have done for the Jewish people, the Orthodox included. Like Kook, Weinberg was confident that when the *ḥalutsim* were properly exposed to traditional Judaism they would adopt it. Weinberg, in agreement with Kook, certainly did not have in mind the form of traditional Judaism found in the Diaspora, in which spirituality, either through prayer or Torah study, is the focus of all efforts. Rather, he was referring to a new form of Orthodoxy which would also be anchored in the physical world.[62] This Orthodoxy would place positive value on building up the Land of Israel and creating a modern country in accordance with Jewish law and ethics. When this occurs, 'we shall all be worthy of seeing those *ḥalutsim*, whose idealism for building up the land was so great, also as the bearers of the banner of Torah'.

In 1936 Weinberg published a collection of essays, aggadic insights, and sermons under the title *Lifrakim*. The homiletic section of this book was intended to meet a great need. As Weinberg explained, halakhic works were held in great esteem, but homiletics, while playing a central role in the *musar* movement, was regarded with scorn by many leading scholars. In their opinion, only those unable to write halakhic treatises would spend time writing homilies. In contrast to this, Weinberg attempted to create a form of homiletics that would help stem the tide of irreligiosity, especially among the younger generation.[63] What stands out most about the

something external, not an external national asset, a means to the end of collective solidarity and the strengthening of the nation's existence, physical or even spiritual. . . . The view of the Land of Israel as only an external value serving as a cohesive force—even when it comes to reinforce the Jewish idea in the Diaspora, to preserve its identity and to strengthen faith, fear [of God] and observance of *mitzvot*—bears no permanent fruit, for this foundation is shaky compared to the holy might of the Land of Israel.' See also Zvi Yehudah Kook, *Bema'arakhah hatsiburit* (Jerusalem, 1986), 129, who elaborates on this notion in an even more extreme fashion.

[60] See Shapiro, *Igerot lare'iyah*, 303–6.

[61] Cf. *SE* ii, p. 156.

[62] In an essay published in 1923 he argued against the negative attitude towards physical labour expressed by many of the Orthodox. In Weinberg's view, the labourer is part of Jewish tradition while the merchant is an aberration brought about by gentile persecution. In this essay Weinberg singled out for criticism the well-known economist and sociologist Werner Sombart, who argued that the Jewish intellect found its natural expression in capitalism. See 'The Scholars and the Workers' Union' (Yid.), *Idisher Lebn*, 13, 20 Apr. 1923.

[63] See *Lifrakim*, 3–8 (although this introduction is signed by the anonymous publisher, a letter of Weinberg to Moses Shulvass, dated 26 Mar. 1937, reveals that Weinberg was really the author); *SE* i, p. 2, iv, pp. 288–9, 342; Weinberg's approbation to Samuel Jacob Rubinstein, *Alfa shemen laner* (Paris, 1959); Etkes, *Rabbi Israel Salanter*, 281–2. Interestingly enough, I found an SS report on *Lifrakim* in the archives of the German Reichssicherheitshauptamt. It is published in my 'Between East and West', 296. Had the SS reader (a Jewish collaborator?) examined the book closely, he would have found the following comment which is surprisingly strong for an author living under Nazi rule:

homiletical section of *Lifrakim* is its modern style. Both the language as well as the structure of Weinberg's homiletics distinguish it from traditional works of this genre, and there is a great deal of stylistic similarity between Weinberg and Rabbi Moses Avigdor Amiel, another modern homilist.

TORAH IM DEREKH ERETZ ON THE DEFENSIVE

Chapter 4 discussed the beginnings of German Orthodox disillusionment with Hirsch's philosophy, and Weinberg's defence of Hirsch's world-view. In the wake of the Nazi exclusion of Jews from German society and culture, it is understandable that Hirsch's teachings should be further challenged, in particular by the young. After all, here was a philosophy which was closely connected to, some would even say dependent on, the manifestations of *Deutschtum* in which Jews no longer had any part.[64] The younger generation, and certainly most of their elders as well, would never dream of blaming the Jews for their own difficulties by arguing that they should have been more successful in showing that it was possible to 'attain a synthesis between Judaism and its eternal forms on the one hand, and the cultural assets of the surrounding world on the other'.[65] On the contrary, most regarded the present exclusion of Jews from 'the cultural assets of the surrounding world' not as a reflection of Jewish failure, but as illustrative of the bankruptcy of the society which advocated these cultural ideals. Now, more than ever before, young men were turning to the east and journeying to yeshivot in greater numbers.[66] Rather than advocating the ideal of Torah im Derekh Eretz, they were adopting the principle of Torah only, or 'Torah and *musar*', in the words of their slogan.[67]

'Only nations that are lacking in religion and faith and empty of all spiritual essence grasp at the ideology of race and blood, since they have no other basis for their national character' (*Lifrakim*, 93 (62)). See also ibid. 69 (40), where Weinberg's reference to 'the wicked regime' is a veiled allusion to the Nazis.

[64] See Kurzweil, *Siyum vereshit*, 63 ff. In 1934 Gershom Scholem penned his sharp critique of Torah im Derekh Eretz, referring to it as Hirsch's 'ghastly accommodation theology'. See *The Messianic Idea in Judaism* (New York, 1971), 329. This article originally appeared as 'Politik der Mystik: Zu Isaac Breuers "Neuem Kusari" ', *Jüdische Rundschau*, 17 July 1934, 1–2.

[65] *Die Laubhütte*, 10 Jan. 1935, quoted in Herbert Freeden, *Die jüdische Presse im Dritten Reich* (Frankfurt, 1987), 130.

[66] According to Rabbi A. I. Bloch's letter of 3 Feb. 1937 to Louis Ginzberg, there were twenty-nine German students studying in Telz. Louis Ginzberg Archives, Jewish Theological Seminary of America, Correspondence (B).

[67] See Breuer, *Autobiography*, 125; Jacob Rosenheim, *Die 'Thora- und Mussar'-Bewegung* (Frankfurt, 1936); Elhanan Blumenthal, *Bekhol derakhekha da'ehu* (Jerusalem, 1995), 22–34. The reorientation of German Orthodoxy did not only move in the direction of the Lithuanian yeshivot. Religious Zionism was also a popular route. The Torah Ve'avodah movement, founded in 1927 by members of Young Mizrachi, quickly built up its membership during the Nazi years as more and more of the young generation rejected the Torah im Derekh Eretz-German bourgeois lifestyle of their parents. See Joseph Walk, 'The Torah Va'Avodah Movement in Germany', *LBIYB* 6 (1961), 236–56, and Tsur, 'Torah im Derekh Eretz'. More detailed discussion of this phenomenon is, however, beyond the scope of this chapter.

This increasing rejection of the Torah im Derekh Eretz philosophy was actively encouraged by east European scholars. In a letter of February 1934 from Grodzinski to Weinberg, the former argued that there was no longer any necessity for German rabbis to study for a doctorate, a practice which still had the complete support of the seminary. He also encouraged Weinberg to transform the seminary into a yeshiva, 'because one must ascend in holiness, not descend'.[68] Similarly, while travelling through Berlin in 1936, the renowned Rabbi Elhanan Wasserman (1875–1941) spoke out against the German Orthodox attitude towards secular studies. He even expressed this opinion in a lecture to the seminary students.[69] Wasserman's main point was that secular studies had utilitarian value and were only permitted when necessary for one's livelihood. However, in complete opposition to Hirsch—a fact acknowledged by Wasserman[70]—he argued that secular studies can never contribute to the religious personality. Not surprisingly, before Wasserman spoke Weinberg pointed out that the position of the seminary with regard to secular studies did not correspond to that of its guest.[71]

[68] See his letter published in *Ḥidushei ba'al 'Seridei esh'*, 578, and see similarly Elhanan Wasserman, *Kovets he'arot* (Jerusalem, 1985), 74*a*. Grodzinski's letter also reveals that there were those in Germany who believed, incorrectly, that Weinberg's heightened emphasis on Talmud study was an attempt to transform the seminary into a traditional yeshiva.

[69] It is interesting that Wasserman refused to pay a visit to Yeshiva College in New York, giving as his reason the fact that the works of Geiger, Zunz, and Weiss were studied there, and blasting it as a 'pseudo-yeshiva' and centre of heresy. Yet he was not reluctant to lecture at the seminary, even though the very works he found objectionable were also studied there. Presumably Weinberg's presence at the institution calmed his fears. See Aaron Rakeffet-Rothkoff, *Bernard Revel: Builder of American Jewish Orthodoxy* (Jerusalem, 1981), 155–6. See also Wasserman's famous essay 'Ikvesa dimeshikha', in Wasserman, *Anthology of Articles and Letters* (Heb., Yid.) (Brooklyn, NY, 1987), 60–1. (This passage has been excised from the Hebrew translation of Wasserman's article, *Ikveta dimeshiḥa* (Jerusalem, 1942), 177.)

[70] This is significant, for as previously noted there was a mistaken belief in eastern Europe that Hirsch's approach was intended only as an emergency measure designed to save German Orthodoxy. Wasserman, however, was aware of the far-reaching nature of Hirsch's Torah im Derekh Eretz philosophy. See his letter in *Kovets he'arot*, 73*b*–74*b*, and Moshe Munk, 'Torah im Derekh Eretz in Our Day' (Heb.), in Yonah Emanuel (ed.), *R. Samson Raphael Hirsch: His Teaching and Method* (Heb.) (Jerusalem, 1962), 214. For his part, Hirsch wrote as follows: 'A good secular education can give our young people substantial new insights, added dimensions that will enrich their religious training. . . . Any supporter of education and culture should deplore the fact that when these secular studies are evaluated in terms of their usefulness to the young, too much stress is often placed on so-called practical utility and necessity. Under such circumstances the young are in danger of losing the pure joy of acquiring knowledge for its own sake, so that they will no longer take pleasure in the moral and spiritual benefits to be obtained from study' (*Collected Writings*, vii. 88). See also p. 90: 'But there is also a spiritual harvest that can be won from secular studies, even for those who seek to grow in the theoretical knowledge of the Jewish religion. Our understanding of the philosophy of life and the *Weltanschauung* taught in the sacred writings of the Jewish religion is dependent in no small measure on our insights into the character and the development of nature and society.' Both these citations come from Hirsch's seminal essay 'The Relevance of Secular Studies to Jewish Education'.

[71] See the reports of Wasserman's visit in *Der Israelit*, 19 Nov. 1936, 14; Pinhas Biberfeld, 'Our Approach to History' (Heb.), in Moses Auerbach (ed.), *Memorial Volume for Rabbi Isaac Halevy* (Heb.) (Benei Berak, 1964), 347–53; and Aharon Sorasky, *Or elḥanan* (Los Angeles, 1978), ii. 26–31. In his letters to the young Aryeh Leib Cohn, dated 7 Sept. 1932 and 19 July 1935, Weinberg urged him to 'walk in the established path' of German Orthodoxy and acquire a secular education.

Public statements like Wasserman's would not have been conceivable a generation or two previously, when east European scholars believed that the Torah im Derekh Eretz philosophy was necessary for ensuring the success of German Orthodoxy. However, times had changed and the east European scholars could not be expected to lend their support to a philosophy which was now being abandoned by many of the German Orthodox themselves. Knowing this, they felt comfortable in expressing their view that the Torah im Derekh Eretz philosophy should now be regarded as an obstacle to true religiosity and the attainment of Torah knowledge, rather than as a shield against the abandonment of tradition.[72]

It was in this context that Rabbi Simon Schwab (1908–95) published his *Heimkehr ins Judentum*.[73] Schwab, a 26-year-old native of Frankfurt, had studied in Lithuanian yeshivot. There he became close to a number of east European sages, whose opposition to secular studies influenced him. His book was the first detailed rejection of the Torah im Derekh Eretz philosophy by one who had grown up in the Hirschian environment.[74] In this book the disillusionment with German culture in general and with Hirsch's Torah im Derekh Eretz philosophy in particular is clear. The author argued that the Hirschian vision was 'meant to be nothing more than a temporary emergency measure, not an ideal state of affairs'. It was designed for nineteenth-century circumstances which were no longer applicable.[75] Schwab also described the Hirschian approach as utopian. Since it was almost impossible for people to achieve greatness in both Torah and secular studies, something had to be given up.[76] In a clear reference to the Nazi era, Schwab added that his critique took on added cogency when there was no connection between the religious and the cultural. In such times, it was only the Torah which could provide comfort and fulfilment.

Another sign of the waning popularity of Torah im Derekh Eretz was Schwab's letter in 1933 to a number of east European sages, asking if it was permissible to study secular subjects.[77] This was an issue which had long since been settled in Germany, but Schwab was questioning whether the conditions that led Hirsch and

[72] As early as 1928, R. Joseph Isaac Schneersohn, the Lubavitcher *rebbe*, publicly declared that the time had come for the German Orthodox to reject 'the curse-bearing bitter water, the approach of Torah im Derekh Eretz'. See his 'Critique', 1–3. See also his *Igerot kodesh* (Brooklyn, NY, 1983), iii, nos. 837 and 839, regarding the dissemination of Habad ideology in Germany.

[73] (Frankfurt, 1934). One of Jacob Katz's first articles was devoted to Schwab's book. See 'Umkehr oder Rückkehr', *Nachlath Zwi*, 5 (1935), 89–95, and *With My Own Eyes*, 96.

[74] He was later to revert to an appreciation of Torah im Derekh Eretz. See his *These and Those* (New York, 1966), and *Selected Speeches* (New York, 1991), 243. He is also the author of the anonymous defence of German Orthodoxy, 'A Letter Concerning "The Frankfurt Approach"' (Heb.), *Hama'ayan*, 6 (Tammuz 5726 [1966]), 4–7.

[75] *Heimkehr ins Judentum*, 114–15.

[76] As mentioned in Ch. 4, Rosenheim had earlier argued this point.

[77] A copy of the letter exists in the Joseph Rozin Archive, Yeshiva University. Contrary to what Schwab told Jacob J. Schacter (see the latter's article 'Torah u-Madda Revisited: The Editor's Introduction', *Torah u-Madda Journal*, 1 (1989), 15 n. 1), this letter is hardly identical to Schwab's article 'Concerning Torah im Derekh Eretz', *Hapardes* (Dec. 1939), 26–8.

Hildesheimer to approve of secular studies still applied. The fact that this letter was sent to the sages of the east meant that the authority of the German rabbinate was no longer sufficient for Schwab and his sympathizers. They sensed that there was a gap between the traditional sources of Orthodoxy and Orthodoxy as practised in Germany.[78]

It is interesting to note that although some scholars responded to Schwab's letter, at least one refused to do so on principle. Rabbi Abraham Mordechai Alter (1866–1948), the *rebbe* of Gur, while believing secular studies to be forbidden, would not allow himself to pen a criticism of the Torah im Derekh Eretz philosophy. As he put it, 'one must be very careful to protect the honour of Rabbi Hirsch'.[79] This is another example of east European admiration for Hirsch combined with rejection of his educational philosophy.

Despite all the opposition to Hirsch's philosophy, Weinberg's attachment to it was not diminished. This is evident from a 1937 lecture which shows how much he had assimilated into his role as a leader of German Orthodoxy.[80] Even though Hirsch and his disciples did not always see eye to eye with the Berlin Orthodox, as noted earlier, this did nothing to lessen Weinberg's veneration for the sage of Frankfurt. In fact, Weinberg went so far as to claim (inaccurately) that there were no real differences between Hirsch and Hildesheimer and that the two simply picked different areas on which to concentrate their efforts. As Weinberg saw it, Hirsch devoted himself to spreading Judaism among the masses, while Hildesheimer's goal was to train rabbis and build up a religious intelligentsia. Furthermore, according to Weinberg, Hirsch was very happy to leave these activities to Hildesheimer. By thus blurring the very real differences between the two, Weinberg enabled the

[78] The four east European rabbis who are known to have replied in writing are Wasserman, Abraham Isaac Bloch, Barukh Ber Leibowitz, and Joseph Rozin. Their replies are printed in Yehudah Levi, *Sha'arei talmud torah* (Jerusalem, 1981), 296–312. One German rabbi of Hungarian origin, Hermann Klein, is also known to have replied; see his *Ḥokhmah im naḥalah* (Bilgoraj, 1935), 99–103. As might be expected, Klein's view was much more favourable to secular studies than were the views of his east European counterparts.

[79] See Grunfeld, *Three Generations*, 48–9; Sorasky, *History*, 147; Yehudah Levi, 'Rabbi Samson Raphael Hirsch: Myth and Fact', *Tradition*, 31 (Spring 1997), 11. See also *Tikun olam* (Munkács, 1935), 144, where even the extremist R. Hayim Eleazar Shapira is able to see something positive in German Orthodoxy's system of education, since it can perhaps 'purify the impure'.

[80] My discussion of Weinberg's view of Hirsch is based on Weinberg's 1937 lecture 'Rabbiner Samson Raphael Hirsch zum Problem Judentum und Weltkultur', which was published that year in the Frankfurt periodical *Nachlath Zwi*. It was reprinted in Weinberg's *Das Volk der Religion*, and it is to this work that I shall refer. His other studies of Hirsch are contained in *SE* iv and in an article entitled 'Torah of Life' (Heb.), in Emanuel, *R. Samson Raphael Hirsch*, 185–99. Although the latter two works were composed after he had left Germany, they reflect his thought as it had developed in his earlier years. There is thus no reason not to regard them as relevant to the period discussed here. I have also drawn on 'Das Jeschiwo-Problem' (1925). Weinberg's article 'Torah of Life' was reprinted in the Nezah publication *Bema'agelei shanah* (Benei Berak, 1966), iii. 11–24. Yet, as Mordechai Breuer has pointed out, 'objectionable' passages of the original article have been altered or simply excised; see his review in *Hama'ayan*, 7 (Tishrei 5727 [1966]), 71–2. A comparison of the two versions of the article reveals other examples of Nezah's tampering which were not noted by Breuer.

Berlin Orthodox to regard themselves as students of Hirsch. They could thus look upon the seminary as an outpost of Hirschian ideology, despite Hirsch's complete opposition to the notion of a rabbinical seminary where Wissenschaft des Judentums was studied.[81]

When it is understood that Weinberg did not see any fundamental contradiction between his own position and the views of Hirsch, a proper appreciation of his exposition and advocacy of Hirsch's thinking is much easier. According to Weinberg, Hirsch was one of Judaism's truly great thinkers whose ideas, despite being couched in difficult language, would never be outdated: 'Not since Abravanel have the Jews possessed a man of such distinction—at once philosopher of religion, Bible commentator, and spiritual leader.'[82]

For Weinberg, Hirsch was the man who prevented German Orthodoxy from fossilizing, which would have led to its disintegration. He had turned it into a living entity able to cope with the challenges of modern society. This was not a type of 'salon Judaism', for he did not wish to make Jews fit for the 'salon', but rather to make 'salon Jews' fit for the *beit midrash*.[83] Those who already had an instinctive appreciation of art and beauty were awakened by Hirsch to a feeling of religious consciousness, an effect which Weinberg claimed also reached into the non-Orthodox community. It was Hirsch who provided answers for those young people seeking meaning in life and, according to Weinberg, there was no reason why he could not do the same for later generations.[84]

Scholars have debated as to whether Hirsch was looking for a synthesis between Torah and the secular, or whether he believed that they should exist independently, each in its own sphere.[85] Weinberg had no doubt that it was a synthesis which Hirsch was seeking, in which all aspects of life are united with the religious life. With such a conception, one cannot separate one's religious commitment from one's 'secular' activity, as each gives meaning to the other. The notion of a 'secular life' simply had no meaning in Hirsch's, or Weinberg's, understanding of Judaism.

After Weinberg had settled in Germany and become acquainted with Hirsch's philosophy, he could no longer retain the ideology of his Pilwishki days. In Germany he came to agree with Hirsch that it was the ghetto which had caused a major distortion in Jewish values. It was the ghetto and other persecutions which

[81] See *Das Volk der Religion*, 71–2, and cf. Kahana, 'Gaon', 6.

[82] *Das Volk der Religion*, 65. It is noteworthy that neither Hirsch nor Abravanel achieved renown in the fields of Talmud and halakhah.

[83] Breuer concludes similarly: 'Hirsch did not want to ease accommodation to a foreign culture for the "old-time pious Jews", but to establish new ties to the old life tradition for the "new pious Jews" already deeply immersed in culture. Every page of his writings testifies to that' (*Modernity within Tradition*, 72).

[84] *Das Volk der Religion*, 67–8, *SE* iv, pp. 360–1, 370; M. Shapiro, 'Letters from Rabbi J. J. Weinberg' (Heb.), *Hama'ayan*, 32 (Tammuz 5752 [1992]), 19.

[85] See Ch. 3 n. 76, where a contradiction on this very point is noted in Breuer's works. Hildesheimer did not advocate a synthesis between Torah and the secular, but believed that each should exist in its own sphere. See Eliav, 'Different Approaches', 52. See also this volume, Ch. 4 n. 2.

had turned Judaism into a religion of ritual and the synagogue. No more did Judaism encompass everyday life and no longer did pious Jews associate religion with science, art, politics, and professional life. Because of this mistaken conception that religion is separate from 'life', the pious strove to avoid the manifestations of modern life as much as possible. They devoted themselves instead to Torah study and ritual, as if this was where Judaism found its only significance.

According to Weinberg, another unfortunate outcome of the Jewish retreat from normal living patterns was that religious feeling was no longer nourished by a healthy appreciation of the world and man's place in it. Instead, it was the fear of divine wrath that became the motivating factor in the psyche of traditional Jews. As Weinberg put it, this notion, while certainly important, was never intended to be at the centre of religious experience or to serve as the sole decisive factor in determining how Jews live their lives. In short, the atmosphere of the ghetto did not allow one to experience Judaism in the most authentic way. Hirsch's philosophy and Weinberg's enthusiastic promotion of it were intended to correct the distortions and misplaced emphases that had become common in Jews' conceptions of their religion. In fact, as Weinberg presented it, Hirschian philosophy actually shared a good deal of common ground with Slobodkaite *musar* in that both of them, in contrast to Novaredok *musar*, stressed the positive in life and the need for a healthy ego.[86]

Yet for all the talk of the importance of the 'secular' which appears in Hirsch's writings, Weinberg, influenced by his love and sympathy for traditional east European Jewish society, advanced a conservative interpretation of Hirsch when he argued that the latter would agree that Judaism did not need to be complemented by the acquisition of culture. In contrast to a feeling widespread among the German Orthodox, Weinberg stressed two points: (1) one who has only studied Torah is not to be regarded as culturally deficient; (2) one need not look outside Torah in order to enrich one's religious personality.[87]

As Weinberg understood Hirsch, he was not interested in simply assimilating elements of general culture into Judaism, for this would diminish authentic Hebrew culture. Rather, he stressed that Judaism, as the highest culture, does not merely concern itself with matters of law, what is permitted and forbidden, but with the whole person in all of his aspects and interactions. In this conception, all aspects of modern society and culture, including the arts and sciences, are

[86] *SE* iv, pp. 365–7.

[87] *Das Volk der Religion*, 73: 'Kein frommer Jude kann sich mit dem Gedanken befreunden, dass, wenn er nur viel Thora gelernt hat, nicht als kulturell vollwertig zu gelten habe, oder dass er zu Bereicherung seiner Persönlichkeit die Kultur ausserhalb der Thora suchen müsse.' Yet there were times when Weinberg, if not contradicting this second point, certainly expressed himself differently. In his letter to Isaiah Wolfsberg, dated 2 Mar. 1956, he wrote, 'I have great satisfaction that I too contributed to the [jubilee] volume in your honour. I did so because of my esteem for your religious personality, in which I see a synthesis of general culture and religious Hebrew culture, something only few have been able to achieve. *In truth, this is the ideal of all thinkers in Israel*' (emphasis added).

significant and must not be ignored, yet they are to be permeated and transformed by the force of the Torah, and not vice versa. Weinberg put this in an Aristotelian light by saying that Torah is the form and *derekh eretz* the matter upon which the Torah works. This matter then itself becomes part of Torah.[88] In Weinberg's opinion, this was the true meaning of the Hirschian synthesis.

It made no sense, Weinberg continued, to say that Hirsch 'permitted' the Orthodox Jew to involve himself with general society, or that his system was an 'emergency measure' dictated by the times. On the contrary, it was the Jew's mission to be involved with general society, and all such activities, when carried out with the proper intentions, were raised to the level of divine service. Weinberg emphasized this to show that, contrary to the opinion of Isaac Heinemann,[89] Hirsch's understanding of Judaism was far removed from that of Mendelssohn. Mendelssohn reduced the religion to a sum of laws, while Hirsch regarded Judaism as an all-encompassing culture.[90]

We have already seen the transformation of Weinberg's thought with regard to the Hirschian world-view. Originally he opposed it, later he granted it a grudging acceptance within Germany, and finally he embraced it totally. In his 1937 lecture Weinberg went even further:

> For us, and I say it with pride, for us eastern Jews Rabbi Hirsch means much more and we believe we have reached a better understanding of him. . . . Precisely we, whose spiritual home is the yeshiva from whose soil we draw our strength . . . feel a strong affinity to Rabbi Hirsch and we shall never allow the teachings of this great guide of Judaism to be confined solely to the secondary school of Frankfurt.[91]

Here is a personal confession testifying to the power of Hirsch's ideology. In Weinberg's mind, it was not the German Jew who grew up in a Torah im Derekh Eretz environment who had the most profound appreciation of Hirsch. In fact, as already noted, many such people were now rejecting his teachings. Weinberg claimed that only those who had spent part of their lives in the exclusively Jewish atmosphere of the yeshiva could discern the genuine greatness of Hirsch's teachings. Whereas the yeshiva promotes Torah study for its own sake as Judaism's highest ideal, an ideal which looks askance at any venture outside the confines of the *beit midrash*, it was Hirsch who challenged these assumptions and demanded that Judaism should not be confined in such a manner. For those, such as Weinberg, who felt that the approach of the yeshiva was not adequate for the mod-

[88] Cf. Kook, *Orot hakodesh*, i. 145: 'Holiness must be erected on a secular base. The secular is the matter, and holiness is the form' (called to my attention by Prof. Lawrence Kaplan).

[89] See Heinemann's introduction to Hirsch, *Igerot tsafun*, trans. Efraim Porat (Jerusalem, 1952), 9.

[90] For the previous paragraphs, see *Das Volk der Religion*, 73–6; *SE* iv, pp. 363–9, 372; *Lifrakim*, 61 (32), 80–1, 322–3 (197–8).

[91] *Das Volk der Religion*, 70. Significantly, however, when actually addressing east European Jews, Weinberg stressed only the practical and professional value of secular education, omitting all mention of Hirsch's conception. See 'Our Educational Questions and Concerns' (Yid.), *Yidishe Togblat*, 21 Sept. 1934, 5.

ern era, Hirsch provided great satisfaction. It was Hirsch who showed that abandonment of the yeshiva ideology need not lead to an abandonment of tradition. On the contrary, Hirschian ideology, properly understood, would lead to a more complete and all-encompassing Orthodoxy, which joined openness to modern society and the most advanced Talmud study as practised in the yeshivot. It was only with such a synthesis that the teachings of Hirsch could be brought to fruition. This is what Weinberg meant when he spoke of the students of the yeshivot having a better appreciation of Hirsch than native German Jews.

Weinberg acknowledged that Hirsch's ideal was a long way from realization, but he did not believe it to be a failure. He recognized that it is always easier to avoid facing the problems of modern civilization, but argued that Orthodoxy, in its higher state, would not choose this path. To do so would condemn it to the role of an uninfluential minority element. Weinberg was hopeful that Hirsch's system would eventually carry the day. He also looked forward to a time when the great sages of eastern Europe would come to recognize that the only way to reach the non-religious and fashion a modern, all-encompassing, Torah society is through the Torah im Derekh Eretz approach.[92] As will be seen in the next chapter, the post-World War II development of Orthodoxy was to be a great disappointment to Weinberg in this regard.

KRISTALLNACHT AND THE WAR YEARS

As mentioned earlier, throughout the Hitler years many Jews came to accept their status as second-class citizens and were content to wait out what they believed would be a temporary phenomenon. As late as October 1938, Weinberg visited Warsaw and expressed hope for the future of German Jewry. Because of this, he rejected any renewed efforts to move the seminary, believing that Germany would have need of rabbis in the future.[93] In another expression of this confidence, he urged German Jews not to emigrate.[94] He and the rest of the country's Jews were totally unprepared for what was to occur on the night of 9 November 1938—'Kristallnacht'. On this night the seminary was locked, never to be reopened.

The next day the young Zionist leader Zorach Warhaftig visited Weinberg and found him mentally crushed, not even capable of carrying on a conversation.[95]

[92] *Das Volk der Religion*, 76–7; 'Zur Auseinandersetzung über S. R. Hirsch und seiner "Thora im Derech Erez Devise"', *Nachlath Zwi*, 7 (1937), 192–3.

[93] See Zorach Warhaftig, *Refugee and Survivor* (Heb.) (Jerusalem, 1984), 344. However, in a letter to M. Z. Levinson, dated 4 Oct. 1937 and sent from Czechoslovakia, Weinberg was somewhat pessimistic: 'We have no hope except a world war, which is certain to occur. We realize this in Germany, but there is a great danger that this wicked regime will, God forbid, be victorious.'

[94] Interview with Joseph Apfel; Zorach Warhaftig's letter in Kressel, 'Hitler', 11. In his letters to Apfel, dated 19 May 1948 and 9 Jan. 1951, Weinberg himself admitted that he had not foreseen what would become of German Jewry—no great revelation. Weinberg's assertion, *Yad sha'ul*, 7–8, that he had no doubt about Hitler's intentions cannot be taken seriously.

[95] *Refugee*, 344–5.

However, a few days later Weinberg had regained his composure. Not realizing that all was lost and that the seminary's closure was irreversible, he wrote to his student Joseph Apfel in Warsaw that 'our seminary is closed for the time being and I do not know when it will open'.[96] However, it was not long before Weinberg himself recognized that Jewish life in Germany was finished. When Apfel visited him a few weeks after Kristallnacht he found a broken man, crying over what had occurred.[97] While the students and faculty members of the seminary were now eagerly seeking out places of refuge, with almost complete success,[98] Weinberg was too ill to travel to the United States, England, or Palestine, from where he had received a number of invitations.[99]

Meanwhile, Kahle, who himself had been forced out of the University of Bonn, was very concerned about Weinberg's situation and wrote to a colleague at the University of Giessen on 25 January 1939. He asked if the university could help Weinberg in finding a new position by granting him some certificate which showed what he had achieved in 1923 towards a doctorate. Not surprisingly, the university refused this request.[100] A couple of months after Kahle wrote this letter, Weinberg was ordered by the Gestapo to leave Germany immediately.[101] 'They did not give

[96] Letter to Joseph Apfel dated 15 Nov. 1938. In his letter to R. Elijah Botchko, dated 23 Nov. 1938, Weinberg also wrote that the seminary was closed 'for the time being', but added, 'I do not know when, or if, it will reopen.'

[97] 'A Portrayal of My Teacher, Rabbi Jehiel Jacob Weinberg' (Heb.), *Hane'eman* (Nisan–Elul 5743 [1983]), 48.

[98] See *Yad sha'ul*, 8; *Hama'ayan*, 32 (Tammuz 5752 [1992]), 7. Weinberg was very involved in efforts to secure such places for his students. For an appeal to the Hebrew University to accept students, see my 'Between East and West', 327–8. In Weinberg's letter to R. Elijah Botchko, dated 23 Nov. 1938, he wrote, 'My first concern is to find places of refuge for my students.' See also Rakeffet-Rothkoff, *Bernard Revel*, 209, where a letter written by Revel on 22 Dec. 1938 is quoted: 'The faculty of the famous and historic Hildesheimer Rabbinical Seminary in Berlin, which the German government closed and disbanded, has turned to us, urging that we take in some members of its faculty, eminent scholars and sages of the Torah, and especially the best of their senior students.' Only one faculty member, Maximilian Landau, was unable to find a place of refuge, and he perished in the Holocaust. Weinberg's 'Zeugnis' on behalf of Landau, dated 1 Dec. 1938, is in the Yeshiva University Archives, Jacob A. Hartstein Administrative Files, Drawer 13/3, Folder: 'Foreign Faculty'.

[99] *Yad sha'ul*, 8; letter to the Corn family, undated but written in 1945; letter to Paul Kahle, dated 10 Feb. 1949.

[100] Information in the University of Giessen Archives. Shortly following this Kahle and his family were forced to flee Germany. The chilling story of their experiences in Germany from Kristallnacht until their escape is told in a small, undated, and privately printed booklet by Kahle's wife Marie, entitled *What Would You Have Done?* Weinberg was deeply moved by this booklet; letter to Paul Kahle, dated 23 Mar. 1947. I thank Kahle's son, Fr. William Kahle of London, for providing me with a copy of the booklet.

[101] *SE* i, p. 1. In a letter dated 27 Dec. 1938 (*Hama'ayan*, 32 (Tammuz 5752 [1992]), 7), Weinberg mentioned that he had been ordered to leave the country within four weeks, but that he had been able to extend the deadline to three months. Similarly, in a letter dated 15 Jan. 1939 (*Hama'ayan*, 33 (Tishrei 5753 [1992]), 38), he mentioned that he had to leave Germany within a few weeks. Since we know that the suddenness of Weinberg's expulsion from Germany took him by complete surprise, one must assume either that the original expulsion order was cancelled, or that Weinberg was suddenly ordered to leave Germany earlier than the date he had been given. We do not know exactly when he

me permission to take one book or garment or any other article. It was only with the clothes on my back that I left the city accompanied by one of my students.'[102] Undoubtedly regretting his earlier opposition to moving the seminary to Palestine, Weinberg asked Esriel Hildesheimer, who was preparing to emigrate there, to contact him if there was a possibility of re-establishing the institution in the Holy Land.[103] Luckily, Weinberg had previously given his student Eliezer Berkovits, who had recently left Germany, a number of his responsa to take out of the country. It is these writings which make up a significant portion of his *Seridei esh*, published later.[104] However, many writings were left in Berlin. Among the works known to have been lost were a great number of responsa and *ḥidushim*, his doctoral dissertation, and three books he had prepared for publication,[105] in addition to the many books he owned, whose loss he would for ever mourn.[106]

In ill health, Weinberg first went to Kovno, where he was treated by doctors who suggested that he should travel to Paris for further treatment. This was impossible, however, since the German consul in Kovno refused to give him a transit visa. He was forced to remain in Kovno for a few more months, until at the beginning of August he travelled to Warsaw in order to consult doctors there. It was presumably on their advice that in mid-August he went for treatment to a spa in the vicinity of Lublin. His mood at this time was one of utter hopelessness. He now believed that Hitler was intent on destroying all of Jewry and that even those in Palestine would not be safe. On 1 September, a few days after Weinberg returned to Warsaw, Germany invaded Poland and World War II had begun.[107]

left Berlin. In *SE* i, p. 1, he wrote that he was expelled approximately six months before the outbreak of war. According to information Weinberg provided in his claim for compensation as a victim of Nazi war crimes (Bayerisches Landesentschädigungsamt, Munich), he was expelled in March. On 12 Mar. 1939 he was still in Berlin, from where he sent Joseph Apfel his certificate of rabbinic ordination (a copy of the *semikhah*, with the above-mentioned date, is in my possession). The official seminary document, which was also signed by Grünberg, was undoubtedly the last pre-war *semikhah* issued by the now defunct institution. (After the war Weinberg and his colleagues conferred ordination on a few more students who had been unable to complete their studies in Berlin; letters to Naftali Berger, dated 8 Jan. 1956, 2 Mar. 1956, 4 June 1956.)

[102] In *Yad sha'ul*, 8, he wrote that he was accompanied by two students.

[103] Interview with Esriel Hildesheimer.

[104] *SE* i, pp. 1, 179; letters to Paul Kahle, dated 23 Mar. 1947 and 10 Feb. 1949.

[105] *SE* i, p. 179, and his letter in *Hane'eman* (Nisan–Elul, 5743 [1983]), 52.

[106] See *SE* iii, no. 71. This responsum is addressed to Moses Rebhun of Haifa, who had been a student at the seminary in its final years. When he left Germany he managed to bring out some books belonging to the seminary library, and he asked Weinberg whether he could keep them. Weinberg replied that he must return the books, but that if the former members of the faculty and governing board decided to give Rebhun some of them as a present, then Weinberg would also agree to this.

[107] *SE* ii, p. 64; *Yad sha'ul*, 8; Warhaftig, *Refugee*, 345; letter to the Corn family, undated but written in 1945; letter to Paul Kahle, dated 23 Mar. 1947; letter to R. Elijah Dessler, dated 14 Aug. 1939. On 26 July 1939, Moses Auerbach wrote to Meir Bar-Ilan seeking the latter's help in securing a certificate of entry to Palestine for Weinberg: Religious Zionist Archives, Mosad Harav Kook, Bar-Ilan papers – 1939. In fact, Weinberg already had the necessary papers, but because of his health could not make the trip; letter to the Corn family, mentioned above.

During the first year of his stay in Warsaw, Weinberg was very ill and often unable to speak or read. In the second year, his health began to improve. It was during this time (on 2 October 1940) that the ghetto was formed. Weinberg, however, was more fortunate than most Jews in the ghetto. Since Lithuania had been taken over by the Soviet Union, he was now a Soviet citizen. As long as Germany and the Soviet Union were at peace, Weinberg was in a protected position and was not subjected to many of the hardships of the other ghetto residents. A notice marking him out as a Soviet citizen was even placed on his clothes and on the door of his home. This presumably explains why as late as February 1941 he was given permission to travel to the Soviet consulate in Königsberg to be issued with a new passport.[108]

After Weinberg's health had improved, he was able to devote much of his time to communal matters. He was elected president of two rabbinic organizations, the Agudat Harabanim of Warsaw and the larger Agudat Harabanim of Poland, as well as president of the supreme rabbinical court of Poland. The Jewish community of Warsaw also offered Weinberg the position of chief rabbi of the city. He refused the offer, explaining that the position would be controlled by the Gestapo.[109] Perhaps it was the Gestapo itself, knowing of Weinberg's importance and wishing to deal with a German-speaking leader, which was responsible for the offer in the first place.

While in Warsaw, Weinberg also served as the head of a committee designed to assist rabbis and yeshiva students. Here he worked closely with the Polish office of the Joint Distribution Committee and the renowned martyr Rabbi Menahem Zemba (1883–1943) in distributing the money and care packages which arrived in Warsaw. From the ghetto, Weinberg sent letters to friends in many countries requesting money, care packages, religious articles, and assistance in arranging for the emigration of rabbis and yeshiva students.[110] In a post-war letter to his family in the United States, Weinberg described his situation in the ghetto:

> My friends and pupils in the whole world overwhelmed me in sending all sorts of things in the form of money, food, and other precious things. My social position in Warsaw reached an extraordinary culmination. I was appointed there to be president of all organizations of rabbis, learned men, and authors. All subsidies went through my hands. I was leader of an office there with many secretaries and supply officials. During my consultation-hour many hundreds of petitioners came to see me. I was able to help each of them. I could give them from the abundance which was placed at my disposal by my pupils.[111]

[108] *SE* ii, p. 64, *Yad sha'ul*, 11–12. The passport is currently in the possession of Abraham Weingort in Jerusalem, and states that Weinberg's picture and signature were authenticated by the consul and secretary in Königsberg.

[109] Letter to the Corn family, undated but written in 1945.

[110] *Yad sha'ul*, 10–12; *SE* ii, pp. 64–5; Weinberg's letter from the ghetto published in *Bita'on Bar-Ilan* (Summer 1974), 22; his letters to Louis Ginzberg and Saul Weingort, published in my 'Between East and West', 334–9; M. Levinson-Lavi's letter in *Bitsaron*, 8 (1943), 278.

[111] Letter to the Corn family, undated but written in 1945. The letter is written in English.

Weinberg also began to edit a volume of halakhic writings from the leading rabbis in Warsaw which was to be published in secret.[112] This publication was to be in remembrance of the 'great miracle' that he had experienced in secretly travelling out of the ghetto.[113] It also was to be in honour of the marriage in Montreux, Switzerland, of one of his dearest pupils, Saul Weingort (1915–46). The significant feature of this volume was that each of the contributions was to be on the same halakhic theme, Maimonides' view of the destruction of *ḥamets* before Passover. The book would have provided a good illustration of the various talmudic methodologies, but unfortunately the events surrounding the outbreak of war with the Soviet Union on 22 June 1941 made publication impossible, and the manuscript was lost.[114]

Recalling the cruelty and torture which were commonplace in the ghetto, Weinberg wrote:

> One cannot describe what happened within the walls of the ghetto. There the German beast showed itself with all its ferocity, violence, and cruelty never seen or heard since the heavens and earth have been created. . . . May I not live to see the consolation of Zion if I have not seen men, women, and children thrown to the ground and trampled by people fleeing for fear of death, or persons having collapsed from hunger and cold and murderous blows. They lay on the ground helplessly and breathed their last with no one to bring them to burial. . . . It was a daily occurrence for German soldiers and officers to roam the streets equipped with iron bars and knock down everyone who came their way.[115]

As for the accusations of the 'heroes of the pen' that the Jews did not rise up against their tormentors, Weinberg asserted that these writers did not understand the Nazis' diabolical methods, which proceeded gradually, 'until at the end not men but shadows were left', full of despair and with but one desire—to give up their lives soon.[116]

In 1941 Hillel Seidman personally witnessed Weinberg's involvement in the following event. It was a Sabbath and Weinberg was returning from prayers when he saw a Jew lying on the pavement, too weak to get up and ignored by all the passers-by. Weinberg quickly ran to his apartment and snatched up some money. Returning to where the man lay, he stood in the centre of the pavement, refusing to allow anyone to pass and demanding that they help him bring the man to a doctor.[117]

With the outbreak of war between Germany and the Soviet Union, Weinberg no longer had any privileged status. He was immediately incarcerated in the

[112] Incidentally, one of these rabbis was Yehiel Meir Blumenfeld, whose criticism of Weinberg is discussed in Ch. 5.

[113] Weinberg did not elaborate on this event.

[114] *Yad sha'ul*, 11; *SE* ii, p. 65; *Hama'ayan*, 32 (Tammuz 5752 [1992]), 8.

[115] *Yad sha'ul*, 8–9. This translation is taken from H. J. Zimmels, *The Echo of the Nazi Holocaust in Rabbinic Literature* (New York, 1977), 124.

[116] *Yad sha'ul*, 9.

[117] 'The Gaon Rabbi Jehiel Jacob Weinberg in the Warsaw Ghetto' (Heb.), *Hapardes* (Feb. 1967), 37.

infamous Pawiak prison, where he remained for two weeks.[118] After this he was placed in a prison reserved for Soviet citizens where the conditions were much better than those at Pawiak. He was able to resume correspondence with friends in neutral countries and continued to supervise the distribution of care packages which arrived in the ghetto.[119] In one letter, dated 26 September 1941, he wrote that he expected to be released soon.[120] However, on 14 October 1941, Weinberg and forty other Lithuanians were transferred to a detention camp reserved for foreign civilians, and later for Soviet prisoners of war, in the Bavarian fortress of Wülzburg, near Weissenburg.[121] According to Weinberg's own testimony, despite having been subjected to forced labour and deprived of adequate nourishment, he was not mistreated in this camp. By this he meant that he was not subjected to any special persecution because he was Jewish, which he attributed to the fact that the camp was controlled by the military, not the SS.[122]

The fact that Weinberg was removed from the Warsaw ghetto and sent to a detention camp in Germany, instead of being sent to a death camp, has always aroused astonishment and suspicion. There are many who are convinced that he must have had an influential friend who was able to secure such special treatment for him. Yet in the absence of any explicit evidence, or testimony from Weinberg, there are no grounds for such an assumption. A more likely explanation for his treatment is that the Nazis, regarding him as the most important rabbi in the ghetto and assuming he would be important to the Soviets, transferred him to

[118] On Pawiak, see the recollections in Abraham Shulman, *The Case of Hotel Polski* (New York, 1981), esp. ch. 4.

[119] See the letters published by Joseph Walk in *Bita'on Bar-Ilan* (Summer 1974), 22.

[120] Ibid. For an unsuccessful attempt by the chief rabbi of Uruguay to secure Weinberg's freedom, see the German government documents published by Joseph Walk, 'A Failed Rescue Attempt' (Heb.), *Ḥadashot universitat bar-ilan* (July 1975), 19–20. Interestingly enough, the documents show that Eichmann himself was informed of the Uruguayan request. Adam Czerniakow, in his diary entry for 13 Sept. 1941, wrote, 'I asked for the release of Rabbi Wajnberg. An interesting personality and an interesting attitude. His outlook was so different from all the other Jews.' See Raul Hilberg *et al.* (eds.), *The Warsaw Diary of Adam Czerniakow* (New York, 1979), 278. (The footnote identifies 'Rabbi Wajnberg' as a certain Rabbi Abraham Weinberg, but as Walk correctly points out, this is clearly an error.)

[121] It is not clear how many of the forty Lithuanians were Jewish. By October 1942 all other nationalities had been removed from Wülzburg and there were 375 Soviet inmates in the camp; Bundesarchiv-Militärarchiv, Freiburg, RW6/v 184, v. 450–3. The Soviets imprisoned in Wülzburg were navy and commercial sailors whose ships were in German ports when the war broke out. Although Weinberg's whereabouts were never a secret, during the war rumours reached London that he had lost his mind and was confined to a hospital in Kovno. See Ze'ev Werba, 'A Centre of Torah Destroyed' (Heb.), *Bitsaron*, 7 (1943), 373.

[122] Information contained in Weinberg's claim for compensation as a victim of Nazi war crimes; *Yad sha'ul*, 11–12; Weinberg's letter to Heinrich Frick, dated 4 June 1946. While at Wülzburg Weinberg began to write his memoirs, but they were confiscated by the authorities. See Ze'ev Hayim Lifschitz, 'Thoughts about the Man in his Era', in *Memorial Volume for Rabbi Jehiel Jacob Weinberg*, 374–5. In his letter to Joseph Apfel, dated 9 Sept. 1965, Weinberg mentioned that he used to trade his meat rations with the Soviet prisoners in exchange for bread. Other than these two pieces of information, we know nothing about his time in Wülzburg.

Wülzburg in order to trade him for German citizens held captive in the Soviet Union.[123] This was the function of the numerous foreign citizens held at the camp, and there is no reason to believe that Weinberg's role was any different. After the decision to implement the Final Solution, Weinberg and his fellow Jewish prisoners, isolated Jews living together with Soviet prisoners of war, were presumably overlooked by the SS, who had more pressing matters on their hands. The only explanation Weinberg himself could give as to why he was miraculously saved was to attribute it to his unworthiness to die a martyr's death.[124]

Weinberg remained in Wülzburg until April 1945. After being freed by American troops, he was brought to Weissenburg, where Jewish soldiers cared for him. At this time he had no knowledge of the Holocaust, which had wiped out his entire family with the exception of one sister. When he was asked where he intended to go now that he had been freed, he replied Warsaw or Kovno, not knowing that there was nothing to return to.[125] When he was informed of what had occurred during the war the shock was too much to bear, and his health took another turn for the worse. He was taken to a hospital in nearby Nuremberg, where he stayed for nine months.[126]

It was not long before word got out about the distinguished patient in Nuremberg, and Weinberg had many visitors, some of them old friends. Herman Dicker recalls visiting Weinberg in the hospital, and that all he could talk about was the fate of the seminary and his library.[127] Warhaftig reports that Weinberg even made plans to return to Berlin to search for his books.[128] It was Dicker who informed the Joint Distribution Committee of Weinberg's condition,[129] and Weinberg himself attempted to contact Samuel Atlas, Abraham Joshua Heschel, Joseph B. Soloveitchik, and other friends to ask for their assistance.[130] Writing to his former colleague Alexander Altmann, then in Manchester, Weinberg expressed his great pessimism about the future and noted that there was no one nearby who could help him through this difficult time. 'In my eyes I am as one who is drowning while his friends and loved ones standing on the shore extend a helping hand, but due to his weakness he is unable to grasp the outstretched hand.'[131]

123 This explanation, which I believe is correct, was suggested to me by Hillel Seidman, former archives director of the Warsaw Judenrat. Professor Christopher Browning has informed me that he too regards it as plausible.

124 *SE* i, p. 1.

125 Atlas, 'Portrayal', 289; letter from 'Herman' (Dicker?) to Weinberg, dated 1 July 1945. In his letter to the Corn family, undated but written in 1945, Weinberg wrote, 'First I wanted to go to Poland to see our relations and to help them. But I am urged from everybody not to go there. It is not worth telling the reason.'

126 *Yad sha'ul*, 13; letter to Heinrich Frick, dated 4 June 1946; letter to Zvi Mathisson, dated 17 Nov. 1952.

127 See his review of M. Carmilly-Weinberger, *Censorship and Freedom of Expression*, in *Judaism*, 27 (1978), 491.

128 *Refugee*, 346.

129 Interview with Dicker.

130 Warhaftig, *Refugee*, 346.

131 Letter to Alexander Altmann, dated 4 Apr. 1946.

At the time that Weinberg wrote this letter, his student Saul Weingort, who throughout the war had been heavily involved with rescue efforts, was desperately trying to help him.[132] In fact, in 1945, shortly after the war's end, the following telegram was sent from Montreux to the chief rabbinates of England and Palestine: 'Just Received Message, Dr. Yechiel Weinberg Former Rector of Rabbi Hildesheimer Seminary Berlin Liberated Camp Weisenburg, Bavaria Stop Procure Immediately Palestine Certificate To Avoid His Repatriation To Russia.'[133] Whether there was any real possibility of Weinberg being sent to the Soviet Union is unknown, since Weingort, after giving assurances that he would be responsible for Weinberg's maintenance, was able to obtain the Swiss government's approval for Weinberg to come and stay with him. His health had improved, and Weinberg was finally able to leave German soil. In June 1946 he journeyed to Montreux, a beautiful and peaceful town on the shores of Lac Leman, where he hoped to find solace.[134]

EXCURSUS: THE CONTROVERSY OVER EXODUS 22: 4

Exodus 22: 4 reads as follows:

כי יַבְעֶר איש שדה או כרם ושלח את בעירה ובער בשדה אחר מיטב שדהו ומיטב כרמו ישלם.

The traditional translation of this verse is, 'If a man cause a field or vineyard to be eaten [by cattle], and shall let his beast loose, and it feed in another man's field; of the best of his own field, and of the best of his own vineyard shall he make restitution.' This verse is of great significance, for it is considered by the Talmud, *Baba Kamma 2b*, as the basis for the two major categories of torts known as שן (tooth) and רגל (foot).[135]

This verse presents important problems, many of which revolve around the rare word יבער.[136] One would have expected יבעיר in the *hiphil* or יְבָעֵר in the *pi'el*. The general consensus is that יבער is a shortened form of the regular *hiphil*. Even after having established the grammatical form of the verb, the problem of its meaning still remains. In general, the root בער in the *hiphil* is in the nature of 'to light a fire', 'to burn', and 'to kindle', and this is how many modern commentators under-

[132] *Yad sha'ul*, 13.

[133] Joseph Friedensohn and David Kranzler, *Heroine of Rescue* (Brooklyn, NY, 1984), 230. The telegram is dated 18 June 1945.

[134] Ibid. 231; information contained in Weinberg's claim for compensation. In the spring of 1946 Weinberg was already well enough to travel to Fürth, where he spent the Passover holiday (interview with Hillel Seidman, who was also in Fürth at this time).

[135] See also *SE* iv, pp. 41–2, where Weinberg argued that the verse is also the basis, in Rav's opinion, for the category of damage known as מבעה (= אדם, man).

[136] Weinberg also discussed other problems, such as the verse's apparent redundancy and the fact that the word 'vineyard' is omitted in the middle of the verse; *SE* iv, pp. 40–7. However, these are of no direct concern in the present discussion.

stand the word. Assuming the verse refers to fire, the proper vocalization of בעירה would be בְּעֵירָה, and not בְּעִירֹה as it is punctuated in the Masoretic text. This reading is particularly appealing, since the following verse also deals with fire. In order to bolster their case, the scholars who hold this view have suggested a variety of textual emendations which would solve all the problems of this verse.

Following in Hoffmann's footsteps by arguing with the non-traditional interpretations rather than ignoring them, Weinberg set out to show that the meaning of the root בער, in this verse, has nothing to do with fire but accords with the traditional talmudic interpretation. In doing so, he attempted to refute all the textual emendations offered. In support of his position he cited Jewish interpreters such as Ibn Janach, Rashi, Ibn Ezra, Rashbam, Kimhi, and S. D. Luzzatto. To counter any criticism that he was not being impartial, he also cited gentile scholars such as Dillman and Kautsch. Finally, he discussed whether talmudic literature contains any indications that this verse refers to fire. Not surprisingly, he strongly denied this. Throughout his various arguments, the dogmatic basis for his views is evident.[137]

When Weinberg dealt with this issue it was anything but a dry academic debate. His discussion followed the publication of some new targumic texts which raised fundamental questions about the nature and function of targumic literature. Until 1930 there were scholars who argued that the root בער in Exodus 22: 4 means 'to kindle'. These scholars based their argument solely on logic and grammar, and their view was no different from the many other hypotheses advanced in explanation of problematic verses in the Bible. Indeed, it had even less to stand on than other suppositions at variance with rabbinic tradition, which could often find support in ancient versions of the Bible such as the Septuagint or the Peshitta. In this case, however, the ancient translations agreed with the rabbinic interpretation.

In 1930 an event occurred which, remarkably, seemed to confirm that the word בער in this verse had once meant 'to kindle', at least for some people. In addition, this surprise confirmation came from a Jewish source. In this year Paul Kahle published the second volume of his famous *Masoreten des Westens*, a book which marked a turning-point in modern targumic studies. Included in this work were fragments from the Genizah containing a small portion of a Palestinian Targum on Exodus. Fortunately, Exodus 22: 4 is among the passages preserved.[138]

[137] For example, after refuting a Pentateuchal emendation on scholarly grounds, he added the following dogmatic-cum-linguistic comment: 'It is clear that this practice of emending and correcting according to "reason" allows the Torah text to be trodden on by all who lack a sense of language, in particular that of the holy tongue' (*SE* iv, p. 46). Cf. Alexander Altmann's judgement that 'Hoffmann's learned and skillful rebuttal of Wellhausen was more in the nature of apologetics than of modern scholarship, no matter how justified were his strictures in details' (*Essays in Jewish Intellectual History* (Hanover, NH, 1981), 289).

[138] See p. 3 in the transcribed texts.

Much to everyone's surprise, the Targum on this verse read as follows:

ארום יבקר גבר חקל או כרם וישלח ית יקידתה ויוכל בחקלה דאחרן בית שפר חקלה ובית שפר כרמה ישלם.

This is to be translated: 'If a man clears (?) a field or vineyard, and sends forth his fire, which [then] destroys another's field; he shall make restitution [from] the best portion of his field and [from] the best portion of his vineyard.'[139] In this Targum, the biblical words ושלח את בעירה are translated as וישלח ית יקידתה, that is, damage done by fire. The author of this Targum thus presumably read בעירה as בְּעֵירָה, and not בְּעִירֹה.

However, for a couple of different reasons, Weinberg rejected the notion that this Targum was referring to fire. His first reason has to do with a technical problem concerning the vocalization of the word יקידתה, which seems to rule out 'fire' as its meaning. Weinberg suggested that יקידתה is an Aramaic neologism meaning 'cattle'. What the Targum has done, therefore, is to imitate the similarity in the Hebrew between the words בעירה in verse 4, meaning 'cattle', and הבערה in verse 5, meaning 'fire'.[140]

Weinberg also offered another suggestion which he believed was more probable, namely, that the word יקידתה is a copyist's error, which arose because the very next targumic verse has the same word, 'fire'. Weinberg supported this

[139] This translation is based on that found in Michael L. Klein, *Genizah Manuscripts of Palestinian Targum to the Pentateuch* (Cincinnati, Oh., 1986), i. 288. The word יבקר is very problematic. According to Weinberg it means 'to graze'. This rendering is rejected by J. L. Teicher, 'A Sixth Century Fragment of the Palestinian Targum?', *Vetus Testamentum*, 1 (1951), 127. A. Toeg, 'Exodus 22: 4: The Text and the Law in the Light of the Ancient Sources' (Heb.), *Tarbiz*, 39 (1970), 226 n. 13, accepts Weinberg's interpretation but ventures the possibility that יבקר is a later correction for the original ייקד! See also Georg Schelbert, 'Exodus xxii 4 im palästinischen Targum', *Vetus Testamentum*, 8 (1958), 256–9. Incidentally, both the superlinear and the sublinear punctuation are either mistaken or illegible in *Seridei esh*. In *Meḥkarim batalmud* they are clear.

[140] Weinberg tried to support this argument in the following manner. The Hebrew word מקנה is derived from the root קנה ('to acquire, own, possess'), even though it has nothing to do with property but means 'cattle'. Onkelos therefore translates it as בעירא. On the other hand, the Peshitta almost always translates מקנה as קנינא, which in Syriac has no meaning other than that of acquisitions and property. Weinberg claimed that the Peshitta had given a new meaning to the word קנינא on the analogy of the Hebrew מקנה.

Yet Weinberg was almost certainly in error, because of the simple fact that languages develop. It was only natural for קנינא to come to mean 'cattle', with no need to posit that the translator of the Peshitta intentionally created a new word along the lines of Hebrew (comment of Dr Sebastian Brock, one of the leading Syriac scholars of our day). It should also be pointed out that the Babylonian Talmud uses קנינא to refer to cattle (*Sotah* 34*b*); see Marcus Jastrow, *A Dictionary of the Targumim, the Talmud Babli and Yerushalmi, and the Midrashic Literature* (New York, 1971), s. v. קנין. See also Joseph A. Fitzmyer, *The Genesis Apocryphon of Qumran Cave 1* (Rome, 1971), 143, where the noun נכסין means both 'possessions' (its meaning in early Aramaic) and 'flocks' (later Aramaic), a perfect example of language development relevant to the issue discussed here. See further Chaim Heller (ed.), *Peshitta* (Berlin, 1927), i. 6 n. 12, and Gad Ben-Ami Sarfatti, 'A New Edition of the *Genesis Apocryphon*' (Heb.), *Leshonenu*, 33 (1969), 123–4.

suggestion by citing Kahle's report that יקידתה appears slightly erased in the manuscript, as if it was intended to be corrected. That there is a textual error in the Targum is also apparent, Weinberg claimed, because the word יקידתה is feminine, yet the verb used with it, ויוכל, is masculine. Weinberg was convinced that readers who took all the evidence into account would conclude that יקידתה is an erroneous word, and not that ויוכל should be emended to read ותוכל.[141]

Without going into the grammatical technicalities involved, suffice it to say that both Weinberg's arguments, and the support they received from J. L. Teicher, have been totally disproved in an article by Georg Schelbert.[142] Furthermore, the entire debate has been rendered superfluous by another amazing occurrence. This was the discovery, in the mid-1950s, of the complete Palestinian Targum known as Targum Neophyti 1. This Targum, which undoubtedly goes back to tannaitic times, translates the verse in question as follows:

ארום יוקד גבר חקל או כרם וישלח יקידתא ויוקד בחקלא דחורן. . . .

'If a man sets fire to a field or a vineyard, and leaves the fire to spread, and [thus] causes fire in the field of another . . .'.[143] We thus see that Neophyti translates the root בער in all its three occurrences with the Aramaic root יקד.[144] A stronger proof of the authenticity of Kahle's Genizah Targum could not be found.[145]

Finally, Weinberg's assertion that Kahle's Targum is corrupt is also mistaken. Schelbert,[146] followed by M. L. Klein,[147] has noted that although Kahle read ויוכל in the Genizah Targum, this is incorrect. In reality, the word which appears is ויוקד.[148] Thus, the Targum reads as follows:

ארום יבקר גבר חקל או כרם וישלח ית יקידתה ויוקד בחקלה דאחרן בית שפר חקלה ובית שפר כרמה ישלם.

All these occurrences of 'to kindle' simply reinforce the point that there was a difference of opinion among the ancient interpreters on how to understand this verse.[149]

141 Teicher, 'Fragment', 126, accepts this argument.

142 'Exodus xxii 4', 253–63.

143 This translation is taken from Alejandro Díez Macho (ed.), *Neophyti 1* (Madrid, 1970), ii. 472.

144 See B. Barry Levy, *Targum Neophyti 1: A Textual Study* (Lanham, Md., 1986), i. 401–2.

145 David Reider's assertion that Neophyti has a 'three-fold error' cannot be taken seriously. See his 'On the Targum Yerushalmi MS Neophyti 1' (Heb.), *Tarbiẓ*, 38 (1969), 85.

146 'Exodus xxii 4', 254–5.

147 *Genizah Manuscripts*, ii. 79.

148 That this is the correct reading can be seen from an examination of the text, ibid., plate 3.

149 Weinberg, *SE* iv, p. 54, insisted that in talmudic literature there is 'not even a tiny hint' that this verse was ever understood to refer to fire. He then considered a number of examples which appear to contradict this claim. Although Weinberg's argumentation is brilliant, it is impossible to agree with him on all counts. This is especially so with regard to his comments in *SE* iv, pp. 60–1, concerning the *Mekhilta derabi shimon ben yoḥai*. For rejections of Weinberg's categorical statement, see Samuel Atlas, 'Hilkhat idit', 70–1; Menahem Kasher, *Torah shelemah*, vol. xviii (New York, 1958), 182–4, and vol. xxiv (Jerusalem, 1975), 111–12; Joseph Heinemann, 'Early Halakha in the Palestinian Targumim', *Journal of Jewish Studies*, 25 (1974), 118–19; Schelbert, 'Exodus xxii 4', 262–3; Toeg, 'Exodus 22: 4', 225–6. Toeg (ibid. 225 n. 12) makes the following interesting observation concerning Weinberg and his critics, with regard to interpreting the relevant talmudic literature: 'This is not the only instance where a *talmid ḥakham*, through his great erudition, supplies evidence for his critics.'

Was there any dogmatic motivation behind Weinberg's strenuous efforts to show that Kahle's Targum was corrupt, or was this genuinely an impartial scholarly discussion on his part? Kahle obviously saw Weinberg's opposition as dogmatically based. Regarding the Targum on Exodus 22: 4, he wrote:

> The fundamental importance of this passage became clear to me through a discussion with my old friend and lecturer from Giessen, Dr. J. J. Weinberg, when I visited him in Berlin where he had become Rector of the Rabbinic Seminary. In the course of our conversation I realized how difficult it must be for a Talmudic Scholar, as he was, to accept an interpretation of a passage of the Bible which conflicted with the rules of the Mishna, even if it was contained in an old Geniza text—the only source available to us at that time.

After placing Weinberg's opposition in a dogmatic light, Kahle concluded: 'we certainly have to take the passage in the way Abraham Geiger has understood similar divergent explanations of the Bible text in the Palestinian Targum'.[150]

Weinberg, on the other hand, strongly asserted that his defence of the traditional rendering of Exodus 22: 4 was due to scholarly and not dogmatic considerations.[151] Indeed, it is a commonplace that there are passages in the various Targumim which contradict accepted halakhah.[152] Furthermore, Weinberg himself discussed this phenomenon in his essay on the Targum, and disputed with Geiger on the implications of these anti-halakhic Targumim.[153] Yet while it is obvious that Weinberg acknowledged the existence of anti-halakhic Targumim, the question which is of concern here is whether he would have been prepared to advocate such a position if there were other interpretative options. All Weinberg's protestations notwithstanding, it seems that he was willing to bend over backwards, some would even say to force the issue, in order to show that the Genizah Targum does not offer an anti-halakhic position. Weinberg did so even though Kahle's approach was much more obvious and straightforward, indicating that there were in fact dogmatic considerations influencing his approach.

While on the topic of dogma and targumic literature, it is worthwhile examining Weinberg's attitude to Rabbi Chaim Heller (1878–1960). Heller was an east European talmudist who made his way to Berlin where, making full use of his brilliant mind and amazing command of ancient languages, he proceeded to write a number of works of biblical scholarship, concentrating on the Targum, Peshitta,

[150] *The Cairo Geniza*, 206–7. In the earlier edition of this book (Oxford, 1941), 123 n. 2, he wrote similarly: 'It is quite interesting to see how a real Talmudic scholar like J. J. Weinberg cannot *admit* that a Targum should translate the Hebrew text in such a way contrary to the Mishna' (emphasis added). Cf. Moise Ohana, 'Agneau pascal et circoncision: Le Problème de la halakha prémishnaïque dans le targum palestinien', *Vetus Testamentum*, 23 (1974), 398–9.

[151] Letters to Paul Kahle, dated 10 Feb. 1949 and 18 Feb. 1949.

[152] Kahle would have been surprised to learn that the arch-traditionalist R. Moses Sofer pointed out a deviation from accepted halakhah in the Targum on Ruth. This led him to wonder whether the Ruth Targum was of Sadducean origin. See *Lishkat soferim* on *Even ha'ezer* 17: 43 (found in standard editions of the *Shulḥan arukh*).

[153] *SE* iv, pp. 270–1.

Septuagint, and Samaritan Pentateuch.[154] Heller did not regard his works as detached scholarship, but rather, as he made clear in his various introductions, as a holy endeavour designed to demonstrate the integrity of the Masoretic text.

The basis of all of Heller's investigations is the dogmatic assumption that the text accepted by Jews—the Masoretic text—is the original and authentic text of the Pentateuch. All variants found in ancient translations or Hebrew manuscripts arose through either the elaborations of the translator or the errors of careless copyists. Heller did not explain why the accepted Masoretic text may not also contain errors, that is, copyists' errors from the original text. Even though numerous earlier authorities, including leading *rishonim*, had recognized that the Talmud contained some readings which differed from the Masoretic text,[155] Heller rejected this. Against irrefutable evidence he firmly held that there is no proof of variant Pentateuchal readings in either talmudic literature or the ancient translations.

Weinberg's approach and methodology were very different, and having studied under Kahle he had a much more critical mind. Furthermore, he saw no basis in tradition for Heller's extreme position, which, as mentioned previously, is contradicted by both traditional authorities and irrefutable evidence. Although, for dogmatic reasons, Weinberg shared Heller's abhorrence of the Higher Criticism, with regard to textual criticism his position was far removed from the hermeneutical acrobatics employed by Heller in order to explain away every ancient variant. In fact, it was precisely due to Heller's methodology that Weinberg had no respect for the former's works. In his mind, they could not even be categorized as scholarship.

Kahle, in his book *The Cairo Geniza*, devoted one footnote to Heller. Concerning the latter's publication of the Peshitta in Hebrew letters, Kahle wrote that it 'cannot be taken seriously. The author is not informed about the real problems; like the other books published by Heller this also is dictated by apologetical tendencies.'[156] Weinberg felt that Kahle had been too mild with this statement. In a letter to Kahle he argued that Heller's writings should not be described as apologetically tendentious, but rather as 'homiletic', in other words, specimens of pseudo-scholarship.[157] He continued:

> That there were, at the time of the [Second] Temple, other texts which deviated from the Masorah can be proved from the fact that, as I demonstrated in my book,[158] at the time of

[154] For biographical and bibliographical information on Heller, see Jacob I. Dienstag, *Ein hamitsvot* (New York, 1968), 46 (this list appears to be complete with the exception of Oscar Rand, *Toledot anshei shem* (New York, 1951), 36–8).

[155] See my 'Maimonides' Thirteen Principles: The Last Word in Jewish Theology?', *Torah u-Madda Journal*, 4 (1993), 197 ff., to which add David Rosenthal, 'The Method of the Sages in Dealing with Variant Versions of the Bible' (Heb.), in Yair Zakovitch and Alexander Rofe (eds.), *Sefer yitsḥak aryeh seeligman* (Jerusalem, 1983), ii. 395–416, and Yeshayahu Maori, 'Rabbinic Midrash as Evidence for Textual Variants in the Hebrew Bible: History and Practice', in Shalom Carmy (ed.), *Modern Scholarship in the Study of Torah: Contributions and Limitations* (Northvale, NJ, 1996), 101–29.

[156] First edition, p. 181 n. 1. A similar note is found on p. 266 in the second edition.

[157] Letter to Paul Kahle, dated 10 Feb. 1949.

[158] See *SE* iv, p. 103.

the Temple corrections were made which were financed by Temple money. If there had not been so-called popular Bibles circulating, the corrections would have been superfluous. Also, Rabbi Akiva in his testament warned his children not to use uncorrected texts of the Bible.[159]

Although academic scholars never took Heller's views into account, Weinberg did discuss them. In fact, he seems to have had a fixation on Heller, for of all the things he could have written about when Kahle sent him his book, he chose to mention an insignificant footnote in order to register his disagreement with Heller. We can speculate about why this was so. It is well known that Heller's works were viewed with great respect in Orthodox circles, and he was regarded as a defender of the faith in the tradition of Hoffmann and Isaac Halevy. However, this type of propaganda came from people who had no training in biblical scholarship. Viewing himself as part of the Orthodox community, Weinberg felt that he had some obligation to set matters straight. It was his duty to show that Heller's writings were actually examples of pseudo-scholarship, and thus not entitled to all the renown they had achieved. This is apart from the fact that Weinberg regarded Heller as a plagiarizer, a view he hinted at very subtly in his *Meḥkarim batalmud*.[160]

Having written his doctoral dissertation on the Peshitta, Weinberg was especially familiar with Heller's own work on this subject, which contained a number of strange views. That Heller believed the Peshitta emanated from a Jewish source[161] was not unusual, for a number of leading scholars had held this position.[162] Yet he went further than this in endowing the Peshitta with a sort of holiness and placing it in the same category as the other Targumim.[163] It was this sentiment that led him to publish an edition of the Peshitta in Hebrew letters. In his extensive notes Heller cited talmudic parallels and attempted to reconstruct the Peshitta's original text, before it was corrupted by the various Christian sects which used it as their Bible.

Because of his reverent attitude towards the Peshitta—which instantly vanished when he discussed the Septuagint, Vulgate, or the Samaritan version—he reached another extreme conclusion. Not only did he assert that none of the variants of the Peshitta testify to the existence of a non-Masoretic text—he claimed this for the other ancient versions too—but he also argued that these variants are actually explanations based on rabbinic exegesis. While Weinberg acknowledged the basic correctness of Heller's point, he recognized that there are many variants which simply cannot be explained along these lines, for they represent real divergences

159 See *Pesaḥim* 112*a*.

160 That Weinberg hinted at Heller's plagiarism is mentioned in his letter to Samuel Atlas, dated 2 Mar. 1961. These hints are found in *SE* iv, p. 50 nn. 8*, 8**, p. 51 n. 12, p. 104.

161 *Untersuchung über die Peschitta* (Berlin, 1911), 3–4; id. (ed.), *Peshitta*, i, p. i.

162 See Kahle, *The Cairo Geniza*, 265 ff.; Peter B. Dirksen, 'The Old Testament Peshitta', in Martin Jan Mulder (ed.), *Mikra* (Assen/Maastricht, 1988), 255–97; Yeshayahu Maori, *The Peshitta Version of the Pentateuch and Early Jewish Exegesis* (Heb.) (Jerusalem, 1995).

163 See Heller, *Peshitta*, i, p. i.

between the Peshitta and the Masoretic text. However, as Weinberg continued, 'So what! Does this, God forbid, put the integrity of our tradition [i.e. the Masoretic text] in doubt? Absolutely not! . . . the responsibility for the Peshitta does not rest with us'.[164]

In his effort to reconcile the Peshitta and the Masoretic text, Heller even claimed that the Peshitta made use of the *at-bash* letter exchange system![165] This was far too much for Weinberg to swallow. While he admitted that the talmudic sages had a tradition regarding the use of *at-bash*, he also added that 'what is permitted for the sages is forbidden for others, for if not you would, God forbid, make the Lord's Torah fraudulent, and, God forbid, nothing will be clear concerning positive and negative commandments'.[166] Furthermore, Weinberg noted, the *at-bash* system is only valid for homiletic purposes but not for scientific study.

For all his criticisms of Heller, Weinberg nevertheless resembled him in one important way. As his continual remarks of 'God forbid' and his use of other dogmatically based catchphrases show, he too was not interested in producing detached scholarship. It is obvious that, as with Heller, he viewed his writings as a defence of the faith. That this defence reached very different conclusions from those of Heller attests to the broadness of his own dogmatic beliefs, rather than to a fundamental difference in scholarly methodology between the two. When dealing with Weinberg, Heller, or any other Orthodox figure—as Kahle himself sensed—one inevitably finds scholarly conclusions being made to conform to dogmatic beliefs. It is the range of the latter which ultimately determines the broadness of the former.

164 *SE* iv, p. 103.

165 *Untersuchung*, 7–8. In the *at-bash* system, the last letter of the alphabet, *tav*, is substituted for the first letter, *alef*; the penultimate letter, *shin*, replaces the second letter, *bet*, and so on. See Joshua Trachtenberg, *Jewish Magic and Superstition* (Cleveland, Oh., 1961), 263.

166 *SE* iv, p. 103.

SEVEN

POST-WAR YEARS (1946–1966)

MONTREUX

WITH HIS WORLD destroyed, the great question before Weinberg was what to do now.[1] He regarded Montreux, with its small yeshiva and Jewish community numbering under a hundred people, as only a temporary stop before he would journey on to a major centre of Jewish life. Because of his fame he received many invitations and could have settled in the United States, France, England, or Palestine–Israel. Although he always expressed a desire to leave Montreux, he was to remain there until the end of his life. Even his lifelong dream of living in, or even visiting, Israel was never to come to fruition. It was during the years in Montreux that Weinberg, who before the war had led a public life, reverted to a very private role. This chapter will examine what brought about this transformation.

As mentioned in Chapter 6, it was Weinberg's student Saul Weingort who was responsible for his teacher's maintenance and who enabled him to take advantage of the pleasant atmosphere of Montreux in order to complete his recuperation. Yet the calm did not last long: on 18 September 1946 tragedy struck when Weingort was killed in a train accident, and Weinberg's health took another turn for the worse.[2] After the initial shock of Weingort's death had passed, Weinberg once again began to reconstruct his life, although his state of depression made this very difficult. During this time he often expressed feelings of hopelessness, claiming that his life had no future.[3]

[1] In seeking to understand Weinberg's thought during this period, I have relied a good deal upon his extensive correspondence with his youthful friend and confidant, Samuel Atlas. Although their careers had diverged drastically, with Atlas becoming professor at the Reform Hebrew Union College, they remained very close. In fact, this type of relationship is unique in the history of outstanding rabbinic figures (*gedolim*). While it is true that one must take into account Atlas's own character in evaluating Weinberg's letters to him, and this can perhaps explain certain emphases which appear here and not elsewhere, these letters are an invaluable source. Only with Atlas did Weinberg feel comfortable enough to reveal his deepest thoughts, feelings, and frustrations. As Weinberg put it in his letter to Atlas, dated 17 Jan. 1950: 'You know that there is no one else besides yourself to whom I can reveal my innermost thoughts.'

[2] See Weinberg's essay in memory of Weingort, *Yad sha'ul*, 3–19; letter to R. Isaac Sher, dated 11 Nov. 1946.

[3] Letter to R. Isaac Sher, dated 11 Nov. 1946; letter to R. Mordechai Shulman, dated 20 Nov. 1946. See *Ḥidushei ba'al 'Seridei esh'*, 580, 604, for letters from Sher and R. Elijah Dessler which attempt to raise Weinberg's spirits.

After acquiring the necessary books,[4] Weinberg was able to return to his talmudic studies and the writing of responsa, which despite all other interests always remained the central focus of his life.[5] However, this activity was more difficult than in the years before the war. As he mentioned in a number of letters, his memory was not what it had been, and he was continuously afflicted by a variety of maladies.[6] Despite this, it was only a short while before he assumed his position as one of the world's foremost *posekim*, whose expertise was sought out even by Israel's Chief Rabbi Isaac Herzog.[7] Although before the war his influence had been limited to Germany, in the post-war years it became international in scope. This was due to a few factors. First, the destructive effect of the Holocaust meant that there were very few world-class halakhists left, and Weinberg was thus able to fill a void. Second, his many students were now scattered throughout the world, carrying his reputation with them.[8] By addressing their questions to Weinberg they enabled him to influence events around the globe. Third, as time went on the segment of Orthodoxy characterized by an openness to modern society, formerly centred in Germany but now scattered throughout the world, began to regard Weinberg as the halakhist best suited to rule on those issues related to the special social circumstances of this community.

From Montreux Weinberg also resumed his correspondence with students, friends, and colleagues, writing many hundreds of letters a year, most of which have been lost to posterity. Although at first his financial situation was somewhat insecure, he soon received a large compensation grant from Germany.[9] With this money he no longer needed to seek paid employment and was able to spend all his time in study and writing. However, being far from any research libraries, it was very difficult for him to engage in serious academic study.[10]

Although Weinberg kept in touch with his sister and nephews in the United States—whose non-Orthodox lifestyle greatly distressed him[11]—the closest thing

14 Many of Weinberg's letters in the first years after the war contain requests for books.

15 See e.g. *SE* iii, p. 256.

16 In *SE* ii, p. 68, Weinberg wrote that his memory loss was so bad that at times he could not remember blessings or prayers. A similar comment is found in his letter to R. Mordechai Gifter, dated 24 Apr. 1961.

17 See e.g. *SE* iii, no. 25.

18 Weinberg took great pride in these students. In his letter to Joseph Apfel, dated 25 June 1948 (excerpt in Apfel, 'Letters', 52), he wrote: 'I have, thank God, many students. . . . They are leaders in both the Mizrachi and Agudat Yisrael, and all of them publicly sanctify God's name. My reward for all my efforts is the joy in my students, who glorify the name of Israel, its Torah, and its faith throughout the world.' See also *SE* i, p. 3. In a letter to his student Alexander Altmann, dated 22 Feb. 1952, Weinberg expressed his hope that Altmann would write a definitive modern philosophical interpretation of Judaism, adding that 'since the time of Hermann Cohen we have not had anyone who has been successful in this area'. In this letter Weinberg also briefly noted some of his objections to Cohen's philosophy.

19 This information has been confirmed by a number of people who knew Weinberg well.

10 Weinberg mentioned this in his letter to Paul Kahle, dated 10 Feb. 1949.

11 Letter to Samuel Atlas, dated 19 Dec. 1958.

he had to a home life was with Weingort's widow and her children, who continued to look after him until his death on 24 January 1966. It was here that Weinberg ate most of his meals and would bring his guests, and he also formed a very close relationship with the youngest of the children, Abraham, who became the son Weinberg had never had,[12] while Weinberg in turn became a father figure to the young Weingort. Yet, despite the many physical comforts available in Montreux, Weinberg was never happy there, often complaining in his letters about his sense of isolation. This was only natural, for from being the rector of an important rabbinical institution he had now been reduced to a private citizen in a small town, in which there were very few people with whom he had anything in common. Although his home was to become a pilgrimage site for friends, students, and admirers from all Jewish religious streams,[13] this clearly did not satisfy him and he was incredibly lonely. Many of his letters include the phrase 'there is no one here with whom I can carry on a conversation'. He also noted that the interests of the teachers at the local yeshiva were confined to talmudic matters, which was not enough to satisfy him.[14] In an undated letter to Samuel Atlas, Weinberg revealed much about his loneliness, and also confessed his unease at the prospect of his own mortality:

> I am alone and isolated here. I have many people who respect and esteem me but no true friends. I have learnt that people befriend only those from whom they are able to receive some benefit. This is part of man's nature, as Hillel said, 'If I am not for myself, who will be for me?' [Mishnah, *Avot* 1: 4]. There are of course exceptions, but they are few and far between. Among the hasidim, the *rebbe*s conquer the hearts of their hasidim and are the recipients of their devotion. They hope for the *rebbe*'s assistance in the next world. Among [non-hasidic] sages there are students who are devoted to their teachers, who warm to their light and feel deep gratitude towards them. However, this feeling lasts only when it does not carry any practical obligations.
>
> In short, I have reached the stage of life when one fights with oneself. This is the end of all men. Only the pure righteous ones are at peace with death, because they believe that it is a gateway from life to life, from degraded life to exalted life, and even they do not want to die. They say about the Vilna Gaon of blessed memory that he cried greatly when his time came. He explained his crying as follows: 'In this world one can perform great *mitsvot* with only a *perutah* [small coin].' This is the saying of the *tanna* 'Against your will you live', but 'against your will you die' [Mishnah, *Avot* 4: 29]. Man does not want destruction. This is one of the forces of life. No belief and no philosophy can comprehend the feeling of dread in the face of destruction.

It was Weinberg's feeling of isolation which explains the steps he took to secure positions in other countries. Yet there is no doubt that his efforts were half-

[12] At the young Weingort's bar mitzvah, Weinberg stated that he was 'more precious to me than a son'. See Abraham Weingort (ed.), *Well of Miriam* (Heb.) (Jerusalem, 1997), 163.

[13] This openness to the non-Orthodox explains why even Louis Finkelstein, chancellor of the Jewish Theological Seminary of America, turned to Weinberg for advice in running his institution; Weinberg's letter to Joseph Apfel, dated 31 Mar. 1959.

[14] Letter to Samuel Atlas, dated 18 Dec. 1958.

Dayan Dr I. Grunfeld (right) with Weinberg (left), Montreux, 1961.
Reproduced by courtesy of Mrs Judith Grunfeld

hearted, and despite numerous opportunities, such as offers of appointments to the London Beth Din, the Paris *beit din*, the professorship of Talmud at Bar-Ilan University, the rectorship of a new rabbinical seminary in Jerusalem, and the directorship of the *Otsar haposekim* project in Jerusalem, he never seriously pursued any of these paths and instead chose to remain in Montreux.[15]

It was in Montreux that Weinberg felt able to preserve a semblance of what life had been like before the war—a life which combined Torah, Western civilization, and academic Jewish studies. The synthesis of Berlin Orthodoxy, whose popularity had plummeted even further in the years after the war, was still an option in Montreux. Weinberg believed that he would have been out of place anywhere else, particularly in Israel, for he would have had to commit himself to a certain philosophy. As he saw it, by becoming a professor at Bar-Ilan University or a lecturer at a yeshiva, he would have been forced to make a choice between the academic world and the traditional yeshiva world. Whichever world he chose would have required him to sever his ties with the other, for he believed that there was little possibility of straddling the two. The right-wing Orthodox, who had a generally negative attitude towards secular studies and often viewed academic Jewish studies as

[15] Weinberg discussed all these job opportunities in his correspondence.

nothing less than sacrilegious, would not have accepted him had he joined the university community. On the other hand, the academic world would have regarded him as an obscurantist if he had cast his lot with the right-wing yeshivot. Similarly, had he moved to Israel he would not have been able to express his Zionist sympathies without risking alienation from the right-wing Orthodox community, to which so many of his friends and colleagues belonged. Such was Weinberg's evaluation of the sociological realities of post-war Orthodoxy. Only by remaining in Montreux could he live the life he had in Berlin, where it had all been so natural. Only in Montreux was Weinberg able to command the respect of right-wing circles through his great Torah knowledge, and at the same time to continue his commitment to Torah im Derekh Eretz, academic Jewish scholarship, and the rebuilding of the Land of Israel.[16]

POST-WAR CHANGES

The changes which occurred in the Orthodox Jewish world in the post-war years were to be a continuous source of disappointment for Weinberg. With the eclipse of the German Orthodox philosophy, a form of Orthodoxy which opposed all secular studies had taken its place. Most irritating to him was the fact that this new trend was able to influence Berlin Rabbinical Seminary graduates to distance themselves both from the philosophy of their earlier years and from the institution where they had received their rabbinical training.[17] Faced with this rising opposition to the ideals of German Orthodoxy, Weinberg thought it necessary to declare: 'It is important to establish for coming generations, that among the German rabbis were pious and outstanding men. If they had been in other countries great numbers would have pursued them in order to benefit from their Torah knowledge and fear of God.'[18] In a private letter which reveals his complete identification with the

[16] In his letter to Samuel Atlas, dated 12 July 1956, he wrote as follows: 'I am afraid to go to the Land of Israel. There are different worlds there, which reject and hate one another. I am part of two worlds, and which one should I choose when I go there? In the end, I will have to remain in solitude. Therefore, it is better for me to be alone in an empty desert than in a noisy and raucous atmosphere.' See Yitzhak Raphael, *Lo zakhiti ba'or min hahefker* (Jerusalem, 1981), 344, where Weinberg's comments about his Zionist sympathies are quoted. In his letters to Ephraim E. Urbach, dated 26 July 1956 (published in *Torah u-Madda Journal*, 7 (1997), 119), and Samuel K. Mirsky, dated 14 Sept. 1959 and 28 Feb. 1960, he expressed his strong commitment to academic Jewish studies. In his letter to Urbach, in which he gave his blessing to the World Congress of Jewish Studies in Jerusalem, he added, 'For from Zion will the Torah come forth', clearly showing how greatly he valued academic Jewish studies. In his letter to Samuel Atlas, dated 25 Mar. 1947, Weinberg mentioned the partisan religious extremism in Palestine in explaining why he did not move there. In his letter to Atlas, dated 1 Jan. 1963, he gave another reason—the fierceness of the dispute between the Israeli religious and secular. In a number of other letters, Weinberg's stated reason for not going to Israel was much simpler—lack of money. Yet even when money was no longer a problem, there were more weighty reasons which prevented him from leaving Switzerland.

[17] These sentiments recur in a number of unpublished letters. See also his letter in *Hama'ayan*, 32 (Tammuz 5752 [1992]), 16–17; and cf. Breuer, 'Agudat Yisrael'.

[18] *SE* ii, p. 53 in the note.

ideals of German Orthodoxy, Weinberg stressed that the German expatriates must remain strong in their adherence to Torah im Derekh Eretz 'in its most wide-ranging sense', and not be led astray by the opponents of this philosophy.[19] In line with this, Weinberg urged European rabbis to establish a non-partisan religious teachers' seminary as well as an Orthodox student union, as had existed in pre-war Germany, complete with its own newspaper which would focus on religious and literary themes. Needless to say, this approach was not shared by 'the rabbis of the old school who have one cure for all problems—support for the yeshivot'.[20]

Weinberg believed that while religious extremism was always harmful, with its anti-Zionism and opposition to secular studies it was now even more dangerous, for it threatened to cripple positive religious development in the newly created State of Israel. Extremist Orthodoxy, which he regarded as entirely lacking in originality of thought, would never be able to present an alternative to the secular vision and would prevent Orthodox Judaism itself from experiencing a rebirth. For those religious figures who paid little regard to Zionism and the State of Israel, such considerations were not of great importance. However, Weinberg regarded the establishment of the state as an event of unparalleled importance. It marked the beginning of the great renewal of the Jewish people, who would no longer be subject to the world's contempt. As he put it, only one whose heart is 'completely frozen' could fail to recognize the importance of the state.[21]

According to Weinberg, the creation of the state was the inauguration of the messianic process which would find its fulfilment in complete redemption. Despite his generally rationalistic outlook, Weinberg specifically rejected Maimonides' view that 'the sole difference between the present and the messianic days is delivery from servitude to foreign powers'.[22] He argued that this view of a non-miraculous messianic era was only an individual opinion and did not reflect the outlook of the rabbinic sages as a whole.[23] As far as Weinberg was concerned 'the messianic era is the hope for a bright future full of the miracles of a general worldwide revolution'.[24] As for the State of Israel, in one letter he confessed that it was only due to its glory that he found the strength to go on, and in another letter he referred to Jewish national independence as 'the joy of my life'.[25]

[19] Undated letter to Yonah Emanuel.

[20] *Hama'ayan*, 34 (Tevet 5754 [1994]), 13; letter to R. Hillel Medalié, dated 29 Oct. 1957.

[21] *SE* iv, p. 375.

[22] *Mishneh torah, Hilkhot melakhim*, 12: 2.

[23] The Talmud quotes this view in the name of Samuel (*Berakhot* 34*b* and parallels). Maimonides, however, quotes this view in the name of the Sages. See Binyamin Ze'ev Benedikt, *Collected Articles* (Heb.) (Jerusalem, 1994), 156–7.

[24] Letter to Isaiah Wolfsberg, dated 5 May 1954.

[25] For the preceding paragraphs see *Das Volk der Religion*, 80; *SE* ii, p. 186, iv, pp. 375, 379; *Musar hamikra vehatalmud*, 23; 'In Expectation of a Great Religious Revival' (Yid.), *Undzer Veg*, 1 Dec. 1950; 'Towards a Religious Revival', *She'arim*, 22 Feb. 1952, 3; 'Jewish Culture and Pagan Culture' (Heb.), *Hapardes* (Jan. 1952), 33–5, and *Hapardes* (Apr. 1966), 6; 'Cette maison doit devenir une forteresse de la Torah pour tous les Juifs de la Diaspora', *Trait d'Union* (Sept. 1958), 5–6; *Hane'eman* (Nisan–Elul 5743 [1983]), 52; Weinberg's letter to an unnamed nephew, dated 28 Feb. 1950; his letter

Despite his great love for Israel, Weinberg believed that it was not wise to encourage all Jews to go on *aliyah*. He feared that this would lead to endless controversy in the new state. Without mentioning Ahad Ha'am, Weinberg adopted his conception that the true ideal was that 'the Land of Israel will be our metropolis, and the Jewish settlements of the Diaspora will be the colonies of the Land of Israel. Their task will be to support and guard our small land so that it can be the spiritual centre for us and the entire world.'[26]

Like many others, Weinberg expected a great spiritual awakening to accompany the rise of the state, and therefore believed it was vitally important to check extremist trends before their negative influence nipped this awakening in the bud. In its wake, it would be possible to think about a revival of the Sanhedrin. Yet as Weinberg explained in a letter to Chief Rabbi Herzog, this step was still premature since the Jewish people, even in Israel, had not yet emancipated themselves from the Diaspora mentality.[27]

Weinberg left this last point unexplained, adding cryptically: 'this is sufficient for the wise [to understand]'. However, there is no doubt that he had in mind the reluctance of the right-wing Orthodox to confront the new realities. Instead, they continued living as if nothing had changed, as if Jewish sovereignty over the Land of Israel was of no great theological or halakhic significance. Indeed, 'the filth of the *galut* is becoming more powerful', Weinberg declared.[28] Similarly, the right wing continued to reject secular studies; this was illustrated most vividly by its opposition to the creation of Bar-Ilan University, even though it was obvious that secular studies were necessary in the modern world.[29] This rejection was nothing less than a hopeless wish 'to turn back the wheels of history'.[30] As Weinberg observed, it was impossible to have a country without a university, so should the Orthodox not also assume the role of training engineers, scientists, and other professionals? Furthermore, only those who lacked all sense could believe that Israel would be able to rely

to Isaiah Wolfsberg, dated 5 May 1954; and his undated letter to Yonah Emanuel. In his letter to Samuel Atlas, dated 4 Aug. 1948, Weinberg wrote: 'Have you read my article on Herzl? In it I also speak of the strength and holiness of the warriors of Israel in the Land of Israel—my only consolation'; see 'The Magical Name—Herzl' (Yid.), *Undzer Veg*, 23 July 1948. See also *SE* iv, p. 375, where he writes that the Land of Israel has become sanctified through the blood of Jewish soldiers. In *Das Volk der Religion*, 83, he refers to Israel's soldiers as 'grandchildren of the Maccabees' and members of 'the national Bar-Kokhba army'. His sympathies did not, however, extend to members of the Irgun and the Stern Group, and he opposed their acts of terrorism directed against the British government (interview with Ze'ev Matzner). For his praise of the Warsaw Ghetto revolt, which was not shared by all rabbinic figures, see *Yad sha'ul*, 10.

[26] Letter to Isaiah Wolfsberg, dated 5 May 1954.

[27] See *Hama'ayan*, 32 (Tammuz 5752 [1992]), 10.

[28] Letter to Samuel Atlas, dated 25 Mar. 1947.

[29] See 'Our Education' (Yid.), *Undzer Veg*, 6 Apr. 1951, 2. In this article, Weinberg also mentioned the need for young people to participate in sports in order to strengthen their bodies. However, unlike Kook's advocacy in *Orot*, ch. 34, Weinberg was not presenting a theological justification.

[30] Letter to Pinhas Biberfeld, dated 8 Apr. 1959.

on gentile doctors or on doctors who had been trained in the Diaspora, which would be the case if the right-wing Orthodox were able to ban the use of cadavers at the university.[31] As for the right-wing argument that secular studies *per se* are dangerous to religious faith, no matter who supervises the instruction, Weinberg responded sharply:

If it were, Heaven forbid, as the opponents of secular education say, it would be a disgrace for the 'wise and understanding nation' [see Deut. 4: 6] that it is not able simultaneously to digest belief and secular education, while other peoples with their foolish beliefs can do so. The Catholics, *lehavdil*, have professors, intellectuals, researchers, and great scientists, and

[31] 'Autopsies in the State of Israel' (Heb.), *Teḥumin*, 12 (1991), 384; *Hapardes* (May 1966), 38. The latter source is a letter from Weinberg to R. Simhah Elberg, a spokesman of right-wing Orthodoxy, in which Weinberg expressed his fear that the university might have a negative impact upon the great yeshivot (a similar view was expressed by Dessler, *Mikhtav me'eliyahu*, iii. 355–8). However, after taking into account everything else known about Weinberg's views during this period, it seems hardly likely that this represented his true feelings. Indeed, the second half of the letter entirely disregards this fear. It would appear that Weinberg's opening words of concern were only intended to establish a common language with his correspondent, after which he could explain why it was essential to open an Orthodox university. See also his letter to Elberg in *Hapardes* (Apr. 1966), 5, where Weinberg expressed his regret at studying for a 'gentile' doctorate. However, once again, this short letter is contradicated by so much else we know about Weinberg's thinking that it certainly does not require us to re-evaluate his views. At best, this letter reflected a fleeting sentiment, but more probably it was tactfully formulated so as to appeal to Elberg's own sensibilities, a trait seen in other letters written by Weinberg to Elberg. See also Weinberg's assertion, *SE* ii, p. 53, that German rabbis did not value the title 'Dr' and only used it when dealing with the government and in their battle against Reform. The fact is, as Weinberg was well aware, that in private vernacular correspondence German rabbis would never omit the title. It was sometimes also used in their Hebrew correspondence. The short note in which Weinberg included this assertion is dedicated to praising, and perhaps even shoring up the legitimacy of German rabbis in the eyes of the increasingly popular right-wing Orthodox. In this context, it is obvious why Weinberg felt the need to downplay one of the characteristics of German Orthodoxy. For a letter negating the significance of secular studies, written before the war to a Hungarian rabbi who had argued that it was forbidden to give a sermon in German, see *SE* ii, p. 364. Once again, in order to appreciate this letter one must not forget to whom it is addressed. In general, the way in which Weinberg's letters are formulated depends on the addressee. For example, when writing to Haredi figures, such as R. Moses Soloveitchik, he portrayed himself as one of their camp, even though in practice this was not how he lived his life. Another good example is the way Weinberg referred to the controversial R. Shelomo Goren: when writing to figures in the yeshiva world he did not refer to Goren as a 'gaon'.

To conclude, it is impossible to make generalizations about Weinberg's positions on the basis of individual letters without taking into account whether these letters are in line with everything else known about his personality. Others have noted the apparent contradictions in Weinberg and explained them by arguing that he was not a harmonious personality (e.g. Moshe Stern, 'Ish eshkolot', *De'ot*, 31 (1967), 23). I cannot accept this interpretation. While it is true that in his early life there was much tension in his personality, no such lack of harmony can be detected in the post-war years. In fact, from as early as the 1920s until his death, Weinberg's *Weltanschauung* was not subject to any significant vacillations or transformations. Quite apart from the fact that not everything he wrote reflected his inner convictions, a careful distinction must also be made between the differing aspects of a unified personality at peace with itself and the contradictions which create tension in this personality. Interestingly enough, Weinberg himself might not have appreciated this judgement, for he wrote: 'A thinker does not regard it as a compliment when it is said concerning him that his soul is "complete", without any contradictions and inner doubts.' See 'Ahad Ha'am' (1920), 120.

they are strong believers and defend their religion with all the weapons of modern philosophy. . . . I am afraid that this fear of secular studies will lead, God forbid, to a disgrace of the Torah. Might one then be able to say that our great divine Torah cannot compete with so-called secular studies, with a little grammar, geography, history, mathematics?[32]

Opposition to secular studies in general, and to a university in particular, showed Weinberg that the right wing was not yet ready to assume the responsibilities of life in a sovereign state. It was not yet ready to create a 'Torah of life' which would leave its imprint on society as a whole. Instead, it was content to occupy a small corner of Jewish life in Israel, a new type of ghetto isolated from the challenges of modernity, rather than striving to assume wide-reaching spiritual leadership in the new state.[33] It was thus obvious to Weinberg that the more weighty question of the creation of a Sanhedrin, and the parameters of its authority, would have to be put off until the more basic problems affecting Orthodox Judaism were solved.[34]

Weinberg's own vision of how Orthodox society should develop is seen in his description of the Berlin Rabbinical Seminary, which was published in 1961.[35] As he put it, the seminary imparted the lesson that, despite their central importance, it was not enough for students to study the laws of *kashrut* and of purity and impurity. Rather, the students' mission, in accordance with the Torah im Derekh Eretz vision of Hirsch, was to enable Judaism to become a decisive spiritual force for humanity. These students were to provide answers for the problems of morality and social justice which confront modern society. They were also to show the emptiness of those aspects of general culture which must be rejected by all faithful Jews. Since only those who understand a civilization are able to affect it, it was imperative that they be acquainted with all fields of modern thought and culture. This would enable them to influence the new generation, which was growing up completely integrated into modern society.[36] It was this approach which Weinberg found sadly lacking in his era, and once again we see his commitment to a vision of

[32] See 'Autopsies'; 'Our Education', 13 Apr. 1951, 2. (A large portion of this paragraph appeared earlier in Weinberg's 'Our Educational Questions and Concerns' (Yid.), *Yidishe Togblat*, 21 Sept. 1934, 5.) See also the continuation of this article, 11 May 1951, 2, where Weinberg defended secular studies but relegated them to a merely utilitarian function. This approach differs from what Weinberg wrote elsewhere, where he stressed the synthesis between the Jewish and the secular. The articles in *Undzer Veg*, which were written for a popular audience, do not develop all of Weinberg's thoughts concerning this interaction. A Hebrew translation of this article appeared in instalments in *She'arim*, 1952 (see bibliography for publication details).

[33] On this mentality, see his 'Our Education', 13 Apr. 1951, 2.

[34] In his letter to Isaiah Wolfsberg, dated 5 May 1954, he wrote: 'Our generation is not capable of establishing a Sanhedrin in its full sense. There is a need for a new method of study, a new outlook, and a new belief.'

[35] *SE* i, introduction.

[36] See also Weinberg's letters in *Hama'ayan*, 6 (Tammuz 5726 [1966]), 66; ibid. 32 (Tammuz 5752 [1992]), 19.

Judaism which is inclusive, as opposed to the yeshiva vision articulated by Dessler, which is élitist.[37]

Since he was always discreet, it is only in Weinberg's private letters that we get a true glimpse of his pessimistic assessment of the times in which he lived and the failure of Orthodox leadership to respond adequately. While in one published responsum he did speak of the inability of east European Orthodoxy, as opposed to German Orthodoxy, to provide an appealing form of Judaism for the young generation,[38] in his private letters he was more strident. Here he blasted the 'blindness' found in this community which, because of its ideology and stringent halakhic rulings, prevented Orthodoxy from having a wide appeal and producing rabbis who could meet the modern challenge, which had been successfully met by the graduates of the Berlin Rabbinical Seminary.[39] 'I know that extremism has assumed a position of strength in contemporary Orthodoxy,' exclaimed Weinberg in a private letter, 'yet in the same measure it has lost its influence on other circles [i.e. the non-Orthodox]. I am concerned with strengthening the religion and not with what will be said by those who have pretences of being its defenders.'[40] The only way to strengthen the religion and stop the trend towards apathy and assimilation, declared Weinberg in another letter, is by spreading the ideology of German Orthodoxy.[41]

For Weinberg, much of contemporary Orthodox Judaism was imbued with hypocrisy and extremism, masquerading as religiosity. This extremism had the power to silence those who wished to speak out against the distortions of Judaism propagated by, among others, 'insignificant hasidic *rebbes*'.[42] Salanter had stressed the need for ethical conduct to be combined with strict punctiliousness in observing Jewish law, and in one of his early essays Weinberg naively claimed that in days past all who were punctilious about observance of the commandments were, in fact, possessed of religiosity.[43] However, he now realized that this was not the case. In the post-war generation he discerned strictness in ritual matters but blatant disregard for ethical conduct and etiquette—the surest way to drive the young generation away from Judaism. Deeply affected by this phenomenon, Weinberg

[37] See also 'Our Education', 13 Apr. 1951, 2, where Weinberg stressed that rabbis must try to influence all young people, regardless of their parents' religious or political affiliation.

[38] *SE* ii, no. 8.

[39] In his letter to Moses Shulvass, dated 12 Apr. 1957, Weinberg wrote: 'You were very brief while the others exaggerate concerning the small yeshivot. Our seminary produced great and renowned men who led communities and large institutions, and virtually all of the leaders of religious Jewry are products of our seminary.' (He is referring to Shulvass's article, 'Rabbinical Seminary'.)

[40] Letter to Joseph Apfel, dated 23 Feb. 1951 (excerpt in Apfel, 'Letters', 53).

[41] *Hama'ayan*, 32 (Tammuz 5752 [1992]), 19. In his letter to Pinhas Biberfeld, dated 8 Apr. 1959, Weinberg wrote: 'We know that it was only the followers of this approach [i.e. Torah im Derekh Eretz] who saved the remnant of Judaism in Lithuania, Poland, and the Holy Land. Just look at those who are in charge of religious education and who have wide-ranging spiritual influence in the land of Israel. The great majority are products of our seminary.'

[42] See Weinberg's letter in Mordechai Eliav and Yitshak Raphael (eds.), *Sefer shragai* (Jerusalem, 1981), 275. See also his letter in *Hama'ayan*, 32 (Tammuz 5752 [1992]), 18.

[43] *Lifrakim*, 374 (148).

asserted that prostration was required at the graves of the hated *maskilim* of old, for it was precisely they who had earlier taken up the fight against religious hypocrisy and the emphasis on the ritual at the expense of the ethical.[44]

Sometimes, in his anger, Weinberg was driven to extremes, as when he poured scorn on those Orthodox who opposed academic Jewish studies, even though he himself admitted that these studies should not be publicized beyond a small circle.[45] He also attacked the right wing for its negative view of gentiles. However, Weinberg realized that matters were more complicated than this, and that the right wing was merely reflecting what appears in ancient sources. It was these very sources which led him to assert that Judaism hates Christianity more than the reverse. He also questioned whether Jews themselves share part of the blame for history's ever-present antisemitism because of their attitude to the non-Jewish world. To illustrate this, he pointed to talmudic laws which discriminate against gentiles, and which he was at pains to justify in his earlier years.[46] He now admitted that these laws, which greatly troubled him, cannot simply be denied or explained away. However, Weinberg was only able to raise the problem and share his frustration that he could not offer any solutions. 'Can the nations resign themselves to such a deprivation of rights? . . . What can we do? Can we uproot our Torah teaching with apologetic formulae or clever deceptions? God knows that I have written this with the blood of my heart, the blood of my soul.'[47]

[44] See Weinberg's letter in Eliav and Raphael, *Sefer shragai*, 275. Some of Weinberg's concerns were shared by R. Joseph B. Soloveitchik. See his letters in Abraham Bick (ed.), *Actual Problems in Light of the Halakhah* (Heb.) (Jerusalem, 1993), 123–5.

[45] See Weinberg's letter to Samuel Atlas, published in my 'Between East and West', 340–2; Weinberg's letter to Atlas, dated 1 Jan. 1963.

[46] A similar explanation for Christian antisemitism was earlier offered by R. Israel Moses Hazzan (1807–63), *Kerakh shel romi* (Livorno, 1876), 4*a*. Cf. also Samuel David Luzzatto, *Studies in Judaism* (Heb.), vol. ii (Warsaw, 1913), 66.

[47] Weinberg's letter to Samuel Atlas, published in my 'Between East and West', 341–2. As an example of anti-gentile discrimination which so distressed Weinberg, he pointed to Rabbenu Tam's view that intercourse with a gentile does not render a woman forbidden to her husband, 'for it is like having intercourse with an animal' (Tosafot, *Ketubot* 3*b* s.v. *velidrosh*). (However, he was willing to make use of Rabbenu Tam's view in a halakhic discussion concerning an adulterous woman. See his responsum in Isser Yehudah Unterman, *Shevet miyehudah* (Jerusalem, 1992), 264–5.) The relevant section of Weinberg's letter reads as follows: 'We regard all the nations as similar to an ass. It is forbidden to save a gentile, it is forbidden to offer him free medical treatment, it is forbidden to violate the Sabbath to save his life, his sexual intercourse does not render a woman forbidden to her husband according to R. Tam. . . . It is permitted to deceive a gentile and cancel his loan and it is forbidden to return his lost object!' For the rabbinic sources upon which these statements are based, see my 'Scholars and Friends: Rabbi Jehiel Jacob Weinberg and Professor Samuel Atlas', *Torah u-Madda Journal*, 7 (1997), 120–1. In his letter to Samuel Atlas, dated 26 Oct. 1964, Weinberg called attention to Maimonides, *Mishneh torah, Hilkhot isurei bi'ah*, 12: 10, as a particularly disturbing example of anti-gentile discrimination. He also pointed out that there is no talmudic source for Maimonides' view. Cf. *Gilyon ne'emanei torah ve'avodah* (Heshvan 5754 [1993]), 25, where Gerald Blidstein recalls the following conversation with R. Joseph B. Soloveitchik: 'I remember that in Israel there was a real problem, do you save a gentile on the Sabbath? One evening during this time I was with the Rav [Joseph B. Soloveitchik] and he said "I have been in Boston many years and I always rule that one saves the lives of gentiles, because if we don't permit this, they won't treat our sick ones." I asked him

In a later letter, however, after declaring that religious hatred between Judaism and Christianity must cease, he advocated unqualified acceptance of Me'iri's view that the talmudic anti-gentile laws are only directed against the idolaters of old. The problem with this, Weinberg added, was that instructors at the right-wing yeshivot, while mouthing agreement with Me'iri, quietly informed their students that this approach was only to be used for apologetic purposes, but did not truly reflect Jewish teaching.[48]

The tension Weinberg was experiencing with regard to the place of gentiles in Jewish law was particularly wrenching, since for him it was not merely a theoretical concern. Unlike his rabbinic contemporaries, Weinberg had a very close friendship with a non-Jew, his teacher Paul Kahle. In this regard, it is worth quoting a passage from his letter to Kahle after the death of the latter's wife, as it shows Weinberg's sensitivity to gentile piety:

> As often as I had the opportunity to meet her, I was strongly impressed by her deep religiosity, her modest demeanour, and her sure judgement—spiritual strengths which make a woman strong and great. Besides its tragic character for her own family, this death of a noble, pious Christian woman also possesses a historically devastating aspect. She was one of the few German women, perhaps even the only one, who found the courage to oppose the overpowering might of the criminal usurpers when it came to standing up for the innocents being persecuted. In the Israeli papers this heroic act of a German woman was lauded as praiseworthy, and I am convinced that many among us keep her in grateful memory.[49]

Pessimistic appraisals of the modern manifestations of Judaism appear throughout Weinberg's private letters, giving a clear picture of a man full of bitterness at not getting what he deserved and eternally suspicious of others' intentions. Charges of dishonest dealings and plagiarism abound in these letters, and Weinberg saw enemies at almost every corner.[50] In a manner which seems almost antisemitic, Weinberg berated the Jewish people for the fraudulence and hypocrisy it harbours, unparalleled in any other nation. For example, he claimed that whereas other nations know how to evaluate creativity and scholarship properly, this is not so with the Jews, who produce more than their share of charlatans and plagiarists who unjustly achieve renown.[51] Even the great intellectual creativity of Rabbi Kook

if this reason satisfied him from a moral standpoint, and he replied, "No, from a moral standpoint it does not satisfy me."'

[48] Letter to Samuel Atlas, dated 26 Oct. 1964. In 'Zum Proselytproblem', *Jüdische Rundschau-Maccabi*, 8 Sept. 1950, 4, Weinberg wrote in an ecumenical vein: 'We believe that a gentile can also be blessed, when he remains true to his religion and faithfully fulfils its precepts.'

[49] Letter to Kahle, dated 25 Jan. 1949.

[50] Those he accused of plagiarism included Chaim Heller, Ezekiel Abramsky, Samuel Bialoblocki, and Hanokh Albeck. See also above, Ch. 4 n. 62, where I mentioned his suspicions of Alexander Sperber. Since Weinberg had such a critical attitude, those who are praised in his letters must have truly impressed him.

[51] A good example of Weinberg's thought in this regard is seen in his letter to Samuel Atlas dated 2 Mar. 1961, parts of which read as follows: 'It seems that this cunning is a national characteristic of

was played down by Weinberg, and Rabbi Jacob Moses Harlap's *Hed harim* aroused his 'spiritual revulsion'.[52]

As mentioned above, Weinberg realized that the problem of Orthodox Jews' negative attitude towards other religions was complicated by the fact that this attitude had its basis in the religion's classical sources. For Weinberg, who adopted the view of Me'iri, it was essential to show that the views advocated in these sources did not apply under contemporary circumstances. To do otherwise would be to disgrace the Torah. Since modern society had come to see religious tolerance as a basic norm, it was essential that Jewish thought and law should also share this advanced point of view. There were a number of other times when Weinberg showed the same concern, asserting that even though certain things are permissible according to Jewish law, they must not be implemented since they were not acceptable in contemporary society. There is ample precedent for this type of concern in earlier rabbinic literature. Although Weinberg did not cite this source, the Talmud points out that while a convert, according to biblical law, is permitted to marry his closest relatives, the Sages forbade this in order to prevent people from saying that standards of morality are more relaxed after conversion than before.[53] Weinberg's originality is found in the cases to which he applied this logic.

One example of this approach concerned a case where a woman's husband had died, leaving her childless. In accordance with Jewish law she was obligated to participate in the *ḥalitsah* ceremony with her brother-in-law. However, the brother-in-law suffered from a physical deformity which, according to many authorities, invalidated the *ḥalitsah* procedure. In earlier generations scholars, including

ours, and this causes the nations of the world to hate us. I have deep thoughts concerning this but am afraid to express them orally, all the more so to put them into writing. . . . We have innumerable *geonim*. Every *meshulaḥ* is a *gaon* and *tsadik*, and everyone with an imagination who knows how to express his thoughts in a literary manner is a philosopher. Yet the outside world does not know how to evaluate us properly.' In his letter to Atlas dated 20 Sept. 1948, he wrote: 'In general, we are afflicted with a despicable charlatanism which is not found among any other peoples.' In his letter to Atlas dated 25 Jan. 1949, he wrote: 'The later scholars repeat what the earlier ones said, but, as is the practice with Jews, do not mention them.' In his letter to Joseph Apfel, dated 8 Dec. 1955, Weinberg wrote: 'The fraudulence which has spread in Israel causes me to feel sad and hopeless. Everything among us is rotten and stench-filled, God have mercy.' Similar sentiments are found in many other letters. Hints of Weinberg's negative view of Jewish scholarly achievement, especially as compared with non-Jewish scholarship, are also found in his published writings from before the war. See *SE* iv, pp. 112, 136 n. 3; and see also his letter in *Hamaor* (July 1953), 19. Cf. the following quotation from Heinrich von Treitschke's 'A Word About Our Jews': 'Among the leading men in the arts and sciences, the number of Jews is not very great; all the stronger do the Semitic talents constitute the host of the third rate. And how firmly these scribblers stick together. How securely they work on the tested business principle of reciprocity, whereby, as in some insurance company dealing in immortality, every Jewish poetaster receives free and clear one day of fame, paid out by the newspapers, without having to pay the premium' (Richard S. Levy, *Antisemitism in the Modern World* (Lexington, Mass., 1991), 71).

52 Letter to Samuel Atlas, dated 2 Mar. 1961.

53 *Yevamot* 22*a*. See also Maimonides, *Mishneh torah, Hilkhot mamrim*, 5: 11, and R. Joseph Caro's commentary, *Kesef mishneh*, ad loc.

Grodzinski,[54] had suggested that, in order to avoid any halakhic problems, the brother-in-law should sleep with the widow, performing *yibum*, and then give her a divorce. However, what had been an option in an earlier generation was now no longer possible. In fact, even to suggest this approach would lead to a 'desecration of God's name and degradation of the Torah', because people would view the entire procedure as giving a halakhic imprimatur to immorality. Although in former times a scholar such as Grodzinski could advocate the procedure, in the face of modern sensibilities only an 'insane' rabbi could offer such a 'foul' suggestion.[55]

Similarly, Weinberg refused to consider the various halakhic arguments for and against the 'sale' of Israeli land to gentiles in the sabbatical year. In his opinion, there was a more important consideration, namely that such a 'sale' would make it appear to both Jews and gentiles as though the Orthodox were trying to evade the laws of the Torah. As this would bring disgrace upon the Torah, as well as weaken the Orthodox in their efforts to expand Torah law in the State of Israel, it must be rejected.[56]

As mentioned above, Weinberg had a very hopeful view of the State of Israel and of what could be accomplished there in religious matters. At the same time, he warned against the state and the land assuming exaggerated importance and becoming ends in and of themselves, since they were only to be regarded as means to an end—observance of the Torah.[57] He often stressed, in particular in his letter to Prime Minister David Ben-Gurion, that the state's new-found glory would dissipate quickly if it did not recognize its heritage and abandon the bankrupt secularism of its leaders. Although he denied that he had any desire for state-instituted religious coercion of individuals, he argued that in religious matters which concern the nation as a whole (e.g. personal status, Sabbath observance in the public sphere), the state must not adopt a neutral role. To do so would be to depart from the basic values of Judaism. Just as every country has certain unshakeable principles

[54] Grodzinski, *She'elot uteshuvot aḥi'ezer*, iii, no. 20.

[55] See *SE* iii, p. 168; *Hama'ayan*, 32 (Tammuz 5752 [1992]), 13, letter to Saul Lieberman, dated 27 July 1954. See also *SE* iii, no. 120. It is unclear whether Weinberg believed that in a Jewish society guided by halakhah and populated only by Orthodox Jews such a 'foul' suggestion would still be viable. It is possible that, on the contrary, he agreed with a popular Modern Orthodox conception that 'new moral insights that have been developed in the world affect our Jewish religious practices'. See Walter S. Wurzburger, 'Confronting the Challenge of the Values of Modernity', *Torah u-Madda Journal*, 1 (1989), 111. See also Alexander Carlebach, 'Saving the Life of a Non-Jew on Shabbat', *Niv Hamidrashia* (Winter 1967), 14: 'The honour of the Torah demands that its interpretation and application should not lag behind such moral standards as set up by Hippocrates or the Declaration of Human Rights.'

[56] See his letter in *Hama'or* (Nov. 1953), 17; Unterman, *Shevet miyehudah*, 265. In the latter source, Weinberg also rejected a suggested procedure whereby a marriage could be annulled retroactively, 'so as not to make the laws of the Torah objects of derision and mockery'. Cf., however, Werner Silberstein, *My Way from Berlin to Jerusalem* (Jerusalem, 1994), 82, where he states that Weinberg expressed support for the sabbatical year 'sale', but would not put this support in writing for fear of how the religious extremists would respond.

[57] See Weinberg's views cited in Ch. 4 n. 112.

upon which it based its existence, so too the State of Israel must make the Torah its foundation, which must not be subject to the whims of popular sentiment.[58]

Weinberg was similarly outspoken on the issue of Reform Judaism. There is no question that he greatly admired a number of Reform rabbis, praising their honourable intentions and committed work on behalf of the Jewish people. In a private letter he even noted sarcastically that a certain Reform rabbi was a 'desecration of God's name', because he demonstrated that one could be a fine and upstanding man without following Jewish law, whereas so many of the Orthodox, who were punctilious with regard to Jewish law, lacked the basic norms of decency. Referring to the recently deceased Reform leaders, Israel Bettan and Leo Baeck, Weinberg declared: 'Every great man who dies leaves a void. Who can replace Dr Baeck? When they are alive we criticize them and search for faults, but when they die we feel what we have lost.'[59] However, statements such as this concerned individuals; as far as the Reform *movement* was concerned, Weinberg felt nothing but scorn. He urged his rabbinic colleagues to reject publicly the validity of Reform Judaism, which he regarded as more akin to Christianity than to Judaism.[60]

Although Weinberg almost always advocated a peaceful approach, especially when dealing with the less religious, when it came to manifestations of the Reform movement he counselled 'war' as the only way to safeguard traditional Judaism.[61] Since extreme steps had to be taken in this battle, Weinberg declared that even *ex post facto* halakhically valid Reform conversions must be rejected as a sign of Orthodoxy's determination not to grant any validity to the heretical movement.[62]

[58] *SE* iii, p. 258, iv, pp. 374 ff.; *Das Volk der Religion*, 89 ff.; Weinberg's essay in *Musar hamikra vehatalmud*, 23–6. See also 'The Fate of One in Confusion', *She'arim*, 20 June 1953, 4–5, written in response to Arthur Koestler's *Promise and Fulfillment*.

[59] Letter to Samuel Atlas, published in my 'Between East and West', 340.

[60] Fuchs, 'Hochschule', 22; letter to Samuel Atlas, dated 16 Oct. 1959; Atlas, 'Portrayal', 286; *Hama'ayan*, 34 (Tevet 5754 [1994]), 13; interview with Professor Alexander Guttmann (Weinberg is mentioned in the preface to Guttmann's book, *The Struggle over Reform in Rabbinic Literature During the Last Century and a Half* (Jerusalem, 1977), xii). See also *SE* iii, p. 42, where Weinberg expresses his concern that negative gossip should not be spread about a Reform rabbi, surely an uncommon sentiment among Orthodox leaders. In a letter to Samuel Atlas, dated 25 Jan. 1949, he mentioned that he had prevented the publication of an attack on Leo Baeck which accused him of having been a German collaborator.

[61] *SE* iii, no. 100. See also 'Zur Frage der Bestattung nicht-jüdischer Ehegatten auf einem jüdischen Friedhof', *Jüdische Rundschau-Maccabi*, 29 Apr. 1955, 1–2. See, however, Weinberg's letter in *Hama'ayan*, 32 (Tammuz 5752 [1992]), 13, where he stressed that his battle with Reform was a quiet one.

[62] *Hama'ayan*, 34 (Tevet 5754 [1994]), 14. That some Reform conversions may be valid was also stated by Weinberg in *SE* iii, no. 100, and in his letter to R. Hillel Medalié, dated 29 Oct. 1957. Weinberg obviously interpreted the talmudic 'acceptance of the commandments', without which no conversion is valid, as meaning something much less than *all* the commandments. This view is actually put forward by his student Eliezer Berkovits in his *Not in Heaven* (New York, 1983), 108–12, though Berkovits does not mention Weinberg in this regard. Weinberg may have believed that acceptance of the commandments is only a *conditio sine qua non* when the convert is informed about them, but that lack of knowledge about the commandments does not invalidate a conversion. See Moshe Tsuriel, 'The Conversion of Russian Immigrants' (Heb.), *Iturei kohanim*, 67 (Tishrei 5751 [1990]), 33–4. Finkelstein, in his extremely comprehensive

It is, of course, only to be expected that he refused to allow Reform rabbis to deliver lectures in Orthodox synagogues.[63] He was also very concerned that Orthodox pulpit rabbis should not institute measures which could lead the right wing to accuse them of reformist tendencies.[64] Yet, as I have pointed out elsewhere, Weinberg believed that the steps to be taken against Reform had to be relevant to the situation then being confronted by Orthodoxy. For example, banning sermons in the vernacular or forbidding prayer in a synagogue which had an unused organ might have been valid responses in former years, but in contemporary times they had no relevance and could do nothing to help the battle against Reform; on the contrary, they created difficulties for Orthodoxy.[65]

Although Weinberg publicly expressed his strong feelings about the State of Israel and Reform, the fact is that he was no longer a fighter, and on many issues he chose to express himself, and offer support, only in private. After the war, in a weakened physical and mental state, he was hardly ever prepared to advocate publicly views which were opposed by other leading scholars and which would have involved him in controversy. For example, in the early 1950s he planned to write an article in support of the institution of national service for young women in Israel. However, after being confronted with opposition he shelved this plan.[66] To give another example, in 1950 Weinberg wrote to M. Freyer, a rabbi in Berlin, encouraging him in his efforts to help rebuild German Jewish life. In this letter Weinberg also rejected calls for a boycott of Jewish settlement in Germany, arguing that making Germany *judenrein* would be granting the Germans their wish. Yet he explained that his support for Freyer would have to remain private, as he was not prepared to face the barrage of criticism which would ensue were he to publicize his view.[67]

As we have already seen, Weinberg's refusal to go to Israel was due to this re-

Proselytism, and Zvi Zohar and Avraham Sagi, *Conversion to Judaism and the Meaning of Jewish Identity* (Heb.) (Jerusalem, 1995), omit any mention of Weinberg's view that Reform conversions may be halakhically valid. In 'Zum Proselytproblem' (1950), 4, Weinberg's view was more restrictive, and here he wrote that non-Orthodox conversions can never be valid. This should not be seen as a contradiction, since the latter source is more of a public policy statement than a halakhic responsum and simply reflected Weinberg's conclusion that the Orthodox, because of meta-halakhic considerations, must not accept *any* Reform conversions. (R. Joseph B. Soloveitchik believed that Reform conversions which were accompanied by circumcision and immersion in a *mikveh* were to be regarded as 'doubtful conversions'. See Walter S. Wurzburger, 'Rav Joseph B. Soloveitchik as *Posek* of Post-Modern Orthodoxy', *Tradition*, 29 (Fall 1994), 14. As with Weinberg, it is obvious that Soloveitchik understood 'acceptance of the commandments' as meaning something less than *all* the commandments. See also R. Hanokh Ehrentreu's view recorded in Ben-Avner, 'Activities', 262.)

[63] See *SE* ii, no. 13.

[64] See ibid., nos. 8, 14.

[65] See ibid., nos. 11, 149; and my 'Sociology and Halakhah', *Tradition*, 27 (Fall 1992), 81.

[66] Interview with R. Bezalel Rakov.

[67] Letter to M. Freyer, dated 8 Nov. 1950. Similar sentiments appear in his letter to Elhanan Scheftelowitz, in the latter's *500 Years*, unnumbered page at the end of the book, and in his letter to Isaiah Wolfsberg, dated 2 Mar. 1956. On the other hand, Weinberg publicly opposed the Israeli government's acceptance of reparations payments from Germany. See his 'The Warsaw Ghetto Revolt and the Protest in the Keneset', *She'arim*, 1 Feb. 1952, 3–4.

luctance to adopt an independent stand which would involve controversy and possibly his subsequent isolation from a segment of Orthodoxy. In response to a request that he become rector of a new rabbinical seminary in Israel, Weinberg stated that because of his age he did not possess the necessary strength to defend the institution against its opponents, who included many old friends, among them Eliezer Judah Finkel and Ezekiel Sarne (1889–1969). Indeed, had Weinberg been strong enough, he would have been very reluctant to jeopardize his friendships by opposing his colleagues on such an important matter. He also would not have wished to jeopardize his standing in the eyes of the so-called yeshiva world, for despite all his criticisms, his deep love for the yeshivot and desire to be accepted by them were never in question. There is no doubt that Weinberg personally supported the creation of a seminary in Israel which would coexist harmoniously with the great yeshivot. For Weinberg, these two institutions would have had different, although equally legitimate, roles. Yet those who hoped for Weinberg's public show of support for a seminary were to be sadly disappointed.[68]

HALAKHIC ACTIVITY

It is true that on occasion Weinberg did take a public stand on matters which threatened to embroil him in controversy with more conservative segments of the Orthodox community. This was particularly so with regard to a number of lenient halakhic rulings that he published, well aware that they were, as he put it, 'daring', and fully prepared for an avalanche of criticism.[69] However, he felt that in these cases he had no choice but to publicize his view, for as he explained, 'it cannot be that only those who are fearful will decide the halakhah'.[70] On another occasion he expressed himself similarly, declaring: 'One must not be afraid of the masses' screaming and of rabbis who wish to glorify themselves with their stringency.'[71]

[68] Letter to R. Hillel Medalié, dated 1 July 1955; letter to Samuel Atlas, dated 7 Mar. 1956; interview with R. Bezalel Rakov. For Finkel's and Sarne's opposition, see the signed protest in *Igerot mibeit halevi*, 125–6. Even Chief Rabbi Herzog was opposed to the creation of a rabbinical seminary in Israel. See his *Constitution and Law in a Jewish State According to the Halakhah* (Heb.) (Jerusalem, 1989), iii. 240. In 'Cette maison' (1958), 5–6, and his letter to Medalié dated 4 Apr. 1958, Weinberg expressed his support for the establishment of Heikhal Shelomo, the seat of the Israeli Chief Rabbinate. For the right-wing opposition, which again included Finkel and Sarne, see *Igerot mibeit halevi*, 115–17, 119.

[69] Letter to Samuel Atlas, dated 18 Dec. 1958. He referred in particular to *SE* iii, no. 25, which deals with women whose husbands converted to Islam and remained in Yemen; these women could not receive a *get*. Weinberg's responsum presented arguments which would allow the women to remarry. His most radical arguments are that one can execute a divorce without the husband's knowledge and that even contemporary rabbis have the power to annul a marriage retroactively. For criticism of this responsum, see Benedikt, *Collected Articles*, 90–107.

[70] Letter to Joseph Apfel, dated 21 Mar. 1963 (excerpt in Apfel, 'Letters', 53).

[71] Letter to Joseph Apfel, dated 26 Apr. 1963 (excerpt in Apfel, 'Letters', 52). Both this comment and the one referred to in the previous note concern Weinberg's approval of the bat mitzvah ceremony.

Because there were always valid halakhic sources to back up his leniencies, he could claim that it was not he who was granting permission, but rather the sources themselves.[72]

However, it more often happened that Weinberg was not prepared to contradict the rulings of outstanding scholars of an earlier generation without the support of other leading contemporary halakhists. In adopting this position, Weinberg took his place with many other *posekim* who are characterized by a lack of confidence in their own authority and hesitancy in reaching significant decisions, in particular concerning matters of personal status. It is only the rare halakhist who can declare that a *posek* must fearlessly answer all queries, and once convinced of the correctness of his argument is obliged to rule in accordance with it.[73] Weinberg's position was much more in line with traditional patterns of halakhic decision-making, which explains why he was reluctant to issue independent rulings in a number of areas, in particular concerning family law, even though he felt strongly that halakhic leniencies were possible and desirable. It was because of his hesitancy that so many of his responsa dealing with important issues, virtually all of which led towards a lenient conclusion, ended with a note that his opinion was not to be acted on in practice until other important scholars expressed their agreement.[74] Even after issuing a ruling he was prepared to retract it if these scholars disagreed.[75]

As he explained in a letter, it was precisely this fear of independent decision-making which prevented solutions to difficult halakhic problems from being found.[76]

[72] See Gavriel Hayim Cohn, 'In Memory of the Gaon Rabbi Dr. Jehiel Jacob Weinberg', *De'ot*, 31 (1967), 13.

[73] Moses Feinstein, *Igerot moshe* (New York, 1959), *Oraḥ ḥayim* i, introduction, v. 58–9.

[74] Sometimes he would not even offer a non-binding decision. See *SE* ii, no. 24. In *SE* iii, no. 6 Weinberg was unable to rule leniently but gave the questioner the option of consulting another authority. With regard to the problem of *agunot*, see also his advice to *posekim* in *No'am*, 5 (1962), 17. Incidentally, a number of *posekim* argue that when an authority writes that his opinion is not to be relied on in practice without the support of other sages, this is simply a sign of modesty and is not to be taken seriously by others; see the sources cited by Hayim Hezekiah Medini, *Sedei ḥemed* (Brooklyn, NY, 1949), ix. 3687–8 (arabic numerals [= '*Kelalei haposekim*' 16: 47]). I have my doubts as to whether this supposition is either historically accurate or methodologically sound. With regard to Weinberg, there is absolutely no question that when he wrote that one should not rely on his view, he was not simply engaging in protestations of modesty but must be taken at his word.

[75] See *SE* iii, p. 350 n. 7, regarding the weighty issue of abortion. (There is some dispute about how to interpret Weinberg's responsum on this topic; see Basil F. Herring, *Jewish Ethics and Halakhah for Our Time* (New York, 1984), 44 n. 18, 45 n. 35.) For another retraction, though without practical halakhic consequences, see *SE* i, p. 361. See also Shapiro, *Igerot lare'iyah*, no. 210, where Weinberg expressed his willingness to retract a decision if Kook were to differ from him. (It is said that R. Abraham Isaiah Karelitz (the Hazon Ish) greatly admired this characteristic of Weinberg, which is very rare among *posekim*; see *Hama'ayan*, 25 (Tishrei 5745 [1985]), 59.)

[76] In this lengthy letter, whose date and addressee are missing, Weinberg wrote: 'I have clear proofs that the marriage can be annulled, but I am also one of the "fearful" and will not under any circumstances rule leniently against the opinion of the *gaon* R. Isaac Elhanan [Spektor] of blessed memory, for I am worthless compared to him. There are indeed many difficult questions which have not found a solution only because we don't have the strength to rule against the authorities who have been accepted by the nation.' On this 'fear', see also *SE* ii, p. 189.

Although he specifically rejected Yeshayahu Leibowitz's call for a 'dynamic' halakhah, he admitted that problems could be solved if there were outstanding authorities willing to take a stand. 'Who would dare oppose a decision by the *gaon* Rabbi Ezekiel Landau? However, if we had in our midst great sages of the level of the *rishonim*, it is possible that they would be lenient.'[77] In his published writings there are also hints of Weinberg's disappointment that he was unable to rule leniently in cases where he thought he had compelling evidence. Rather than assuming the role of apologist and justifying the prohibitions, Weinberg frankly acknowledged that he was pained by the fact that previous authorities had ruled stringently.[78] In one striking passage, unparalleled in recent rabbinic literature, Weinberg even admitted that a prohibition of the *Shulḥan arukh* caused him great anguish.[79]

This same trait of hesitancy on Weinberg's part is seen in his approbation to Eliezer Berkovits's book *Conditional Marriage and Divorce*.[80] In this book Berkovits argued in favour of a certain form of conditional marriage which would eliminate the possibility of women becoming *agunot* because of their husbands' refusal to grant a divorce. In a lengthy approbation Weinberg elaborated on the importance of Berkovits's book, particularly in contemporary times when more and more husbands were refusing to grant their wives Jewish divorces and the wives were remarrying nonetheless, in civil ceremonies. He also urged scholars to examine the material Berkovits presented in favour of conditional marriages, noting that the crux of the dispute over this issue had more to do with conceptions of how Jewish marriage should be structured—a meta-halakhic issue—than with technical halakhic points.[81] The question which must confront scholars examining Berkovits's book was formulated by Weinberg thus:

> Is it more important to maintain the holiness and permanence of Jewish marriage in the sense of 'I will betroth thee unto me for ever' [Hosea 2: 21], so that also in religious circles purity of marital life should not suffer the slightest impairment, or to consider the widespread difficult circumstances which exist today—an important consideration which must not be downplayed in the slightest?

Although he may have had some specific objections to Berkovits's proposals, Weinberg left no doubt that he approved of the latter's general approach to finding

[77] In this letter Weinberg pointed to two examples where 'it is possible, and indeed necessary' for halakhah to be responsive to modern developments. He argued that it should now be permissible to drink non-Jewish milk which is produced under government supervision, and to shave during the intermediate days of the festivals. As Weinberg noted, both of these suggestions had already been offered by earlier scholars. They can also be justified by authoritative halakhic sources, whereas what Leibowitz was advocating was nothing less than a reconstruction of the entire halakhic process.

[78] *SE* iii, p. 113.

[79] Ibid., no. 54. What made the *Shulḥan arukh*'s ruling so frustrating to Weinberg is the fact that R. Joseph Caro had gone against his own principle and ruled in accordance with Rabbenu Asher, despite the fact that Alfasi and Maimonides ruled differently.

[80] Heb. (Jerusalem, 1967).

[81] A similar point was made in his letter to R. Leo Jung, dated 19 June 1957.

a satisfactory method of conditional marriage.[82] Yet in the end, blaming ill health, Weinberg was unwilling to involve himself in any serious discussion of Berkovits's proposals, or of conditional marriage in general. This is another example of his reluctance to chart new halakhic ground independently.[83] As with all great

[82] Weinberg's approval of certain types of conditional marriages and his belief that halakhists should continue work in this area are seen in his letter to R. Leo Jung, dated 19 June 1957. In the questionable letter to R. Menahem Kasher (see next note), Weinberg explained that his sympathetic attitude towards Berkovits's endeavour was due to his being unaware that the issue had already been the focus of a major dispute in the United States between the Orthodox and the Conservative rabbinates, with the Orthodox forbidding conditional marriages.

[83] Weinberg's letter is cited by Israeli Supreme Court Justice Moshe Silberg in one of his decisions; see *Piskei din shel beit hamishpat ha'elyon leyisrael*, 22 (1968), 37–8. Silberg argues that, despite Weinberg's outward refusal to adopt a stance, a close reading of his approbation reveals his identification with Berkovits's position and his strong criticism of those who refuse to explore halakhic ways of solving the modern problems of marriage and divorce. It is worth noting that, according to R. Moshe Tendler, as quoted by R. Leo Jung in an undated letter to Berkovits, R. Moses Feinstein expressed theoretical approval of Berkovits's position.

There has been some dispute regarding Weinberg's approbation ever since R. Menahem Kasher, in the midst of a strident attack on Berkovits's book ('Concerning Conditional Marriage' (Heb.), *No'am*, 11 (1969), 338–53), published a letter from Weinberg in which the latter expressed regret over writing this approbation. Despite Berkovits's claim that this letter was a forgery, Kasher never produced the original. (Berkovits's final statement on this issue is found in his *Jewish Women in Time and Torah* (Hoboken, NJ, 1990), 111: 'I regret to say that my work has not been given serious consideration, and instead all kinds of statements have been made maintaining that my teacher, Rabbi Y. Y. Weinberg, *z.l.*, withdrew the moral support that he gave to the work. I have to declare that in all these statements and rumors there is not the slightest truth.') Although it is impossible for me to offer any definitive evidence that Weinberg's retraction was a forgery perpetrated by Kasher, the following points do not reflect well upon Kasher's credibility.

1. Berkovits's book was originally going to be published in *No'am*, the halakhic annual edited by Kasher, until the latter, presumably because of fear of the religious right, decided this could not be done. The work, with a good portion of it already in print, was then transferred to Mosad Harav Kook which completed publication. These facts are never mentioned by Kasher in his attack on Berkovits's book, in which, by the way, he refuses to mention Berkovits's name, referring to him instead as 'a certain rabbi'. (Soon after Berkovits's book was published, Kasher sent him a letter, a copy of which is in my possession, congratulating him on the appearance of the book!) Nor does Kasher mention the fact that Weinberg's approbation was actually addressed to *him*, and not to Berkovits (a copy of Weinberg's original letter is in my possession). According to Berkovits, Kasher refused to publish the work without this approbation (interview with Berkovits).

2. A letter (in English) from R. Moses Botchko to R. Leo Jung, dated 31 Dec. 1965, a mere three weeks before Weinberg's death when he was too ill to write personally, reads:

> Rabbi Weinberg has received your telegram as well as your letter in connection with the work of Dr. B. However, he is not well at all these days—May the Almighty grant him a Refuah Shelemo. He asked me to write to you on his behalf, and to let you know, that he has not changed his mind at all, and he thinks that it is a very good thing, that the work should be printed in the Hanoam, to stimulate the discussion and the clarification on the matter. He asked me, to state it in unequivocal terms, that he stands 100% to his previous mind, and he really does not understand what has made Rabbi Kasher suddenly change his mind, since he wrote to Rabbi Weinberg that he is thrilled with the work.

When, therefore, is Weinberg supposed to have written his letter of retraction to Kasher? Nevertheless, as noted above, there is no *direct* evidence that Kasher forged the letter. The possibility still exists that Weinberg wrote one thing to Jung and another to Kasher. As I have already pointed out, it

talmudists, however, this hesitancy was confined to practical halakhah. In theoretical discussions he had no qualms about rejecting the opinions of earlier scholars,[84] even the greatest among them, and his criticisms can at times be quite sharp.[85]

In 1961 Weinberg published his first volume of responsa, *Seridei esh* ('Remnants from the Fire'). Although it includes some rabbinic articles he wrote after the war, the bulk of the work consists of his responsa and those of other rabbis concerning the *sheḥitah* question. In his introduction he explained that for several years he had refused to publish the work, fearing that the institution of *sheḥitah* might be endangered if its opponents were to learn that there was a halakhist who argued in favour of the permissibility of stunning. It was for this reason that Chief Rabbi Herzog had requested that he should not publish the responsum. However, the great historical significance of the work, the important talmudic expositions it contained, and the need to set the record straight in the face of those who claimed that he had permitted stunning in practice, convinced him that the work should be published.[86] This volume was soon followed by two more, which combine the responsa saved by Berkovits as well as those he wrote after the war.

TALMUDIC STUDIES

Even though, as mentioned previously, Weinberg was not able to devote himself to modern Jewish scholarship to the extent he would have liked, his training in Wissenschaft des Judentums methodologies was manifested in his talmudic studies. Throughout his writings, including those devoted to practical halakhah,[87] Weinberg continued to stress the importance of using critically established texts and to point out how earlier scholars had been misled by faulty texts.[88] To this end, he did not

was not unheard of for Weinberg to write different things to different people, although in this case it appears highly unlikely.

[84] See *SE* iii, p. 27, for Weinberg's formulation of the difference between theory and practice.

[85] See e.g. *SE* ii, p. 123 and no. 109. See also *SE* i, p. 46, in the note, where Weinberg claimed that his interpretation is obvious to all who know how to read the Tosafists carefully. As Weinberg himself noted, those to whom this interpretation was not obvious included two of the greatest talmudic commentators, R. Samuel Edels and R. Meir of Lublin. For an example of similar self-confidence, see *SE* i, p. 33.

[86] Ibid., pp. 6–7; letter to Pinhas Biberfeld, dated 8 Apr. 1959; letter of Samson Raphael Weiss to Weinberg, dated 22 Feb. 1960, and Weinberg's reply, dated 28 Feb. 1960. See also his letter in Munk and Munk, *Edut ne'emanah*, 249, that Herzog later agreed that publishing the responsum would not create difficulties.

[87] I emphasize this because R. David Zvi Hoffmann, despite being Orthodoxy's leading critical talmudic scholar, did not use his Wissenschaft des Judentums knowledge in formulating halakhic decisions. Even questions regarding proper texts were not taken up by him in his practical halakhic writings. This is the conclusion of Daniel Gordis, who has written a detailed study of Hoffmann's responsa entitled 'Dialectics of Community, Continuity, and Compassion: The Legal Writings of Rabbi David Zevi Hoffmann and their Philosophical Foundations' (Ph.D. diss., University of Southern California, 1992), 151–2.

[88] See *SE* ii, p. 263, iii, p. 253, his review in *Hapardes* (Feb. 1953), 26, and his letters in *No'am*, 16 (1973), 160–4.

hesitate to suggest many textual emendations, which led Eliezer Berkovits to remark, 'I doubt there was anyone among the talmudical authorities of his generation who spent so much effort in establishing a correct reading, and who was able to solve as many problems by ascertaining the right *Girsa*.'[89] Weinberg believed that it was preferable to base these emendations on solid textual support, and he quoted Rabbenu Tam's view that one must not emend a text simply because of a difficulty.[90] However, on occasions when textual support was not available, and an emendation appeared logically convincing, Weinberg would suggest this approach.[91]

Weinberg often emphasized that rabbinic texts must be explained in accordance with their 'true' meaning, which he identified as their original intent, rather than used as a starting-point for brilliant, but misguided, dialectics, which are sometimes even based on faulty texts.[92] In striving to discover the original intent, Weinberg also warned against a common pitfall of modern rabbinic exegesis, that of anachronism. Good illustrations of this aspect of Weinberg's approach appear in

[89] 'Rabbi Yechiel Yakob Weinberg: My Teacher and Master', *Tradition*, 5 (Summer 1966), 7.

[90] *SE* iii, p. 255. Rabbenu Tam's view appears in a variety of places. See esp. his *Sefer hayashar*, ed. F. Rosenthal (Berlin, 1898), 75, 105, and *Sefer hayashar lerabeinu tam: Ḥelek haḥidushim* (Jerusalem, 1959), introduction. See also Irving A. Agus, 'R. Jacob Tam's Stringent Criticism of R. Meshullam of Melun, in its Historical Setting', in Abraham I. Katsh and Leon Nemoy (eds.), *Essays on the Occasion of the Seventieth Anniversary of The Dropsie University* (Philadelphia, Pa., 1979), 1–10; Yaakov Shmuel Spiegel, *Chapters in the History of the Jewish Book* (Heb.) (Ramat Gan, 1996), ch. 5. It must be noted, however, that Rabbenu Tam was concerned with making corrections in a manuscript, a consideration which is not directly relevant to modern scholars.

[91] Similarly, despite Rabbenu Tam's harsh denunciation of those who emended talmudic texts, scholars long ago pointed out that he himself did just that; see Isaac Hirsch Weiss, *Dor dor vedoreshav* (Vilna, 1904), iv. 301, and Avigdor Aptowitzer, *Mavo lesefer ra'avyah* (Jerusalem, 1938), 359. As Aptowitzer has explained, and Weinberg obviously agreed, 'one must certainly distinguish between [different types of] emendations'. See also Nahman Greenspan, *Pilpulah shel torah* (London, 1935), pp. xvi–xxi. For examples of Weinberg's emendations, based upon both textual support and logic, see *SE* i, p. 364, ii, pp. 93–4, iii, no. 33 (see also the criticism of Yehudah Herzl Henkin, *Benei vanim* (Jerusalem, 1981), 91); *SE* iii, pp. 177, 346, 401–8, iv, pp. 143, 249; *Yad sha'ul*, 62–87; 'An Unclear Passage in the Jerusalem Talmud' (Heb.), *Hapardes* (June 1950), 3. In his letter to Saul Lieberman, dated 8 Dec. 1955, Weinberg wrote, with reference to the former's edition of the Tosefta, 'It will remove all the falsifications and distortions that arose because of faulty texts. . . . The modern commentators are happy when they find a mistaken text upon which they can base their distorted *ḥidushim*.'

[92] Weinberg's writing contains numerous comments of this sort. See e.g. *SE* ii, p. 57 and no. 162, iii, p. 346. See also *SE* iii, p. 249, for Weinberg's comments regarding R. Abraham Isaiah Karelitz. When Weinberg used the term *pilpul* he was referring to its extreme version, which throughout history has been a target for criticism by many leading scholars. See Dov Rapel, *The Dispute over Pilpul* (Heb.) (Jerusalem, 1979). As Weinberg never tired of pointing out, moderate *pilpul* is an essential element of Talmud study. See 'Talmudic Pilpul' (1911), *Lifrakim*, 260–1 (117–18); *SE* iii, p. 356, iv, p. 223; 'Die Jeschiwoth' (1916), 116–18, esp. 116: 'What is the entire Babylonian talmudic literature if not *pilpul*?' (Cf. Kaplan, *Be'ikvot hayirah*, 208–9, *Divrei talmud*, i. 23; and Amiel, *Hamidot*, chs. 1–2 of the introduction.) See *SE* ii, p. 57, which shows that Weinberg saw some intellectual value even in extreme *pilpul*, a sentiment which also appears in *SE* iv, p. 232. See similarly Hoffmann's introduction to *Melamed leho'il*; Salanter's introduction to his *Tevunah* (Königsberg, 1861), also found in Salanter's *Or yisrael* (Vilna, 1900), 40 (Hebrew numerals); and the discussion in Etkes, *Rabbi Israel Salanter*, 231–5.

his letters to Samuel Atlas (1899–1977). Although Weinberg admitted that a number of suggestions advanced by Atlas were masterful in showing how talmudic concepts could be expressed in modern scientific language, they were nevertheless *pilpul* of a different sort, 'scientific *pilpul*', for these explanations were based on concepts which would have been foreign to the authors being interpreted. In one of his letters to Atlas, Weinberg quoted the popular yeshiva saying attributed to Rabbi Hayim of Volozhin, 'one doesn't die from a question'.[93] That is, it is better to be left with a question than to interpret the Talmud in an unsuitable manner.[94]

It was Weinberg's emphasis on original intent which was responsible for his criticism of Rabbi Hayim Soloveitchik's Analytic Method, which by the post-war years had become the norm in Lithuanian yeshivot. As Weinberg put it, 'While the ideas of Rabbi Hayim Soloveitchik are true from the standpoint of profound analysis, they are not always so from a historical standpoint, that is, with regard to the true meaning of Maimonides, whose way of study was different from that of Rabbi Hayim Soloveitchik. This does not detract from the value of this intellectual genius who is worthy of being called a "new Maimonides", though not always as an interpreter of Maimonides.'[95] On a number of occasions, Weinberg rejected interpretations made by Soloveitchik and others since they were based on methods of analysis which would have been foreign to Maimonides or were simply not grounded in the latter's words.[96]

93 See Weinberg's letter in Atlas, *Pathways in Hebrew Law* (Heb.) (New York, 1978), 154, and Reuven Katz, *Degel re'uven* (Jerusalem, 1949), iii. 62*b*. See also Ephraim E. Urbach, *From the World of the Sages* (Heb.) (Jerusalem, 1988), 42 n. 189, quoting R. Ezekiel Landau.

94 Letter to Gavriel Hayim Cohn, dated 1 Jan. 1965; *SE* ii, pp. 197–8. See also ibid. 199, where after rejecting an explanation proposed by Atlas, Weinberg wrote: 'It is too modern to insert into the words of Rava.' See also *SE* iii, p. 94, Weinberg's letter in Atlas, *Pathways*, 154, and his article 'Sources of the Mishnah and its Method of Organization' (Heb.), *Talpiot*, 7 (1958), 73. In *Meḥkarim batalmud* S. D. Luzzatto and G. Hoffmann are similarly criticized; see *SE* iv, pp. 43, 56, and his general comments ibid., p. 134. In his letter to Atlas, dated 5 May 1957, Weinberg wrote: 'I did not express disagreement with your logic, which is very good, but only stated that you cannot insert it as an "explanation"—not in the Mishnah, the Jerusalem Talmud, or Maimonides. You are not a teacher at one of the yeshivot and do not need to show your sharpness. Rather, you should explain in a scientific fashion and in accordance with the simple meaning.' In his letter to Abraham Arazy, dated 21 Oct. 1953, Weinberg wrote: 'I prefer a grain of truth to mountains of *pilpul* and *ḥarifut*.' In general, Weinberg thought very highly of Atlas's scholarship, and in his letter to Atlas, dated 25 Mar. 1947, he wrote: 'Your *ḥidushim* and notes excel in their clarity and profundity.' Weinberg's attitude should be compared with that of a noted right-wing *posek*, R. Menasheh Klein, *Mishneh halakhot* (Brooklyn, NY, 1992), second series, *Yoreh de'ah*, nos. 212–13, who discusses whether it is halakhically permissible even to read Atlas's comments.

95 *SE* ii, no. 144, letter to Gavriel Hayim Cohn, dated 1 Jan. 1965. In his letter to Cohn, dated 28 Nov. 1965, Weinberg stated flatly that R. Hayim Soloveitchik was not an interpreter of Maimonides. See also my 'The Brisker Method Reconsidered', *Tradition*, 31 (Spring 1997), 78–102.

96 See *SE* iii, p. 343 and nos. 132–3; *Hama'ayan*, 34 (Tevet 5754 [1994]), 19; his letters in Atlas, *Pathways*, 138, 154; and Abraham Weingort, 'Reflections on the Teachings of Rabbi Weinberg' (Heb.), *Hama'ayan*, 37 (Nisan 5757 [1997]), 28. A motivation similar to that of Weinberg seems to be behind R. Abraham Isaiah Karelitz's well-known criticisms of Soloveitchik; see Lawrence Kaplan, 'The Hazon Ish: Haredi Critic of Traditional Orthdoxy', in

In a private letter Weinberg responded quite sharply to what he regarded as the exaggerated importance granted to Rabbi Hayim Soloveitchik by his followers. The most eloquent statement of the uniqueness of Rabbi Hayim and his method of study is found in Rabbi Joseph B. Soloveitchik's famous eulogy for his uncle, Rabbi Isaac Ze'ev Soloveitchik, son of Rabbi Hayim.[97] In this eulogy not only is the brilliance of Rabbi Hayim extolled, but Talmud study which is not pursued in accordance with the Analytic Method—i.e. as it was pursued by talmudic scholars throughout most of Jewish history—is portrayed as lacking in intellectual sophistication and rigour. As far as Weinberg was concerned, the younger Soloveitchik's essay, while possessing a masterful style, was as full of hyperbole as if written by a member of a sect about his leader. (Weinberg specifically referred to the writings of the Habad and *musar* movements as parallel examples of this tendency.) Weinberg continued the letter with a most interesting passage, which, incidentally, also offered a suggestion as to why the Analytic Method so quickly conquered the yeshiva world:

From his article one gets the impression that the Torah was not given through Moses, God forbid, but rather through Rabbi Hayim. It is true that Rabbi Hayim brought a new type of logical *pilpul* into the yeshivot. Anyone can have a grasp of logic, and therefore all yeshiva students can come up with novel insights in this fashion. This is not so with regard to the approach of the Shakh [Rabbi Shabbetai ben Meir Hakohen, 1621–62] and Rabbi Akiva Eger [1761–1837], concerning which one needs to have great erudition in order to be a little sharp-witted [*ḥarif*]. Therefore, since all yeshiva students want to be 'creators' [of such insights] they prefer Rabbi Hayim to all the sages who preceded him. I once asked Rabbi Joseph Baer [Soloveitchik] when he was in Berlin: Who was greater, the Vilna Gaon or Rabbi Hayim of Brisk? He replied that Rabbi Hayim had a greater understanding than even the Vilna Gaon. But this is not true. The Vilna Gaon searched for the simple truth, but not Rabbi Hayim. His logic and reasoning cannot be integrated with the language of the Talmud or with the language of Maimonides.[98]

Not surprisingly, Weinberg's concerns with original intent and proper methodology were more pressing when dealing with issues of practical halakhah. In this realm there are well-established principles which must not be abandoned, the most important being that it is forbidden to issue halakhic rulings which have no sound basis in earlier rabbinic authorities or which are contradicted by the *Shulḥan arukh*

Jack Wertheimer (ed.), *The Uses of Tradition* (New York, 1992), 154–5. Referring to these criticisms, one observer has perceptively remarked that Karelitz judged Soloveitchik's interpretations of Maimonides 'by the wrong criterion; he wanted to determine if they were true!' See ibid. 155 n. 33. The same comment could be made with regard to Weinberg. Incidentally, in his letter to R. Mordechai Gifter, dated 24 Apr. 1961, Weinberg expressed regret that he had never troubled to make the acquaintance of Soloveitchik: 'Because of this I deprived myself of growth and lost something that can never be replaced.'

[97] The eulogy, which originally appeared in *Hado'ar*, 15 Sept. 1963, has been reprinted in J. B. Soloveitchik, *Divrei hagut veha'arakhah* (Jerusalem, 1982), 57–97.

[98] Letter to Gavriel Hayim Cohn, dated 28 Nov. 1965.

and its standard commentaries.[99] We have already seen echoes of this view in Weinberg's dispute with Rabbi Joseph Rozin, who violated both of these principles. Rozin viewed himself as bound only by the rulings of Maimonides, leading Weinberg to declare, 'In Lithuania they did not establish the halakhah in accordance with his opinion, since it was well known that he had his own method and did not show regard for the greatest *posekim*.'[100]

In Weinberg's efforts to understand the true meaning of rabbinic sources, it was crucial that no relevant information should be ignored. This is a significant view, for as is well known, the renowned Rabbi Abraham Isaiah Karelitz argued that textual variants contained in recently discovered manuscripts of ancient and medieval texts—manuscripts either of standard works or of previously unpublished works—must not enter the halakhic decision-making process. Even when dealing with the theoretical analysis of a *sugya* and its medieval commentaries, Karelitz opposed emending texts which had been in use for generations. He simply ignored all of the variant talmudic readings which are recorded in Rabbi Raphael Nathan Rabbinovicz's *Dikdukei soferim*, about which earlier scholars had been enthusiastic. Karelitz further argued that, in formulating halakhic decisions, one should not take into account opinions of medieval authorities whose works had only been published in recent years, since they had not been part of the halakhic tradition.

We have already seen that, in areas of theoretical analysis, Weinberg had few qualms about emending texts. He also opposed Karelitz when issues of practical halakhah were concerned, for he believed in making use of manuscripts when they preserve halakhically significant textual variants or important halakhic opinions. With regard to textual variants, Karelitz had a somewhat mystical view of the accuracy of texts which had been in use for generations. As he saw it, the texts which have come down to us and have been accepted by previous generations of scholars are the product of divine providence which has prevented error from creeping in—even when these texts contradict each other! 'Providence decreed that some texts be preserved for posterity and that some be relegated to obscurity.'[101]

[199] See e.g. *SE* iii, p. 15, where Weinberg criticized R. Judah Leib Zirelson for deriving a halakhic ruling from a biblical verse. See also *SE* i, pp. 26, 41, 202, 272, ii, pp. 19, 20, 233, 257–8, iii, pp. 46, 184, 341.

[100] *SE* i, p. 245. Weinberg's opposition to exclusive reliance on Maimonides is also found in *SE* ii, p. 139.

[101] Moshe Bleich, 'The Role of Manuscripts in Halakhic Decision-Making: Hazon Ish, his Precursors and Contemporaries', *Tradition*, 27 (Winter 1993), 44. For further discussion of Karelitz's views, which are more complicated than appear at first sight and contain exceptions and perhaps even contradictions, see Shnayer Z. Leiman, 'Hazon Ish on Textual Criticism and Halakhah—A Rejoinder', *Tradition*, 19 (Winter 1981), 301–10; Zvi Yaakov Halevi Lehrer, 'Manuscripts of Early Commentaries and their Qualification to Rule on Jewish Law' (Heb.), *Tsefunot*, 16 (1992), 72–3; David Matzger's introduction to his edition of *Perushei rabeinu ḥananel bar ḥushiel latalmud: Berakhot* (Jerusalem, 1990), 23 n. 44; id., 'Tovah tsiparnam shel rishonim', *Hama'ayan*, 35 (Tevet 5755 [1995]), 1–10; Daniel Sperber, 'On the Legitimacy, or Indeed Necessity, of Scientific Disciplines for True "Learning" of the Talmud', in Shalom Carmy (ed.), *Modern Scholarship in the Study of Torah: Contributions and Limitations* (Northvale, NJ, 1996),

Weinberg did not share this view, and pointed out that even Rabbi Joseph Caro, author of the *Beit yosef* and *Shulḥan arukh*, did not always have access to uncorrupted manuscripts. Does this mean that modern scholars, who now have access to more accurate texts, can go so far as to reject rulings by Caro which were based on faulty texts? Although when dealing with other halakhists the answer is clearly yes, Caro's rulings, if not opposed by major figures among his contemporaries, have been endowed with a special authority. This complicates matters immensely, and it is no doubt because of this that Weinberg, who himself raised the question, did not offer a definitive answer.[102]

Although in a work of this sort it is not possible to go into any detail concerning Weinberg's *ḥidushim*, it would be remiss not to give at least a few examples, admittedly in greatly simplified form, since so much of Weinberg's scholarly effort was devoted to this endeavour. In one particularly fascinating *ḥidush* we see Weinberg's modern sensibilities come to the fore.[103] The Talmud, *Kidushin* 3*a*, states that a wife may not be acquired through barter. The reason for this is that although barter is possible with something worth less than a *perutah*, 'a woman will not cede herself [in marriage] for less than a *perutah*'s worth [Rashi: For it is derogatory to her dignity, therefore all barter is invalid, even with an object worth a *perutah*]'.

Weinberg pointed out that Rashi's opinion is difficult to understand, because it is also degrading for a woman to be acquired with a mere *perutah*. Weinberg explained that in reality one cannot 'acquire' a wife with any amount of money, and the fact that a *perutah* is enough to effect this acquisition is itself proof that the money is just a *symbol* of the holy transaction which effects the *kidushin*, and which serves to render the woman forbidden to all other men. This explains why barter is not valid for effecting *kidushin*, because it is a form of exchange used in commerce, and a woman is not an object of commerce.[104]

In another responsum Weinberg considered the theological significance of the Sabbath, and quoted Maimonides' *Guide* ii. 31 that it is designed to teach the principle of the world's divine creation. Taking this as his starting-point, Weinberg declared that Jews do not rest on the Sabbath because God rested on that day

214–15; Moses Lipshitz's comment in Rafael Rosenbaum, *Rabbi Moses Lipshitz Memorial Volume* (Heb.) (New York, 1996), 127; Spiegel, *Chapters*, 488–95. For a rejection of Karelitz's approach, see Menahem Kasher, 'The Appearance of Two Volumes of the Comprehensive Talmud Project' (Heb.), *No'am*, 16 (1973), 165–82. According to Walter Wurzburger, R. Joseph B. Soloveitchik was also opposed to using newly discovered manuscripts of medieval sages for halakhic purposes. See his 'Rav Joseph B. Soloveitchik', 6.

102 Letter to R. Isaac Herzog, dated 16 Oct. 1950. See also *SE* ii, p. 22 in the note, and iii, p. 179; *Hama'ayan*, 32 (Tammuz 5752 [1992]), 14.

103 *SE* iii, no. 56; *Ḥidushei ba'al 'Seridei esh'*, no. 11, with Weingort's extensive commentary and his additional comments, ibid. 508–13.

104 If the money is only a symbol for effecting the *kidushin*, what actually causes the *kidushin* to be binding? Surprisingly enough, Weinberg did not explain this, but Weingort offers a plausible suggestion. See *Ḥidushei ba'al 'Seridei esh'*, 66.

(*imitatio Dei*), but rather because 'God blessed and hallowed this day so that we might testify to His creation of the world during the six days of creation.'[105]

With this understanding of the significance of the Sabbath, i.e. that the Jew's rest is not related to God's rest, Weinberg was able to explain why there is a concept of *tosefet shabat* (extending the Sabbath) even though God only rested for twenty-four hours. The behaviour of humans in this regard is simply not intended to correspond to God's actions during the creation. Furthermore, Weinberg continued, in essence the concept of *tosefet shabat* is not even related to the Sabbath. Rather, there is a separate, and general, commandment to add holiness to the profane. Because of its general nature, *tosefet shabat* is not a time-bound commandment from which women are exempt. The 'adding on' of holiness is a commandment which is unrelated to considerations of time, although it just so happens that the holiness of the Sabbath and holidays *is* bound by considerations of time.

With this subtle distinction, Weinberg was also able to clarify a different issue.[106] Nahmanides claimed that the biblical commandment to count the *omer* was not a positive time-bound commandment from which women are exempt. This is a difficult position to understand, as what could be more 'time-bound' than the commandment to count forty-nine days? Weinberg offered a new understanding of time-bound commandments which is profound in its simplicity. According to him, a time-bound commandment is one which has a definite time within which the commandment must be fulfilled, such as the commandments of matzah, *lulav*, *sukkah*, etc. This is not the case with regard to the counting of the *omer*. Here the element of time is not simply the framework of the commandment, but is the essence of the commandment itself. Such a commandment is not a 'time-bound' commandment, but literally a commandment of time itself.

As with virtually all major *posekim* in the modern era, Weinberg dealt with the question of the halakhic status of civil marriage.[107] A significant, though minority, block of opinion views a civil marriage followed by cohabitation as creating a binding tie, whose termination requires a religious divorce. The majority of *posekim* oppose this stance, and Weinberg agreed with them that a religious divorce is unnecessary following a civil marriage. Yet there is a significant position in Weinberg's responsum on the topic which was noted by David Novak and Elyakim G.

[105] *SE* ii, no. 20.

[106] Ibid., no. 116, *Ḥidushei ba'al 'Seridei esh'*, no. 17, with Weingort's commentary.

[107] *SE* iii, no. 22, and Gavriel Hayim Cohn, 'A Note to the Dispute Concerning the Law of Marriage and Divorce' (Heb.), *De'ot*, 7 (1958), 56 n. 12. For detailed discussion of the halakhic status of civil marriage, see Abraham Hayim Freimann, *Seder kidushin venisuin* (Jerusalem, 1945), 362 ff.; Elyakim G. Ellinson, *Marriage Not in Accord with Jewish Law* (Heb.) (Tel Aviv, 1975); David Friedman, 'The Status of Non-Halachic Marriage', *Journal of Halacha and Contemporary Society*, 8 (Fall 1984), 118–28; Meir Issachar Mazuz, 'Civil Marriage and the Consequences', *Shenaton hamishpat ha'ivri*, 3–4 (1976–7), 233–70; David Novak, 'The Marital Status of Jews Married under Non-Jewish Auspices', *Jewish Law Association Studies*, 1 (1985), 61–77; and Eliezer Waldenberg, *Tsits eli'ezer* (Jerusalem, 1985), ii. 19. Regarding Reform marriages, in which the issues are very similar, see Norman E. Frimer and Dov I. Frimer, 'Reform Marriages in Contemporary Halakhic Responsa', *Tradition*, 21 (Fall 1984), 7–39.

Ellinson.[108] Whereas previous discussions regarded civil marriage either as unlawful fornication or, because of the parties' public cohabitation, as effecting a valid Jewish marriage, Weinberg adopted a middle position not considered by other *posekim*.

Weinberg argued that a distinction must be made between people who simply live together and those united by a civil marriage, since the latter shows that the parties have made a commitment to one another. The civil marriage, in this interpretation, is equivalent to a non-Jewish marriage. Although there is no religious element in such marriages, the connection established between man and wife means that the woman is not permitted to anyone else. Divorce for gentiles consists simply of the separation of the partners, which in modern times is followed by a civil divorce. Weinberg claimed that the same pattern existed with regard to civil marriage. There was no religious element to it, but there was nevertheless a connection established between the partners in that the woman was to be regarded as a concubine with the rights and duties this implies, a situation which would not exist if the partners were simply living together. To end a relationship between a concubine and her 'husband', no religious divorce was needed. A simple separation, as with a gentile marriage, was sufficient. Yet as long as they remained together in a state of civil marriage, the halakhah would recognize them as a unit. Unlike other *posekim*, who focus on the fact that the parties are living together and attribute no legal significance to the civil marriage *per se*, Weinberg showed 'a tacit recognition (although not approval) of the legal reality of a secular system of marriage, initiated and terminated on its own grounds'.[109]

One of the most discussed passages in Maimonides' *Mishneh torah* appears in *Hilkhot rotseaḥ ushemirat hanefesh* 1: 9:

> This, too is a [Negative] Commandment: Not to take pity on the life of a pursuer. Therefore the Sages ruled that when a woman has difficulty in giving birth, one may dismember the child in her womb—either with drugs or by surgery—because he is like a pursuer seeking to kill her. Once his head has emerged, he may not be touched, for we do not set aside one life for another; this is the natural course of the world.[110]

This passage is very problematic, for Maimonides brings in the argument of pursuit to justify abortion (actually embryotomy) when the sense of the Mishnah[111] and Talmud[112] is that abortion is permitted because the foetus is not yet a person. Numerous explanations of Maimonides' words have been suggested.[113]

[108] Novak, 'Marital Status', 74–5; id., *Law and Theology in Judaism* (New York, 1974), 38–9; Ellinson, *Marriage*, 186.

[109] Novak, *Law and Theology*, 39. The logic of this responsum is praised by Klein, *Mishneh halakhot*, vol. x (1987), 236. See also Novak, *Law and Theology*, 159 n. 26; id., 'Marital Status', 75; id., *The Image of the Non-Jew in Judaism* (New York, 1983), 209–10, who points to a halakhic difficulty in Weinberg's responsum.

[110] This translation is taken from David M. Feldman, *Marital Relations, Birth Control and Abortion in Jewish Law* (New York, 1974), 276.

[111] *Oholot* 7: 6.

[112] *Sanhedrin* 72*b*, and see Rashi.

[113] Feldman, *Marital Relations*, 277–81, discusses thirteen different approaches. His description of Weinberg's view is inadequate, however.

Weinberg offered an original solution to this problem.[114] He called attention to *Mishneh torah, Hilkhot ḥovel umazik*, 8: 4, where Maimonides rules that if someone surrenders money or property belonging to another upon threat of death he must nevertheless compensate the owner. Yet Maimonides also rules that if the property itself is causing the danger to life, no compensation is necessary. Thus, if someone is on a ship in danger of sinking because of its heavy load, and he throws something overboard in order to lighten this load, he is not obligated to pay back the owner. What he has thrown overboard is regarded as a 'pursuer' (ibid. 8: 15).

Weinberg explained that the 'pursuer' argument, in addition to its technical applicability, is also used rhetorically to describe a case when something is causing danger to another. This is obvious according to Weinberg, for the law of pursuit cannot, strictly speaking, be applied to material overloading a boat. Similarly, with regard to Maimonides' formulation concerning abortion where the word 'pursuer' also appears, the term is not used in its technical sense and there is therefore no need to say that by invoking the argument from pursuit, Maimonides differs from the commonly accepted view that a foetus is not considered a human life.

According to Weinberg, the argument from pursuit teaches us another law, namely, that the husband is not entitled to monetary compensation as is normally the case when a foetus is destroyed (Exodus 21: 22). When the mother's life is in danger the destroyed foetus is considered a 'pursuer' in the broad sense of the term, and as such no monetary compensation is forthcoming, just as, in the parallel case of the sinking ship in which the cargo is the 'pursuer', there is no compensation. That this is Maimonides' intention, Weinberg added, can also be seen by a close examination of his words. In discussing the abortion procedure he does not say that one is *obligated* to destroy the foetus. This would be expected since we are dealing with a case of life and death. Rather, he says that one is *permitted* (*mutar*) to destroy the foetus. By saying so, Maimonides is establishing that there is complete permission (*heter gamur*) to destroy the foetus without incurring any obligation to pay the father.

Among Weinberg's non-halakhic writings of the post-war years, a particularly important place is occupied by his essays on the *musar* movement and its major figures, in which he was able to draw on personal recollections. In fact, it was in these studies that Weinberg advanced the incorrect notion, which he helped popularize, that Salanter preceded Freud in discovering the unconscious. Weinberg also wrote the first study of the dispute concerning *musar*, and, as with his earlier studies, never lost his objectivity. Despite his undisguised partisanship, he presented even the strongest opponents of *musar* in a sympathetic light.[115]

[114] *SE* i, p. 315, iii, no. 127, *Ḥidushei ba'al 'Seridei esh'*, no. 40, with Weingort's commentary.

[115] *SE* iv, pp. 296–340. Regarding Salanter and Freud, see Etkes, *Rabbi Israel Salanter*, 326 ff. See also *Ḥidushei ba'al 'Seridei esh'*, 4–5, for Weinberg's letter urging Dov Katz to write about the *musar* dispute.

MODERN SCHOLARSHIP

Although in the post-war years Weinberg was able to write productively on talmudic and halakhic themes, as mentioned previously it was much more difficult for him to be involved with modern Jewish scholarship. Being far from any significant libraries, and lacking essential books, he was not able to continue work on his *Meḥkarim batalmud*, studies of the Targum, or any of the other projects he had begun in Berlin. It was only through the kindness of friends that he was able to obtain such basic texts as those by Nahman Krochmal, Zechariah Frankel, and Isaac Halevy. Weinberg briefly considered travelling to Oxford, where he would have been able to work together with Kahle on academic projects, but because of the problem of obtaining kosher food he was forced to abandon this plan. Yet he continued his correspondence with Kahle, which, incidentally, allowed him to express himself in a freer manner than did his correspondence with traditional Jewish scholars.[116]

In spite of the logistical difficulties, Weinberg was never totally removed from modern Jewish scholarship, and it was important to him that his views should find favour in the academic community.[117] With this end in mind, he wrote a number of studies concerning the formation and nature of the Mishnah.[118] Weinberg began these studies by returning to a point he often stressed, namely, that even in pre-modern times traditional scholars were interested in the questions posed by modern scholarship. He continued that although it was only with Wissenschaft des Judentums scholars such as Krochmal and Frankel that one first found extended and detailed treatment of these topics carried out in accordance with modern scholarly standards,[119] even in medieval works there were comments which shed light on the formation of the Mishnah. This is certainly true of traditional works which focus on issues of methodology, such as *Sefer keritut, Halikhot olam*, and *Yad malakhi*. Yet, as Weinberg was well aware, there is a fundamental difference between the modern scholars and their predecessors in that modern scholars view the Mishnah as a document to be interpreted on its own terms, rather than through the Talmud's eyes.

[116] In Weinberg's letter to Paul Kahle, dated 18 Feb. 1949, he wrote: 'The kabbalistic vision of the Messiah as the redeemer of all mankind is the Jewish counterpart to Christ, yet the question must still be solved as to who might have influenced whom.' Portions of a letter from Weinberg to Kahle are printed in Matthew Black, *An Aramaic Approach to the Gospels and Acts* (Oxford, 1967), 238.

[117] Letter to Samuel K. Mirsky, dated 14 Sept. 1959.

[118] *SE* i, pp. 364–9, iii, no. 134, iv, pp. 222–66; 'Sources' (1958), 72–88, 290–316. These articles were intended to be part of a book of studies on the Mishnah, which Weinberg mentioned in a number of letters. In his letter to Samuel Atlas dated 14 Jan. 1954, he wrote that he had sent the entire manuscript to London so that it could be typed and corrected. Instead, it was lost, once more subjecting Weinberg to the pain he had suffered at the earlier loss of his manuscripts.

[119] On their approach, see Joel Gereboff, 'The Pioneer: Zecharias Frankel', and William Scott Green, 'The Talmudic Historians: N. Krochmal, H. Graetz, I. H. Weiss, and Z. Jawitz', in Jacob Neusner (ed.), *The Modern Study of the Mishnah* (Leiden, 1973), 59–75, 107–21.

It is significant that Weinberg was prepared to grant legitimacy to explanations of the Mishnah which were not in accordance with the Talmud, as long as practical halakhah was not thereby affected. In support, he quoted Rabbi Yom Tov Lipmann Heller's earlier approval of this approach,[120] and the fact that Rabbi Saadiah Gaon, Rabbi Hai Gaon, Rabbenu Hananel, Maimonides, and the Vilna Gaon also suggested explanations that were not in accordance with the Talmud.[121] It has previously been pointed out that Weinberg rejected Rabbi Joseph Duenner's similar explanations, but this was because Duenner's arguments were based on the view that the *amoraim* had *misunderstood* the Mishnah.[122] Isaac Hirsch Weiss had suggested this view earlier,[123] and had also argued that there were times when the *amoraim* deliberately misinterpreted the Mishnah in order to bring it into line with their own decisions.[124] These are the positions which Weinberg rejected on dogmatic grounds. It is because of this traditionalism that he cannot be characterized as an academic talmudist along the lines of Abraham Weiss or David Halivni Weiss.[125]

In presenting his own view of how the *amoraim* interpreted the Mishnah, a view motivated by traditionalism—which, of course, does not mean that it is incorrect—Weinberg followed the path charted by the Vilna Gaon.[126] He argued that the *amoraim* treated the Mishnah in the same way they treated the Bible, applying the method of *derash* to 'derive' a great deal of halakhic information from the

[120] Commentary on *Nazir* 5: 5.

[121] *SE* iv, pp. 150, 237. See also the sources cited in Kalman Kahana, *Ḥeker ve'iyun* (Tel Aviv, 1960), 132–52; David Weiss Halivni, *Mekorot umesorot: Nashim* (Tel Aviv, 1968), introduction; id., 'Abraham Geiger and Talmud Criticism', in Jakob Petuchowski (ed.), *New Perspectives on Abraham Geiger* (New York, 1975), 31–41; Irwin H. Haut, *The Talmud as Law or Literature* (New York, 1982), 49; and Yaakov Elman, 'Progressive *Derash* and Retrospective *Peshat*: Nonhalakhic Considerations in Talmud Torah', in Shalom Carmy (ed.), *Modern Scholarship in the Study of Torah: Contributions and Limitations* (Northvale, NJ, 1996), 240 ff. Although it is generally accepted that Maimonides and the Vilna Gaon offered explanations which do not accord with the Talmud, there has been some dispute about this. See Meshullam Roth, *Kol mevaser* (Jerusalem, 1972), ii. 120–1, 129.

[122] Not noted by Weinberg is the fact that the Tosafists sometimes argue that the later *amoraim* did not understand the views of their predecessors. See the sources cited by Ephraim Kanarfogel, 'The Tosafist Œuvre and Torah u-Madda', *Torah u-Madda Journal*, 2 (1990), 58 n. 18, to which add *Yevamot* 8*a* s.v. *ki*. With regard to Aggadah, one is confronted with entirely different issues, and Weinberg was comfortable in stating that there are *aggadot* which were understood by later sages as being historical although this was not what the creators of these *aggadot* had in mind. See *SE* iv, p. 274.

[123] *Dor dor vedoreshav*, iii. 193–4 (= 219 in the New York/Berlin, 1924 edition used by Weinberg).

[124] See ibid. ii. 191 (215 in the New York/Berlin edition). Surprisingly enough, this view also seems to have been held by R. Naftali Zvi Judah Berlin. See *Ha'amek she'alah* (Jerusalem, 1961), 128, no. 1 (63*a*): 'It is the manner of the Gemara to contort the explanation of the Mishnah in order to bring it into line with the final halakhah.'

[125] Cf. Sperber, 'Legitimacy', 206–8.

[126] See Benjamin Rivlin, *Gevi'i gevia hakesef* (Warsaw, 1898), 23*b*: 'I heard from my master, the Gaon of blessed memory, that the Mishnah is interpreted as *peshat* and *derash*.'

mishnaic text. By doing so, they did not mean to disregard the text's simple meaning or to imply that the actual source of the information was to be found in the Mishnah.[127]

Despite a number of important comments found in Weinberg's articles, which include strikingly new interpretations of some *mishnayot*, he did not offer any original approach to solving the major issue with which he was concerned, that of Mishnah redaction. For the most part, he was content with summarizing the views of earlier scholars, in particular those of Hanokh Albeck (1890–1972), to which he added his own critical observations.[128] In discussing the formation of the Mishnah, Weinberg followed Hoffmann, who placed the work's original composition in the days of Hillel.[129] This is in opposition to Halevy, who claimed that the first redaction of the Mishnah was the work of the Men of the Great Assembly, in the first centuries of the Second Commonwealth.[130] Halevy felt compelled to argue in favour of such an early dating for ideological reasons, yet Weinberg, like Hoffmann earlier,[131] was adamant in insisting that enquiries into the origin of the Mishnah are literary-historical and do not in any way compromise the integrity of the halakhic system.[132]

Yet having said this, the fact remains that Weinberg's approach to Mishnah redaction was not that of detached scholarship, but contained elements of traditionalism. For example, in explaining his rejection of Albeck's well-known view that Rabbi Judah the Prince, in redacting the Mishnah, did not exercise any editorial discretion in order to ensure a coherently structured work, Weinberg wrote as follows: 'In the main I protested against the view that Rabbi [Judah] did not edit or arrange the Mishnah but merely gathered from various collections without distinguishing, *Heaven forbid. Despite my anger at the defamation of our holy Rabbi's honour*, I tried not to offend Albeck' (emphasis added). It is this type of exclamation which shows that Weinberg was unable, and indeed had no wish, to reject

127 See *SE* iv, p. 18, for Weinberg's earlier formulation of this point, and Yonah Emanuel, '*Peshat* and its Meaning in the Mishnah' (Heb.), *Hama'ayan*, 12 (Tishrei 5732 [1971]), 27 ff., for comments on Weinberg's approach. See also Yaakov S. Spiegel, 'Elliptical Language of the Tannaim and Concerning *Peshat* and *Derash* in the Mishnah' (Heb.), *Asupot*, 4 (1990), 20 ff., and Elman, 'Progressive *Derash*', 240 ff.

128 Albeck in turn referred to Weinberg as a '*ba'al pilpul*'; see his *Introduction to the Mishnah* (Jerusalem, 1959), 276. In Albeck's system of terminology, this refers to one who errs in obvious matters. See Albeck, 'Criticism or Sophistry' (Heb.), *Sinai*, 46 (1960), 237. Regarding Albeck's views, see Gary G. Porton, 'Hanokh Albeck on the Mishnah' (Heb.), in Neusner, *Modern Study*, 209–24.

129 On Hoffmann's views, see Charles Primus, 'David Hoffmann's *The First Mishnah*', in Neusner, *Modern Study*, 122–34.

130 On Halevy's views, see Baruch Micah Bokser, 'Y. I. Halevy', in Neusner, *Modern Study*, 135–54.

131 See *The First Mishnah* (Heb.), trans. Samuel Grünberg (Berlin, 1914), 3.

132 See *SE* iv, p. 266, and cf. ibid., pp. 119–20, where Weinberg states that analysis of the formation of *sugyot* does not threaten the basis of the halakhic system.

traditionalism completely in favour of detached objectivity. Even in Mishnah studies, his ideology precluded the acceptance of certain opinions.[133]

As for Halevy, his entire scholarly endeavour was really an ideologically driven polemic, as is obvious upon reading his work. This explains his extremely negative attitude towards Krochmal, Frankel, and other Wissenschaft des Judentums scholars. Since Halevy did not agree with their view of tradition, and regarded them as nothing less than heretics, he automatically disqualified their scholarly conclusions.[134] Weinberg, on the other hand, distinguished between religious beliefs and scholarly conclusions. He therefore refused to condemn the Wissenschaft des Judentums scholars as Halevy did, noting that there is no place for religious polemics in the realm of scholarship.[135] Furthermore, Weinberg did not agree with the substance of Halevy's religious polemics, as can be seen in how he related to Frankel.

In Weinberg's opinion, Frankel was far from being a heretic. He called him 'Rabbi' and affixed the phrase *zikhrono livrakhah* (of blessed memory) after his name, a sure sign of respect and one that was notably missing when he mentioned Geiger. Weinberg claimed that Halevy's attacks implied that Frankel, 'a very wise man whose work benefits all, including Halevy', as well as Krochmal, were complete heretics who intentionally aimed at destroying Judaism. Weinberg would not accept this.[136] In fact, a fitting equivalent of Frankel in Weinberg's day was Louis Ginzberg (1873–1953), and because of the way the Conservative movement had

[133] Letter to R. Charles B. Chavel, dated 21 Jan. 1960. See also *Yad sha'ul*, 87, where one of his reasons for rejecting Albeck's view is that it undermines the foundations of the Talmud. It is worth noting that in his early essay 'Die Jeschiwoth' (1916), 124, Weinberg rejected the method of Talmud study advocated by Tchernowitz. He claimed that it undermined the foundations of Jewish law, which were based upon traditional methods of study. In the post-war years Weinberg did not hold such a negative view of Tchernowitz's work, and in his letters to Samuel Atlas dated 4 Aug. 1948 and 20 Sept. 1948 he praised Tchernowitz's studies of halakhah.

[134] Halevy, who opposed Hoffmann's view of Mishnah redaction just as adamantly as he opposed the views of Krochmal and Frankel, would not dare attack the Orthodox Hoffmann in the same fashion as he did the latter two. In fact, as Albeck has pointed out, he did not even mention Hoffmann by name, instead referring to him as 'those who rely on Krochmal'. See Albeck, *Untersuchungen über die Redaktion der Mischna* (Berlin, 1923), 92 n. 1.

[135] This attitude was a hallmark of the Berlin Rabbinical Seminary's ideology, which was sharply criticized by Halevy. See Ch. 4 n. 27. Interestingly enough, in the section of Halevy's work published posthumously and edited by Moses Auerbach, Weinberg's colleague at the seminary, the editor informs us that he has removed Halevy's harsh comments directed at other scholars. See Auerbach, *Memorial Volume*, part ii, 5. This book also reprints Weinberg's previously published article on Halevy, with the deletion of his negative comments about the latter's approach.

[136] See *SE* iii, pp. 364–5, iv, pp. 224, 228, 233. In a youthful letter to Zvi Mathisson, dated 5 Dec. 1904, Weinberg also referred to Krochmal as 'R. Nahman Krochmal of blessed memory'. In a letter to Joseph Apfel, dated 4 July 1956, Weinberg discouraged him from translating Frankel's *Darkhei hamishnah* into English. One of the reasons he gave is as follows: 'I am afraid that the zealots in England will attack you, for they regard R. Zechariah Frankel as a *min* and *epikoros* because R. Samson Raphael Hirsch battled against him.'

developed, Ginzberg could be questioned on religious grounds in a way that could not be done with Frankel.[137] Yet, as with Frankel, Weinberg made a point of referring to Ginzberg as 'Rabbi L. Ginzberg of blessed memory'.[138]

Throughout Weinberg's writings great respect is accorded to academic Talmud scholars such as Ginzberg, Saul Lieberman,[139] and Samuel Atlas.[140] When he strongly rejected the work of Albeck and other modern scholars, it was because he believed that they were unable to grasp the intricacies of talmudic argumentation. Weinberg was convinced that the key to all academic study of the Talmud is an understanding of the inner dynamics of a *sugya*, and that this could only be achieved after having mastered the traditional study of Talmud as practised in the yeshivot[141]—a mastery that Albeck and other modern scholars never acquired.[142]

POST-WAR RESPONSA

It is now time to turn our attention to the most important aspect of Weinberg's writings, his responsa. In earlier chapters several halakhic rulings given by Weinberg were mentioned, but it was only in the post-war years that his rulings began to have an international influence, which was not diminished by his death. As it is impossible to discuss all aspects of Weinberg's responsa here, I will concentrate on the most significant characteristics of his work.

Attention has already been drawn to the tension between Weinberg's desire to

[137] Unlike Frankel, Ginzberg also accepted some of the tenets of Higher Biblical Criticism, as seen in his article 'Codification of Jewish Law', published in the *Jewish Encyclopaedia*, and reprinted in his *On Jewish Law and Lore* (New York, 1970), 153–84. It is doubtful whether Weinberg was aware of this.

[138] *SE* iii, p. 179. See also my 'Sociology', 80–1, 84 n. 28.

[139] In his letter to Saul Lieberman, dated 8 Dec. 1955, Weinberg heaped praise on his work on the Tosefta.

[140] See Weinberg's letter to Atlas in the latter's *Pathways*, 154, where he was unrepentant about including a responsum to Atlas in *SE* ii, no. 78. He also offered to include material from Atlas in vol. 3 of his responsa, 'even though by doing so I will arouse against myself the anger of the complaining zealots, who have not forgiven me for including your words in volume 2 of *Seridei esh*'. In a letter to Joseph Apfel, dated 10 May 1963, Weinberg stated that Simhah Elberg was correct in believing that his letter to Atlas should not have been included in *Seridei esh*, but that since he was such good friends with Atlas he could not leave it out. It seems clear that even if Weinberg meant what he said here, it was only a passing sentiment which did not reflect his dominant outlook.

[141] See his letters to Samuel Atlas, dated 4 Aug. 1948, 22 Aug. 1948, and 25 Jan. 1949. See also his comment recorded in Joseph Apfel, *Yad yosef* (Lakewood, NJ, 1996), 492. Cf. Ginzberg, *On Jewish Law*, 49: 'Great as the achievements of the *Wissenschaft des Judentums* are in all other branches of Jewish learning, it failed in the field of the Talmud—I am using the name in a broad sense including both Talmuds as well as cognate halakhic writings—because its study was superficial and limited to generalities.'

[142] Weinberg's harshest criticisms of Albeck, which include accusations of plagiarism, are contained in his letters to Samuel Atlas, dated 20 Sept. 1948, and Yehoshua Brand, dated 15 Jan. 1960 and 23 Mar. 1960. In the first letter to Brand, Weinberg wrote: 'Scholars of Albeck's sort dislike *pilpul* not because they have no desire for it, but because of their lack of ability. Superficial erudition . . . does not enable one to achieve profound understanding.'

rule leniently in a number of cases and his hesitancy about issuing such rulings. Bearing this in mind, we must ask why he broke with this pattern to issue several ground-breaking rulings, which departed from precedent and did not have the support of contemporary sages. The answer is that there is a crucial difference between the cases on which he hesitated to rule and those about which he had no reservations. In the former type, although he believed that halakhic evidence was on his side, since previous scholars examining the same evidence had come to different conclusions, Weinberg did not feel confident enough in his own standing to challenge them. These were matters of 'pure' halakhic argumentation.

However, in the examples where Weinberg disagreed with the other sages and charted new halakhic ground, he believed that he was more qualified to issue the ruling than his predecessors and colleagues. In these responsa the dispute between Weinberg and his opponents was not so much a dispute about halakhah, in which case Weinberg would have deferred to them, as a dispute about sociology. It was a dispute about which rulings would best ensure the survival of Orthodoxy. In such a fundamental dispute, which revolved around meta-halakhic considerations, Weinberg saw no need to defer to others, or to request their concurrence. He felt that he understood the issues confronting Orthodoxy better than his colleagues, and was strong in his belief that the halakhic solutions he offered would be a positive force. It was with reference to such cases that Weinberg declared: 'It cannot be that only those who are afraid will decide the halakhah',[143] and 'One must not be afraid of the masses' screaming, and of rabbis who wish to glorify themselves with their stringency.'[144]

The most famous of Weinberg's post-war responsa is his decision to grant a religious imprimatur to the bat mitzvah celebration, which was beginning to become popular in Orthodox circles but had not yet received rabbinic sanction. In dealing with such a phenomenon, particularly in an era rife with Reform and Conservative innovations, it was natural for *posekim* to forbid the celebration, with many falling back upon Rabbi Moses Sofer's well-known phrase, 'What is new is forbidden by the Torah.'[145] That is, all religious innovations, even the halakhically innocuous, must be opposed, for in the present era of religious crisis a reactionary approach is the only way to safeguard the religion. Even Weinberg at times fell into this mode and argued that something should be forbidden, even though there was no clear halakhic prohibition, simply because it was an unwarranted innovation to traditional practice.[146]

[143] Letter to Joseph Apfel, dated 21 Mar. 1963 (excerpt in Apfel, 'Letters', 53).

[144] Letter to Joseph Apfel, dated 26 Apr. 1963 (excerpt in Apfel, 'Letters', 52). In a letter to Joseph Apfel dated 24 Nov. 1959, he wrote of 'impassioned zealots who do not acknowledge the truth, but are stringent in accordance with their understanding and feelings. One should not argue with them. They are also suspected of shedding the blood of those who are lenient, and this is sufficient for the wise [to understand].'

[145] Conerning this phrase, see Louis Jacobs, *A Tree of Life* (Oxford, 1984), 255–6.

[146] See *SE* ii, no. 9 (concerning prayers in the vernacular), iii, no. 96 (concerning the use of general anaesthesia during circumcision), iii, no. 111 (concerning planting flowers on graves).

However, there is another model which a *posek* can use, formulated in Rabbi Kook's poetic words as 'the old will be renewed and the new will be sanctified'.[147] This approach does not oppose modern trends, but, assuming there is no halakhic impediment, seeks to integrate them into Orthodoxy. This approach had also been the hallmark of German *posekim* from the mid-nineteenth century onwards. Hirsch, Hildesheimer, and their colleagues realized that without adjustments and innovations in Orthodox practice, German Orthodoxy would not survive the onslaught of modernity.[148] As Mordechai Breuer has pointed out, 'they produced reforms out of their overwhelming desire to hold fast to Orthodoxy'.[149] They also realized, to adapt Chesterton's formulation, that in order to reform one must adhere to Orthodoxy,[150] for any reforms suggested by the non-Orthodox, even if they were halakhically justified, were *ipso facto* invalid in the eyes of the Orthodox. Weinberg followed this German tradition, applying its ideological assumptions to new challenges. In so doing he became a very creative *posek*.

Of course, it was impossible for Weinberg to integrate all features of modernity into Orthodoxy. As noted above, there were times when, even though there was no specific halakhic prohibition, Weinberg believed that tampering with tradition would have a negative impact and must be resisted. But this was not a general rule, and in line with the German halakhic ideology Weinberg often argued that creativity and innovations were necessary. To give one example where Weinberg parted company with the right-wing Orthodox led by Rabbi Karelitz and Rabbi Isaac Ze'ev Soloveitchik,[151] he called for the establishment of a national day of mourning for victims of the Holocaust.[152] This was a dynamic step and was understandably opposed by the right wing, who, motivated largely by religious conservatism even if this was not always explicitly stated, viewed all such innovations as incompatible with Jewish tradition. Yet Weinberg, despite his own opinion, was not prepared to support the creation of this memorial day without securing the approval of the right wing, for he strongly believed that in such national matters there needed to be general agreement among Orthodox leaders. Similarly, despite his strong feelings

[147] *Igerot hare'iyah*, i. 214.

[148] See Mordechai Breuer, 'The German Rabbinic Approach towards Halakhic Decision-Making during the Era of Emancipation' (Heb.), *Sinai*, 100 (1987), 166–86.

[149] *Modernity within Tradition*, 30.

[150] See *Orthodoxy*, 134.

[151] See Abraham Isaiah Karelitz, *Collected Letters* (Heb.) (Benei Berak, n.d.), i, no. 97; Sternbuch, *Teshuvot*, ii, no. 721; Feinstein, *Igerot moshe* (Jerusalem, 1996), *Yoreh de'ah* iv. 289; Yoel Schwartz and Yitshak Goldstein, *The Holocaust* (Heb.) (Jerusalem, 1987), 285–97; Eleazar Halevi Schulzinger, *Al mishkenot haro'im* (Benei Berak, 1988), 202–3. Karelitz's letter is directed in particular at the institution of a fast day in memory of the Holocaust, but it is known that he opposed all forms of special commemoration. It is worth noting that R. Joseph B. Soloveitchik agreed with his uncle, R. Isaac Ze'ev, and even cited the same proof-text. See Zvi Schachter, *Nefesh harav* (Jerusalem, 1994), 197–8.

[152] *SE* ii, p. 53. See Joel B. Wolowelsky, 'Observing Yom Hasho'a', *Tradition*, 24 (Summer 1989), 46–58.

about the State of Israel he did not accept the Israeli chief rabbinate's declaration that Israel Independence Day was a new holiday. As he explained in a letter, without the consensus of a broad spectrum of religious leaders, including the leaders of the right-wing yeshiva world, any innovations which would affect the Jewish people as a whole must be shunned.[153]

In another example of their conservatism, the right-wing Orthodox regarded the practice of military funerals, complete with the firing of volleys, as a gentile practice and therefore forbidden. Weinberg obviously granted the fact that the Israeli army had adopted this practice in imitation of other armies. However, as far as he was concerned there was no reason to forbid it, since there is sufficient halakhic support to permit the imitation of gentile practices which are not idolatrous and have a good rationale.[154] In truth, the difference between Weinberg and the right wing did not concern talmudic dialectics, but rather an attitude towards modernity and change. The right wing began by forbidding the innovation and then finding halakhic texts to support its position. Weinberg, for his part, was able to find other halakhic sources to justify his view. Here, as in so many other examples in halakhic history, it was the ideological position which created the halakhic argument.

A similar phenomenon may be observed with regard to the question of the halakhic permissibility of the Israeli census.[155] Weinberg's halakhic ruling permitting the census is based on the fact that national defence, and even economic planning, are a necessity for any government. They therefore constitute a 'purpose', which Nahmanides requires in order to permit such a counting. Once again, Weinberg's argument with the other halakhists was, in large part, one of outlook, in particular with regard to his view that economic planning is an important consideration from the standpoint of halakhah. Through this ruling Weinberg established a distinction between individuals, who are forbidden to count other Jews, and a government, which is permitted to do so. Not surprisingly, those *posekim* who had a negative approach towards the State of Israel were unanimously opposed to any such leniency.

[153] *Hapardes* (Apr. 1966), 6. In his letter to R. Moses Soloveitchik, dated 8 Mar. 1951, Weinberg stressed the importance of including the leaders of the yeshiva world in the discussions of Jewish law taking place in the fledgling State of Israel. He mentioned that in a letter to Chief Rabbi Herzog he had recommended, in place of a Sanhedrin, the establishment of a supreme *beit din* composed of R. Abraham Isaiah Karelitz, R. Isser Zalman Meltzer, and R. Isaac Ze'ev Soloveitchik. It seems clear that Weinberg was referring to his letter to Herzog published in *Hama'ayan*, 32 (Tammuz 5752 [1992]), 8–12, which includes the main points mentioned in his letter to Soloveitchik. However, in this letter he wrote that the supreme *beit din* should be under the authority of the Israeli chief rabbis. Furthermore, it is extremely unlikely that Weinberg could have written to Herzog and, in effect, asked him to relinquish the authority of the chief rabbinate in favour of the three scholars mentioned above, one of whom (Soloveitchik) was a complete anti-Zionist while another (Karelitz) granted the State of Israel only grudging acceptance.

[154] *SE* iii, pp. 297–8.

[155] For discussion of this issue see Bleich, *Contemporary Halakhic Problems*, iii, ch. 13.

In another responsum which also distinguishes between individuals and the state, Weinberg discussed autopsies.[156] Here he explicitly stated that it is difficult for halakhists to come to any agreement on this issue since their decisions depend, in large measure, on their attitudes to modern medicine and on how they regard the State of Israel and its institutions. In line with this approach, Weinberg cited halakhic arguments in favour of autopsies as well as the sociological considerations that make a lenient decision a necessity for the new state. There is thus an admission on Weinberg's part of the point I have already made, which will also be seen in his responsa dealing with women's issues: namely, that the dispute between him and his colleagues was more a dispute of world-view than of halakhah. Had the other *posekim* shared Weinberg's assessment of the times and his concern that without anatomical instruction it would be impossible for advanced medicine under Jewish auspices to thrive in Israel, they too would have availed themselves of the halakhic support he offered.

The most important area where Weinberg felt that adjustments must be made to tradition concerns the status of women. Weinberg freely admitted that some traditional practices which were considered proper in earlier generations were no longer tenable, and if enforced would have the effect of driving women away from Orthodoxy.[157] A crucial concern of his was to show that Jewish law does not treat women as 'Canaanite slaves', and he actually used this logic in one responsum where he refused to permit a man, whose barren wife would not agree to a divorce, to marry another woman. Since this man knew his wife's age when he married her, he was not permitted simply to discard her when he felt like it.[158]

Weinberg's best-known responsum concerning women's issues deals with the bat mitzvah celebration, which aimed at redressing the imbalance between boys and girls with regard to the public celebration of the attainment of adulthood.[159] Interestingly enough, the bat mitzvah celebration did not become a controversial issue in Orthodoxy until the mid-twentieth century,[160] although as early as the

156 'Autopsies in the State of Israel', *Teḥumin*, 12 (1992), 382–4.

157 *SE* ii, no. 14. Weinberg's responsum concerns the demand of Hungarian rabbis, such as the Satmar *rebbe*, that women stay home rather than attend a synagogue in which the separation between the sexes is minimal enough to enable the men to see them. See also *SE* iii, no. 95, where Weinberg was asked by a rabbi what he should do regarding women who dress immodestly, and apparently also come to services this way. Weinberg replied that it is most important not to take any steps which will drive these women away from the synagogue.

158 *SE* iii, no. 6.

159 *SE* iii, no. 93. The most comprehensive treatment of the halakhic issues concerning bat mitzvah is found in Erica Brown, 'Bat Mitzvah: A Case Study in Halakhic Innovation' (MA diss., Jews' College-University of London, 1990). See also Alfred S. Cohen, 'Celebration of the Bat Mitzvah', *Journal of Halacha and Contemporary Society*, 12 (Fall 1986), 5–16.

160 The oft-repeated report that R. Jacob Ettlinger sanctioned the bat mitzvah service does not appear to be accurate. See Yehudah Horowitz's note in his edition of Ettlinger's *She'elot uteshuvot ha'arukh laner* (Jerusalem, 1989), ii. 145 n. 1. See also Judith Bleich, 'Jacob Ettlinger, his Life and Works: The Emergence of Modern Orthodoxy in Germany' (Ph.D. diss., New York University, 1974), 167–75.

mid-nineteenth century German Orthodoxy had recognized the changed status and role of women and in line with this began to stress women's education. In 1863 Hirsch warned that the very future of Western Orthodoxy rested on providing religious education for girls, for only then would they learn to 'prefer Isaiah and Amos over Goethe and Shakespeare'.[161] Hildesheimer was also very concerned with women's education and Salanter praised him for this, while pointing out that his approach would be improper if instituted in eastern Europe.[162]

Weinberg acknowledged that the issue of women's education was the most difficult of all problems facing the Orthodox,[163] and it is only to be expected that concerning this matter he shared the sentiments of Hirsch, Hildesheimer, and German Orthodoxy as a whole. As he put it in an early essay, 'the female students of Rabbi Samson Raphael Hirsch have set right that which Mendelssohn's daughters corrupted'.[164] While pointing with great pride to the thirst for Jewish knowledge found among the young women of Frankfurt, Weinberg lamented the lack of education for women in the east, confessing that 'no party has ignored women as much as the east European Orthodox'.[165] In another early essay he again showed how concerned he was with this issue, mentioning the great fallacy, often expressed precisely by women, that a learned woman could not be pious.[166]

Weinberg followed in the German Orthodox tradition which recognized the legitimacy of women's religious development and regarded education as essential to this development. In this conception women's education came to be regarded as an intrinsically positive manifestation, not merely an unavoidable measure taken to prevent religious breakdown, which was the attitude of so many east European supporters of the Beth Jacob movement.[167] It is thus no surprise that Weinberg embraced other halakhically permissible innovations, such as the bat mitzvah celebration, which, together with education, he regarded as essential to women's religious growth in contemporary times. However, he shared the sentiments of Salanter that when dealing with communities which have had very little exposure

[161] See his letter in Mayer Herskovics (ed.), *Parnas ledoro* (Hoboken, NJ, 1992), 37. See also the discussion in Breuer, *Jüdische Orthodoxie*, 116–20.

[162] See Reines, *Shenei hame'orot*, 48 (first pagination); Eliav, *Hildesheimer Briefe*, letter 86 (German section); 'Unveröffentliche Sche'eloth und Teschuwoth des Raw Esriel Hildesheimer von Berlin', *25 Jahre Jüdische Schule Zürich* (Jerusalem, 1980), 84–5; Ellenson, *R. Esriel Hildesheimer*, 122–3. Ellenson cites a book by Hildesheimer entitled *Etwas über den Religionsunterricht der Mädchen* (Berlin, 1871). This appears to be a non-existent work. Ellenson is presumably referring to Hildesheimer's 'Unterricht der Mädchen im Urtext der "heiligen Schrift"', *Israelitischer Lehrer und Cantor*, supplement to *Die Jüdische Presse*, 41 (1910), no. 7.

[163] See *Lifrakim*, 214.

[164] 'Don't Forget the Jewish Woman!' (Yid.), *Idisher Lebn*, 22 Feb. 1924.

[165] Ibid.

[166] See *Lifrakim*, 211–14. See also *SE* iii, p. 237, for Weinberg's praise of the Beth Jacob movement.

[167] See Breuer, *Jüdische Orthodoxie*, 117. Hildesheimer was an exception among the German Orthodox, as he shared the view of the east European supporters of Beth Jacob. See Eliav, *Hildesheimer Briefe*, letter 86 (German section): 'In earlier times, religiosity could certainly always be inculcated by parental example, but times have unfortunately changed very much.'

to the challenges of modernity, a slower and more cautious approach is called for before introducing any innovations.[168]

Before writing a responsum on the bat mitzvah, there was an important consideration which Weinberg had to take into account. To justify the bat mitzvah would be to give a halakhic imprimatur to an innovation of Mordecai Kaplan.[169] Moreover, this innovation was itself an outgrowth of the confirmation service instituted at the beginning of the last century by various Reform leaders in conscious imitation of the Christian ceremony.[170] Confirmation, in which both boys and girls participated, was designed to achieve equality between the sexes. It was also supposed to take the place of the bar mitzvah ceremony, which was thought to have deteriorated and did not give the opportunity for young Jews to make a solemn declaration of their religious commitment in the face of the widespread erosion of Jewish identity.[171]

The origin of the bat mitzvah creates great halakhic difficulties for any *posek* who wishes to permit it, for just as halakhah forbids imitation of gentile practices, it also forbids imitation of the practices of heretics, the category into which Reform leaders fall. Indeed, an examination of nineteenth- and twentieth-century halakhic literature leads to the following conclusion: any practice that was an innovation was suspect, but a practice introduced by the Reformers, even with halakhic support, was almost always regarded as invalid, if only because of its origin. In addition to this, *posekim* had raised another problem with the bat mitzvah, arguing that it was an imitation of the Christian ritual of confirmation and thus forbidden because of *ḥukot ha'amim*, the prohibition against imitating gentile practices. Thus, the bat mitzvah was viewed as either a Reform custom or a gentile custom—in either case absolutely forbidden.[172]

[168] See e.g. *SE* ii, p. 17.

[169] See Walter Jacob (ed.), *American Reform Responsa* (New York, 1983), 88; Carole S. Kessner, 'Kaplan and the Role of Women in Judaism', in Emanuel S. Goldsmith (ed.), *The American Judaism of Mordecai M. Kaplan* (New York, 1990), 335–56.

[170] See Mordechai Eliav, *Jewish Education in Germany in the Period of Enlightenment and Emancipation* (Heb.) (Jerusalem, 1960), ch. 10; W. Gunther Plaut, *The Rise of Reform Judaism* (New York, 1963), 171–7; Michael A. Meyer, 'Christian Influence on Early German Reform Judaism', in Charles Berlin (ed.), *Studies in Jewish Bibliography, History, and Literature in Honor of I. Edward Kiev* (New York, 1971), 298; id., *Response to Modernity*, 39–40; and Paula E. Hyman, 'The Introduction of Bat Mitzvah in Conservative Judaism in Postwar America', *YIVO Annual*, 19 (1990), 133 ff. There were a few Orthodox rabbis who conducted confirmations, but they were not halakhic authorities. See Eliav, *Jewish Education*, 269–70; Steven M. Lowenstein, *The Mechanics of Change: Essays in the Social History of German Jewry* (Atlanta, Ga., 1992), 91 n. 9.

[171] See Meyer, *Response to Modernity*, 40; David Philipson, 'Confirmation in the Synagogue', *Year Book of the Central Conference of American Rabbis*, 1 (1890–1), 43–58, esp. 48–9: 'The Bar Mitzvah ceremony is a remnant of rabbinism.' Philipson goes on to say that it is 'a soulless ceremony without any signification', an 'old and worn tradition', and a practice which 'has lived its day'.

[172] Particularly noteworthy is the reaction of R. Aaron Walkin, Weinberg's short-lived successor to the rabbinate of Pilwishki and a leading supporter of the Beth Jacob movement (see his *Zekan aharon*, ii, no. 66). After detailing his strong opposition to the innovative practice, Walkin adds: 'Certainly, one who permits this is a *zaken mamre* [rebellious elder].' See *Zekan aharon*, i, no. 6. One exception to the opponents of the ceremony was the 19th-cent. R. Abraham Musafia of

On the other hand, before issuing his ruling Weinberg also had to take into account the fact that not all innovations borrowed from the Reformers, or from non-Jews for that matter, are necessarily bad.[173] In addition, there is a difference between taking over a Reform custom immediately after it is instituted and adopting it years later when it is no longer identified as being related to Reform. Finally, Weinberg had to consider whether *not* introducing the Reform innovation might harm Orthodoxy.

Although Weinberg's responsum contains a lengthy discussion of the parameters of the law against imitating gentiles, it is clear that he did not give the issue an objective and detached treatment. He had made up his mind that the bat mitzvah celebration was a positive manifestation, and he then set out to find the means of justifying it halakhically. This lends support to Emanuel Rackman's comment that 'in the deepest strata of halakhic thinking, logical judgment is preceded by value judgment, and intuitive insight gives impetus to the logic of argument'.[174]

Weinberg did not simply present halakhic arguments, but, just as important, gave full details of the meta-halakhic factors which stood behind his decision. With reference to those who opposed the bat mitzvah on the grounds that it went against tradition, he wrote:

In truth, this is no claim, for in previous generations they did not have to be concerned with the education and training of girls. At that time all Jews were full of Torah and God-fearing and every city was full of the spirit of Judaism. Girls who were raised in a Jewish home absorbed the spirit of Judaism without any active deed, almost taking it in with their mothers' milk. But now, a great change has occurred. The influence of the street removes every spark of Judaism from the hearts of boys and girls, and the girls are being educated at non-Jewish or secular schools which do not try to implant in the hearts of their students a love for Torah and the holy practices of authentic Judaism. It is incumbent upon us to concentrate all our strength on the education of girls. It is disappointing that in general education—the study of languages, secular literature, science, and the humanities—we concern ourselves with girls as much as with boys, but we totally neglect religious education,[175] i.e.

Jerusalem; see R. Isaac Nissim's summary of his manuscript responsum in *No'am*, 7 (1964), 4–5. Had Weinberg known of Musafia's position when he wrote his own responsum, he would certainly have highlighted the latter's concurring view. However, as is clear from his responsum, Musafia was unaware of the circumstances surrounding the origin of the bat mitzvah.

173 See the famous responsum of R. Isaac bar Sheshet, *Teshuvot rivash* (Jerusalem, 1993), no. 158, which Weinberg himself noted. With reference to the German Orthodox practice of wearing clerical robes, see Marcus Horovitz, *Mateh levi* (Frankfurt, 1932), ii, *Oraḥ ḥayim*, no. 6; Meier Hildesheimer (ed.), *Rabbiner Dr Israel Hildesheimer Gesammelte Aufsätze* (Frankfurt, 1923), 20, 25–6; and Breuer, *Jüdische Orthodoxie*, 42.

174 'Halakhah: Orthodox Approaches', *Encyclopaedia Judaica Year Book: 1975–1976* (Jerusalem, 1976), 141.

175 See Eliav, *Hildesheimer Briefe*, letter 86 (German section): 'It is a true scandal and a humiliation of our sacred faith that girls—and today this is not only true of the so-called "upper classes"—learn Hungarian in German areas, and German in Hungarian areas, and often French, English, and dancing as well, but have not the faintest knowledge of the sources of their own religion.'

Bible study, the *musar* literature of our sages, and instruction concerning the commandments in which women are obligated.[176] . . . From the standpoint of logic and pedagogy it is almost imperative to celebrate the attainment of the age of *mitsvot* for girls too. Moreover, the discrimination (*haflayah*) which occurs between boys and girls with regard to the celebration of maturity makes a very hurtful impression on the feelings of the maturing girl, who in other areas has been granted equality, so to speak.

It was these considerations which led Weinberg to offer his support to the bat mitzvah, on the condition that those who wished to institute it were motivated by the good intentions he described, rather than intending to imitate the Reformers. He also urged the more right-wing members of the community to make their peace with the celebration, and to accept the fact that the advocates of the bat mitzvah were motivated by good intentions.

Both in this responsum and in a subsequent letter in which he defended his decision,[177] Weinberg claimed that since he limited his permission to having the bat mitzvah celebration in a home, and not in the synagogue, his view was in accordance with that of Rabbi Moses Feinstein, a *posek* who was greatly respected among the right-wing Orthodox.[178] Presumably Weinberg stressed this point in order to forestall any attacks on his view from the more conservative segments of Orthodoxy. However, anyone who reads the responsa of Weinberg and Feinstein will immediately see the great difference between the two, even though in practice they agree. Feinstein's responsum is purely halakhic and does not take into account any of Weinberg's social and educational considerations. In fact, Feinstein had a completely negative view of the celebration, opposing its adoption and calling it 'nonsense'.[179] It was only if the community insisted upon having the bat mitzvah that Feinstein specified that it must not take place in the synagogue. On the other hand, Weinberg had a very positive view of the celebration and elaborated on its crucial importance for young Jewish women being raised in Western society. Here we have a good example of Weinberg following in the path of previous German *posekim* who believed, as with Kook, in sanctifying the new rather than rejecting it outright, which was the approach of Sofer and his followers.

Weinberg's enthusiasm for expanding the religious opportunities available to women was so strong that it even led him to adopt a halakhic stance which contradicts a position he held elsewhere. In *Seridei esh*, ii, no. 80, he discusses the use of an organ at a cemetery, a practice initiated by the Reformers. Weinberg could have argued that this was a custom which had a good reason, namely, to arouse feelings commensurate with the occasion. As Weinberg noted, Rabbi Joseph Colon, a leading medieval halakhist, had ruled that imitation of gentile practices was permitted

[176] Note that Weinberg does not refer to women studying Talmud, a phenomenon which did not exist in his time.

[177] *Hapardes* (July 1966), 36.

[178] *Igerot moshe*, *Oraḥ ḥayim* i, no. 104.

[179] In a later responsum, *Igerot moshe* (New York, 1982), *Oraḥ ḥayim* iv: 36 (addressed to Meir Kahane), Feinstein argued that the ceremony has no value in bringing girls closer to Judaism.

if the practice had a valid reason and was not associated with idolatry or immodest conduct, a position with which Isserles agreed.[180] Weinberg acknowledged that, if this opinion were to be accepted, it would be possible to permit the use of an organ at a cemetery. However, without pointing to any analytical weakness in Colon's view, Weinberg rejected it and instead adopted the Vilna Gaon's opinion that any gentile practice which Jews would not have instituted on their own is forbidden regardless of whether it has a good reason.[181]

Yet in discussing the bat mitzvah issue, Weinberg specifically rejected the Vilna Gaon's position, without demonstrating why it is mistaken,[182] and adopted the view of Colon, thus enabling him to permit the celebration. In other words, even if the bat mitzvah celebration was taken from gentiles or from the Reformers, as long as the Orthodox intended to achieve something positive through it there was no religious objection. As for the fact that confirmation is a Christian ceremony, Weinberg rather surprisingly denied that confirmation has any religious character, claiming that it was merely a celebratory rite of passage! Here we have a good example of the 'fluidity' of the halakhic system. In the responsum concerning the organ, where Weinberg had important meta-halakhic reasons to forbid it, he adopted the Vilna Gaon's opinion. In the responsum dealing with bat mitzvah, where Weinberg had important meta-halakhic reasons to permit it, he adopted Colon's opinion.[183] Acceptance or rejection of these views was not based on analyses of their inherent strengths and weaknesses, but on overriding meta-halakhic considerations.[184]

There is another responsum in which the same sensitivity to women's issues appears, as well as the belief that, within halakhic parameters, Orthodoxy must adapt to the times in order both to ensure the continued loyalty of its adherents and to achieve the educational objectives made necessary by modernity. In *Seridei esh*,

[180] *She'elot uteshuvot maharik hashalem* (Jerusalem, 1988), no. 88; *Shulḥan arukh*, *Yoreh de'ah*, 178: 1.

[181] *Yoreh de'ah*, 178: 7.

[182] Quoting R. Moses Schick, Weinberg answered the objection that the Vilna Gaon raised against Colon. He then explained how the Vilna Gaon's view is based on a reading of the Talmud which differs from that of Colon. However, Weinberg did not attempt to refute the Vilna Gaon's interpretation.

[183] At the end of the responsum, and almost as an aside, Weinberg advanced the dubious suggestion that if the bat mitzvah is used to impart important lessons in Judaism to young women, it can be seen as consistent even with the Vilna Gaon's position on the adoption of gentile practices. However, as already noted, his main method of proving the legitimacy of the bat mitzvah is to reject the Vilna Gaon's position in favour of Colon's view.

[184] Weinberg's responsum, especially the reasoning behind it relating to the sensitivities of women and the validity of breaking with traditional practice when the need is great, is cited in Wayne R. Allen (ed.), *Tomekh kehalakhah* (Mount Vernon, NY, 1986), i, no. 6, in order to support the halakhic validity of women's prayer groups. See, however, Zvi Schachter, 'Go Thy Way Forth by the Footsteps of the Flock' (Heb.), *Beit yitsḥak*, 17 (1985), 128, who argues against this view, citing Weinberg's great regard for traditional custom in *SE* iii, no. 96. (Surprisingly, Schachter does not mention Weinberg's responsum on bat mitzvah.) Berkovits, *Jewish Women*, 79–81, denies that the logic of *SE* iii, no. 96, compels one to admit that Weinberg would have forbidden women's prayer groups.

ii, no. 8, Weinberg discusses the halakhic propriety of the Yeshurun youth group in France. This organization, which was modelled on German Orthodox youth groups, was co-educational and allowed girls to sing at its gatherings. Both of these characteristics made it the subject of attack by right-wing segments of the French Orthodox—attacks which Weinberg believed were symptomatic of their short-sightedness and lack of concern for the larger community. He responded very sharply to these opponents, noting that even though they were only concerned about their own children, they had no way of ensuring that the latter would not also be swept away by the anti-religious trends pervading French Jewry.[185]

In Weinberg's responsum justifying the actions of Yeshurun it is clear, just as with his responsum on the bat mitzvah, that he had convinced himself what his ruling must be. The only obstacle to overcome was finding the sources to justify it. 'He knows only too well that some conclusions are ruled out from the beginning even if these appear convincing from the point of view of abstract logic and pure legal theory.'[186] In a fashion unheard of in responsa literature, Weinberg explained at great length the educational and sociological importance of this organization and the psychological state of French youth, especially young women who take offence at being excluded from singing. It was these considerations which led Weinberg to conclude that in modern times there was an obligation to create youth groups such as Yeshurun. Only they would be able to provide a connection to Judaism, and, in turn, spark a religious revival for the overwhelming majority of modern Jewish youth.

Weinberg's meta-halakhic considerations are set out even before he reaches his halakhic arguments, which are based on the notions that (1) it is permitted to listen to women singing as part of a group, and (2) the prohibition against hearing a woman sing does not apply to holy songs.[187] This order of presentation is important, because by showing how critical Yeshurun was for the survival of French Orthodoxy, Weinberg was setting the stage for the use of minority opinions which would not be taken into account in a halakhic decision that did not have such extenuating circumstances.

A *posek* is not 'objective' when dealing with issues of *agunah* or *mamzerut*, but on the contrary has a set goal—freeing the bound women or removing restrictions from the children. He devotes all his energy to finding a halakhic way to reach this goal, and usually succeeds. Similarly, when the fate of thousands of young Jews was in the balance, Weinberg did not consider pros and cons objectively. Rather, he approached the discussion with a set goal and went about finding the halakhic sources to justify it. It is therefore to be expected that those authorities who did not

[185] In *SE* ii, no. 14, Weinberg again referred harshly to the right-wing French Orthodox.

[186] Jacobs, *Tree of Life*, 12–13.

[187] See also *SE* ii, no. 14 (end), where Weinberg repeated these arguments. Saul Berman, 'Kol Isha', in Leo Landman (ed.), *Rabbi Joseph H. Lookstein Memorial Volume* (New York, 1980), 63–5, shows the significance of Weinberg's halakhic views within the development of the prohibition of *kol ishah*.

share Weinberg's general outlook would oppose his responsum and cite numerous halakhic sources to buttress their opposition. But these opponents were missing the point, for Weinberg too was well aware of the halakhic authorities in opposition to his view. Indeed, he cited a number of them. Yet because of the critical importance of the issue he was confronting, he chose to ignore these authorities and to rely on minority opinions. Halakhic interpretation was not in dispute, but rather how the needs of contemporary Orthodoxy were to be evaluated and what the role of the *posek* should be in responding to those needs.

Weinberg continued by pointing out that the leaders of pre-war German Orthodoxy, who approved of co-educational groups such as Yeshurun, were able to pass on the tradition successfully to their children. They succeeded because they knew how to present Orthodoxy in a fashion which was consistent with the spirit of modern times. However, the sages of Lithuania and Poland had failed in this regard, a fact they freely admitted.[188] Weinberg's public identification with the ideals and method of education of German Orthodoxy, at the expense of east European Orthodoxy, was never made clearer.[189]

Weinberg's method in this responsum, as in so many others, followed the German halakhic tradition. To give one example from this tradition which relates to issues Weinberg discussed, Jacob Rosenheim, a leading follower of Hirsch, explained that the latter showed 'tolerant, cautious reserve (if judged by the moral rigour of the divine Law and of rabbinical teaching) towards those very objectionable forms of conduct of the sexes on the parquet floors of the salons, towards תערובת נשים עם אנשים[190] [and] towards קול באשה ערוה[191] at public examinations in the higher grades'.[192] Both Hirsch and Weinberg were forced to compromise. The sociological realities of their time compelled them to explore the outer limits of halakhic propriety. However, they were prepared to do so, for the alternative would have been much worse.[193]

[188] See e.g. Moses Auerbach, 'Concerning an Orthodox College for Women' (Heb.), *Hama'ayan*, 4 (Nisan 5724 [1964]), 1.

[189] See the comments on this responsum in Joel B. Wolowelsky, 'Modern Orthodoxy and Women's Changing Self-Perception', *Tradition*, 22 (Spring 1986), 66–7.

[190] The mixing of the sexes.

[191] 'A woman's voice is considered nakedness [i.e. licentious]' (*Berakhot* 24*a*).

[192] Rosenheim, *Samson Raphael Hirsch's Cultural Ideal*, 60. (I have corrected the punctuation to agree with the original German, *Das Bildungsideal S. R. Hirschs und die Gegenwart*, 65. This passage has been excised in the Hebrew translation of Rosenheim's essay, *Rabi shimshon rafa'el hirsh: Mevaser umagshim ḥazon ha'aḥdut hanitsḥit*, trans. Chaim Weissman (Benei Berak, 1965), and published by Nezah Publications.)

[193] On this theme, see Breuer, *Jüdische Orthodoxie*, 368 n. 26, who calls attention to a report in *Jeschurun*, 18 (1885), 11, of a public function at the Orthodox school in Frankfurt at which a teenage girl sang in the presence of a crowded audience. See also Unna, *Sho'alin vedorshin*, no. 2, who defends the practice of unmarried girls singing in front of men. Unlike Weinberg, he does not restrict his permission to singing in groups or singing holy songs. I would also call attention to a picture of a group of girls found at the end of Sinasohn, *Adass Jisroel Berlin* (32 in the unpaginated pictures). They are participating in a co-educational Adass Jisroel event, apparently a sports

One of the characteristics of the German halakhic tradition has been described by Breuer as follows: 'How the inquirer will respond to the decision which is given to him was often no less decisive, with regard to the ultimate halakhic ruling, than

exhibition, and are not dressed in the fashion one might expect of members of the separatist Orthodox community. See also the picture in Mario Offenberg (ed.), *Adass Jisroel: Die Jüdische Gemeinde in Berlin (1859–1942)* (Berlin, 1986), 202.

After publishing his responsum, Weinberg was pleased to learn that Karelitz shared his outlook, See *Hapardes* (Feb. 1967), 38 (Karelitz's opinion was expressed with regard to the co-educational Ezra movement in Israel). As with his responsum on the bat mitzvah, this responsum has stimulated a great deal of discussion. Abraham David Horowitz, *Kinyan torah behalakhah* (Strasbourg, 1976), i, no. 85, completely rejects Weinberg's view permitting girls to sing (the issue of co-educational groups is not considered). He also expresses doubt that any German *posek* ever ruled leniently in this matter, and goes so far as to say that Weinberg's old age was blinding him to reality, in that he assumed that the young men of Yeshurun would not enjoy hearing the young women sing holy songs. It is clear from Horowitz's letter that Weinberg had written to him privately before he gave his decision. Presumably, Weinberg expected opposition to his view among segments of the French Orthodox, and therefore wished to enlist the support of Horowitz, the *ḥaredi* rabbi of Strasbourg. (Horowitz is currently a member of the *beit din* of the Edah Haḥaredit in Jerusalem.) A more concise version of Horowitz's responsum appears in *SE* iii, p. 194 (with the passage of time, Horowitz probably added to his original letter). Waldenberg, *Tsits eli'ezer*, xiv. 20; Meir Amsel, 'Concerning the "Yeshurun" Organization in France', *Hama'or* (Nov. 1955), 15–17, (Dec. 1955), 13–15, (Mar. 1956), 14–17; Meir Isaacson, *Mevaser tov* (Brooklyn, NY, 1986), ii, no. 74; R. Yosef Shalom Eliashiv and R. Jacob Kaminetzky as quoted in Aryeh Ze'ev Ginzberg, *Divrei ḥakhamim* (Brooklyn, NY, 1986), 253; and Menasheh Klein, *Mishneh halakhot*, second series, *Oraḥ ḥayim*, no. 54, and *Even ha'ezer*, no. 26, also dispute Weinberg's conclusions. Eliashiv claims that even according to Weinberg his responsum cannot be applied to other cases. However, he is apparently unaware of Weinberg's comments on women singing at the end of *SE* ii, no. 14. Isaac Jacob Fuchs, *Halikhot bat yisra'el* (Jerusalem, 1984), 89 n. 16, is similarly unaware of these comments. Weinberg reaffirmed his position in his letter to Meir Amsel, dated 13 Nov. 1957. For positive reactions to Weinberg's responsum, see R. Elimelekh Bar-Shaul in Shmuel Katz, *Kedoshim tiheyu* (Jerusalem, 1980), 244, who relies on Weinberg to permit mixed singing. See also Elyakim G. Ellinson, *Hatsnea lekhet* (Jerusalem, 1981), 42–3 n. 117, who quotes Weinberg's view in support of religious co-educational youth movements. In *Kedoshim tiheyu*, 248–9, R. Shlomo Aviner cites Weinberg in order to establish the halakhic validity of the co-educational Bnei Akiva and Ezra movements in Israel. See also Aviner, *Ḥesed ne'urayikh* (Jerusalem, 1991), 76, where he sharply restricts Weinberg's comments, claiming that Weinberg did not support the broad conclusions that many drew from his responsum. This same view is expressed by Aviner's teacher, R. Zvi Yehudah Kook; see Aviner, *Gan na'ul* (Jerusalem, 1985), 22. In his *Torat imekha* (Jerusalem, 1991), 238, Aviner asserts that Weinberg's view is not shared by any other authority. See also *Bemareh habezek* (Jerusalem, 1995), ii. 19, where Weinberg's view is relied upon to permit group-singing by women.

J. Simcha Cohen, *Intermarriage and Conversion: A Halakhic Solution* (Hoboken, NJ, 1987), 101–3, cites Weinberg in order to permit women to join men in song during synagogue services. On Weinberg's ruling, he writes: 'The problem with this decision is that it appears to be based primarily upon a perception of life-style and a cultural milieu rather than a purely halakhic source' (p. 102). Cohen is troubled by this and tries to suggest a 'pure' halakhic reason for the permission of Hirsch and Hildesheimer for women to join men in song, upon which Weinberg relied. However, Cohen's comments are very strange. To begin with, Weinberg never said that there were *no* halakhic sources to back up his ruling. In *SE* ii, nos. 8 and 14, he stated that Hirsch and Hildesheimer were guided by the halakhic notion of 'two voices are not heard' and the view that holy songs do not lead to impure thoughts. Furthermore, although Cohen is correct in

the pure halakhic argumentation.'[194] Weinberg shared this characteristic, and the tendency to take into account modern social and educational issues is constantly present in his responsa. This distinguishes him from many other *posekim*, who choose either to ignore or to fight against these manifestations of modern society. Weinberg's responsa are also unusual in that he was explicit about the meta-halakhic factors which led him to his decisions, whereas with other *posekim* the halakhic historian usually has to read between the lines or speculate about possible influences. Weinberg very often cited these meta-halakhic factors in order to bolster a decision even when there was no need to do so, since the halakhic sources were themselves sufficient.[195]

Another issue discussed by Weinberg which was related to women was female suffrage, whose permissibility was at one time subject to great halakhic dispute. Although it is common today for even ultra-Orthodox women to vote in various elections, this was not always the case. When, in 1918, the Jewish Agency granted women the right to vote and hold office, most of the world's leading rabbis, including Kook, Israel Meir Hacohen, and Grodzinski, strongly opposed this.[196] Their negative stand was supported by Germany's Orthodox newspaper, *Der Israelit*,[197] as well as by prominent German religious leaders.[198] Hoffmann disagreed with

sensing that Weinberg's decision was based primarily upon 'a perception of life-style and a cultural milieu', there is no 'problem' with this. Since there were halakhic sources to justify his position, it was precisely the 'perception of life-style and cultural milieu' which impelled Weinberg to make use of this halakhic support.

[194] See Breuer, 'German Rabbinic Approach', 167.

[195] There are so many examples of this that it would be impossible to do justice to them in a single chapter. One typical example is *SE* ii, no. 157, where Weinberg was asked whether it was necessary to recite *kiddush* in the synagogue. It seems that during World War II, owing to a lack of wine, this custom was abolished and the rabbi did not want to reinstate it because of the *Shulḥan arukh*'s disapproval (*Oraḥ ḥayim* 269). After citing a number of halakhic sources in support of the custom, Weinberg also noted the educational importance of sanctifying the Sabbath in public, as this could inspire people to recite the prayer at home. Thus, even though there are authoritative halakhic sources in support of this position, not to mention long-standing custom, Weinberg was not content with this. He felt that it was just as important to emphasize the educational factor. In *SE* ii, no. 5, Weinberg showed that it is halakhically acceptable for a bar mitzvah boy to chant the Torah reading in the Sephardi pronunciation even though the community uses the Ashkenazi method. He then added that there are meta-halakhic factors—education of the bar mitzvah boy and the need for peace in the community—which support his decision. See also *SE* iii, no. 95, where Weinberg added a paragraph dealing with modern pedagogy, even though the halakhic issues were clear.

[196] The dispute has been described in detail by Menahem Friedman, *Society and Religion* (Heb.) (Jerusalem, 1978), chs. 6, 7, and by Zohara Bozich Hertzig, 'The Controversy over Women's Suffrage at the Beginning of the Mandate' (Heb.) (MA diss., Bar-Ilan University, 1990). See also Michael Z. Nehorai, 'Halakhah, Metahalakhah, and the Redemption of Israel: Reflections on the Rabbinic Rulings of Rav Kook', in Lawrence J. Kaplan and David Shatz (eds.), *Rabbi Abraham Isaac Kook and Jewish Spirituality* (New York, 1995), 138–44.

[197] See 3 Dec. 1925, 1. See also 6 Nov. 1919, 1, for a German translation of an article by Kook on this question.

[198] See Meier Lerner of Altona (1857–1930), *Hadar hakarmel* (London, 1975), ii, *Ḥoshen mishpat*, nos. 8 and 9 (the original German version of this last responsum appears in Ina Lorenz, *Die Juden in Hamburg zur Zeit der Weimarer Republik* (Hamburg, 1987), ii. 1250–1); Moses Auerbach,

these rabbis on the question of women voting, yet he too agreed that they were not permitted to hold office.[199] For the opponents of women's suffrage, the halakhic arguments they marshalled were secondary to the fundamental reason for their opposition, namely, that women voting, and holding office, did not conform to traditional Jewish conceptions of modesty.

Since this was an issue which would not go away, it is not surprising that Weinberg was also asked to rule on it. In his first responsum,[200] dated 1932, he stated that at a meeting of the Vereinigung's Halakhah Commission he had refuted Hoffmann's proofs and shown that there was no halakhic prohibition against women holding office. However, as far as practical halakhah was concerned, he agreed with his colleagues that for reasons of modesty it was improper for women to do so.[201] With regard to women voting, he advised his questioner to adopt the permissive view of Hoffmann, who, according to Weinberg, was the only authority who based his decision on halakhic sources as opposed to preconceived notions of female modesty. Weinberg concluded his responsum by noting that if following Hoffmann's view would destroy the peace and unity of the community, then the community could adopt his own position, which allowed women to be elected to office. Here again, we find Weinberg arguing that there is room for halakhic innovation if it becomes increasingly difficult to fulfil the halakhah in the best possible manner because of pressing sociological considerations.

In a second responsum dealing with this issue,[202] dated 1960, Weinberg was more cryptic. After quoting authorities on both sides of the dispute, he refused to give a ruling, even with regard to women voting. Instead, he suggested that the matter be left alone as it would eventually be worked out by itself.[203] He then listed the reasons given by those who forbade female participation. These are based on traditional conceptions of female modesty as well as on rabbinic sources. Weinberg

From Halberstadt to Petaḥ Tikvah, 144; Abraham Samuel Benjamin Spitzer of Hamburg (1872–1934), 'Ketorah ya'aseh', *Festschrift für Jacob Rosenheim*, 1–43 (Hebrew section). Alone among German rabbis, R. Nehemiah Anton Nobel of Frankfurt (1871–1922) ruled that women could vote and be elected to office. His motivations were largely meta-halakhic in nature. Nobel stated that he did not issue his ruling for the sake of the women of Frankfurt, but for the women of Palestine. It was crucial not to alienate the latter in any way, for, as he put it, 'we cannot build the Land [of Israel] without our women and girls'. See Ernst Simon, 'N. A. Nobel als Prediger', in id., *Brücken: Gesammelte Aufsätze* (Heidelberg, 1965), 380.

199 'Ein Gutachten', *Jeschurun*, 6 (1919), 262–6, and 'Über Frauenwahlrecht in jüdischen-Gemeinden', ibid. 515–22.

200 *SE* ii, no. 52.

201 The minutes of this 5 June 1930 meeting are preserved in the Institute for Holocaust Research, Bar-Ilan University, File 105/3:67. They also reveal that Weinberg insisted that his refutation of Hoffmann should not be made public knowledge.

202 *SE* iii, no. 105.

203 This, by the way, is exactly what happened in Israel; see my 'Further on Women's Hair Covering', *Judaism*, 40 (Winter 1991), 92 n. 6. In his letter to Isaiah Wolfsberg, dated 5 May 1954, Weinberg wrote: 'The problem of Torah and the state will be solved by the next generation.' I am unaware of any responsa by Agudah figures justifying women's suffrage, yet Agudah women vote in Israeli elections. Throughout the rest of the world, Agudah women have no electoral influence on the affairs of their community, in accordance with the rulings of the Agudat Yisrael leadership earlier in the century.

concluded that one could debate the relevance of the rabbinic sources, 'but [in this case] there is no value in talmudic dialectics since there are more profound reasons' at the heart of the dispute.

What Weinberg was saying is that, in essence, there was nothing forbidden about women voting or being elected to office. At that time (1960), Weinberg was prepared, by refusing to issue a ruling, to deny women electoral involvement. He chose this course since many authorities opposed women's electoral involvement and this policy did not threaten the coherence of the traditional community or the religious loyalty of women. However, he felt that if in the future the situation changed, there would be no reason to oppose an expansion of women's involvement in community affairs. At such a time there would be much to lose, in terms of the religious allegiance of women, and nothing to gain by maintaining what was only a stringency.[204] Just as the Mishnah preserves the opinion of an individual, even if it is not adopted, in order to enable a future court to rely on this view,[205] so too Weinberg left open the possibility that the time would come when the prevailing majority view should be set aside.[206]

In conclusion, it is worthwhile to call attention to one more responsum, for it too reveals a great deal about Weinberg's ideological outlook. In my discussion of the responsa dealing with bat mitzvah and the Yeshurun group, I noted Weinberg's view that, when the practice under consideration is halakhically questionable but has important communal value, the *posek* should do his utmost to find ways to justify the practice. We find another example of this approach in a short responsum in which Weinberg dealt with the practice of those mourners who, instead of performing the ritual tearing of a garment, tear a small tie.[207] In this case there was no way in which the practice could be justified, for tearing a ribbon has no halakhic validity. Yet Weinberg counselled restraint. If the rabbi is unable to persuade the mourners to change their practice he should remain silent, since it is better that they tear the ribbon, so that the practice is not entirely forgotten, than not tear anything at all. Weinberg concluded with a very interesting passage: 'In general, one should be careful not to cause an argument because of these things, and they [the Sages] have

[204] He expressed the same view at the 1930 meeting of the Vereinigung's Halakhah Commission. After agreeing that the striving for women's suffrage was part of a larger alienation from the halakhic system, Weinberg's position was summed up in the Commission's minutes: 'With a prohibition one would push away and alienate the women. He is for the retention of the exclusion of women in Orthodox communities where they raise no claim. However, he opposes fighting against women's suffrage in places where they have already achieved this. . . . Winning over the women can strengthen the power of conservatism. Among the Catholics, for instance, women are an important factor in the maintenance of conservative thought.'

[205] *Eduyyot* 1: 5; see the commentaries of Rabad, Meiri, R. Samson of Sens and *Tosafot yom tov*. See also Tosefta, *Eduyyot* 1: 4.

[206] See Menahem Elon's decision in the Leah Shakdiel case, published in Dov Rapel (ed.), *Hapeninah* (Jerusalem, 1989), 104–5, and Yonah Ben-Sasson, 'The Significance of Social Reality in Halakhah' (Heb.), in Menahem Kahana (ed.), *Beḥevlei masoret*, 65. Elon and Ben-Sasson offer alternative readings of *SE* iii, no. 105, neither of which corresponds to my own interpretation.

[207] *SE* ii, p. 278.

already said (Mishnah, *Pesaḥim* 50*b*) that we are obligated to follow the custom of the locality in order to avoid arguments, and see Rabbenu Asher there.'[208]

What is surprising about Weinberg's citation of *Pesaḥim* 50*b* and Rabbenu Asher is that both of these sources refer to the adoption of halakhically valid customs. It is only in such circumstances that one is not supposed to depart from local practice.[209] However, in the case discussed by Weinberg, the mourners were violating halakhah rather than following a valid custom. Normally, in cases such as this, one would have expected Weinberg to cite the phrase, 'Just as it is a *mitzvah* for a person to say something that will be listened to, so too it is a *mitzvah* to refrain from saying something that will not be listened to',[210] or 'Leave Israel alone, better that they should sin in ignorance than deliberately.'[211]

Although the evidence does not suggest any definitive answer to this problem, it is possible that the rabbinic responses mentioned here were viewed by Weinberg as applying to cases where there is no redeeming value in the people's actions. However, in this case, even though tearing the tie has no *halakhic* significance, and indeed is in violation of a rabbinic commandment, it still has *religious* significance in that it prevents the ceremony from being entirely forgotten.[212] Therefore, the mistaken practice of the masses is still entitled to a degree of respect, and Weinberg related it to valid customs from which one should not depart for fear of creating controversy, a consideration which is found in many of his responsa.[213]

[208] The reference is to Rabbenu Asher's comments to *Pesaḥim* 51*a* (also referred to in *SE* ii, p. 12).

[209] In a responsum Rabbenu Asher states explicitly that if a local custom involves a halakhic infraction it must be abolished. See Asher ben Yehiel, *She'elot uteshuvot lerabeinu asher ben yeḥiel* (Jerusalem, 1994), 55: 10.

[210] *Yevamot* 65*b*. See *SE* ii, no. 67 (end).

[211] *Shabbat* 148*b*, *Betzah* 30*a*. See *SE* ii, pp. 156, 157. On this principle, see Yehudah Herzl Henkin, ' "Better Unintentional Sinners than Deliberate Ones" in Contemporary Times' (Heb.), *Teḥumin*, 2 (1981), 272–80, and Gershon C. Bacon, 'Leave Israel Alone: Better Unintentional Sinners than Deliberate Ones: Some Rabbinic Responses to Communal Disregard of the Law', in J. Leonard Romm and Leonard Levy (eds.), *Halakhah and the Modern Jew: Essays in Honor of Horace Bier* (n.p., 1989), 9–17.

[212] Cf. *Mishneh berurah* 649: 54 (reflecting earlier sources) regarding the use of a non-kosher *lulav* without a blessing in order to prevent the ritual from being forgotten.

[213] This notion of ensuring communal peace and unity is a basic consideration, not merely in Weinberg's responsa, but in Jewish law in general. However, because of its vague nature, which allows it to be applied at a *posek*'s discretion, I believe that it too should be described as a meta-halakhic, rather than a halakhic, consideration. What one *posek* views as an obligatory ruling, whatever the cost to communal peace, another *posek* opposes precisely because of the damage to communal peace. The tension between these two tendencies is seen clearly in a comment by Meier Lerner, *Hadar hakarmel*, ii, *Yoreh de'ah*, no. 71, in justification of a ruling which would destroy communal peace and unity: 'The Sages who said "Do not separate yourself from the community", also said "Distance yourself from a bad neighbour and do not associate with a wicked person".' See similarly Jacob Ettlinger, *Minḥat ani* (Jerusalem, 1963), 105*a*: 'Even though peace between a man and his neighbour is important, nevertheless it is better for there to be peace between the people of Israel and their Father in heaven. Therefore, one who is zealous for God and the Torah is a pursuer of peace.' See also Klugman, *R. Samson Raphael Hirsch*, 136–7, 158–9. Despite the overriding value he attributed to communal peace, as seen throughout his writings, Weinberg also had to draw the line somewhere. See e.g. *SE* ii, p. 32, iii, no. 100.

AFTERWORD

WEINBERG'S LIFETIME coincided with a series of dizzying changes in the Jewish community. As we have seen, he was affected by a number of these changes, and the story of his life gives us a better understanding of them. It is the issue of Weinberg's lasting importance which we must now address. Though several of his colleagues, despite much renown during their lifetime, are without influence today, Weinberg's case is different.

Because Weinberg's form of Orthodoxy has been forced on to the defensive in recent years, it is no surprise that the so-called Modern Orthodox look towards him as a guiding light in their encounter with modernity. His name is often brought up in Modern Orthodox writings, for he identified with the ideals of this 'movement'. Weinberg believed that Orthodox Jews should not run away from modern society but should educate themselves so that they can be a part of this society. He regarded the creation of the State of Israel as an event of unparalleled importance. He believed that Jewish women's changing self-perception must be acknowledged. Rather than fighting this new manifestation, he chose to work within the halakhic system to see how far the desires of women could be legitimated. He believed in a halakhah which responded to social change wherever possible, and was frightened by the rising extremism in Orthodoxy. It is only to be expected, therefore, that the Modern Orthodox claim Weinberg as one of their own, and draw inferences from his published opinions to cases which were not yet relevant in his time (for example, women's prayer groups). Together with David Zvi Hoffmann, Isaac Herzog, and Joseph B. Soloveitchik, Weinberg stands out as an icon of Modern Orthodoxy, and shows that this brand of Orthodoxy has its own authority figures whose renown must be acknowledged in all circles.

Having said this, it is not surprising that the more conservative elements of Orthodoxy have also been quick to claim Weinberg. Because of his undisputed halakhic greatness and his close friendships with many in right-wing Orthodox circles, it would have been too much for the right wing to concede him to the more liberal segments of Orthodoxy. The dispute over Weinberg's image centres on whether he was a traditional *rosh yeshiva* who happened to receive a secular education which he regarded as of little significance, or whether he was an advocate of German-style Orthodoxy who stressed the importance of secular studies and

Zionism and integrated these elements into his *Weltanschauung*. This dispute was already seen at his funeral and in the many eulogies published after his death. It continues in our own generation and in some ways it is Weinberg himself, by not publicizing his true feelings on important issues of the day, who allowed the opposing segments to lay claim to him. In fact, it is probably unavoidable that the legacy of outstanding Modern Orthodox sages will lead to such disputes, and the contemporary controversy over how to characterize Joseph B. Soloveitchik's *Weltanschauung* is particularly relevant in this regard.

Through an impartial examination of Weinberg's views and by focusing particularly on his private correspondence, it is hoped that this book has made some contribution to clarifying his outlook. It is true that not every detail falls neatly into place, but the overall picture is unambiguous. Perhaps only now can we begin to appreciate Weinberg's significance and speak of the legacy that he bequeathed.

APPENDIX I

Lebenslauf—Autobiographical Note

My name is Chilko Jakob Weinberg and I was born in Pilwishki in 1884, the son of the merchant Moses Weinberg and his wife Scheine Rivke.

As a child, I attended the Jewish Elementary School, and later the Jewish Talmudic College (Yeshiva) in Kovno. I obtained my rabbinical licence at the age of 17. When I was 20, I was appointed rabbi in Pilwishki and later I also became the crown rabbi, having passed the state examination (equivalent to the German matriculation) in Lomza.

Since then, I have published historical, talmudic, and pedagogic papers in various scientific journals.

In 1914 I moved to Germany, taking up the post of rabbi in Berlin.

With the permission of the Prussian Ministry of Education and Cultural Affairs, I attended lectures at the Berlin philosophical faculty during the winter term of 1920. There I heard Professors Erdmann, Riehl, Stumpf, and Strack.

Having obtained the university entrance certificate in Kovno after passing the requisite examinations, I enrolled in the University of Giessen. Here I attended the lectures of Professors Kahle, Messer, Hölscher, Kinkel, Aster, Hans Schmidt, and others.

For the past 2½ years I have been employed as a lecturer in Judaica at the University of Giessen.

I would express my sincerest thanks to all my highly esteemed teachers for the part they played in my academic education, especially to Herr Professor Kahle, my esteemed teacher, who did so much to advance my academic studies and also enriched this present work with valuable suggestions.

Giessen, 25 July 1923

University of Giessen Archives. Appendices I–III have been translated from the German by Arnold J. Pomerans. Translations © The Littman Library of Jewish Civilization 1999.

APPENDIX II

Letter to Hitler

Frankfurt am Main, 4 October 1933

The Herr Reich Chancellor,
Berlin.

The undersigned, the most respectful Free Association for the Interests of Orthodox Jewry, has the honour, also on behalf of the two co-signatory organizations, to submit a memorandum on the German Jewish question in the hope that it may receive favourable consideration.

With humble respects
FREE ASSOCIATION
FOR THE
INTERESTS OF ORTHODOX JEWRY
Dr S. Ehrmann

MEMORANDUM

TO THE HERR REICH CHANCELLOR

The undersigned Orthodox Jewish organizations, representing that section of German Jewry which considers the Jewish religion as the sole ground and justification of the historical existence of the Jewish people,* feel compelled, Herr Reich Chancellor, to set forth openly and honestly their attitude to the Jewish question. In the wake of the National Revolution and the measures taken by your government, this question has become so burning an issue that it must be resolved in one way or another if German Jewry, and ultimately Germany herself, are not to suffer the most serious damage. *Struggling* National Socialism lumped Judaism, Marxism, and Communism together and ignored the Jewish religion. *Victorious* National Socialism will be unable to solve the Jewish question without taking the Jewish religion into consideration, if, that is, the solution is to reflect the principles of justice.

Federal Archives Potsdam R/43 II 602, L383445, L383446–L383452.

* Whenever the term 'nation' or 'people' is applied to the Jewish community in this memorandum, it should not—according to the teachings of Orthodox Judaism—be interpreted as mere blood kinship. On the contrary, the Jewish tradition considers Jewry as a community sharing a *religious* calling, admittedly on a *national basis*, but with so strong a *primacy of the religious aspect* that by assuming the *religious* obligations of the community, foreigners, too, *acquire* the right of being included in the nation.

This fact compels us to speak out, and also fills us with hope that our voice will be heard.

I

Marxist materialism and Communist atheism have nothing whatever in common with the spirit of the affirmative Jewish religious tradition, with true, historical Judaism, with the Orthodox Jewish doctrine binding on the Jewish people.

For as long as can be remembered, we have, in speech and in writing, been battling against this anti-religious attitude. In the instruction of our youth, in public lectures and from the pulpit, and in the Orthodox religious press, we have always countered the corrupting spirit of materialism with religious idealism, by stressing man's responsibility to God and the nation. We have declared war on the atheist movement and engaged it in combat. We have raised up the Orthodox Jewish law as a rampart against depravity and dissipation and against capitalist excesses, a law that calls for the strictest morality in the conduct of life, that opposes the pursuit of gain for its own sake and demands the most trenchant renunciation of material advantages for the sake of religious and ethical principles.

II

Precisely because we have been fighting against the threat of subversion with all the means at our disposal since long *before* the beginning of the National Revolution, we are entitled to ask: have these mistakes and these excesses really been committed by people of Jewish descent alone? Is it really the Jewish extraction that must be pilloried as the source of these evils?

Are non-Jewish citizens and their way of thinking really free from these errors? Were Jews alone active in preaching materialism and godlessness? No, the soulless European materialism which fostered spiritual decay, which caused corruption and treason to flourish and which, morally and materially, underpinned all these currents was a general affliction of our age.

Could not enough names be cited of politicians and writers here and abroad who are not of Jewish descent but use every means to encourage godlessness and immorality, who support materialistic ideas and destroy the national spirit? In the Second International, which constitutes the foundation of Marxism, as also in the related Third International, the Comintern, only some of the active members are Jews. The Politburo, which governs Russia, is led by the Georgian, Stalin, and in its ranks there is but a single Jew. We therefore feel justified in decisively rejecting the allegation of our enemies that Judaism and materialistic Marxism are identical. No! By its true nature, its spiritual attitude, its traditional Orthodox approach, Judaism is the staunchest opponent of materialism and atheism and of the intellectual construct of class struggle and bloody violence which prevails in Russia today, destroying a nation of 150 million people but above all the Orthodox core of Russian Jewry.

III

The German National Socialist party claims that the Jewish race is pernicious and inferior. We would be going too far were we to question the evidence and results of scientific race theory. There is just one thing we would be so bold as to assert:

The Jewish people are *no unknown strangers* to Germans, even in the intellectual field. The Jewish Bible and the Books of the New Testament, conceived and written by Jews, have been impressing indelible traces on the German essence for a thousand years, have shaped and determined it from within. Who is to say whether the Psalms of David and the exalted morality of the Jewish Prophets have a larger or smaller share in the soul that German people, German artists, and German spiritual leaders have inherited from humble and pious mothers and fathers than the Nordic blood of the Vikings and the heritage of German heroes?

Yet the call for liberation from alien Jewish influences is being applied even to the Bible by some individuals in the National Socialist camp.

However, we can see how greatly the new Germany esteems and protects the Church as a mighty and indispensable spiritual bastion in the construction of a healthy national life, and no Christian Church, be it ever so nationalistically inclined, can demolish the bridge to its own *Heilsgeschichte* [the interpretation of history stressing God's saving grace and viewing Jesus as central in redemption].

When we are reproached with the fact that Jewish hyper-intellectualism, the oversubtle carping of a superannuated people, injects a dangerous germ of decay into the German essence, when the attempt is made to represent this as a natural taint of Jewish blood, and when, in support of this claim, the work of modern Jewish writers and scientists, journalists and artists is cited, then we rightly contend that all these people are products of the modern rationalist spirit. The true Jewish blood, the true Jewish race, as it has been shaped by the unrivalled discipline and education provided by the Jewish religion over three thousand years, is represented by no one less than it is by deracinated Jews, people whose intellectual outlook stamps them as twentieth-century Europeans, not as Jews.

The true Jewish people, who continue to live their own life to this day in millions of quiet and pious homes, are a deeply religious people pursuing sacred ideals, a community spiritually unsullied in their youthful mysticism, one living in the expectation of a pure and ideal future. The Jewish people, guided by their traditional religion, are a virtuous and helpful nation pursuing their path through life with calmness and modesty.

In the fight against the materialistic spirit of Marxism, only the revival of the religious mainsprings, only the return of society to God, will be crowned with success. In this struggle, the true, religious Jewish people could stand shoulder to shoulder with the German people, guided by faith in God, renewed and rejuvenated.

IV

In attacks on the Jewish community, the atrocity propaganda spread in countries hostile to Germany plays a crucial role.

The National Socialist Party must surely realize that by declaring war on the entire Jewish race it has caused Jews all over the world to feel that their honour, their noblest ideals, and their feelings have been impugned. It would have been unnatural had that slur on their honour not elicited a strong reaction from every single Jew, wherever he was to be found. Germany's enemies have been quick to exploit this indignation.

The National German Government found itself on the defensive. Unfortunately it, or rather the NSDAP [the National Socialist Party], thought it right to discharge their entire anger on German Jewry, mounting an economic boycott against it. We do not shrink from calling these measures a catastrophic error and a grave injustice. At no time did German Jewry bear the least responsibility for the behaviour of Jews in other countries. Wherever foreign Jews have committed the wrong of spreading atrocity propaganda, they have done so on their own initiative, out of their own sense of injured honour. In reality, this propaganda war has been largely unleashed by radicals, Marxists, and Communists in all countries and of all races. Yet the boycott of German Jewish businesses has struck a blow at the German economy at large. The incidents of this boycott campaign, greatly magnified and distorted, have been used throughout the world, isolated and regrettable episodes being inflated to add fuel to the flames of the campaign against Germany's National Movement.

The great majority of German Jews did whatever they could from the very outset of the atrocity propaganda campaign to prevent these deplorable manifestations. We could produce a host of attested evidence of the steps German Jewish organizations and individual spiritual leaders have taken by letter and telegram to intervene with our co-religionists abroad. We implored them most earnestly to do their utmost to ensure that this propaganda campaign, so harmful to Germany and to German Jewry as a whole, be called off. As an example of our intervention we enclose the following telegram sent from Berlin by Dr Esra Munk, rabbi of the Berlin Orthodox community, to the Orthodox Rabbi Jung in New York.

It reads as follows:

25.3.1933
New York, 131 West 86th Street.

Dear Rabbi Jung,

Reports, flagrantly in conflict with the facts, of atrocities against the Jews in Germany have caused me, with the full agreement of all my colleagues, to direct this appeal to you as a friend of long standing, a visitor frequently seen at the local schools of higher learning and one familiar with the German people, imploring you to denounce, categorically and with the utmost emphasis, such reports as criminal, because they are contrary to the truth and monstrous exaggerations of the excesses of individuals during the elections. Please ensure the immediate and widest possible notification of the contents of this telegram to the American newspapers for this coming Monday.

Rabbi Dr E. Munk.

This telegram was sent to counterbalance the demonstration in New York planned for Monday, 27 March in New York *before the announcement* and the implementation of the anti-Jewish boycott in Germany. But neither it nor our other steps have been able to stave off the disastrous days when the entire Jewish population was blatantly held up to public scorn. We could add much further evidence of our attempts to mould international public opinion in Germany's favour—in particular we would draw attention to the continuous efforts in that direction, in the Dutch, English, and American press, of the president of the international Orthodox organization 'Agudas Jisroel', who lives in Germany, and the successful intervention of the selfsame organization to prevent a religious ban against German goods planned in Poland—but it would not be honest were we to claim at this moment that the world had grown calmer, that the boycott of German goods was no longer being advocated by anti-German propagandists, albeit less stridently than before. Undeniable, too, is the fact that the agents of the Second and Third Internationals often hide behind the mask of Judaism when directing their damaging work against Germany, falsely appearing before world public opinion as our friends and defenders. We have repeatedly drawn the attention of our co-religionists abroad to this threat.

Our Orthodox Jewish organizations are ready to send a special delegation abroad in order to convey a correct picture of events in Germany. We shall give it instructions to protest publicly against the attempts by malicious persons to exacerbate the difficult situation of Germany and of German Jewry by interfering in the relations between German Jews and the National Government.

The delegation will be able to explain that Orthodox German Jewry will itself openly and loyally defend its civil and human rights before the National Government.

German Jewry rejects most decisively any interference by non-German bodies in its internal affairs. It considers all external pressure on the German National Government a source of lasting damage to itself.

V

Before we refer to the current situation of German Jewry, we must, however diffidently, make mention of the immense blood sacrifice by Jews during the difficult days of the world war, a sacrifice proportionally as great as that of other Germans.

The *Commemorative Volume of Jewish Casualties in the German Army, the German Navy and the German Colonial Forces*, accompanied by a cordial letter of recommendation by Herr von Hindenburg, president of the German Reich, refutes in the most deeply affecting way once and for all the allegation that Jews shirked military service. It contains endless lists of men who remained loyal unto death in battle, first in alphabetical order and then arranged as a gazetteer, giving the place of residence, place of birth, date of birth, date of death, military rank, military unit, and official casualty report. With the assistance of the Central Office of Information in Spandau, it could be established that the war losses of German Jewry amounted to more than 12,000 dead. Ten thousand and sixty Jewish names, including 322 officers and 185 medical officers, could be identified in the casualty lists at the Spandau office; the rest were identified in other ways. A great many war victims were not even included because at their death they were no longer attached to any military formation. Of the 545,000 Jewish souls present in the German Reich in 1914, some 100,000 served in the army, navy and the colonial forces during the war. If we compare these figures with the German total we obtain the same proportion of war casualties for both population groups. The Jewish toll of lives was as great and as uncontrovertible as the Aryan, and as clear a sign of unswerving loyalty.

The fact that in their individual feats of valour, too, Jews did not lag behind their comrades-in-arms, is borne out by the Jewish Airmen's Book, in which 164 Jewish war pilots are identified, men who, in countless aerial battles, proved their readiness to lay down their lives for their country, and of whom thirty died a hero's death. The Jewish Flight-Lieutenant Franke, who was killed in action, was one of the first to be awarded the Ordre pour le Mérite [one of the highest German distinctions].

It was not to elicit thanks for this blood sacrifice that we have presented these facts. We know that the allowances to the dependent survivors of Jewish soldiers who fell at the front, enshrined in the laws of the National Government, are only accepted by the beneficiaries with strong inner scruples and because they help them to survive. Like them, *all German Jews* without exception, and this has to be stressed, did their duty to the full when their monarch called. That is why the legal restrictions imposed upon them by the very German people for whom they were ready to lay down their lives have dealt them a double blow.

VI

As it is, the present situation of German Jewry, as created for them by the German people, is a *completely intolerable one, in respect of their legal position and also of their economic existence, their good name, and their scope for religious activity*.

The legal position of German Jews after the implementation of the laws passed by the National Government may be summed up as follows. Jews are excluded from government and municipal service, from cultural life, from educational institutions and the academic establishments. No more than a limited number of the

Jewish students and pupils at universities and secondary schools will be admitted to some, but not all, examinations. Jewish lawyers are not allowed to represent public and local government organizations. Jewish doctors have lost the right to work for health insurance plans, and have been removed from public hospitals. The exemptions issued to the special category of front-line soldiers and their dependants do not alter the hopeless situation of the future generation of Jewish medical practitioners. Jews are almost everywhere excluded from the corporate structures of the new Reich.

Beyond that, economic activity, even when there are no laws restricting it, is being hampered most severely. Although the activity of Jews in the economic sphere has not been limited by direct legislation, *an anti-Jewish boycott is being applied throughout Germany*. It involves all state, government, municipal, and public enterprises, and, on orders of the Party leadership, all members of the NSDAP. In many cases, moreover, ordinary Jewish employees, to say nothing of Jewish members of the administration, have been removed from business enterprises.

As a result of these legal and actual restrictions, tens of thousands of German Jews have suddenly been deprived of their livelihood. The livelihood of tens of thousands of others has been destroyed as an indirect result. While the removal of Jews from the civil service, the liberal professions and commerce ought logically to have led to the deliberate redirection of Jewish manpower into various trades and into agriculture, that is, if the Jews were to be left with any *Lebensraum* at all, no such efforts by the government can be detected. On the contrary, the anti-Jewish boycott is being waged with the utmost vigour even in the trade organizations; nor are many opportunities for work on the land being made available to Jews.

In other words, German Jewry has been condemned to a slow but certain death from starvation.

Beyond that, there is the *defamation* of Jews, whose honour is constantly impugned, the population being incited against them and depriving them of room in which they can live and breathe. In official proclamations, Jews are equated with the coloured races. In schoolbooks Jews, without exception, are depicted as the epitome of evil, and German youth is being taught from the earliest age to hate the Jews. In the press, on the radio, and in speeches, every lapse by a Jewish individual is held up as typical of Jewish criminality at large, and all Jewry is identified with it.

Even religious life, which might serve as a source of moral education and elevation, is being obstructed. Purely religious education no longer enjoys the support of the state; the religious school system is breaking down, and religious congregations, the sole and ultimate means of turning their members into noble, God-imbued human beings, cannot continue for lack of state support and the destruction of the livelihood of their members.

Above all, the ban on ritual slaughter imposes the most severe personal restriction on Orthodox Jews.

The situation of German Jewry must therefore strike the objective observer throughout the world as plainly desperate, and it is understandable that the German National Government is only too easily suspected of deliberately planning the destruction of German Jewry. *This mistaken view must be refuted with concrete evidence, if any attempt to enlighten the outside world is to prove successful.*

Orthodox Jewry has no wish to abandon its conviction that the German government does not seek the destruction of German Jewry. Even if some individuals do have this objective, we do not believe that it meets with the approval of the Führer, or of the German government.

VII

But if we are wrong, if you, Herr Reich Chancellor, and the National Government you lead, if the responsible members of the Reich leadership of the NSDAP, should indeed have made it their objective to eradicate German Jewry from the German body politic, then we would rather cease nurturing illusions and learn the bitter truth.

To tell us the truth openly is in your interest, and in that of the entire German people. We would then consider your intentions a matter of fact and accommodate ourselves to them. We confess that for us this would be an unimaginable tragedy. We have learned to love the German soil. It holds the graves of our forebears, of many great and holy sons and daughters of the Jewish people. During two thousand years of our history we have grown close to this soil; we have learned to love the German sun; for all these centuries it has allowed our children to grow and has endowed their Jewishness with many fine and special traits. And we have learned to love the German people. They have occasionally caused us sorrow, especially during the Middle Ages. But we also shared in their resurrection. We have close bonds with their culture. It is part of our spiritual life and has set a special stamp upon us German Jews.

And yet, if we have to, we shall have the courage to shoulder our tragic fate and leave the outcome confidently to the God of history.

VIII

If, however, the German National Government is not seeking to destroy the spirit of German Jewry, if it wants merely to restrict our power to shape public policy and to reserve that power exclusively for those of Germanic descent, while yet granting us a place in the resurgence of the German nation, if it wants to preserve the moral core of Judaism, the arch-enemy of materialism, then let it tell us so frankly.

In view of the prevailing atmosphere we shall not ask the German government to abrogate all the restrictions imposed on the Jews overnight, although we consider such restrictions to be a considerable historical error. We have no wish, however, to create difficulties for the National Government.

Albeit with grieving hearts, we accept that we shall have to resign ourselves to today's many frustrations. Orthodox Jews have never sought economic supremacy, something that is in any case precluded by the religious command to keep the Sabbath, which guards Jews against materialism. Moreover, Orthodox Jewry has always vigorously opposed baptism and mixed marriages.

On the other hand, we require some *Lebensraum* within the *Lebensraum* of the German people, and a chance *to practise our religion and our calling in safety and without being vilified*. Our religion commands us to be loyal to the National Government. In accordance with our religious obligations we shall always remain loyal to the government of the country. As part of the German people, the German Jew will gladly help in the reconstruction of the German nation, and do what he can to gain it friends outside the German borders.

In presenting these comments, Herr Reich Chancellor, for your fair-minded consideration, we, as representatives of the undersigned organizations, which have for decades protected the religious interests of Orthodox German Jewry, beg you to favour us with the opportunity of an early exchange of views. We are convinced that such an exchange would, not least, serve the wider domestic and foreign-policy interests of Germany, which make imperative a clarification of the prevailing relations and a gradual relaxation of the tensions arising from the present situation.

In anticipation of a favourable reply to our request, we remain, most respectfully,

REICH ALLIANCE OF LAW-ABIDING* SYNAGOGUE CONGREGATIONS IN HALBERSTADT

signed: *Rabbi Dr M. Schlesinger*, Halberstadt
Rabbi Dr. E. Munk, Berlin

FREE ASSOCIATION FOR THE INTERESTS OF ORTHODOX JEWRY IN FRANKFURT AM MAIN

signed: *Dr S. Ehrmann* signed: *Dr J. Breuer*

NATIONAL AGUDAS JISROEL ORGANIZATION IN GERMANY

Rabbi Dr M. Auerbach, Berlin
Jacob Rosenheim, Frankfurt am Main

Frankfurt am Main, Halberstadt, and Berlin, October 1933

* i.e. observant of Jewish law.

APPENDIX III

Letter from Jacob Rosenheim

Frankfurt am Main, 14 May 1934

Copy 83–72 4/5

Agudas Jisroel
Head Office:
26, Leopoldgasse, Vienna II.

The undersigned President of the Agudas Jisroel World Organization intends, together with his colleagues, the advocate Dr I. Breuer of Frankfurt am Main, and the dentist Dr S. Ehrmann of Frankfurt am Main, to be present at a meeting of the central council of our Organization to be held in Warsaw on 28 May. The meeting will be devoted primarily to matters connected with the activities of our Organization dedicated to the religious reconstruction of the Holy Land and to the promotion of the religious schooling and educational systems, to which Agudas Jisroel has been committed in many different countries.

Together with his colleagues, the undersigned has already sought during the last year, by word of mouth and in writing, to stem the virulent boycott of German goods that is being mounted abroad, by emphasizing the irrational nature of this campaign, even when it is considered from a purely Jewish standpoint.

Our efforts in this field have met with undeniable success in Western countries, inasmuch as those Orthodox circles in particular that are close to us are by degrees withdrawing from the boycott campaign.

The situation is more difficult in the East, especially in Poland. Last September we sent a prominent figure from our circle, Rabbi Dr M. Hildesheimer, to Warsaw, for the express purpose of resolving the situation, but without achieving any significant result.

We now intend to take advantage of the occasion of our participation in the Warsaw meeting once again to moderate and enlighten public opinion, and we make bold to enquire whether there is any material that might perhaps be put at our disposal by the Foreign Ministry or whether we might count on receiving any useful advice that may help to further our objective. If necessary, we should be prepared, if that were considered appropriate, to contact the German Embassy in Warsaw. However, in view of the prevailing mood in that country, we would have to proceed with caution and above all with discretion.

Political Archives of the Foreign Ministry, Bonn, Internal Affairs II A/B 'Jewry' (General) Vol. 1, R 99330, K330029–K330030 (fiche no. 5302).

I should be most grateful if we could possibly receive a reply to this enquiry not later than 24 May.

most respectfully yours,
signature
[Jacob Rosenheim]
PRESIDENT OF THE
AGUDAS JISROEL WORLD ORGANIZATION

To the Foreign Ministry, Berlin.

Glossary

aggadah (pl. *aggadot*). Non-legal portions of the Talmud.

Agudat Yisrael. Orthodox religious movement and political party.

agunah (pl. *agunot*). A woman who cannot remarry because her husband is missing or refuses to grant her a divorce.

aliyah. Immigration to Israel.

amora (pl. *amoraim*). Rabbinic teacher of talmudic period.

Austritt. German Orthodox separatism.

beit din. Court of Jewish law.

beit midrash. House of study.

Congress Poland. Areas of Poland annexed to the Russian Empire in 1815.

derash. Rabbinic exposition of Scripture in a non-literal fashion.

epikoros. Heretic.

eruv. Wire surrounding an area which creates an enclosure enabling one to carry on the Sabbath.

gadol (pl. *gedolim*). Rabbinic sage.

galut. Diaspora.

gaon. Genius.

Gemeinde (or *Grossgemeinde*). Jewish community, encompassing both Orthodox and Reform; often used in contrast with *Austrittsgemeinde*, a separatist Orthodox community.

geonim. Scholars who flourished in Babylonia from the seventh to eleventh centuries.

get. Jewish divorce.

gezerah shavah. Rabbinic hermeneutical method.

girsa. Talmudic text.

Habad. Hasidic movement founded by R. Shneur Zalman of Lyady.

ḥalitsah. Ceremony performed in lieu of *yibum*, enabling the woman to marry.

ḥalutsim. Pioneer settlers in the Land of Israel.

ḥaredi (pl. *ḥaredim*). Ultra-Orthodox.

ḥarifut. Sharpness of mind.

Haskalah. 18th–19th cent. movement for 'enlightenment' within Jewry.

ḥeder. School for Jewish youth.

ḥerem. Excommunication.

heter. Halakhic permission.

Hevrah Shas. Group dedicated to the study of Talmud.

Hibbat Zion. Movement of early, pre-Herzl Zionists.

ḥidush (pl. *ḥidushim*). Rabbinic novellae.

ḥukot ha'amim. Forbidden gentile practices.

kiddush. Prayer recited over wine on Sabbath and festivals.

kidushin. 'Betrothal', first stage of marriage.

kittel. White garb worn on Yom Kippur.

kohen (pl. *kohanim*). Priest.

kol ishah. A woman's singing voice.

kollel. Institution which supports married men who devote themselves to Torah study.

lehavdil. 'To distinguish', used when comparing things of unequal value.

mamzerut. Halakhic illegitimacy; the offspring of an incestuous relationship is called a *mamzer*.

maskil (pl. *maskilim*). Adherent of Haskalah.

Masoretic text. The traditionally accepted text of the Bible.

melamed (pl. *melamedim*). Teacher of children.

meshulaḥ. Yeshiva fund-raising emissary.

Midrash (pl. midrashim). Rabbinic interpretation of Scripture.

mikveh (pl. *mikvaot*). Ritual bath.

min. Heretic.

mitzvah. Commandment.

Mizrachi. Religious Zionist movement and political party.

musar. Ethical literature, usually associated with *musar* movement founded by Israel Salanter.

Ostjuden. East European Jews.

perutah. Least valuable coin.

peshat. Plain, literal meaning of a biblical or talmudic passage.

Peshitta. Syriac version of the Bible.

pilpul. Sharp dialectical form of Talmud study.

posek (pl. *posekim*). Halakhic authority.

rebbe. Hasidic leader.

Rishonim. Medieval sages.

rosh yeshiva (pl. *rashei yeshiva*). Head of a yeshiva.

saboraim. Scholars who flourished in Babylonia during the sixth and seventh centuries CE.

Sanhedrin. Assembly of ordained scholars in Temple days.

semikhah. Rabbinic ordination.

Septuagint. Greek version of the Bible.

sheḥitah. Ritual slaughter.

sugya. A theme discussed in the Talmud.

tallit. Four-cornered prayer shawl with fringes.

talmid ḥakham. Scholar.

tanna (pl. *tannaim*). Rabbinic teacher of mishnaic period.

Targum (pl. Targumim). Aramaic translation of the Bible.

Torah im Derekh Eretz. The German Orthodox approach which combined adherence to Torah values and openness to modern culture.

Torah vemusar. 'Torah and Musar', a German organization founded in the 1930s.

Wissenschaft des Judentums. Scientific study of Judaism.

yibum. Levirate marriage.

zaken mamre. Rebellious elder.

zikhrono livrakhah. 'Of blessed memory', often abbreviated as *z"l*.

Bibliography

WRITINGS OF JEHIEL JACOB WEINBERG

Books and Pamphlets

Pinui atsamot metim (Frankfurt, 1925).

Lifrakim (Bilgoraj, 1936; second abridged edition, Jerusalem, 1967). When cited in the text, the first page number refers to the Bilgoraj edition and the number in parentheses to the Jerusalem edition.

Meḥkarim batalmud (Berlin, 1937–8).

Das Volk der Religion (Geneva, 1949).

Ed., with Pinhas Biberfeld, *Yad sha'ul* (Tel Aviv, 1953). Not included in *Seridei esh* are Weinberg's introductory essay, pp. 3–10; 'Kohanei hamishmar', pp. 62–87; notes to an article by R. Ezekiel Sarne, pp. 92–9; and notes to an article by R. Moses Botchko, pp. 404–5.

Et aḥai anokhi mevakesh, trans. Aharon Sorasky (Benei Berak, 1966). Originally published as 'Verständigung: Ein Wort für Nichtorthodoxe', *Israelit*, 21, 28 June, 5, 12, 26 July, 2, 9 Aug. 1921.

Die Vorbereitung für das Pessachfest (Basle, n.d.).

Seridei esh, 4 vols. (Jerusalem, 1977).

Ḥidushei ba'al 'Seridei esh', ed. Abraham Abba Weingort (Jerusalem, 1995), includes Weingort's lengthy introduction and commentary.

Articles

Articles, responsa, and letters which have been reprinted in *Lifrakim, Das Volk der Religion*, and *Seridei esh* are not listed, except when Weinberg published them in Yiddish or French translations. All the articles with English titles appeared in Hebrew or Yiddish.

1910

'The Issue of the Rabbinate and the Hebrew Newspapers', *Hamodia*, 27 Iyar 5670.

1911

'Concerning Orthodox Literature', *Yagdil torah*, 3: 20–3, 43–5, 81–4, 101–2.

'Talmudic Pilpul', *Ha'ivri*, 31 Mar.

'Clarifying the Essence of Jewish Ethics', *Ha'ivri*, 9 Sept.

'Response to Criticism', *Hamodia*, 22 Adar 5671.

'Concerning the Yeshivot', *Hamodia*, 12 Sivan 5671.

'Concerning the Rabbinate', *Hamodia*, 10 Av 5671.

'Concerning the Rabbinate (2)', *Hamodia*, 13 Tishrei 5672.

'Keneset Yisrael (1)', *Hamodia*, 12 Heshvan 5672.

'Keneset Yisrael (2)', *Hamodia*, 19 Heshvan 5672.

Letter to the Editor, *Hamodia*, 6 Kislev 5672.

1912

Review of Hayim Plansberg's edition of Hasdai Crescas, *Or hashem, Ha'ivri*, 26 Jan.

'The Righteous and the Wise in the Sages' Conception', *Ha'ivri*, 24 May.

'The Essence of Judaism', *Ha'ivri*, 14 June.

'The Yeshivot (1)', *Hamodia*, 6 Shevat 5672.

'The Yeshivot (2)', *Hamodia*, 20 Shevat 5672.

'The Yeshivot (3)', *Hamodia*, 9 Iyar 5672.

'Rabbi Israel Salanter and His Musar Teachings', in Judah Elbinger (ed.), *Halevanon* (Warsaw, 1912), 1–8.

1913

'At Home and Outside', *Hamodia*, 26 Adar II 5673.

1915

'Ein russisch-jüdischer Gaon: Zum Gedächtnis R. David Karliners', *Die Jüdische Presse*, 23 Apr.

1916

'Die Jeschiwoth in Russland', *Jeschurun*, 3: 52–9, 107–26.

'Schulfragen im Ostjudentum', *Jeschurun*, 3: 445–58, 490–505.

'Eine rabbinische Residenz und ihr letztes Fürst', *Jeschurun*, 3: 320–40.

'Li-"Terei temiḥei demidkar dekhiri"', *Jüdische Monatshefte*, 3: 282–3.

'Eine Rosch-Haschanah Predigt an die jüdische Frau', *Der Israelit*, 7 Sept.

'Vom Geiste des Ostens', *Der Israelit*, 23 Nov.

'Zum Pessach-Feste', *Die Jüdische Presse*, 14 Apr.

1917

'Der "Masmid"', *Jeschurun*, 4: 425–30.

'Rettet die Jeschiwoth', *Der Israelit*, 11 Jan.

'Über Opferwesen und Opfergebete', *Die Jüdische Presse*, 21, 28 Dec. 1917; 4, 11 Jan. 1918.

1918

'Von den litauischen "Moralisten" ihrer Ideenwelt und ihrem ersten Führer', *Jeschurun*, 5: 478–84, 585–606.

'Die Democratisierung der Orthodoxie', *Der Israelit*, 20 June.

'Eine Rede zur Tagung der Agudath-Yisroel in Frankfurt a. M.', *Die Jüdische Presse*, 1 Feb.

'Rosch-Hashonoh-Gedanken', *Die Jüdische Presse*, 6 Sept.

'Das frohe Volk', *Die Jüdische Presse*, 20 Sept.

1920

'R. Jisroel Salanter und die Mussar Bewegung', *Jeschurun*, 7: 597–605.

'Piety and Observance of the Commandments', *Jeschurun*, 7: 8–11.

'Ahad Haam as Thinker and Guide', *Jeschurun*, 7: 118–22.

'The Yeshivot in Russia', *Hatsefirah*, 31 Aug., 1, 2, 5 Sept.

1921

'R. Jisroel Salanter und die Mussar Bewegung', *Jeschurun*, 8: 52–62, 162–8.

'The New Hebrew Literature and its Champions', *Jeschurun*, 8: 31–9.

'Verständigung: Ein Wort für Nichtorthodoxe', *Der Israelit*, 21, 28 June, 5, 12, 26 July, 2, 9 Aug. This work was published in Hebrew as *Et aḥai anokhi mevakesh*, trans. Aharon Sorasky (Benei Berak, 1966).

'From our Jewish Treasures', *Idisher Lebn*, 8 July.

1923

'The Scholars and the Workers' Union', *Idisher Lebn*, 13, 20 Apr.

'In Hidden Corners', *Idisher Lebn*, 18 June.

1924

'Eine ר"ה Predigt für meine ostjüdischen Brüder', *Der Israelit*, 25 Sept.

'Rabbi Jizchok Jakob Reines z'l', *Jüdisches Wochenblatt*, 17 Apr.

'Zur Geschichte der Targumim', *Jüdisches Wochenblatt*, 14, 28 Aug., 11 Sept.

'Lenin and MacDonald', *Idisher Lebn*, 15 Feb.

'Don't Forget the Jewish Woman!', *Idisher Lebn*, 22 Feb.

1925

'Elucidations of the Talmud', *Jeschurun*, 12: 102–4.

Notes to H. N. Telem's 'Be'urim biyerushalmi', *Jeschurun*, 12: 105–8.

'Das frohe Volk', *Der Israelit*, 1 Oct.

'Das Jeschiwoh-Problem', *Jüdisches Wochenblatt*, 14 Aug.

1926

'Removing a Stumbling Block', *Jeschurun*, 13: 16.

Comments on David Golomb's notes to Weinberg's *Pinui atsamot metim*, *Jeschurun*, 13: 14–16.

1928

'Zum siebenten Adar: Aus den Gedankengängen des Rabbi Israel Salanter', *Der Israelit*, 15 Feb.

'The Scholar', *Hane'eman* (Tevet 5688), 3–5.

1929

'From the Treasures of the People', *Hane'eman* (Iyar–Sivan 5689), 29–30.

1931

'Zur Geschichte der Targumim: Eine Darstellung der Entstehung und Entwicklung der aramäischen Targumim', *Festschrift für Jacob Rosenheim* (Frankfurt, 1931), 237–58.

'Sefer Hilleli', *Otsar haḥayim*, 7: 126.

1933

'Our Program', *Yidishe Tsaytung*, 24 Mar.

'An Advocate, But for Whom', *Yidishe Togblat*, 19 June.

'From my Eulogy for the Rabbi of Lublin', *Lubliner Togblat*, 28 Nov.

1934

'Jewish Joy', *Yidishe Togblat*, 3 Apr.

'Our Educational Questions and Concerns', *Yidishe Togblat*, 21 Sept.

1935

'Old and Young', *Yidishe Togblat*, 15 Mar.

'Herzl, the Man of Religion', *Ha'olam*, 18 July.

With Paul Kahle, 'The Mishna Text in Babylonia, Fragments from the Geniza', *Hebrew Union College Annual*, 10: 185–222.

1936

Letter concerning the death of R. Jeruham Levovits, *Der Israelit*, 11 June.

1937

'Zur Auseinandersetzung über S. R. Hirsch und seiner "Thora im Derech Erez Devise"', *Nachlath Zwi*, 7: 186–93.

1938

'From the Lectures of the Elder', *Keneset Yisrael* (Shevat 5698), 30–2.

1948

'The Magical Name—Herzl', *Undzer Veg*, 23 July.

1949

'A Rosh Hashanah Sermon for the Jewish Woman', *Undzer Veg*, 23 Sept.

1950

'An Unclear Passage in the Jerusalem Talmud' *Hapardes* (June), 1–4.

'Zum Proselytproblem', *Jüdische Rundschau Maccabi*, 8 Sept.

'The Religious Worker's Movement', *Undzer Veg*, 13 Oct.

'In Expectation of a Great Religious Revival', *Undzer Veg*, 1 Dec.

'The Great Teacher', *She'arim*, 14 Dec.

1951

'Israelis and Jews', *Hatsofeh*, 16 Mar.

'Basugya dilemafrea hu kadosh', *Hane'eman* (Nisan 5711), 6–8.

'Our Education', *Undzer Veg*, 6, 13, 20, 27 Apr., 4, 11 May.

1952

'Jewish Culture and Pagan Culture', *Hapardes* (Jan.), 33–5.

'The Warsaw Ghetto Revolt and the Protest in the Keneset', *She'arim*, 1 Feb.

'Towards a Religious Revival', *She'arim*, 22 Feb.

'Our Education', *She'arim*, 28 Feb., 14 Mar., 4, 9 Apr., 9, 23 May, 6 June.

'Sacrifices—The Foundation of Judaism', *She'arim*, 28 Mar.

'The Fate of One in Confusion', *She'arim*, 20 June.

'Herzl's Spiritual Profile', *Hatsofeh*, 11 July.

1953

Review of Hayim Zvi Taubes, *Likutei r. yitsḥak ben yehudah ibn giat: Masekhet berakhot im perush iyun tsevi, Hapardes* (Feb.), 24–7.

Letter in *Hama'or* (July), 19.

'Artificial Insemination and the Sale of the Land of Israel', *Hama'or* (Nov.), 16–17.

1954

'Simḥat Torah with Rabbi Israel Salanter', *Undzer Veg*, 22 Oct.

'Kampf und Sieg des Geistes', *Jüdische Rundschau Maccabi*, 24 Dec.

1955

'Zur Frage der Bestattung nicht-jüdischer Ehegatten auf einem jüdischen Friedhof', *Jüdische Rundschau Maccabi*, 29 Apr.

'Combat et victoire de l'esprit', *Trait d'Union* (Oct.–Nov.), 2–4.

1956

'A Note to Rabbi A. Y. Neumark's Article', *Hane'eman* (Adar–Nisan 5716), 14.

'Meine Geschöpfe versinken im Meer . . .', *Jüdische Rundschau Maccabi*, 23 Mar.

1957

'Rabbi Samuel Aaron Halevi Pardes', *Hapardes* (Feb.), 1–2.

'Culture juive et culture païenne', *Trait d'Union* (Nov.–Dec.), 4–9.

1958

'Sources of the Mishnah and its Method of Organization', *Talpiot*, 7: 72–88, 290–316.

'Cette maison doit devenir une forteresse de la Torah pour tous les Juifs de la Diaspora', *Trait d'Union* (Sept.), 5–6.

1959

'Notes to Rabbi Nahshoni's Article', *Hane'eman* (Tishrei–Kislev 5719), 7–11; repr. in *Ḥidushei ba'al 'Seridei esh'*, no. 8.

1961

'Jewish Spiritual Treasures', *Hadarom* (Elul 5721), 320.

1962

'Torah of Life', in Yonah Emanuel (ed.), *Harav shimshon rafael hirsh: Mishnato veshitato* (Jerusalem, 1962), 185–99.

1965

'Can One Include a Deaf Man Who Can Speak in a Minyan?', *Shanah beshanah*, 125–8.

'The Gaon Rabbi Eliezer Yehudah Finkel', *Hama'ayan*, 6 (Tishrei 5726), 45.

Posthumous

1982

'Testimony by a Single Witness', *Moriah* (Tammuz 5742), 34–5.

1984

Responsum concerning Torah radio broadcasts, *Moriah* (Kislev 5745), 64–6.

1992

'Autopsies in the State of Israel', *Teḥumin*, 12: 382–4.

Introductions and Approbations in the Following Works

KLEIN, ZE'EV ZVI (HERMANN), *Kahana mesayea kahana* (Berlin, 1938).

RUBINSTEIN, SAMUEL JACOB, *She'erit menaḥem* (Paris, 1954), vols. iii–iv.

—— *Alfa shemen laner* (Paris, 1959).

REZNICK, ABRAHAM ABBA, *Kelei sharet* (Netanya, 1957).

ARIELI, GERSHON, *Torat hamelekh* (Jerusalem, 1958).

HOFFNER, NAFTALI, *Sefer halakhah: Dinei birkhot hanehenin* (Monsey, 1960).

—— *Mafteaḥ lehilkhot terefot* (Benei Berak, 1980).

EISENSTADT, MENAHEM ZVI, *Perush haramban al hatorah*, vol. ii (New York, 1962).

BERKOVITS, ELIEZER, *Tenai benisuin uveget* (Jerusalem, 1967).

PINES, SHLOMO ZALMAN, *Musar hamikra vehatalmud* (Jerusalem, 1977).

LEIZEROWSKI, BARUCH, *Ta'am barukh* (New York, 1979).

NEUWIRTH, JOSHUA ISAIAH, *Shemirat shabat kehilkhatah* (Jerusalem, 1979).

Letters, Responsa, and Notes in the Following Works

Horovitz, Marcus, *Mateh levi* (Frankfurt, 1932), ii. 137–9.

Atlas, Samuel (ed.), *Ḥidushei harabad al masekhet bava kama* (London, 1940), 362–85.

Klein, Ze'ev Zvi (Hermann), *Oraita begaluta* (Buenos Aires, n.d.), letter in unpaginated introduction.

Breisch, Mordekhai Jacob, *Ḥelkat ya'akov* (Jerusalem, 1951), i. 20.

Taubes, Hayyim Zvi, *Likutei r. yitsḥak ben yehudah ibn giat: Masekhet berakhot im perush iyun tsevi* (Zurich, 1952), 80–2.

Blumenfeld, Meir, *Mishnat yisra'el* (New York, 1960), 5*b*–6*a*.

—— *Sha'ar hamelekh* (New York, 1976), letter in unpaginated introduction.

Keneset beit yitsḥak (Jerusalem, n.d.), 151–2.

Chavel, H. D., 'Letters from Rabbi Weinberg' (Heb.), *Hadarom*, 24 (1966), 16–20.

Hapardes (Apr. 1966), 4–6; (May 1966), 38–9; (June 1966), 38–40; (July 1966), 36–7; (Nov. 1966), 33–4; (Dec. 1966), 42; (Jan 1967), 39–40; (Feb. 1967), 38; (Mar. 1967), 39; (May 1967), 40; (June 1967), 37; (Oct. 1967), 38; (Jan. 1968), 42.

Rabiner, Ze'ev Aryeh, *Raza deshabata* (Tel Aviv, 1965), letter in unpaginated introduction.

—— *Maran rabeinu meir simḥah hakohen* (Tel Aviv, 1967), 293–9.

—— *Hagaon rabi eli'ezer gordon* (Heb.) (Tel Aviv, 1968), 18.

No'am, 16 (1973), 160–4.

Munk, E., and Munk, M. L. (eds.), *Edut ne'emanah* (Jerusalem, 1974), 195–6, 246–9.

—— *Shechita: Religious and Historical Research on the Jewish Method of Slaughter* (New York, 1976), 64–6.

Bita'on Bar-Ilan (Summer 1974), 22.

Atlas, Samuel, *Netivim bamishpat ha'ivri* (New York, 1978), 137–9, 153–5.

Leizerowski, Baruch, *Ta'am barukh* (New York, 1979), nos. 22, 25, 28, 81.

Eliav, Mordechai, and Raphael, Yitshak (eds.), *Sefer shragai* (Jerusalem, 1981), 275.

Ilan, Mordechai, *Ner mordekhai* (Benei Berak, 1982), 289–90 (bound with Jacob David Ilan, *Shitah mekubetset al masekhet tamid*).

Apfel, Joseph, 'Letters from Rabbi Jehiel Jacob Weinberg' (Heb.), *Hane'eman* (Nisan–Elul 5743 [1983]), 51–4 (slightly enlarged in Apfel's *Yad yosef* (Lakewood, NJ, 1996), 453–68).

Auerbach, Moses, *From Halberstadt to Petaḥ Tikvah* (Heb.) (Jerusalem, 1987), letter in middle of book (unpaginated).

Felder, Gedaliah, *Gilyonei yeshurun* (New York, 1989), 51–2.

Shapiro, Ben Zion (ed.), *Igerot lare'iyah* (Jerusalem, 1990), nos. 79, 81, 210, 214, 347.

Unterman, Isser Yehudah, *Shevet miyehudah* (Jerusalem, 1992), 261–7.

Rosenberg, Meir Joshua, *Kur hamivḥan* (Jerusalem, 1992), letter in unpaginated introduction.

Shapiro, Melekh (Marc), 'Letters from Rabbi J. J. Weinberg' (Heb.), *Hama'ayan*, 32 (Tammuz 5752 [1992]), 6–20.

—— 'Letters from Rabbi David Zvi Hoffmann, Rabbi Moses Feinstein and Rabbi J. J. Weinberg' (Heb.), *Hama'ayan*, 34 (Tevet 5754 [1994]), 9–20.

Hama'ayan, 33 (Tishrei 5753 [1992]), 38.

Ḥidushei ba'al 'Seridei esh', 4–6 (first pagination), 453–5, 566, 568–9.

SCHEFTELOWITZ, ELHANAN, *500 Years, The History of a Jewish Family* (Heb.) (Jerusalem, n.d.), letter at end of book (unpaginated).

Letters by Weinberg referred to in this book in the possession of the author (MS) *and in public archives* (*listed by name of recipient*)*

Alexander Altmann MS

Erwin Altmann MS

Meir Amsel MS

Joseph Apfel MS

Abraham Arazy MS

Samuel Atlas Jewish Theological Seminary of America, Autograph Collection; selections from these letters appear in English translation in my 'Scholars and Friends: Rabbi Jehiel Jacob Weinberg and Professor Samuel Atlas', *Torah u-Madda Journal*, 7 (1997), 105–21

Naftali Berger MS

Pinhas Biberfeld MS

Elijah Botchko Saul Weingort papers, Institute for Holocaust Research, Bar-Ilan University

Yehoshua Brand MS

Charles B. Chavel MS

Aryeh Leib Cohn MS

Gavriel Hayim Cohn MS

Corn family MS

Elijah Dessler MS

Albert Einstein Albert Einstein Correspondence, Boston University and the Hebrew University of Jerusalem

Yonah Emanuel MS

M. Freyer MS

Heinrich Frick MS

Mordechai Gifter MS

Louis Ginzberg Jewish Theological Seminary of America, Louis Ginzberg Collection

Hayim Ozer Grodzinski MS

Isaac Herzog Heikhal Shelomo, Jerusalem

Leo Jung MS

Paul Kahle Paul Kahle Archives, University of Turin; several of these letters have now been published in my article 'On Targum and Tradition: J. J. Weinberg, Paul Kahle and Exodus 4: 22', *Henoch*, 19 (1997), 215–32

Dov Katz MS

*All other non-archival correspondence mentioned in the book is in the possession of the author.

Moshe Klein MS

Sheftel Kramer MS

M. Z. Levinson-Lavi Genazim, Tel Aviv

Saul Lieberman Jewish Theological Seminary of America Saul Lieberman Collection

Zvi Mathisson Genazim, Tel Aviv

Hillel Medalié MS

Isser Zalman Meltzer MS

Samuel K. Mirsky MS

Moses Schlesinger Institute for Holocaust Research, Bar-Ilan University, Files 105/3: 53, 105/3: 110, 105/4: 58

Isaac Sher MS

Mordechai Shulman MS

Moses Shulvass MS

Moses Soloveitchik MS

Town leaders of Pilwishki YIVO Archives, Lithuanian Towns, File 846 no. 36646

Isak Unna Central Archives for the History of the Jewish People, Jerusalem, File P131/5; Institute for Holocaust Research, Bar-Ilan University, Files 102/4: 63, 102/4: 145, 102/6: 72, 102/6: 87, 102/7: 4, 102/10: 63

Ephraim Urbach MS

Saul Weingort Saul Weingort papers, Institute for Holocaust Research, Bar-Ilan University

Samson R. Weiss MS

Isaiah Wolfsberg Jewish National and University Library, ARC. 4° 1735

SECONDARY LITERATURE

Newspaper articles are not cited individually.

ABRAMSKY, EZEKIEL, *Collected Articles* (Heb.) (Jerusalem, 1994).

ADLER-RUDEL, S., *Ostjuden in Deutschland 1180–1940* (Tübingen, 1959).

AGNON, SHMUEL YOSEF, *Lifnim min haḥomah* (Jerusalem, 1976).

Agudas Jisroel: Berichte und Materialien (Frankfurt, [1912]).

AGUS, IRVING A., 'R. Jacob Tam's Stringent Criticism of R. Meshullam of Melun, in its Historical Setting', in Abraham I. Katsh and Leon Nemoy (eds.), *Essays on the Occasion of the Seventieth Anniversary of The Dropsie University* (Philadelphia, Pa., 1979), 1–10.

AHREN, YITZHAK, 'Rabbiner Breuers Frankfurter Jeschiwo', *Udim*, 14–15 (1990), 28–37.

AHREND, MOSHE, 'German Orthodox Spokesmen Before the Holocaust' (Heb.), in Mordechai Breuer (ed.), *Torah im Derekh Eretz* (Ramat Gan, 1987), 133–46.

ALBECK, HANOKH, *Untersuchungen über die Redaktion der Mischna* (Berlin, 1923).

—— *Introduction to the Mishnah* (Heb.) (Jerusalem, 1959).

Albeck, Hanokh, 'Criticism or Sophistry' (Heb.), *Sinai*, 46 (1960), 235–55.

Albeck, Shalom, *Kofer ha'eshkol* (Warsaw, 1911).

Alfasi, Yitshak, *The Great Sage* (Heb.) (Tel Aviv, 1985).

Allen, Wayne R. (ed.), *Tomekh kehalakhah* (Mount Vernon, NY, 1986).

Alon, Gedalyahu, 'The Lithuanian Yeshivas', in Judah Goldin (ed.), *The Jewish Expression* (New Haven, Conn., 1976), 452–68.

Alter, Abraham Mordechai, *Collected Letters* (Heb.) (Jerusalem, 1988).

Altmann, Alexander, 'Theology in Twentieth Century German Jewry', *Leo Baeck Institute Year Book*, 1 (1956), 193–216.

—— 'The German Rabbi 1910–1939', *Leo Baeck Institute Year Book*, 19 (1974), 31–50.

—— *Essays in Jewish Intellectual History* (Hanover, NH, 1981).

Altmann, M., 'Rabbi Abraham Elijah Kaplan' (Heb.), in Samuel K. Mirsky (ed.), *Ishim udemuyot beḥokhmat yisra'el* ([New York], 1959), 324–37.

Amiel, Moses Avigdor, *Hamidot leḥeker hahalakhah* (Jerusalem, 1939).

—— *Linevukhei hatekufah* (Brooklyn, NY, 1980).

Amsel, Meir, 'Concerning the "Yeshurun" Organization in France' (Heb.), *Hama'or* (Nov. 1955), 15–17, (Dec. 1955), 13–15, (Mar. 1956), 14–17.

Apfel, Joseph, 'A Portrayal of My Teacher, Rabbi Jehiel Jacob Weinberg' (Heb.), *Hane'eman* (Nisan–Elul 5743 [1983]), 46–54, 60.

—— *Yad yosef* (Lakewood, NJ, 1996).

Aptowitzer, Avigdor, *Mavo lesefer ra'avyah* (Jerusalem, 1938).

Aschheim, Steven E., *Brothers and Strangers: The East European Jew in German and German Jewish Consciousness, 1800–1923* (Madison, Wis., 1982).

Asher ben Yehiel, *She'elot uteshuvot lerabeinu asher ben yeḥiel* (Jerusalem, 1994).

Atkin, Abraham, 'The Beth Jacob Movement in Poland (1917–1939)' (Ph.D. diss., Yeshiva University, 1959).

Atlas, Samuel, 'Lishe'elat hilkhat idit', *Ḥorev*, 9 (1946), 59–78.

—— 'A Portrayal of the Gaon Rabbi Jehiel Jacob Weinberg' (Heb.), *Sinai*, 58 (1966), 281–92.

—— *Pathways in Hebrew Law* (Heb.) (New York, 1978).

Auerbach, B. H., *Die Geschichte des 'Bund gesetzestreuer jüdischer Gemeinden Deutschlands' 1919–1938* (Tel Aviv, 1972).

Auerbach, Moses (Abuha di Samuel), 'Jüdischer Nationalismus und gesetzestreues Judentum', *Jeschurun*, 4 (1917), 625–32.

—— 'Die Bildungsfrage in der Thora-Treuen Judenheit Deutschland', in A. E. Kaplan and Max Landau (eds.), *Vom Sinn des Judentums: Ein Sammelbuch zu Ehren Nathan Birnbaums* (Frankfurt, 1925), 225–33.

—— 'Seligmann Bär Bamberger', *Jeschurun*, 15 (1928), 524–38.

—— 'Zur geistigen Struktur der deutschen Orthodoxie der Gegenwart', *Festschrift für Jacob Rosenheim* (Frankfurt, 1931), 196–211.

—— 'Ziel und Wege der heutigen Rabbinerausbildung', *Der Israelit*, 15 Sept. 1932, 1–3; 19 Sept. 1932, 6; 22 Sept. 1932, 6.

—— 'Concerning an Orthodox College for Women' (Heb.), *Hama'ayan*, 4 (Nisan 5724 [1964]), 1–2.

—— *From Halberstadt to Petaḥ Tikvah* (Heb.) (Jerusalem, 1987).

—— (ed.), *Memorial Volume for Rabbi Isaac Halevy* (Heb.) (Benei Berak, 1964).

AUERBACH, RAPHAEL, 'Rabbi Kook and his Relation to the Torah im Derekh Eretz Approach and its Advocates' (Heb.), in Hayim Hamiel (ed.), *Be'oro* (Jerusalem, 1986), 528–48.

AVINER, SHLOMO, 'Rabbi Kook and the Distinction between Holy and Profane' (Heb.), *Hama'ayan*, 22 (Tishrei 5742 [1981]), 66–9.

—— *Gan na'ul* (Jerusalem, 1985).

—— *Ḥesed ne'urayikh* (Jerusalem, 1991).

—— *Torat imekha* (Jerusalem, 1991).

AVINERI, REUVEN, 'Agnon's Wedding' (Heb.), *Ma'ariv*, 6 May 1988.

AVITAL, MOSHE, *The Yeshiva and Traditional Education in the Literature of the Hebrew Enlightenment Period* (Heb.) (Tel Aviv, 1996).

BABAD, DAVID MENAHEM MAINISH, *Ḥavatselet hasharon* (Bilgoraj, 1938).

BACON, GERSHON C., 'Agudath Israel in Poland: An Orthodox Jewish Response to the Challenge of Modernity' (Ph.D. diss., Columbia University, 1979).

—— 'Leave Israel Alone—Better Unintentional Sinners than Deliberate Ones: Some Rabbinic Responses to Communal Disregard of the Law', in J. Leonard Romm and Leonard Levy (eds.), *Halakhah and the Modern Jew: Essays in Honor of Horace Bier* (n.p., 1989), 9–17.

BAECK, LEO, *The Essence of Judaism*, trans. Irving Howe (New York, 1961).

BAKER, LEONARD, *Days of Sorrow and Pain: Leo Baeck and the Berlin Jews* (New York, 1978).

BAMBERGER, M. L., 'Seligmann Baer Bamberger', in Leo Jung (ed.), *Jewish Leaders* (New York, 1953), 179–95.

BAMBERGER, SELIGMANN BAER, *Collected Writings* (Heb.) ([Israel], 1992).

BAMBERGER, SIMHAH, *Zekher simḥah* (Frankfurt, 1925).

BAR-ILAN, MEIR, *From Volozhin to Jerusalem* (Heb.) (Tel Aviv, 1971).

BARNAI, YA'AKOV, 'Rabbi Rabinowitz of Poltava's Change of Mind on Zionism' (Heb.), *Sinai*, 70 (1972), 282–8.

BARTAL, ISRAEL, 'Jacob Lifshitz's *Zikhron ya'akov*—Orthodox Historiography?' (Heb.), *Millet*, 2 (1985), 409–14.

BARTH, JACOB, 'Die Entstehungzeit des Buches Hiob', in *Jahres-Bericht des Rabbiner-Seminars für das Orthodoxe Judentum pro 5636 (1875–76)* [Berlin, 1876].

BAT-YEHUDAH, GEULAH, *Ish hame'orot* (Jerusalem, 1985).

BAUMINGER, ARYEH, *et al.*, *Sefer krakov* (Jerusalem, 1959).

BECHTOLDT, HANS-JOACHIM, *Die jüdische Bibelkritik im 19. Jahrhundert* (Stuttgart, 1995).

Bemareh habezek, vol. ii (Jerusalem, 1995).

BEN-AVNER, YEHUDAH, 'Activities of Orthodox Rabbis in Germany' (Heb.), *Sinai*, 91 (1982), 140–55.

BEN-AVNER, YEHUDAH, 'Unity and Separatism in German Orthodoxy in 1934–5' (Heb.), *Keshev*, 1 (Dec. 1985), 5–14.

—— *Vom orthodoxen Judentum in Deutschland zwischen zwei Weltkriegen* (Hildesheim, 1987).

—— 'The Dispute over the Rabbinate of Frankfurt's Adass Jeschurun in the 1920s' (Heb.), *Sinai*, 106 (1990), 72–9.

—— 'Antisemitism in the Weimar Republic as Reflected in the Jewish Newspapers' (Heb.), *Sinai*, 107 (1991), 265–83.

BEN-DAVID, DAVID, 'A Portrayal of Rabbi Weinberg as a *Posek*' (Heb.), *Hadarom*, 24 (1966), 12–15.

BEN-SASSON, HAIM HILLEL, *Hagut vehanhagah* (Jerusalem, 1959).

BEN-SASSON, YONAH, 'The Significance of Social Reality in Halakhah' (Heb.), in Menahem Kahana (ed.), *Beḥevelei masoret utemurah* (Rehovot, 1990), 51–74.

BENAYAHU, MEIR, *Shaving on Ḥol Hamo'ed* (Heb.) (Jerusalem, 1995).

BENEDIKT, BINYAMIN ZE'EV, *Collected Articles* (Heb.) (Jerusalem, 1994).

BENZ, WOLFGANG, *Die Juden in Deutschland 1933–1945* (Munich, 1988).

BERGMAN, ISSACHAR DOV, 'Biography of the Author of *Naḥal eshkol*' (Heb.), in Sidney B. Hoenig and Leon D. Stitskin (eds.), *Joshua Finkel Festschrift* (New York, 1974), 59–79.

BERKOVITS, ELIEZER, *Was ist der Talmud?* (Frankfurt am Main, 1962).

—— 'Rabbi Yechiel Yakob Weinberg: My Teacher and Master', *Tradition*, 5 (Summer 1966), 5–14.

—— *Conditional Marriage and Divorce* (Heb.) (Jerusalem, 1967).

—— *Not in Heaven* (New York, 1983).

—— *Jewish Women in Time and Torah* (Hoboken, NJ, 1990).

BERLIN, NAFTALI ZVI JUDAH, *Ha'amek she'alah* (Jerusalem, 1961).

—— *Meshiv davar* (Brooklyn, NY, 1987).

BERMAN, JEREMIAH J., *Shehitah: A Study in the Cultural and Social Life of the Jewish People* (New York, 1941).

BERMAN, SAUL J., 'Kol Isha', in Leo Landman (ed.), *Rabbi Joseph H. Lookstein Memorial Volume* (New York, 1980), 45–66.

BIALOBLOCKI, SAMUEL, *Em lamasoret* (Tel Aviv, 1971).

BIBERFELD, PINHAS, 'Our Approach to History' (Heb.), in Moses Auerbach (ed.), *Memorial Volume for Rabbi Isaac Halevy* (Heb.) (Benei Berak, 1964), 347–53.

—— 'In Memory of the Gaon Rabbi Jehiel Jacob Weinberg' (Heb.), *Hane'eman* (Tishrei 5727 [1966]), 30–2.

—— 'Leo Deutschländer z'l: Bildnis eines Erziehers', in *25 Jahre Jüdische Schule Zürich Festschrift* (Jerusalem, 1980), 223–30.

BICK, ABRAHAM, 'Rabbi Zalman Barukh Rabinkow' (Heb.), in Yitshak Raphael (ed.), *Sefer aviad* (Jerusalem, 1986), 89–91.

—— (ed.), *Actual Problems in Light of the Halakhah* (Heb.) (Jerusalem, 1993).

BLACK, MATTHEW, *An Aramaic Approach to the Gospels and Acts* (Oxford, 1967).

BLAU, JOSHUA, 'Jacob Barth' (Heb.), in S. Federbush (ed.), *Ḥokhmat yisrael bema'arav eiropah* (Jerusalem, 1958), 47–52.

BLAU, MOSHE, *Al ḥomotayikh yerushalayim* (Benei Berak, 1967).

—— *Writings* (Heb.) (Jerusalem, 1983).

BLEICH, J. DAVID, *Contemporary Halakhic Problems*, vols. ii–iii (New York, 1983, 1989).

BLEICH, JUDITH, 'Jacob Ettlinger, His Life and Works: The Emergence of Modern Orthodoxy in Germany' (Ph.D. diss., New York University, 1974).

—— 'The Emergence of an Orthodox Press in Nineteenth Century Germany', *Jewish Social Studies*, 42 (1980), 323–44.

—— 'Rabbinic Responses to Nonobservance in the Modern Era', in Jacob J. Schacter (ed.), *Jewish Tradition and the Nontraditional Jew* (Northvale, NJ, 1992), 37–115.

—— 'Between East and West: Modernity and Traditionalism in the Writings of Rabbi Yehi'el Ya'akov Weinberg', in Moshe Z. Sokol (ed.), *Engaging Modernity* (Northvale, NJ, 1997), 169–273.

BLEICH, MOSHE, 'The Role of Manuscripts in Halakhic Decision-Making: Hazon Ish, his Precursors and Contemporaries', *Tradition*, 27 (Winter 1993), 22–55.

The Blessing of Eliyahu (London, 1982).

BLUMENFELD, KURT, *Erlebte Judenfrage. Ein Vierteljahrhundert deutscher Zionismus* (Stuttgart, 1962).

BLUMENTHAL, ELHANAN, *Bekhol derakhekha da'ehu* (Jerusalem, 1995).

BOAS, JACOB, 'The Jews of Germany: Self-Perceptions in the Nazi Era as Reflected in the German Jewish Press 1933–1938' (Ph.D. diss., University of California–Riverside, 1977).

BOKSER, BARUCH MICAH, 'Y. I. Halevy', in Jacob Neusner (ed.), *The Modern Study of the Mishnah* (Leiden, 1973), 135–54.

BOLKOSKY, SIDNEY M., *The Distorted Image: German Jewish Perceptions of Germans and Germany, 1918–1935* (New York, 1975).

BORNSTEIN, ABRAHAM, *Avnei nezer* (Tel Aviv, 1964).

BREIMAN, S., 'The Dispute over Religious Reforms in Hebrew Literature' (Heb.), *He'avar*, 1 (1953), 115–32.

BRENNER, MICHAEL, 'East and West in Orthodox German-Jewish Novels (1912–1934)', *Leo Baeck Institute Year Book*, 37 (1992), 309–23.

—— *The Renaissance of Jewish Culture in Weimar Germany* (New Haven, Conn., 1996).

BRESLAUER, S. DANIEL, *The Hebrew Poetry of Hayyim Nahman Bialik (1873–1934) and a Modern Jewish Theology* (Lewiston, NY, 1991).

BREUER, ISAAC, 'Rückblick auf das Jahr 5662', *Der Israelit*, 3 Dec. 1903.

—— *Programm oder Testament* (Frankfurt, 1929).

—— *Moriyah* (Jerusalem, 1982).

—— *Autobiography* (Heb.) (Jerusalem, 1988).

BREUER, MORDECHAI, 'Agudat Yisrael and Western Orthodoxy' (Heb.), *Hama'ayan*, 5 (Tishrei 5725 [1964]), 15–18.

BREUER, MORDECHAI, Review of New Books Published by Nezaḥ (Heb.), *Hama'ayan*, 7 (Tishrei 5727 [1966]), 64–72.

—— *The 'Torah-Im-Derekh-Eretz' of Samson Raphael Hirsch* (Jerusalem, 1970).

—— Review of Noah H. Rosenbloom, *Tradition in an Age of Reform*, in *Tradition*, 16 (Summer 1977), 140–7.

—— 'Emancipation and the Rabbis', *Niv Hamidrashia*, 13 (1978–9), 26–51.

—— 'Changes in the Attitude of German Orthodoxy towards Zionism during the First World War' (Heb.), *Proceedings of the Seventh World Congress of Jewish Studies: History of the Jews in Europe* (Jerusalem, 1981), 167–79.

—— 'Miba'ad limeḥitzah', *Hama'ayan*, 21 (Nisan 5741 [1981]), 37–45.

—— 'Three Orthodox Approaches to Wissenschaft' (Heb.), in Shaul Yisraeli *et al.* (eds.), *Sefer yovel likhvod moreinu haga'on rabi yosef dov halevi soloveitchik*, vol. ii (Jerusalem, 1984), 856–65.

—— *Jüdische Orthodoxie im Deutschen Reich 1871–1918* (Frankfurt, 1986). In English: *Modernity within Tradition*, trans. Elizabeth Petuchowski (New York, 1992).

—— 'Orthodoxy and Change' (Heb.), in id. (ed.), *Torah im Derekh Eretz* (Ramat Gan, 1987), 85–95.

—— 'The German Rabbinic Approach towards Halakhic Decision-Making during the Era of Emancipation' (Heb.), *Sinai*, 100 (1987), 166–86.

—— 'Orthodox Rabbis from Germany in Poland and Lithuania during the German Occupation (1914–1918)' (Heb.), *Bar-Ilan Annual*, 24–5 (1989), 117–53.

—— 'Samson Raphael Hirsch Today: Conceptions and Misconceptions', *Jewish Action* (Summer 1989), 7–10.

—— 'Four Eulogies for Theodor Herzl by an Opponent' (Heb.), *Hama'ayan*, 36 (Tammuz 5756 [1996]), 7–16.

—— 'Orthodoxy in Germany and its Eastern Counterpart at the Turn of the Century', *Leo Baeck Institute Year Book*, 41 (1996), 75–86.

BREUER, RAPHAEL, *Die fünf Megilloth: Hoheslied* (Frankfurt, 1912).

—— *Zur Abwehr* (Frankfurt, 1912.

—— *Lied der Lieder* (Frankfurt, 1923).

BROWN, ERICA, 'Bat Mitzvah: A Case Study in Halakhic Innovation' (MA diss., Jews' College–University of London, 1990).

BUECHLER, SIMEON, *Shai lamoreh* (Budapest, [1895]).

CALVARY, MOSES, *Bein zera liketsir* (Tel Aviv, 1947).

CARLEBACH, ALEXANDER, 'A German Rabbi Goes East', *Leo Baeck Institute Year Book*, 6 (1961), 60–121.

—— *Adass Yeshurun of Cologne* (Belfast, 1964).

—— 'Saving the Life of a Non-Jew on Shabbat', *Niv Hamidrashia* (Winter 1967), 7–14.

—— 'Were Rabbi Esriel Hildesheimer's Educational Initiatives Failures?' (Heb.), *Niv Hamidrashia* (1972), 200–8.

—— *Men and Ideas* (Jerusalem, 1982).

Carlebach, Julius, 'Orthodox Jewry in Germany: The Final Stages', in Arnold Paucker (ed.), *The Jews in Nazi Germany 1933–1943* (Tübingen, 1986), 75–93.

—— 'The Foundations of German-Jewish Orthodoxy: An Interpretation', *Leo Baeck Institute Year Book,* 33 (1988), 67–91.

Carlebach, Naphtali, *Joseph Carlebach and his Generation* (New York, 1959).

Carmy, Shalom, 'R. Yehiel Weinberg's Lecture on Academic Jewish Scholarship', *Tradition*, 24 (Summer 1989), 15–23.

Chajes, Zvi Hirsch, *Collected Writings* (Heb.) (Jerusalem, 1958).

Chesterton, G. K., *Orthodoxy* (New York, 1990).

Cochavi, Yehoyakim, 'German Jewish Cultural and Religious Activities (1933–1941) as a Response to the Challenge of the Nazi Regime' (Heb.) (Ph.D. diss., Hebrew University of Jerusalem, 1986).

Cohen, Aaron, *Keneset hagedolah*, vol. ii (Alexandria, 1904).

Cohen, Alfred S., 'Celebration of the Bat Mitzvah', *Journal of Halacha and Contemporary Society,* 12 (Fall 1986), 5–16.

Cohen, J. Simcha, *Intermarriage and Conversion: A Halakhic Solution* (Hoboken, NJ, 1987).

Cohn, Gavriel Hayim, 'A Note to the Dispute Concerning the Law of Marriage and Divorce' (Heb.), *De'ot*, 7 (1958), 54–7.

—— 'In Memory of the Gaon Rabbi Dr. Jehiel Jacob Weinberg' (Heb.), *De'ot*, 31 (1967), 7–18.

Darkah shel torah (Vilna, 1902).

Dawidowicz, Lucy S., *The Golden Tradition* (New York, 1967).

—— *The War Against the Jews* (New York, 1975).

—— *A Holocaust Reader* (West Orange, NJ, 1976).

Dessler, Elijah, *Mikhtav me'eliyahu*, vol. iii (Benei Berak, 1977).

Dicker, Herman, Review of M. Carmilly-Weinberger, *Censorship and Freedom of Expression*, in *Judaism*, 27 (1978), 489–91.

Dienstag, Jacob I., *Ein hamitsvot* (New York, 1968).

Dinur, Ben-Zion, *Bemifneh hadorot* (Jerusalem, 1953).

Dippel, John V. H., *Bound Upon a Wheel of Fire* (New York, 1996).

Dirksen, Peter B., 'The Old Testament Peshitta', in Martin Jan Mulder (ed.), *Mikra* (Assen/Maastricht, 1988), 255–97.

Domb, Yerahmiel Yisrael Yitshak, *Ha'atakot* (Jerusalem, 1990).

Düwell, Kurt, 'Jewish Cultural Centers in Nazi Germany: Expectations and Accomplishments', in Jehuda Reinharz and Walter Schatzburg (eds.), *The Jewish Response to German Culture* (Hanover, NH, 1985), 294–316.

Dvortz, Israel Zissel, *The Gaon Rabbi Moshe Mordechai Epstein* (Heb.) (Tel Aviv, n.d.).

Edelheim-Muehsam, Margaret T., 'Reactions of the Jewish Press to the Nazi Challenge', *Leo Baeck Institute Year Book*, 5 (1960), 308–29.

Eichenstein, Menasheh, *Alfei menasheh* (Przemysl, 1895).

EISNER, ISI JACOB, 'Reminiscences of the Berlin Rabbinical Seminary', *Leo Baeck Institute Year Book*, 12 (1967), 32–52.

EIZ, HAYIM, 'Concerning Agudat Yisrael' (Heb.), *Hamodia*, 23 Shevat 5673 [1913], 267–8.

ELIAV, MORDECHAI, 'Torah im Derekh Eretz in Hungary' (Heb.), *Sinai*, 51 (1959), 127–42.

—— *Jewish Education in Germany in the Period of Enlightenment and Emancipation* (Heb.) (Jerusalem, 1960).

—— 'Rabbi Esriel Hildesheimer and his Influence on Hungarian Jewry' (Heb.), *Zion*, 27 (1962), 59–86.

—— 'Different Approaches to Torah im Derekh Eretz' (Heb.), in Mordechai Breuer (ed.), *Torah im Derekh Eretz* (Ramat Gan, 1987), 45–55.

—— 'Das orthodoxe Rabbinerseminar in Berlin', in Julius Carlebach (ed.), *Wissenschaft des Judentums* (Darmstadt, 1992), 59–73.

—— (ed.), *Rabbiner Esriel Hildesheimer Briefe* (Jerusalem, 1965).

ELLENSON, DAVID, *Rabbi Esriel Hildesheimer and the Creation of a Modern Jewish Orthodoxy* (Tuscaloosa, Ala., 1990).

—— 'German Jewish Orthodoxy: Tradition in the Context of Culture', in Jack Wertheimer (ed.), *The Uses of Tradition* (New York, 1992), 5–22.

—— and JACOBS, RICHARD, 'Scholarship and Faith: David Hoffmann and his Relationship to *Wissenschaft des Judentums*', *Modern Judaism*, 8 (Feb. 1988), 27–40.

ELLINSON, ELYAKIM G., *Marriage Not in Accord with Jewish Law* (Heb.) (Tel Aviv, 1975).

—— *Hatsnea lekhet* (Jerusalem, 1981).

ELMAN, YAAKOV, 'Progressive *Derash* and Retrospective *Peshat*: Nonhalakhic Considerations in Talmud Torah', in Shalom Carmy (ed.), *Modern Scholarship in the Study of Torah: Contributions and Limitations* (Northvale, NJ, 1996), 227–87.

EMANUEL, YONAH, '*Peshat* and its Meaning in the Mishnah' (Heb.), *Hama'ayan*, 12 (Tishrei 5732 [1971]), 27–37.

—— 'Chapters in the Biography of Rabbi Jacob Ettlinger' (Heb.), *Hama'ayan*, 12 (Tevet 5732 [1972]), 24–36.

—— (ed.), *Rabbi Samson Raphael Hirsch: His Teaching and Method* (Heb.) (Jerusalem, 1962).

Emet leya'akov (Berlin, 1937).

Encyclopaedia Judaica (Jerusalem, 1971).

EPSTEIN, BARUKH, *Mekor barukh* (Vilna, 1928).

EPSTEIN, MOSES MORDECHAI, *Levush mordekhai: Baba kamma* (New York, 1924).

—— *Levush mordekhai: Baba metsia* (Jerusalem, 1929).

—— *She'elot uteshuvot levush mordekhai* (Jerusalem, 1946).

ETKES, EMANUEL, 'The Approach and Actions of R. Hayim of Volozhin as a Response of "Mitnagdic" Society to Hasidism' (Heb.), *Proceedings of the American Academy for Jewish Research*, 38–9 (1972), 1–45.

—— *Rabbi Israel Salanter and the Beginning of the Musar Movement* (Heb.) (Jerusalem, 1984).

—— 'Talmudic Scholarship and the Rabbinate in Lithuanian Jewry', in Leo Landman (ed.), *Scholars and Scholarship: The Interaction between Judaism and Other Cultures* (New York, 1990).

—— *Lithuania in Jerusalem* (Heb.) (Jerusalem, 1991).

Ets ḥayim (Haderah, 1985).

ETTLINGER, JACOB, *Minḥat ani* (Jerusalem, 1963).

—— *She'elot uteshuvot ha'arukh laner* (Jerusalem, 1989).

FEDERBUSH, SIMEON, *Binetivot hatalmud* (Jerusalem, 1957).

FEHRS, JÖRG H., *Von der Heidereutergasse zum Roseneck* (Berlin, 1993).

FEINER, SHMUEL, 'The Modern Jewish Woman: A Test Case in the Relationship between Haskalah and Modernity' (Heb.), *Zion*, 58 (1993), 453–99.

FEINSTEIN, MOSES, *Igerot moshe* (New York/Benei Berak/Jerusalem, 1959–96).

FELDMAN, DAVID M., *Marital Relations, Birth Control and Abortion in Jewish Law* (New York, 1974).

Festschrift für Jacob Rosenheim (Frankfurt, 1931).

Festschrift in Honour and Memory of Rabbi Abraham Dov Weisfisch (Heb.) (Jerusalem, 1992).

FINKELSTEIN, MENAHEM, *Proselytism: Halakhah and Practice* (Heb.) (Ramat Gan, 1994).

FISCHER, PHILIP, *In seinen Spuren* (Sátoraljaújhely, 1922).

FISHMAN, DAVID, 'Musar and Modernity: The Case of Novaredok', *Modern Judaism*, 8 (Feb. 1988), 41–64.

FITZMYER, JOSEPH A., *The Genesis Apocryphon of Qumran Cave 1* (Rome, 1971).

FRAENKEL, ABRAHAM A., *Lebenskreise* (Stuttgart, 1967).

FRANKEL, ZECHARIAH, *Darkhei hamishnah* (Warsaw, 1923).

FREEDEN, HERBERT, *Die jüdische Presse im Dritten Reich* (Frankfurt, 1987).

FREIMANN, ABRAHAM HAYIM, *Seder kidushin venisuin* (Jerusalem, 1945).

FRIEDENSOHN, JOSEPH, 'Beth Jacob Schools in Poland' (Heb.), in *Haḥinukh vehatarbut ha'ivrit be'eiropah* (New York, 1957), 43–59.

—— and KRANZLER, DAVID, *Heroine of Rescue* (Brooklyn, NY, 1984).

FRIEDLÄNDER, SAUL, *Nazi Germany and the Jews* (New York, 1997).

FRIEDMAN, DAVID, 'The Status of Non-Halachic Marriage', *Journal of Halacha and Contemporary Society*, 8 (Fall 1984), 118–28.

FRIEDMAN, DOV A., 'Ḥazut kashah', *Hamagid*, 30 July 1885, 257–9.

FRIEDMAN, ELIEZER ELIJAH, 'The History of the *Musar* Sect' (Heb.), *Hator*, 29 Jan. 1926, 8–10.

FRIEDMAN, HAYIM BARUKH, 'Repentance in the Thought of Rabbi Dr. J. J. Weinberg' (Heb.), in *Teshuvah veshavim* (n.p., 1980), 109–15.

FRIEDMAN, MENACHEM, *Society and Religion* (Heb.) (Jerusalem, 1978).

—— 'The Haredim and the Holocaust', *Jerusalem Quarterly*, 53 (Winter 1990), 86–114.

FRIEDMAN, MOSES, *Da'at moshe hashalem* (Jerusalem, 1983).

FRIEDRICH, OTTO, *Before the Deluge: A Portrait of Berlin in the 1920s* (London, 1974).

FRIMER, NORMAN E., and FRIMER, DOV I., 'Reform Marriages in Contemporary Halakhic Responsa', *Tradition*, 21 (Fall 1984), 7–39.

FUCHS, ABRAHAM, *The Holocaust in Rabbinic Sources* (Heb.) (Jerusalem, 1995).

FUCHS, ISAAC JACOB, *Halikhot bat yisra'el* (Jerusalem, 1984).

FUCHS, RICHARD, 'The "Hochschule für die Wissenschaft des Judentums" in the Period of Nazi Rule', *Leo Baeck Institute Year Book*, 12 (1967), 3–31.

FUENN, SAMUEL JOSEPH, 'The Haskalah and the Halakhah' (Heb.), *Hakarmel*, 7 (1868), 105–6.

GERBER, REUVEN, 'The Development of National Vision in Rabbi Kook's Philosophy' (Heb.) (Ph.D. diss., Hebrew University of Jerusalem, 1991).

GEREBOFF, JOEL, 'The Pioneer: Zecharias Frankel', in Jacob Neusner (ed.), *The Modern Study of the Mishnah* (Leiden, 1973), 59–75.

GILLIS-CARLEBACH, MIRIAM, *Education and Faith* (Heb.) (Tel Aviv, 1979).

—— 'The Concept of the Yeshiva and the Distinctiveness of the Lithuanian Yeshiva in the Eyes of Rabbi Dr. Joseph Zvi Carlebach' (Heb.), in Mordechai Breuer (ed.), *Torah im Derekh Eretz* (Ramat Gan, 1987), 147–60.

GILMAN, SANDER, 'The Rediscovery of the Eastern Jews: German Jews in the East 1890–1918', in David Bronsen (ed.), *Jews and Germans from 1860–1933* (Heidelberg, 1979), 338–65.

GINZBERG, ARYEH ZE'EV, *Divrei ḥakhamim* (Brooklyn, NY, 1986).

GINZBERG, LOUIS, *Students, Scholars and Saints* (Philadelphia, Pa., 1943).

—— *On Jewish Law and Lore* (New York, 1970).

GOLDBERG, HILLEL, *Between Berlin and Slobodka: Jewish Transition Figures from Eastern Europe* (Hoboken, NJ, 1989).

GOLDSCHMIDT, S. 'Die Gründung und Bedeutung des Rabbiner-Seminars', *Jeschurun*, 7 (1920), 216–55.

GORDIS, DANIEL, 'Dialectics of Community, Continuity, and Compassion: The Legal Writings of Rabbi David Zevi Hoffmann and their Philosophical Foundations' (Ph.D. diss., University of Southern California, 1992).

GORDON, H. L., 'After the Death of Rabbi Jehiel Jacob Weinberg' (Heb.), *Hado'ar*, 11 Feb. 1966. Contains the Letter to Gordon referred to in the text.

GOTTLIEB, MOSHE, *American Anti-Nazi Resistance, 1933–1941* (New York, 1982).

GOTTLIEB, SAMUEL NOAH, *Ohalei shem* (Pinsk, 1912).

GRAETZ, HEINRICH, *Geschichte der Juden* (Leipzig, 1876).

GREEN, WILLIAM SCOTT, 'The Talmudic Historians: N. Krochmal, H. Graetz, I. H. Weiss, and Z. Jawitz', in Jacob Neusner (ed.), *The Modern Study of the Mishnah* (Leiden, 1973), 107–21.

GREENBERG, HAYIM HAIKEL, *One of the Great Ones of the Generation* (Heb.) (Tel Aviv, 1967).

—— *Kovets rabani torani: 'Aḥi'ezer'—'Torat ḥayim'* (Tel Aviv, n.d.).

GREENSPAN, NAHMAN, *Pilpulah shel torah* (London, 1935).

GREENWALD, LEOPOLD, *The History of the Religious Reformation in Germany and Hungary* (Heb.) (Columbus, Oh., 1948).

GRODZINSKI, HAYIM OZER, *Collected Letters* (Heb.) (Benei Berak, 1967–70).

—— *She'elot uteshuvot aḥi'ezer* (Jerusalem, 1986).

GROSSBERG, MOSHE, *Tsefunot harogochovi* (Jerusalem, 1976).

GRUENBAUM, ISAAC, *The Wars of Polish Jewry* (Heb.) (Tel Aviv, 1941).

GRUNFELD, I., *Three Generations: The Influence of Samson Raphael Hirsch on Jewish Life and Thought* (London, 1958).

—— 'The "Ba'al Seride Esh"', in Nisson Wolpin (ed.), *The Torah Personality* (Brooklyn, NY, 1980), 99–105.

GUTTMANN, ALEXANDER, *The Struggle over Reform in Rabbinic Literature During the Last Century and a Half* (Jerusalem, 1977).

HACOHEN, ISRAEL MEIR, *Collected Writings* (Heb.) (Brooklyn, NY, 1989).

HALEVY, ISAAC, *Dorot harishonim* (Jerusalem, 1967).

HALEVY, ZVI, *Jewish Schools under Czarism and Communism* (New York, 1976).

Halikhot hagrah (Jerusalem, [1996]).

HALIVNI, DAVID WEISS, *Mekorot umesorot: Nashim* (Tel Aviv, 1968).

—— 'Abraham Geiger and Talmud Criticism', in Jakob Petuchowski (ed.), *New Perspectives on Abraham Geiger* (New York, 1975), 31–41.

—— 'Contemporary Methods of the Study of Talmud', *Journal of Jewish Studies*, 30 (1979), 192–201.

HALKIN, A. S., 'The Medieval Jewish Attitude toward Hebrew', in Alexander Altmann (ed.), *Biblical and Other Studies* (Cambridge, Mass., 1963), 233–48.

HAMBURGER, WOLFGANG, 'The Reaction of Reform Jews to the Nazi Rule', in Herbert A. Strauss and Kurt R. Grossmann (eds.), *Gegenwart im Rückblick* (Heidelberg, 1970), 150–64.

HARLAP, JACOB MOSES, *Hed harim* (Jerusalem, 1953).

HARRIS, JAY M., *Nachman Krochmal: Guiding the Perplexed of the Modern Age* (New York, 1991).

HAUT, IRWIN H., *The Talmud as Law or Literature* (New York, 1982).

HAZZAN, ISRAEL MOSES, *Kerakh shel romi* (Livorno, 1876).

HEILPRIN, ISRAEL, *Pinkas va'ad arba aratsot* (Jerusalem, 1990).

HEINEMANN, JOSEPH, 'Early Halakha in the Palestinian Targumim', *Journal of Jewish Studies*, 25 (1974), 114–22.

HEINEMANN, YITSHAK, 'The Relationship between S. R. Hirsch and his Teacher Isaac Bernays' (Heb.), *Zion*, 16 (1941), 44–90.

—— 'R. Mordechai Halevi Horovitz and his Perception of Judaism' (Heb.), *Sinai*, 14 (1944), 162–71.

—— *The Reasons for the Commandments in Jewish Literature* (Heb.) (Jerusalem, 1993).

HELLER, CHAIM, *Untersuchung über die Peschitta* (Berlin, 1911).

—— (ed.), *Peshitta*, vol. i (Berlin, 1927).

HENKIN, JOSEPH ELIJAH, *Writings* (Heb.), vol. i (Jerusalem, 1989).

HENKIN, YEHUDAH HERZL, *Benei vanim* (Jerusalem, 1981).

Henkin, Yehudah Herzl, '"Better Unintentional Sinners than Deliberate Ones" in Contemporary Times' (Heb.), *Teḥumin*, 2 (1981), 272–80.

Henshke, David, 'A Dispute for the Sake of Heaven' (Heb.), *Hama'ayan*, 13 (Tammuz 5733 [1973]), 41–51.

Herring, Basil F., *Jewish Ethics and Halakhah for our Time* (New York, 1984).

Herrmann, Klauss J., *Das Dritte Reich und die deutsch-jüdischen Organisationen 1933–1934* (Cologne, 1969).

Herskovics, Mayer, *Rabbi Zvi Hirsch Chajes* (Heb.) (Jerusalem, 1972).

—— (ed.), *Parnas ledoro* (Hoboken, NJ, 1992).

Hertzig, Zohara Bozich, 'The Controversy over Women's Suffrage at the Beginning of the Mandate' (Heb.) (MA diss., Bar-Ilan University, 1990).

Herzog, Isaac, *Constitution and Law in a Jewish State According to the Halakhah* (Heb.) (Jerusalem, 1989).

Heuberger, Rachel, 'Nehemias Anton Nobel: Ein orthodoxer Rabbiner zwischen deutschem Patriotismus und religiösem Zionismus', *Trumah*, 3 (1992), 151–74.

—— 'Orthodoxy versus Reform: The Case of Rabbi Nehemiah Anton Nobel of Frankfurt a. Main', *Leo Baeck Institute Year Book*, 37 (1992), 45–58.

Hilberg, Raul, *et al.*, *The Warsaw Diary of Adam Czerniakow* (New York, 1979).

Hildesheimer, Azriel, 'The Central Organization of German Jewry During the Years 1933–1945' (Heb.) (Ph.D. diss., Hebrew University of Jerusalem, 1982).

—— 'Rabbi Esriel Hildesheimer's Conception of Torah im Derekh Eretz' (Heb.), in Mordechai Breuer (ed.), *Torah im Derekh Eretz* (Ramat Gan, 1987), 75–82.

Hildesheimer, Esriel, 'Rede zur Eröffnung des Rabbiner-Seminars', *Jahres-Bericht des Rabbiners-Seminars für das orthodoxe Judenthum pro 5634 (1873–74)* (Berlin, [1874]), 84–9.

—— 'Unterricht der Mädchen im Urtext der "heiligen Schrift"', *Israelitischer Lehrer und Cantor*, supplement to *Die Jüdische Presse*, 41 (1910), no. 7.

—— 'A Selection of Letters between Rabbi Esriel Hildesheimer and Rabbi Samson Raphael Hirsch and his Supporters' (Heb.), in Jehiel Jacob Weinberg and Pinhas Biberfeld (eds.), *Yad sha'ul* (Tel Aviv, 1953), 248–51.

—— 'Unveröffentliche Sche'eloth und Teschuwoth des Raw Esriel Hildesheimer von Berlin', *25 Jahre Jüdische Schule Zürich* (Jerusalem, 1980).

—— and Kahana, Kalman (eds.), *Memorial Volume for Rabbi Jehiel Jacob Weinberg* (Heb.) (Jerusalem, 1969).

Hildesheimer, Meier (ed.), *Rabbiner Dr. Israel Hildesheimer Gesammelte Aufsätze* (Frankfurt, 1923).

Hildesheimer, Meir, 'Writings Regarding the Founding of the Rabbinical Seminary of Berlin' (Heb.), *Hama'ayan*, 14 (Tevet 5734 [1974]), 12–37.

Hirsch, Samson Raphael, *Neunzehn Briefe über Judentum* (Altona, 1836). In Hebrew: *Igerot Tsafun*, trans. Moses Ahronson (Vilna, 1891); trans. Efraim Porat, with an introduction by Isaac Heinemann (Jerusalem, 1952). In English: *The Nineteen Letters of Ben Uziel*, trans. B. Drachman (New York, 1942); *The Nineteen Letters*, trans. Karin Paritzky with a commentary by Joseph Elias (Jerusalem, 1995).

—— *Gesammelte Schriften* (Frankfurt, 1912).

—— *Meitav higayon*, trans. Isaac Eleazar Hirschowitz (Vilna, 1913).

—— *Shemesh marpeh* (New York, 1992).

—— *Collected Writings of Rabbi Samson Raphael Hirsch*, vol. vii (New York, 1992).

HOFFMANN, DAVID ZVI, *Mar samuel* (Leipzig, 1873).

—— *Der Schulchan Aruch und die Rabbinen über das Verhältnis der Juden zu Andersgläubigen* (Berlin, 1894).

—— *Die wichtigsten Instanzen gege die Graf-Wellhausensche Hypothese* (Berlin, 1904).

—— *Leviticus* (Berlin, 1905).

—— *The First Mishnah* (Heb.), trans. Samuel Grünberg (Berlin, 1914).

—— 'Ein Gutachten', *Jeschurun*, 6 (1919), 262–6.

—— 'Über Frauenwahlrecht in jüdischen-Gemeinden', *Jeschurun*, 6 (1919), 515–22.

—— 'Thora und Wissenschaft', *Jeschurun*, 7 (1920), 497–504.

—— *Melamed leho'il* (New York, 1954).

HOFFSEYER, BENJAMIN, 'Rabbi Chaim Tchernowitz, "Rav Tsa'ir", and the Odessa Yeshiva' (Heb.) (Ph.D. diss., Yeshiva University, 1967).

HOLTZMAN, AVNER, *El hakera shebalev* (Jerusalem, 1995).

HONIGMANN, PETER, 'Jüdische Studenten zwischen Orthodoxie und moderner Wissenschaft: Der Heidelberger Talmudistenkreis um Salman Baruch Rabinkow', in Julius H. Schoeps (ed.), *Menora* (Munich, 1992), 85–96.

HOROVITZ, MARCUS, *Mateh levi*, vol. ii (Frankfurt, 1932).

HOROWITZ, ABRAHAM DAVID, *Kinyan torah behalakhah*, vol. i (Strasbourg, 1976).

HORWITZ, RIVKA, 'Voices of Opposition to the First World War among Jewish Thinkers', *Leo Baeck Institute Year Book*, 33 (1988), 233–59.

HUTNER-DAVID, BRURIAH, 'The Dual Role of Rabbi Zvi Hirsch Chajes: Traditionalist and *Maskil*' (Ph.D. diss., Columbia University, 1971).

HYMAN, PAULA E., 'The Introduction of Bat Mitzvah in Conservative Judaism in Postwar America', *YIVO Annual*, 19 (1990), 133–46.

Igerot mibeit halevi (Benei Berak, 1993).

In Zwei Welten: Siegfried Moses zum fünfundsiebzigsten Geburtstag (Tel Aviv, 1962).

ISAAC BAR SHESHET, *Teshuvot rivash* (Jerusalem, 1993).

ISAACSON, MEIR, *Mevaser tov*, vol. ii (Brooklyn, NY, 1986).

JACOB, WALTER (ed.), *American Reform Responsa* (New York, 1983).

JACOBS, LOUIS, *A Tree of Life* (Oxford, 1984).

JACOBSON, BINYAMIN ZE'EV, *Memoirs* (Heb.) (Jerusalem, 1953).

—— *Esa de'i lemeraḥok* (Benei Berak, 1967).

Jahres-Bericht des Rabbiner-Seminars zu Berlin, 1873–1937.

JAKOBOVICS, BENZIYON, *Zekhor yemot olam*, vol. ii (Benei Berak, 1989).

JAKOBOVITS, IMMANUEL, '*Torah im Derekh Eretz*', in Moses Rischin and Raphael Asher (eds.), *The Jewish Legacy and the German Conscience* (Berkeley, Calif., 1991), 157–70.

JASTROW, MARCUS, *A Dictionary of the Targumim, the Talmud Babli and Yerushalmi, and the Midrashic Literature* (New York, 1971).

Jüdisches Lexicon (Berlin, 1930).

JUNG, LEO (ed.), *Men of the Spirit* (New York, 1964).

KAGAN, BERL, *Jewish Towns and Villages in Lithuania* (Yid.) (New York, 1990).

KAHANA, KALMAN, *Ḥeker ve'iyun* (Tel Aviv, 1960).

—— 'The Gaon Rabbi Esriel Hildesheimer and his Seminary' (Heb.), *Hama'ayan*, 29 (Tammuz 5749 [1989]), 1–8.

KAHANA, MENAHEM, 'Talmudic Research at the University and Traditional Yeshiva Study' (Heb.), in id. (ed.), *Beḥevlei masoret utemurah* (Reḥovot, 1990), 113–42.

KAHLE, MARIE, *What Would You Have Done?* (n.p., n.d.).

KAHLE, PAUL, *Masoreten des Westens*, 2 vols. (Stuttgart, 1927 and 1930).

KAMELHAR, MOSHE, *Rabbi Dov Ber Meisels* (Heb.) (Jerusalem, 1970).

KANARFOGEL, EPHRAIM, 'The Tosafist Œuvre and Torah u-Madda', *Torah u-Madda Journal*, 2 (1990), 51–60.

KAPLAN, ABRAHAM ELIJAH, *Divrei talmud*, vol. i (Jerusalem, 1958).

—— *Be'ikvot hayirah* (Jerusalem, 1988).

—— and LANDAU, MAX (eds.), *Vom Sinn des Judentums: Ein Sammelbuch zu Ehren Nathan Birnbaums* (Frankfurt, 1925).

KAPLAN, LAWRENCE, 'The Hazon Ish: Haredi Critic of Traditional Orthodoxy', in Jack Wertheimer (ed.), *The Uses of Tradition* (New York, 1992), 145–73.

—— 'Rabbi Joseph B. Soloveitchik's Conception of Repentance' (unpublished).

KARELITZ, ABRAHAM ISAIAH, *Collected Letters* (Heb.) (Benei Berak, n.d.).

—— *Ḥazon ish: Even ha'ezer* (Benei Berak, 1958).

KARLINSKY, HAYIM, *The First in the Brisk Dynasty* (Heb.) (Jerusalem, 1984).

KASHER, MENAHEM, *Torah shelemah*, vol. xviii (New York, 1958), vol. xxiv (Jerusalem, 1975).

—— *Mefane'aḥ tsefunot* (New York, 1959).

—— 'Concerning Conditional Marriage' (Heb.), *No'am*, 11 (1969), 338–53.

—— 'The Appearance of Two Volumes of the Comprehensive Talmud Project' (Heb.), *No'am*, 16 (1973), 165–82.

KASHER, MOSHE SHLOMO, *The Rogochover Gaon and his Teachings* (Heb.) (Jerusalem, 1958).

—— *Introduction to the Teachings of the Rogochover* (Heb.) (Jerusalem, 1966).

—— *The Teachings of Rabbi Joseph Rozin* (Heb.) (Jerusalem, 1976).

KATZ, DOV, *The Musar Controversy* (Heb.) (Jerusalem, 1972).

—— *The Musar Movement* (Heb.) (Jerusalem, 1982).

KATZ, JACOB, 'Umkehr oder Rückkehr', *Nachlath Zwi*, 5 (1935), 89–95.

—— 'Tsevi Hirsh Kalischer', in Leo Jung (ed.), *Guardians of our Heritage* (New York, 1958), 207–27.

—— *Halakhah in Straits* (Heb.) (Jerusalem, 1992).

—— *The Unhealed Breach* (Heb.) (Jerusalem, 1995).

—— *With My Own Eyes*, trans. Ann Brenner and Zipora Brody (Hanover, NH, 1995).

KATZ, REUVEN, 'Concerning the Rabbinate in Palestine' (Heb.), *Hahed* (Shevat 5694 [1934]), 9–10.

—— *Degel re'uven*, vol. iii (Jerusalem, 1949).

KATZ, SHMUEL, *Kedoshim tiheyu* (Jerusalem, 1980).

KATZENELSON, GIDEON, *The Literary Battle Between the Orthodox and the Maskilim* (Heb.) (Tel Aviv, 1954).

KAULLA, RUDOLF, *Der Liberalismus und die deutschen Juden: Das Judentum als konservatives Element* (Munich, 1928).

KAZDAN, H. S., *From Ḥeder and 'Schools' to the Central Jewish School Organization* (Yid.) (Mexico, 1956).

KESSNER, CAROLE S., 'Kaplan and the Role of Women in Judaism', in Emanuel S. Goldsmith (ed.), *The American Judaism of Mordecai M. Kaplan* (New York, 1990), 335–56.

KIERKEGAARD, SØREN, *Journals*, trans. Alexander Dru (London, 1938).

KIRSCHBAUM, MENAHEM MENDEL, *Tsiyun limenaḥem* (New York, 1965).

KIRSCHNER, ROBERT, *Rabbinic Responsa of the Holocaust Era* (New York, 1985).

KLATZKIN, ELIJAH, *Devar halakhah: Miluim* (Lublin, 1923).

—— *Even pinah* (Jerusalem, 1930).

—— *Devarim aḥadim* (Jerusalem, 1931).

KLEIN, HERMANN, 'Das Judenthum in seinen Grundzügen', *Der Israelit*, 5 Dec. 1904.

—— 'Das Ostjuden-Problem', *Jüdische Monatshefte*, 3 (1916), 91–9.

—— *Ḥokhmah im naḥalah* (Bilgoraj, 1935).

—— *Kahana mesayea kahana* (Berlin, 1938).

—— *Oraita begaluta* (Buenos Aires, n.d.).

KLEIN, MENASHEH, *Mishneh halakhot* (Brooklyn, NY, 1987–96).

KLEIN, MICHAEL L., *Genizah Manuscripts of Palestinian Targum to the Pentateuch* (Cincinnati, Oh., 1986).

KLUGMAN, ELIYAHU MEIR, *Rabbi Samson Raphael Hirsch* (New York, 1996).

KOOK, ABRAHAM ISAAC, *Igerot hare'iyah* (Jerusalem, 1962).

—— *Orot hakodesh* (Jerusalem, 1964).

—— *Da'at kohen* (Jerusalem, 1969).

—— *Arpilei tohar* (Jerusalem, 1983).

—— *Orot* (Jerusalem, 1992); English trans. Bezalel Naor (Northvale, NJ, 1993).

KOOK, ZVI YEHUDAH, *Bema'arakhah hatsiburit* (Jerusalem, 1986).

—— *Lehilkhot tsibur* (Jerusalem, 1987).

—— *Tsemaḥ tsevi* (Jerusalem, 1991).

KRESSEL, GETZEL, *Guide to the Hebrew Press* (Zug, Switzerland, 1979).

KRESSEL, GETZEL, 'Hitler Only Persecutes Zionists' (Heb.), *Ma'ariv*, 15 Oct. 1985.

KROCHMAL, NAHMAN, *Moreh nevukhei hazeman* (Lemberg, 1851).

KUPFER, EFRAIM, *Ber Meisels* (Yid.) (Warsaw, 1952).

KURZWEIL, BARUCH, *Bema'avak al erkhei hayahadut* (Jerusalem, 1970).

KURZWEIL, ZVI, *Siyum vereshit* (Tel Aviv, 1992).

LAMM, HANS, 'Über die innere und äussere Entwicklung der deutschen Judentums im dritten Reich' (Ph.D. diss., University of Erlangen, 1951).

LAMM, LOUIS, *Verzeichnis jüdischer Kriegsschriften* (Berlin, 1916).

LANDAU, MENAHEM MENDEL, *Mekits nirdamim* (Petrokov, 1903).

LAVUT, ABRAHAM DAVID, *Kav venaki* (Brooklyn, NY, 1985).

LAZARUS, M., *The Ethics of Judaism*, trans. Henrietta Szold (Philadelphia, Pa., 1900).

LEDERHENDLER, ELI, *Jewish Responses to Modernity* (New York, 1994).

LEHRER, ZVI YAAKOV HALEVI, 'Manuscripts of Early Commentaries and their Qualification to Rule on Jewish Law' (Heb.), *Tsefunot*, 16 (1992), 68–73.

LEIB, ZEBULUN, 'Dover shalom', *Halevanon*, 9 (1872), 226–7.

LEIBOWITZ, BARUKH BER, *Birkat shemuel* (New York, 1964).

LEICHTER, SINAI, and MILKOV, HAYIM (eds.), *Olei hasertifikatim* (Jerusalem, 1993).

LEIMAN, SHNAYER Z., 'Hazon Ish on Textual Criticism and Halakhah: A Rejoinder', *Tradition*, 19 (Winter 1981), 301–10.

LEONI, ELIEZER (ed.), *Ciechanowiec Memorial Volume* (Heb.) (Tel Aviv, 1964).

LERNER, MEIER, *Hadar hakarmel* (London, 1975).

LEVI, YEHUDAH, *Sha'arei talmud torah* (Jerusalem, 1981).

—— 'Rabbi Samson Raphael Hirsch: Myth and Fact', *Tradition*, 31 (Spring 1997), 5–22.

LEVI, ZVI, 'Gaon, Man of Character, Educator' (Heb.), *Hatsofeh*, 13 Jan. 1967.

LEVINE, HOWARD I., 'Enduring and Transitory Elements in the Philosophy of Samson Raphael Hirsch', *Tradition*, 5 (Fall 1962), 278–97.

LEVINSON-LAVI, M., Letter in *Bitsaron*, 8 (1943), 278.

—— 'Pilvishok', in Mendel Sudarsky *et al.* (eds.), *Lithuania* (Yid.), vol. i (New York, 1951), 1533–6.

LEVITATS, ISAAC, *The Jewish Community in Russia 1844–1917* (Jerusalem, 1981).

LEVY, B. BARRY, *Targum Neophyti 1: A Textual Study*, vol. i (Lanham, Md., 1986).

LEVY, JACOB, 'Youthful Memories from the Adass Jisroel Community in Berlin' (Heb.), *Hama'ayan*, 4 (Tammuz 5724 [1964]), 3–15.

LEVY, RICHARD S., *Antisemitism in the Modern World* (Lexington, Mass., 1991).

LEWIN, ISAAC, *et al.*, *Religious Freedom: The Right to Practice Shehita* (New York, 1946).

LIBERLES, ROBERT, *Religious Conflict in Social Context: The Resurgence of Orthodox Judaism in Frankfurt am Main, 1838–1877* (Westport, Conn., 1985).

LIFSCHITZ, ZE'EV HAYIM, 'Thoughts about the Man in his Era' (Heb.), in Esriel Hildesheimer and Kalman Kahana (eds.), *Memorial Volume for Rabbi Jehiel Jacob Weinberg* (Jerusalem, 1969), 363–87.

LIFSHITZ, A. M., 'The Ḥeder' (Heb.), *Hatekufah*, 7 (1920), 294–352.

LIFSHITZ, HAYIM, *Shivḥei hare'iyah* (Jerusalem, 1979).

LIFSHITZ, JACOB, 'Haseder vehama'aseh', *Halevanon*, 8 (1872), 17–19.

—— 'Lahat haḥerev hamithapekhet', *Halevanon*, 9 (1873), 273–5.

—— *Maḥazikei hadat* (Petrokov, 1903).

—— 'Habit Becomes Second Nature' (Heb.), *Hamodia*, 5 Tevet 5671 [1911], 168–72.

—— *Zikhron ya'akov* (Israel, 1968).

LIFSHITZ, ZVI ELEAZAR, 'Concerning the Appointment of Rabbis' (Heb.), *Yagdil Torah*, 2 (1910), 16–18.

Lithuanian Jewry (Heb.) (Jerusalem, 1959).

Lithuanian Jewry (Heb.), vol. iii (Tel Aviv, 1967).

LITVIN, A., *Yidishe neshomes* (New York, 1917).

LORENZ, INA, *Die Juden in Hamburg zur Zeit der Weimarer Republik* (Hamburg, 1987).

LOWENSTEIN, STEVEN M., *The Mechanics of Change: Essays in the Social History of German Jewry* (Atlanta, Ga., 1992).

LOWENTHAL, ERNST G., 'In seinen Hörern noch lebendig . . . Das Rabbiner Seminar zu Berlin', *Emuna*, 9 (1974), 103–10.

LURIA, SOLOMON, *Yam shel shelomo* (New York, 1953).

LUZ, EHUD, *Parallels Meet*, trans. Lenn J. Schramm (Philadelphia, Pa., 1988).

LUZZATTO, SAMUEL DAVID, *Studies in Judaism* (Heb.), vol. ii (Warsaw, 1913).

MANN, ISAAC H., 'The Prohibition of Teaching Non-Jews Torah: Its Historical Development', *Gesher*, 8 (1981), 122–73.

MÄNNCHEN, JULIA, *Gustaf Dalmans Leben und Wirken in der Brüdergemeinde, für die Judenmission und an der Universität Leipzig 1855–1902* (Wiesbaden, 1987).

MANOR, ALEXANDER, *et al.*, *Sefer lida* (Tel Aviv, 1970).

MA'ORI, YESHAYAHU, *The Peshitta Version of the Pentateuch and Early Jewish Exegesis* (Heb.) (Jerusalem, 1995).

—— 'Rabbinic Midrash as Evidence for Textual Variants in the Hebrew Bible: History and Practice', in Shalom Carmy (ed.), *Modern Scholarship in the Study of Torah: Contributions and Limitations* (Northvale, NJ, 1996), 101–29.

MARGALIOT, ABRAHAM, 'The Dispute over the Leadership of German Jewry (1933–1938)', *Yad Vashem Studies*, 10 (1974), 129–48.

MARKOWITZ, YEHOSHUA, 'Rabbi David Zvi Hoffmann' (Heb.) (MA diss., Bar-Ilan University, 1968).

MARX, ALEXANDER, *Essays in Jewish Biography* (Philadelphia, Pa., 1947).

MATHISSON, ZVI, 'The Tragedy of a Great Man' (Heb.), *Hado'ar*, 4 Mar. 1966.

MATZGER, DAVID (ed.), *Perushei rabeinu ḥananel bar ḥushi'el latalmud: Berakhot* (Jerusalem, 1990).

—— 'Tovah tsiparnam shel rishonim', *Hama'ayan*, 35 (Tevet 5755 [1995]), 1–10.

MAURER, TRUDE, *Ostjuden in Deutschland 1918–1933* (Hamburg, 1986).

MAYER, EUGEN, 'Räumet, räumt, macht Bahn!' in *Gabe: Herrn Rabbiner Dr. Nobel zum 50. Geburtstag* (Frankfurt, 1922), 85–7.

MAZUZ, MEIR ISSACHAR, 'Civil Marriage and the Consequences' (Heb.), *Shenaton hamishpat ha'ivri*, 3–4 (1976–7), 233–70.

MEDINI, HAYIM HEZEKIAH, *Sedei ḥemed* (Brooklyn, NJ, 1949).

MELTZER, IMMANUEL, 'The Anti-German Economic Boycott by Polish Jewry in 1933–1934' (Heb.), *Gal-ed*, 6 (1982), 129–48.

MEYER, MICHAEL A., 'Jewish Religious Reform and Wissenschaft des Judentums', *Leo Baeck Institute Year Book*, 16 (1971), 19–41.

—— 'Christian Influence on Early German Reform Judaism', in Charles Berlin (ed.), *Studies in Jewish Bibliography, History, and Literature in Honor of I. Edward Kiev* (New York, 1971), 289–304.

—— *Response to Modernity* (Oxford, 1988).

MIKHAELZON, ZVI EZEKIEL, *Pinot habayit* (Petrokov, 1925).

MILLER, ISRAEL DAVID, *Toledot menaḥem* (Petrokov, 1913).

MITTLEMAN, ALAN L., *The Politics of Torah: The Jewish Political Tradition and the Founding of Agudat Israel* (Albany, NY, 1996).

MORGAN, MIRIAM, 'The Traditional Aspect in the Views of Ahad Ha'am and Berdyczewski' (Heb.) (MA diss., Bar-Ilan University, 1979).

MORGENSTERN, MATTHIAS, '*Von Frankfurt nach Jerusalem*': *Isaac Breuer und die Geschichte des 'Austrittsstreits' in der deutsch-jüdischen Orthodoxie* (Tübingen, 1995).

MUNK, ELIE, *Judentum und Umwelt* (Frankfurt, 1933).

MUNK, ELIYAHU, and MUNK, MICHAEL L., *Edut ne'emanah* (Jerusalem, 1974).

—— *Shechita: Religious and Historical Research on the Jewish Method of Slaughter* (Brooklyn, NY, 1976).

MUNK, MICHAEL L., 'Austrittsbewegung und Berliner *Adass Jisroel*-Gemeinde 1869–1939', in Herbert A. Strauss and Kurt R. Grossmann (eds.), *Gegenwart im Rückblick* (Heidelberg, 1970), 130–49.

MUNK, MOSHE, 'Torah im Derekh Eretz in our Day' (Heb.), in Yonah Emanuel (ed.), *Harav shimshon raphael hirsch: Mishnato veshitato* (Jerusalem, 1962), 200–33.

NEHORAI, MICHAEL Z., 'Halakhah, Metahalakhah, and the Redemption of Israel: Reflections on the Rabbinic Rulings of Rav Kook', in Lawrence J. Kaplan and David Shatz (eds.), *Rabbi Abraham Isaac Kook and Jewish Spirituality* (New York, 1995), 120–56.

NERIYAH, MOSHE ZVI, *Siḥot hare'iyah* (Tel Aviv, 1979).

NEUWEDAL, S. T., 'The Humiliation of Judaism Due to the Negligence of the Orthodox' (Heb.), *Hamodia*, 2 Heshvan 5671 [1910], 23–5.

NIEDERLAND, DORON, *German Jews: Emigrants or Refugees* (Heb.) (Jerusalem, 1996).

NIEWYK, DONALD L., *The Jews in Weimar Germany* (Baton Rouge, La., 1980).

NOVAK, DAVID, *Law and Theology in Judaism* (New York, 1974).

—— *The Image of the Non-Jew in Judaism* (New York, 1983).

—— 'The Marital Status of Jews Married under Non-Jewish Auspices', *Jewish Law Association Studies*, 1 (1985), 61–77.

OFFENBERG, MARIO (ed.), *Adass Jisroel: Die Jüdische Gemeinde in Berlin (1859–1942)* (Berlin, 1986).

OHANA, MOISE, 'Agneau pascal et circoncision: Le Problème de la halakha prémishnaïque dans le targum palestinien', *Vetus Testamentum*, 23 (1974), 385–99.

OSTROVESKI, MOSHE (ed.), *Ish yerushalayim* (Jerusalem, 1937).

OVSAY, YEHOSHUA, *Collected Articles* (Heb.) (New York, 1947).

PERLOW, BERNARD, 'Institutions for the Education of the Modern Rabbi in Germany' (Ph.D. diss., Dropsie College, 1954).

PHILIPSON, DAVID, 'Confirmation in the Synagogue', *Year Book of the Central Conference of American Rabbis*, 1 (1890–1), 43–58.

PINEAS, M., 'Zum Tode von Rabbiner Dr Weinberg', in Max Sinasohn (ed.), *Adass Jisroel Berlin* (Jerusalem, 1966), 175–7.

PLAUT, W. GUNTHER, *The Rise of Reform Judaism* (New York, 1963).

PORTON, GARY G., 'Hanokh Albeck on the Mishnah' (Heb.), in Jacob Neusner (ed.), *The Modern Study of the Mishnah* (Leiden, 1973), 209–24.

POSEN, ELIEZER, 'The Frankfurt Yeshiva', in *Ateret Zvi: Jubilee Volume Presented in Honor of the Eightieth Birthday of Rabbi Dr. Joseph Breuer* (New York, 1962), 149–54.

POSNER, AKIVA, 'The Monthly *Jeschurun* Edited by Dr. Wohlgemuth' (Heb.), in Y. Tirosh (ed.), *Shai liyeshayahu* (Tel Aviv, 1955), 73–8.

—— 'The Study of Talmud in the Rabbinical Seminary of Berlin' (Heb.), *Hadarom*, 12 (1960), 184–94.

PRIMUS, CHARLES, 'David Hoffmann's *The First Mishnah*', in Jacob Neusner (ed.), *The Modern Study of the Mishnah* (Leiden, 1973), 122–34.

PRINZ, JOACHIM, *Wir Juden* (Berlin, 1934).

—— 'A Rabbi under the Hitler Regime', in Herbert A. Strauss and Kurt R. Grossmann (eds.), *Gegenwart im Rückblick* (Heidelberg, 1970), 231–8.

'Protokollbuch des seminarischen Vereins "Dibbuk Chawerim"', Jewish Theological Seminary of America, MS no. 3675.

RABIN, DOV (ed.), *Encyclopaedia of the Diaspora: Grodno* (Heb.) (Jerusalem, 1973).

RABINER, ZE'EV ARYEH, *The Gaon Rabbi Eliezer Gordon* (Heb.) (Tel Aviv, 1968).

RACKMAN, EMANUEL, 'Halakhah: Orthodox Approaches', *Encyclopaedia Judaica Year Book: 1975–1976* (Jerusalem, 1976), 134–44.

RAFAEL, YITSHAK, *Rishonim ve'aḥaronim* (Tel Aviv, 1957).

—— *Lo zakhiti ba'or min hahefker* (Jerusalem, 1981).

—— (ed.), *Sefer aviad* (Jerusalem, 1986).

RAGOLER, ELIJAH, *Yad eliyahu* (Jerusalem, 1969).

RAKEFFET-ROTHKOFF, AARON, 'The Spiritual Legacy of Rabbi Jehiel Jacob Weinberg', *Niv Hamidrashia*, 11 (1974), 91–103.

—— *Bernard Revel: Builder of American Jewish Orthodoxy* (Jerusalem, 1981).

RAPEL, DOV, *The Dispute over Pilpul* (Heb.) (Jerusalem, 1979).

—— (ed.), *Hapeninah* (Jerusalem, 1989).

RAPHAEL, SHILO, 'The Gaon Rabbi Jehiel Jacob Weinberg: Sage and *Posek*' (Heb.), *Sinai*, 58 (1966), 293–6.

REICHEL, ASHER (ed.), *Letters of Rabbi Isaac Halevy* (Heb.) (Jerusalem, 1972).

REIDER, DAVID, 'On the Targum Yerushalmi MS Neofiti 1' (Heb.), *Tarbiz*, 38 (1969), 81–6.

REINES, ISAAC JACOB, *Shenei hame'orot* (Petrokov, 1913).

REISNER, ERWIN, *Die Juden und das Deutsche Reich* (Erlenbach, 1966).

RHEINS, CARL JEFFREY, 'German Jewish Patriotism 1918–1935: A Study of the Attitudes and Actions of the *Reichsband Jüdischer Frontsoldaten*, the *Verband Nationaldeutscher Juden*, the *Schwarzes Fahnlein*' (Ph.D. diss., SUNY Stony Brook, 1978).

RIVLIN, BENJAMIN, *Gevi'i gevia hakesef* (Warsaw, 1898).

ROSENBAUM, RAFAEL (ed.), *Rabbi Moses Lipshitz Memorial Volume* (Heb.) (New York, 1996).

ROSENBLOOM, YEHOSHUA, *My City, Ciechanowiec* (Heb.) (Tel Aviv, 1951).

ROSENBLUTH, MARTIN, *Go Forth and Serve* (New York, 1961).

ROSENHEIM, JACOB, *Oholai Ya'akov: Ausgewählte Aufsätze und Ansprachen* (Frankfurt, 1930).

—— *Das Bildungsideal Samson Raphael Hirschs und die Gegenwart* (Frankfurt, 1935).

—— *Die 'Thora- und Mussar'-Bewegung* (Frankfurt, 1936).

—— *Memoirs* (Heb.) (Tel Aviv, 1955).

—— *Erinnerungen: 1870–1920* (Frankfurt, 1970).

ROSENTHAL, DAVID, 'The Method of the Sages in Dealing with Variant Versions of the Bible' (Heb.), in Yair Zakovitch and Alexander Rofe (eds.), *Sefer yitsḥak aryeh seeligman*, vol. ii (Jerusalem, 1983), 395–416.

ROSKIES, DIANE, *Heder: Primary Education among East European Jews* (New York, 1977).

ROTH, MESHULLAM, *Kol mevaser* (Jerusalem, 1972).

ROZENBLIT, MARSHA L., 'Jewish Identity and the Modern Rabbi: The Cases of Isak Noah Mannheimer, Adolf Jellinek, and Moritz Güdemann in Nineteenth-Century Vienna', *Leo Baeck Institute Year Book*, 35 (1990), 103–32.

ROZIN, JOSEPH, *Tsafenat paneaḥ* (Jerusalem, 1968).

RUBENSTEIN, AVRAHAM, *A Movement in an Era of Change* (Heb.) (Jerusalem, 1981).

RUBENSTEIN, SHMUEL T., 'Men Who Cannot be Circumcised Due to Health Reasons: Can They Convert?' (Heb.), *Torah shebe'al peh*, 29 (1988), 28–32.

RUDNICKI, SZYMON, 'Ritual Slaughter as a Political Issue', *Polin*, 7 (1992), 147–60.

SALANTER, ISRAEL, *Tevunah* (Königsberg, 1861).

—— *Or yisra'el* (Vilna, 1900).

SALMON, YOSEF, 'The First Reform in East European Yeshivot' (Heb.), *Molad*, 4 (1971), 161–72.

—— 'The Yeshiva of Lida: A Unique Institution of Higher Learning', *YIVO Annual*, 15 (1974), 106–25.

—— *Religion and Zionism* (Heb.) (Jerusalem, 1990).

SAMET, MOSHE, 'Moses Mendelssohn, N. H. Wessely, and the Rabbis of their Generation' (Heb.), in A. Gilboa *et al.* (eds.), *Meḥkarim betoledot am yisra'el ve'erets yisra'el lezekher tsevi avneri* (Haifa, 1970), 233–57.

—— 'R. Nahman Berlin's Views on Society and History' (Heb.), in Yehezkel Cohen (ed.), *Ḥevrah vehistoriyah* (Jerusalem, 1980), 125–35.

SAPERSTEIN, MARC, 'War and Patriotism in Sermons to Central European Jews: 1756–1815', *Leo Baeck Institute Year Book*, 38 (1993), 3–14.

SARFATTI, GAD BEN-AMI, 'A New Edition of the *Genesis Apocryphon*' (Heb.), *Leshoneinu*, 33 (1969), 115–28.

SAVITSKY, MORDEKHAI, *Nezir eḥav* (n.p., 1988).

SCHACHTER, ZVI, 'Go Thy Way Forth by the Footsteps of the Flock' (Heb.), *Beit yitsḥak*, 17 (1985), 118–34.

—— *Nefesh harav* (Jerusalem, 1994).

SCHACTER, JACOB J., 'Reminiscences of Shlomo Barukh Rabinkow', in Leo Jung (ed.), *Sages and Saints* (Hoboken, NJ, 1987), 93–132.

—— 'Torah u-Madda Revisited: The Editor's Introduction', *Torah u-Madda Journal*, 1 (1989), 1–22.

—— 'Haskalah, Secular Studies and the Close of the Yeshiva in Volozhin in 1892', *Torah u-Madda Journal*, 2 (1990), 76–133.

SCHARFSTEIN, ZVI, *The Ḥeder in the Life of our People* (Heb.) (New York, 1953).

—— *The History of Jewish Education in Recent Generations* (Heb.), vol. i (Jerusalem, 1960).

SCHATZKER, CHAIM, 'The German-Jewish Attitude of Jewish Youth in Germany during the First World War and the Influence of the War on this Attitude' (Heb.), in B. Oded *et al.* (eds.), *Meḥkarim betoledot am yisra'el ve'erets yisra'el*, vol. ii (Haifa, 1972), 187–215.

SCHEFTELOWITZ, ELHANAN, *500 Years, The History of a Jewish Family* (Heb.) (Jerusalem, n.d.).

SCHEIDERMAN, HARRY, and CARMIN, ITZHAK J., *Who's Who in World Jewry* (New York, 1955).

SCHELBERT, GEORG, 'Exodus xxii 4 im palästinischen Targum', *Vetus Testamentum*, 8 (1958), 253–63.

SCHENIRER, SARA, *Em beyisra'el* (Tel Aviv, 1956).

SCHICK, MOSES, *She'elot uteshuvot maharam schick* (New York, 1961).

SCHMELKES, ISAAC, *Beit yitsḥak* (Przemysl, 1892).

SCHNEERSOHN, JOSEPH ISAAC, 'A Critique of the Educational Approach of German Orthodoxy' (Heb.), *Hahed* (Av 5688 [1928]), 1–3.

—— *Igerot kodesh*, vol. iii (Brooklyn, NY, 1983).

SCHNEERSOHN, SHOLOM DOV BER, *Igerot kodesh*, vols. ii–v (Brooklyn, NY, 1982–87).

SCHOLEM, GERSHOM, *The Messianic Idea in Judaism* (New York, 1971).

—— *From Berlin to Jerusalem* (Heb.) (Tel Aviv, 1982).

SCHULMAN, B., 'The Revolutionary Spirit in the Yeshivot' (Heb.), *He'avar*, 12 (1965), 134–46.

SCHULZINGER, ELEAZER HALEVI, *Al mishkenot haro'im* (Benei Berak, 1988).

SCHWAB, HERMANN, *The History of Orthodox Jewry in Germany, 1830–1945* (London, [1950]).

SCHWAB, SIMON, *Heimkehr ins Judentum* (Frankfurt, 1934).

—— 'Concerning Torah im Derekh Eretz', *Hapardes* (Dec. 1939), 26–8.

SCHWAB, SIMON, *These and Those* (New York, 1966).

—— 'A Letter Concerning "The Frankfurt Approach"' (Heb.), *Hama'ayan*, 6 (Tammuz 5726 [1966]), 4–7.

—— *Selected Speeches* (New York, 1991).

SCHWADRON, SHALOM, *Da'at torah* (Toltshava, 1911).

SCHWARTZ, DANIEL R., 'Early but Opposed—Supported but Late: Two Berlin Seminaries which Attempted to Move Abroad', *Leo Baeck Institute Year Book*, 36 (1991), 267–83.

SCHWARTZ, YOEL, and GOLDSTEIN, YITSHAK, *The Holocaust* (Heb.) (Jerusalem, 1987).

SCHWARZ, LEO W., *Wolfson of Harvard: Portrait of a Scholar* (Philadelphia, Pa., 1978).

SEGEV, TOM, *The Seventh Million*, trans. Haim Watzman (New York, 1993).

SEIDMAN, HILLEL, 'The Gaon Rabbi Jehiel Jacob Weinberg in the Warsaw Ghetto' (Heb.), *Hapardes* (Feb. 1967), 36–7.

SHAKH, ELEAZAR, *Letters and Articles* (Heb.), vol. vi (Benei Berak, 1996).

SHAPIRA, BERAKHYAH BEREKH, *Zera berakh* (Amsterdam, 1730).

SHAPIRA, HAYIM ELEAZAR, *Minḥat ele'azar* (Brooklyn, NY, 1991).

SHAPIRO, BEN-ZION (ed.), *Igerot lare'iyah* (Jerusalem, 1990).

SHAPIRO, MARC B., 'The Herem on Spain: History and Halakah', *Sefarad*, 49 (1989), 381–94.

—— Review of Benziyon Jakobovics, *Zekhor yemot olam, Tradition*, 25 (Fall 1989), 97–9.

—— 'Further on Women's Hair Covering', *Judaism*, 40 (Winter 1991), 89–94.

—— 'Sociology and Halakhah', *Tradition*, 27 (Fall 1992), 75–85.

—— 'A Letter of Criticism Directed against the Yeshiva of Eisenstadt' (Heb.), *Hama'ayan*, 34 (Tishrei 5754 [1993]), 15–25.

—— 'Maimonides' Thirteen Principles: The Last Word in Jewish Theology?' *Torah u-Madda Journal*, 4 (1993), 187–242.

—— 'Between East and West: The Life and Works of Rabbi Jehiel Jacob Weinberg' (Ph.D. diss., Harvard University, 1995).

—— 'Rabbi David Zvi Hoffmann on *Torah u-Madda*', *Torah u-Madda Journal*, 6 (1995–6), 129–37.

—— 'Scholars and Friends: Rabbi Jehiel Jacob Weinberg and Professor Samuel Atlas', *Torah u-Madda Journal*, 7 (1997), 105–21.

—— 'The Brisker Method Reconsidered', *Tradition*, 31 (Spring 1997), 78–102.

SHAZAR, ZALMAN, *Or ishim* (Jerusalem, 1973).

SHIFMAN, YAIR, 'The Dispute between the Orthodox and the Zionists from the First Zionist Congress until the Appearance of *Hapeles*' (Heb.) (MA diss., Hebrew University of Jerusalem, n.d.).

SHOCHAT, AZRIEL, *The Institution of the 'Crown Rabbinate' in Russia* (Heb.) (Haifa, 1976).

SHULMAN, ABRAHAM, *The Case of Hotel Polski* (New York, 1981).

SHULVASS, MOSES, 'The Rabbinical Seminary of Berlin' (Heb.), in S. Mirsky (ed.), *Mosedot torah be'eiropah* (New York, 1956), 689–713.

SIEGEL, SEYMOUR, 'The War of the *Kitniyot* (Legumes)', in A. A. Chiel (ed.), *Perspectives on Jews and Judaism* (New York, 1978), 383–408.

SILBER, MICHAEL, 'The Historical Experience of German Jewry and its Impact on the Haskalah and Reform in Hungary', in Jacob Katz (ed.), *Toward Modernity: The European Jewish Model* (New Brunswick, NJ, 1987), 107–57.

SILBERSTEIN, WERNER, *My Way from Berlin to Jerusalem* (Jerusalem, 1994).

SIMON, ERNST, 'Jewish Adult Education in Nazi Germany as Spiritual Resistance', *Leo Baeck Institute Year Book*, 1 (1956), 68–104.

—— *Brücken: Gesammelte Aufsätze* (Heidelberg, 1965).

SINASOHN, MAX, *Die Berliner Privatsynagogen und ihre Rabbiner 1671–1971* (Jerusalem, 1971).

—— (ed.), *Adass Jisroel Berlin* (Jerusalem, 1966).

SMOLAR, ISSER, 'The Cultural State of the Jews of Ciechanowiec at the End of the Nineteenth Century' (Heb.), in Eliezer Leoni (ed.), *Ciechanowiec Memorial Volume* (Tel Aviv, 1964), 337–9.

SOFER, HAYIM, *Kol sofer* (Munkács, 1882).

—— *Kan sofer* (London, 1963).

SOFER, MOSES, *She'elot uteshuvot ḥatam sofer* (Jerusalem, 1991).

SOFER, SOLOMON (ed.), *Igerot soferim* (Tel Aviv, 1970).

SOFER, YAAKOV HAYIM, *Tal ḥayim* (Jerusalem, 1994).

SOLOMON, NORMAN, *The Analytic Movement* (Atlanta, Ga., 1993).

SOLOVEITCHIK, JOSEPH B., *Ish hahalakhah: Galui venistar* (Jerusalem, 1992).

SOLOVEITCHIK, JOSEPH DOV, *Divrei hagut veha'arakhah* (Jerusalem, 1982).

SORASKY, AHARON, *The History of Torah Education* (Heb.) (Benei Berak, 1967).

—— *Or elḥanan* (Los Angeles, 1978).

SOROTZKIN, ZALMAN, *Hade'ah vehadibur*, vol. iii (Jerusalem, 1965).

SPEKTOR, ISAAC ELHANAN, *Ein yitsḥak* (Vilna, 1889).

SPERBER, ALEXANDER, 'Peschitta und Onkelos', in Salo W. Baron and Alexander Marx (eds.), *Jewish Studies in Memory of George A. Kohut* (New York, 1935), 554–64.

SPERBER, DANIEL, 'On the Legitimacy, or Indeed Necessity, of Scientific Disciplines for True "Learning" of the Talmud', in Shalom Carmy (ed.), *Modern Scholarship in the Study of Torah: Contributions and Limitations* (Northvale, NJ, 1996), 197–225.

SPIEGEL, YAAKOV S., 'Elliptical Language of the Tannaim and Concerning *Peshat* and *Derash* in the Mishnah' (Heb.), *Asupot*, 4 (1990), 9–26.

—— *Chapters in the History of the Jewish Book* (Heb.) (Ramat Gan, 1996).

SPITZER, ABRAHAM SAMUEL BENJAMIN, 'Ketorah ya'aseh', *Festschrift für Jacob Rosenheim* (Frankfurt, 1931), 1–43.

STAMPFER, SHAUL, 'Three Lithuanian Yeshivot in the Nineteenth Century' (Heb.) (Ph.D. diss., Hebrew University of Jerusalem, 1981).

—— '*Heder* Study, Knowledge of Torah, and the Maintenance of Social Stratification in Traditional East European Jewish Society', *Studies in Jewish Education*, 3 (1988), 271–89.

—— *The Lithuanian Yeshiva* (Heb.) (Jerusalem, 1995).

STANISLAWSKI, MICHAEL, *For Whom Do I Toil? Judah Leib Gordon and the Crisis of Russian Jewry* (Oxford, 1988).

STERN, ELIEZER, *The Educational Ideal of Torah im Derekh Eretz* (Heb.) (Ramat Gan, 1987).

STERN, MOSHE, 'Ish eshkolot', *De'ot*, 31 (1967), 23.

STERNBUCH, MOSHE, *Teshuvot vehanhagot* (Jerusalem, 1989–92).

STRAUSS, HERBERT A., 'Jewish Emigration from Germany: Nazi Policies and Jewish Responses', *Leo Baeck Institute Year Book*, 25 (1980), 313–61; 26 (1981), 343–409.

Studien und Prüfungsordnung des Rabbiner-Seminars zu Berlin (Berlin, 1928).

SUDARSKY, MENDEL, *et al.* (eds.), *Lithuania* (Yid.) (New York, 1951).

SULZBACH, CARLA, 'David Zvi Hoffmann's *Die wichtigsten Instanzen gegen die Graf-Wellhausensche Hypothese*' (MA diss., McGill University, 1996).

SWIFT, MOSES, '"External Books" in the Halakhah' (Heb.), in H. J. Zimmels *et al.* (eds.), *Essays Presented to Chief Rabbi Israel Brodie on the Occasion of his Seventieth Birthday* (London, 1967), 205–8.

SZAJKOWSKI, ZOSA, 'The Struggle for Yiddish During World War I: The Attitude of German Jewry', *Leo Baeck Institute Year Book*, 9 (1964), 131–58.

Takanot agunot (Odessa, 1887).

TAM, JACOB, *Sefer hayashar*, ed. F. Rosenthal (Berlin, 1898).

—— *Sefer hayashar lerabeinu tam: Ḥelek haḥidushim* (Jerusalem, 1959).

TCHERNOWITZ, CHAIM (Rav Tsa'ir), *Memoirs* (Heb.) (New York, 1945).

—— *Autobiography* (Heb.) (New York, 1954).

TEICHER, J. L., 'A Sixth Century Fragment of the Palestinian Targum?' *Vetus Testamentum*, 1 (1951), 125–9.

TEITELBAUM, JOEL, *Al hage'ulah ve'al hatemurah* (Brooklyn, NY, 1982).

TENENBAUM, MENAHEM MENDEL, *The Method of Study of the Rogochover* (Heb.) (n.p., 1987).

Tikun olam (Munkács, 1935).

TOEG, A., 'Exodus 22: 4: The Text and the Law in the Light of the Ancient Sources' (Heb.), *Tarbiz*, 39 (1970), 223–31.

TOR, MALKAH, 'Germany Jewry's Spiritual and Intellectual Resistance to the Nazi Regime, with Special Emphasis on the Response of the Orthodox' (Heb.) (MA diss., Hebrew University of Jerusalem, n.d.).

TRACHTENBERG, JACOW, *Atrocity Propaganda is Based on Lies Say the Jews of Germany Themselves* [Berlin, 1933].

TRACHTENBERG, JOSHUA, *Jewish Magic and Superstition* (Cleveland, Oh., 1961).

TSUR, YAAKOV, 'German-Jewish Orthodoxy and its Relationship to Organized Jewry and to Zionism' (Heb.) (Ph.D. diss., Hebrew University of Jerusalem, 1982).

—— 'Torah im Derekh Eretz and Torah ve'avodah' (Heb.), in Mordechai Breuer (ed.), *Torah im Derekh Eretz* (Ramat Gan, 1987), 97–107.

TSURIEL, MOSHE, 'The Conversion of Russian Immigrants' (Heb.), *Iturei kohanim*, 67 (Tishrei 5751 [1990]), 33–7.

TWERSKY, ISADORE, *Rabad of Posquières* (Cambridge, Mass., 1962).

TZIHAN, E. L., untitled article, *Hapeles*, 5 (1905), 424–31.

TZINOVITZ, MOSHE, *Mir* (Heb.) (Tel Aviv, 1981).

UNNA, ISAK, 'Zeitgemässe Mahnungen', *Jeschurun*, 3 (1916), 703–9.

—— 'Das Trennungsprinzip und die Zusammenarbeit der Gesetztreuen', *Jeschurun*, 13 (1926), 403–18.

—— 'Die Frage des Trennungsprinzips: Eine Replik', *Jeschurun*, 14 (1927), 87–90.

—— *Sho'alin vedorshin* (Tel Aviv, 1964).

—— *Lema'an ha'aḥdut vehayiḥud* (Jerusalem, 1975).

Unser Dibbuk (Berlin, 1899).

UNTERMAN, ISSER YEHUDAH, *Shevet miyehudah* (Jerusalem, 1992).

URBACH, EPHRAIM E., *From the World of the Sages* (Heb.) (Jerusalem, 1988).

VELTZ, ISRAEL, *Divrei yisra'el*, vol. ii (Benei Berak, 1980).

Verzeichnis der Mitglieder des Bundes Jüdischer Akademiker nach dem Stande vom 1. Februar 1929 (Berlin, 1929).

VOSS, CARL HERMANN, 'Letters from Stephen S. Wise to a Friend and Colleague: Morton Mayer Berman', in Charles Berlin (ed.), *Studies in Jewish Bibliography, History, and Literature in Honor of I. Edward Kiev* (New York, 1971), 479–94.

WALDENBERG, ELIEZER, *Tsits eli'ezer* (Jerusalem, 1985).

WALK, JOSEPH, 'The Torah Va'Avodah Movement in Germany', *Leo Baeck Institute Year Book*, 6 (1961), 236–56.

—— 'A Failed Rescue Attempt' (Heb.), *Ḥadashot universitat bar-ilan* (July 1975), 19–20.

WALKIN, AARON, *Zekan aharon* (New York, 1977).

WARHAFTIG, YERUHAM ASHER, *Shalmei yeruḥam* (Jerusalem, 1941).

WARHAFTIG, ZORACH, 'The Historical and Legal Struggle over *Sheḥitah*' (Heb.), *Torah she-be'al peh*, 5 (1963), 151–9.

—— *Refugee and Survivor* (Heb.) (Jerusalem, 1984).

Was will, Was ist Agudas Jisroel (Hamburg, [1919?]).

WASSERMAN, ELHANAN, *Kovets he'arot* (Jerusalem, 1985).

—— *Anthology of Articles and Letters* (Heb., Yid.) (Brooklyn, NY, 1987).

WASSERMAN, MOSES SAMSON, *She'elat moshe* (Tel Aviv, 1957).

WECHSLER, HILE, *A Warning to Israel* (Heb.), ed. Rivka Horwitz (Jerusalem, 1991).

WEINBERG, ZVI, 'The Lectures of Jacob Barth on the Book of Isaiah at the Rabbinical Seminary of Berlin' (Heb.), in Uriel Simon and Moshe Goshen-Gottstein (eds.), *Iyunei mikra unfarshanut* (Ramat Gan, 1980), 229–41.

—— 'Jacob Barth's Notes to Isaiah, Song of Songs and Ecclesiastes', *Beit Mikra*, 31 (1986), 78–87.

WEINBERGER, BERISH (ed.), *Igerot shapirin* (Brooklyn, NY, 1983).

WEINBERGER, DAVID NETANEL (ed.), *The Elder of Slobodka* (Heb.) (Brooklyn, NY, 1986).

WEINGORT, ABRAHAM ABBA 'From Rabbi Jehiel Jacob Weinberg's Method of Study' (Heb.), *De'ot*, 31 (1967), 19–22.

—— 'Concerning the Essence of Acquiring a Wife' (Heb.), *Hama'ayan*, 24 (Tammuz 5744 [1984]), 41–57.

—— 'Reflections on the Teachings of Rabbi Weinberg' (Heb.), *Hama'ayan*, 37 (Nisan 5757 [1997]), 24–32.

—— (ed.), *Well of Miriam* (Heb.) (Jerusalem, 1997).

WEISS, ISAAC HIRSCH, *Dor dor vedoreshav* (Vilna, 1904).

WELTSCH, ROBERT, *An der Wende des modernen Judentums* (Tübingen, 1972).

WERBA, ZE'EV, 'A Center of Torah Destroyed' (Heb.), *Bitsaron*, 7 (1943), 245–54, 364–73.

WERTHEIMER, JACK, *Unwelcome Strangers: East European Jews in Imperial Germany* (Oxford, 1987).

WILENSKY, MICHAEL, 'Be'inyan hilkhat idit', *Ḥorev*, 10 (1948), 35–56.

WILOVSKY, JACOB DAVID, *Beit ridbaz* (Jerusalem, 1995).

—— *Kerem ridbaz* (Jerusalem, 1995).

WININGER, S., *Grosse Jüdische National Biographie* (Czernowitz, n.d.).

WISE, STEPHEN, *Challenging Years* (New York, 1949).

WOHLGEMUTH, JOSEPH, 'Beiträge zu einer jüdischen Homiletik', in *Jahres-Bericht des Rabbiner-Seminars zu Berlin für 1903/1904* (Berlin, [1905]), 1–107.

—— 'Unser Kaiser', *Jeschurun*, 2 (1915), 1–18.

—— *Der Weltkrieg im Lichte des Judentums* (Berlin, 1915).

—— *Krieg und Judentum* (Frankfurt, 1916).

—— 'Deutschland und die Ostjudenfrage', *Jeschurun*, 3 (1916), 1–19, 65–95, 177–210.

—— 'Erziehungsfragen in Ost und West', *Jeschurun*, 4 (1917), 1–13, 65–75, 129–53.

—— 'Zionismus, Nationaljudentum, und gesetzestreues Judentum', *Jeschurun*, 5 (1918), 1–31, 133–73, 257–88.

—— 'Nachwort des Herausgebers', *Jeschurun*, 7 (1920), 505–12.

—— 'Westjüdisches und ostjüdisches Empfinden', *Jeschurun*, 10 (1923), 1–8.

—— 'R. Awrohom Elijo Kaplan', *Jeschurun*, 11 (1924), 233–45.

WOHLGEMUTH, JUDA ARI, 'Joseph Wohlegemuth', in Leo Jung (ed.), *Guardians of Our Heritage* (New York, 1958), 533–50.

WOLF, JOSEPH ABRAHAM, *The Era and Its Problems* (Heb.) (Benei Berak, 1965).

WOLFSBERG, ISAIAH, 'Lithuanian Jewry and German Jewry' (Heb.), *Talpiot*, 3 (1947), 7–31.

—— Introduction to Abraham Berliner, *Selected Writings* (Heb.) (Jerusalem, 1969), pp. vii–xvi.

—— 'Autobiography' (Heb.), in Yitshak Rafael (ed.), *Sefer aviad* (Jerusalem, 1986), 4–65.

WOLFSON, HARRY A., *Crescas' Critique of Aristotle* (Cambridge, Mass., 1929).

WOLOWELSKY, JOEL B., 'Modern Orthodoxy and Women's Changing Self-Perception', *Tradition*, 22 (Spring 1986), 65–81.

—— 'Observing Yom Hasho'a', *Tradition*, 24 (Summer 1989), 46–58.

WURZBURGER, WALTER S., 'Confronting the Challenge of the Values of Modernity', *Torah u-Madda Journal*, 1 (1989), 104–12.

—— 'Rav Joseph B. Soloveitchik as *Posek* of Post-Modern Orthodoxy', *Tradition*, 29 (Fall 1994), 5–20.

YERUSHALMI, SHMUEL, *Rabbi Naḥum the Tsadik* (Heb.) (Jerusalem, 1970).

ZEVIN, SHELOMO YOSEF, 'Tsiyurim ketanim', *Hamodia*, 21 Kislev 5671 [1910].

—— *Le'or hahalakhah* (Tel Aviv, 1957).

—— *Authors and Books* (Heb.) (Tel Aviv, 1959).

—— *Outstanding Men and their Intellectual Approaches* (Heb.) (Tel Aviv, 1966).

ZIMMELS, H. J., *The Echo of the Nazi Holocaust in Rabbinic Literature* (New York, 1977).

ZIPPERSTEIN, STEVEN J., 'Transforming the Heder: Maskilic Politics in Imperial Russia', in Zipperstein and Ada Rapoport-Albert (eds.), *Jewish History: Essays in Honour of Chimen Abramsky* (London, 1988), 87–109.

ZIRELSON, JUDAH LEIB, *Lev yehudah* (Jerusalem, 1961).

ZOHAR, ZVI, and SAGI, ABRAHAM, *Conversion to Judaism and the Meaning of Jewish Identity* (Heb.) (Jerusalem, 1995).

Zum hundertjährigen Geburtstage des Rabbiners und Seminardirektors Dr Israel Hildesheimer (Berlin, 1920).

Zur Agudas-Jisroel Jugendbewegung (Frankfurt, 1913).

Index

Page numbers in bold refer to illustrations